An HISTORICAL ATLAS of SUFFOLK

Revised and Enlarged Edition

John Denston of Denston Hall (died 1473-4), and his daughter and heiress Anne (died 1481), wife of John Broughton,
founders of the superbly proportioned church at Denston, as depicted in the medieval glass of Long Melford church.
Two of the medieval inhabitants of Suffolk who helped to endow the county with a rich legacy of fields, moats, houses and churches.

An HISTORICAL ATLAS of SUFFOLK

edited by

David Dymond and Edward Martin

with a foreword by

Christopher Taylor

and contributions by
Philip Aitkens, Leigh Alston, John E. Archer, Mark Barnard, Gordon Blackwood,
John Blatchly, Sylvia Colman, Peter Dolman, David Dymond, Nesta Evans,
Eric Fernie, Roger A. Freeman, Frank Grace, Birkin Haward, Rosemary Hoppitt,
Peter Kent, Michael Lane, Alan Mackley, Robert Malster, Edward Martin,
Joanna Martin, Pat Murrell, Peter Northeast, Clive Paine, Charles Pankhurst,
Judith Plouviez, Oliver Rackham, John Ridgard, Brian K. Roberts, Alistair Robertson,
Joy Rowe, Norman Scarfe, Jonathan Theobald, Gwyn Thomas, Hilary Todd,
Keith Wade, Stanley West, Tom Williamson and John Wymer

Maps drawn by
Henry Skinner, Rebecca Archer, Robert Garnham, Sue Holden,
Edward Martin, Hazel Milbourne, David Nuttall and Glenys Wade

SUFFOLK COUNTY COUNCIL, ENVIRONMENT & TRANSPORT
SUFFOLK INSTITUTE OF ARCHAEOLOGY & HISTORY

First edition published 1988
Second edition 1989
Third edition, revised and enlarged, published 1999 by
>   The Archaeology Service,
>   Environment and Transport,
>   Suffolk County Council,
>   St Edmund House,
>   County Hall,
>   Ipswich   IP4 1LZ
>   (e-mail: archaeology@et.suffolkcc.gov.uk)

>   in conjunction with
>   The Suffolk Institute of Archaeology and History

© Suffolk County Council &
Suffolk Institute of Archaeology and History 1999

>   ISBN 0 86055 252 7 (hardback)
>   0 86055 253 5 (paperback)

Printed in Great Britain by The Lavenham Press, Water Street,
Lavenham, Sudbury, Suffolk. CO10 9RN.

Acknowledgements:
Front cover and frontispiece supplied by NPA Satellite Mapping.
Illustrations for the text pages were supplied by
Philip Aitkens (Maps 79, 81 and 82); Rebecca Archer (Map 12); C. Howlett and Dr K Brown (Map 65); Dr Oliver Rackham (Map 27); Robert Malster (Maps 58, 62 and 69); John Wymer (Map 11); the Bury Past & Present Society-Spanton Jarman Collection (Map 67); the Suffolk Record Office, Suffolk County Council (rear cover, Maps 26, 33, 57 and 66); the remainder were supplied by the Archaeology Service of Suffolk County Council.

Index compiled by Nesta Evans

Book design by Edward Martin

REAR POCKET : This contains two large maps of Suffolk
1. The civil parishes as they were in the 19th century, based on the Ordnance Survey's diagram of Sanitary Districts, 1888.
2. The civil parishes as they are today, based on the Ordnance Survey's diagram of administrative areas, 1:1000,000.
These maps can be used to identify unnamed places on the smaller parish outline maps in the *Atlas*.

NOTE: the two maps have slightly different shapes because of the different projections used to create the original maps.

FRONTISPIECE (opposite): An image of Suffolk taken by the American Landsat 5 satellite on the 15 July 1989 from an altitude of 705km (438 miles). It was captured in Thematic Mapper mode at a resolution of 30m, producing false colour image.
The colour representation is:
>   very dark red, almost black = coniferous trees
>   deep red = deciduous trees
>   bright red = healthy green vegetation (crops or grass)
>   black/blue = water
>   blue = urban areas or bare soil
>   purple = agricultural land (vegetation and soil mixture)
>   green/yellow = grass, heathland or ripe crops.

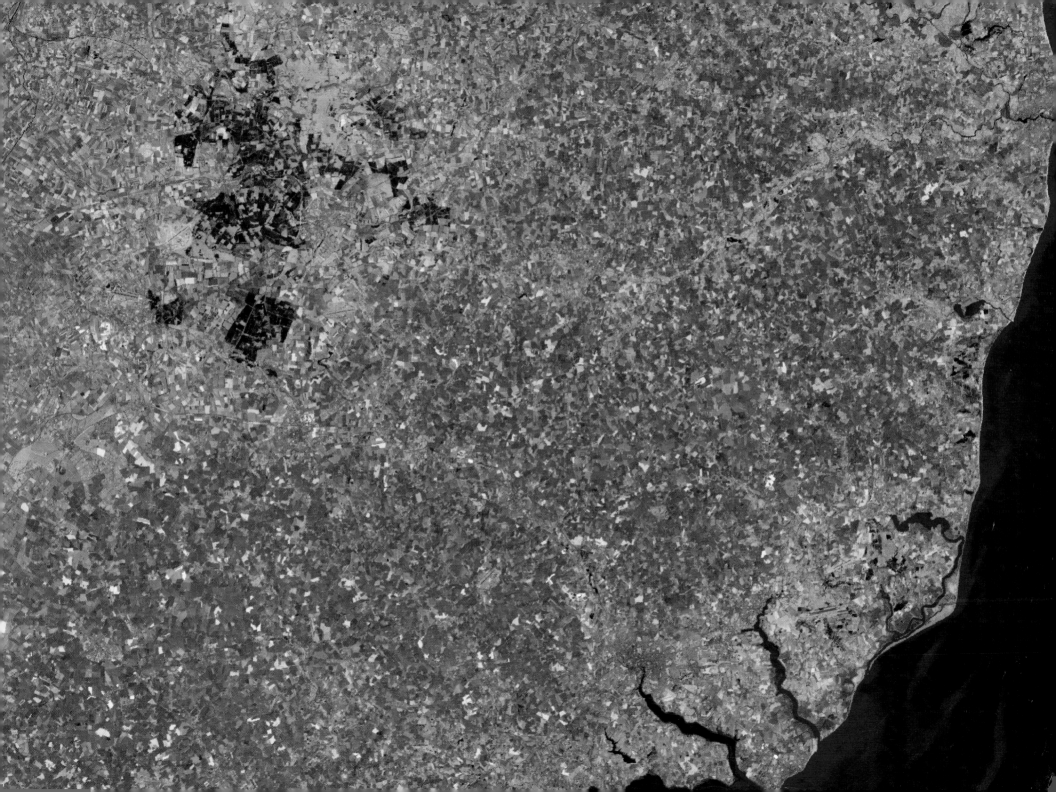

CONTENTS

Gold bracteate (pendant) dating from *c*. AD 450-500, found at Undley, Lakenheath, in 1981. The design is based on a Roman coin of the 330s, with a helmeted head on one side and a wolf and twins on the other. The runic inscription is reversed and can be read as 'gæ go gæ mægæ medu'. One suggested translation is: '[this] she-wolf [i.e. the bracteate, with its depiction of a she-wolf] [to a] kinswoman [for a] reward, but this is very unsure. The inscription is however of great significance because the 'o' rune in the second bind-rune (g and o together) only occurs in England and Frisia, and these few words are probably earliest piece of writing in the English language. Original is 23mm in diameter. **See Map 6.**

CONTRIBUTORS

Philip Aitkens	Historic buildings consultant
Leigh Alston, MA	Medieval and architectural historian
John E. Archer, PhD, FRHistS	Lecturer, Edge Hill University College, Ormskirk, Lancashire
Mark Barnard, DipEP, DipCons(AA), IHBC	Historic Buildings Officer, Suffolk County Council
Gordon Blackwood, DPhil, FRHistS	Early retired Head of History, Felixstowe College
John Blatchly, MA, PhD, HonLittD, FSA	Former Headmaster of Ipswich School; President of the Suffolk Institute of Archaeology and History
Sylvia Colman, BSc (Econ)	Retired Historic Buildings Adviser, Suffolk County Council
Peter Dolman, FRICS	Writer and lecturer on mills; Secretary of Suffolk Mills Group
David Dymond, MA, FSA, FRHistS	Formerly of the Board of Continuing Education, University of Cambridge; Vice-President of the Suffolk Institute of Archaeology & History
Nesta Evans, MA, MPhil, FSA	Historian and local history lecturer
Professor Eric Fernie, CBE, BA, FSA, FRSE	Director of the Courtauld Institute of Art, London
Roger A. Freeman	Writer and lecturer on 2nd World War aviation
Frank Grace, MA	Historian, local history lecturer and editor of the *Suffolk Review*
Birkin Haward, OBE, FRIBA, Hon MA, FSA	Retired architect
Rosemary Hoppitt, BA, PhD	Lecturer in Geography, Suffolk College, Ipswich
Peter Kent, MA	Author and illustrator
Michael Lane	Writer and engineering historian
Alan Mackley, BA, BSc, PhD	Senior Research Associate, Centre of East Anglian Studies, University of East Anglia
Robert Malster	Publications consultant and industrial archaeologist
Edward Martin, BA, FSA, MIFA	Archaeological Officer, Suffolk County Council; Vice-President of the Suffolk Institute of Archaeology and History
Joanna Martin, PhD	Historian and genealogist
Pat Murrell, PhD	Historian and local history lecturer
Peter Northeast, FSA	Historian and local history lecturer; Vice-President of the Suffolk Institute of Archaeology & History
Clive Paine, BEd	Education Officer, Suffolk Record Office
Charles Pankhurst	Industrial archaeologist
Judith Plouviez, BA, FSA	Archaeological Officer, Suffolk County Council

Oliver Rackham, OBE, PhD — Fellow of Corpus Christi College, Cambridge

John Ridgard, MA, PhD — Historian; former Tutor-Organiser for WEA in Suffolk

Professor Brian K. Roberts, PhD — Professor of Geography, University of Durham

Alistair Robertson — Former Local Studies Librarian, Suffolk Record Office

Joy Rowe, BA — Former Archivist, West Suffolk Record Office

Norman Scarfe, MBE, MA, HonLittD, FSA — Historian; Vice-President of the Suffolk Institute of Archaeology and History; former General Editor of the Suffolk Records Society

Jonathan Theobald, MA — Post-graduate student, Centre of East Anglian Studies, University of East Anglia

Gwyn Thomas, MA — Senior Archivist, Suffolk Record Office

Hilary Todd, BA — Former Local History Compiler, Archaeology Service, Suffolk County Council

Keith Wade, BA, FSA — Principal Archaeological Officer, Suffolk County Council

Stanley West, MA, PhD, FSA — Retired Principal Archaeological Officer, Suffolk County Council

Tom Williamson, MA, PhD — Lecturer in Landscape History, Centre of East Anglian Studies, University of East Anglia

John Wymer, MA, HonDSc, FBA, FSA, MIFA — Palaeolithic archaeologist; Vice-President of the Suffolk Institute of Archaeology & History

Hengrave Hall, the great mansion built 1525-*c*.1540 for Sir Thomas Kytson, a wealthy London merchant. As with most of the other major houses being built in suffolk at this date, it wae made mainly of brick, but exceptionally, in this case the bricks were white and were meant to give the impression of costly limestone. The moat that originally surrounded the house would have further enhanced the facade by reflecting the walls and making them seem even taller. By the mid-17th century it was largest house in Suffolk - **see map 40.**

FOREWORD

The appearance of the third edition of this atlas is especially welcome. For it confirms the success of the previous editions in terms of the great interest in the history of Suffolk that they have generated and of the original historical research that they have encouraged. Both of the previous editions have explained many aspects of the history of the county not fully appreciated before, and they have also posed questions to which the historians of the county are now finding answers.

The *Historical Atlas of Suffolk* was the first in what is becoming a series of similar county atlases which will soon cover much of eastern England and, hopefully eventually, extend to the rest of the country. The very fact that Suffolk's lead has been taken up elsewhere means that the principal drawback of such an atlas, that it is limited to an administrative county however ancient, is overcome. The wider perspective of the history of the region and beyond is now being realised.

The contributors and editors are to be congratulated on their continuing achievement in explaining the history of Suffolk to its inhabitants and to those who do not know the county well. The Suffolk Institute of Archaeology and History and the Environment and Transport Department of Suffolk County Council have encouraged and supported the compilation and production of this atlas. Their generosity and far-sightedness merit special mention.

CHRISTOPHER TAYLOR, FBA, FSA
former Principal Investigator of the Royal
Commission on Historical Monuments (England),
founding President of the Society for Landscape Studies

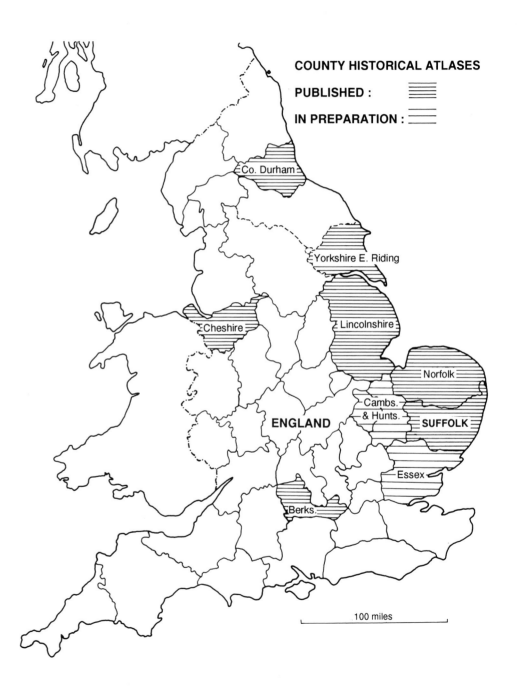

Map showing the English counties for which an historical atlas is either published or in preparation.

INTRODUCTION

David Dymond & Edward Martin

We believe that this *Atlas*, which first appeared in 1988, was only the second to have been published for any English county.[1] Our faith was vindicated when it was favourably reviewed, sold well, and was hailed as a useful tool for those interested in local landscape, archaeology, history and architecture. Librarians and archivists tell us that the *Atlas* has been used by large numbers of people including schoolchildren, sixth-formers, teachers, undergraduates, postgraduates, adult students, local historians and, of course, general readers. It has been quoted frequently in books, academic journals and dissertations, and we ourselves have seen some very tattered copies in local libraries and record offices! Although a slightly amended second edition was brought out in May 1989, stocks were exhausted by the end of 1993 and the book could only be obtained, if at all, second-hand.

The most pleasing result, however, has been the publication of historical atlases in other parts of the country. This has already been likened to a 'benign virus' creeping up the eastern side of England, and likely to erupt elsewhere.[2] Since the Suffolk volume appeared in 1988, similar atlases have been published for County Durham (1992), Norfolk (1993), Lincolnshire (1993), East Yorkshire (1996) and Berkshire (1999), and others are in preparation or under consideration (see the map opposite).[3] Of course, the formula has the serious disadvantage of implying that county boundaries have been significant at all times and in every aspect of life. This is patently untrue when, for example, one considers prehistoric cultures, the spread of major industries, or the development of transport networks.[4] For that reason, another important landmark will be the appearance of the first *regional* atlas: an *Historical Atlas of South-West England* is now imminent. Nevertheless, the county atlas still offers one of the best ways of summarising and marketing new research of a localised kind. If more

of these compilations appear, we fervently hope that every effort will be made to cover the same themes as in neighbouring counties, using methods which are comparable and complementary. In that way, we shall have a much better chance of identifying the historical 'regions' which lie both *within* and *across* county boundaries, and thus of lessening our obsession with administrative boundaries in general.

Since 1988-9 important new discoveries and interpretations have continued to change most of the subjects covered in the *Atlas*, and some entirely new themes have shot into prominence. These trends, coupled with a steady commercial demand, made the case for a third edition irresistible. In 1994, therefore, contributors and editors began work on revising and expanding the book, which now re-appears after an interval of ten years. Out of total of 86 subjects 26 are new, and the number of contributors—all specialists in their fields—has risen from 27 to 39. The basic format remains the same: a distribution map is normally given on the right of each opening, with an explanatory text of no more than 900 words to the left. Each contributor was also asked to provide extra notes which appear at the back of the volume: these describe the sources used to compile the map and may include any appropriate references, bibliography or tables. Although these extra contributions vary greatly in length, they now form a larger block and give readers the chance of investigating subjects to greater depth.

As before, the main aim has been to present in succinct form the results of new thinking and recent research, much of which is incomplete and previously unpublished. Indeed, most of the maps are interim statements; in effect they invite others to contribute and take the work further. In some cases we have been able to include subjects previously omitted, for example in

maritime and military history. Even so, plenty of gaps are left for future researchers. One major omission, for example, is the massive transformation of Suffolk's agricultural landscapes and of its rural communities since the end of the Second World War.

As general editors, we would like to thank all contributors for their interest, time and hard work. With amazing forbearance they have put up with five years of badgering, interference and delay. We can only give the usual excuse that we have gone as fast as other commitments allowed, and hope that both contributors and readers will think the final result worth waiting for. Lastly, it needs emphasising that this book is still not *THE* but *AN* historical atlas of Suffolk. Everyone concerned with the project knows how fast our knowledge has changed in the last thirty years, and confidently expects that it will change even more rapidly and profoundly in the exciting years ahead. For example, all the maps in this *Atlas* were drawn by hand, but their successors in future publications are likely to be computer generated. Already a project has been started, using a 'geographical information system' (GIS) on a computer, to map the various types of historic landscape in Suffolk and to present the results in many different ways.[5]

---

[1] The first historical atlas to set this pattern of multiple distribution maps with short explanatory texts was D. Sylvester & G. Nulty (eds), *The Historical Atlas of Cheshire* (1958).

[2] *Agric. Hist. Rev.*, 46, pt ii (1998), 226-7.

[3] For example, Cambridgeshire and Essex. The completion of these volumes will give coverage of the whole East Anglian region and beyond.

[4] The basic format is also capable of being adapted to smaller urban and industrial environments, as is shown by the *Historical Atlas of Trafford* (1996).

[5] This is the first part of an 'Historic Landscape Characterisation Project' for East Anglia, sponsored by English Heritage.

1. EARLY PRINTED MAPS OF SUFFOLK

John Blatchly

Maps of Suffolk are to be found in all the great county atlases, beginning with Christopher Saxton's *Atlas of England and Wales*, published in London in 1579. That thorough survey was undertaken by the command and at the expense of Thomas Seckford, Master of Requests to Queen Elizabeth and owner of fine houses in Ipswich and Woodbridge. The Suffolk map entitled 'Suffolciae Comitatus', engraved by Lenaert Terwoort in 1575 at three miles to the inch, has many features which persist in the work of later cartographers: hills on the Breckland, widespread woodland and 28 parks which are an important record of Elizabethan landowning. Parks are shown by a fence around a tree but with no house.[1] As on the map of Norfolk and three others, hundred boundaries are shown, and many bridges, two over 'Orwell flu' at Ipswich and others at Snape, Mutford and 'Catiwade'. Easton Ness is prominent and shown correctly with its church, but Aldringham and Thorpe are transposed.[2] All 35 county maps in Saxton's atlas have the Royal Arms and Seckford's quarterly; the map of Suffolk is one of five with the motto 'pestis patriae pigrities' ('sloth is the bane of a country'). Saxton's plates were reused, scarcely revised or improved, for almost two centuries. At least the acknowledged copy of Saxton for Camden's *Britannia* of 1607 was re-engraved by William Kip (3.5 miles[3]); he ignored woodland and missed four parks, but tabulated the 21 hundreds.

John Speed, tailor and antiquary, aimed his *Theatre of the Empire of Great Britaine* at a more popular market, with English titling, prominent decorative features, copious heraldry and town plans. His 'Suffolke described' of 1610 is still a lavish copy of Saxton at the same scale with, for example, all Saxton's parks except one near Cavendish, but he did move two parishes into their correct hundreds.[4] In the margins are the arms of four dukes and earls of 'Clare' (Clarence) and five of Suffolk,

as well as the earliest town plan of Ipswich (supported by the figures of Boadicia and Q. Petillius Cerialis who tried unsuccessfully to rescue Colchester from her grasp) which may be Speed's own work. The same nine shields and a blank hang like washing over Joan Bleau's map of 1645, but the next year Jan Jansson merely omitted the Royal Arms and the blank; both, with Speed's 27 parks, are at 2.5 miles and are pure plagiarism. Richard Blome's map of 1673 at 3.75 miles, a crude copy of Speed, is dedicated to Thomas Tymperley Esq. of Hintlesham Hall, and the version of 1685 to Charles Lord Cornwallis, Baron of Eye.

Robert Morden first showed counties with roads in 1676 on a pack of playing cards, only a year after John Ogilby's published his atlas of strip maps following the main post roads.[5] For Bishop Edmund Gibson's edition of Camden's *Britannia* (1695), Robert Morden produced a new series of maps with added roads, the first to use the meridian of London throughout.[6] Herman Moll's maps of 1724 owe much to Morden and show antiquities excavated in the county: some Saxon coins on his Suffolk map are fanciful but still interesting as evidence of rare specimens he must have seen. The bird's-eye-view map of the county in George Bickham's *British Monarchy* (1752) has a vantage point above Newmarket, looking over Bury and Hadleigh to the coastline.

There is greater interest and far more information in the large-scale maps produced only for this county by Kirby and Hodskinson, original surveys of 1736, 1766 and 1783 of the highest quality, beauty and usefulness. After three years on the road John Kirby, schoolmaster and surveyor, published a small gazetteer and road book entitled *The Suffolk Traveller* in 1735. What few realise, because copies are so rare, is that subscribers were also offered his survey in map form at one or two miles to the inch. R. Collins, who also worked for

Thomas Warren on his plans for Bury St Edmunds, engraved the larger, dated 1736 and sold at ten shillings. The map, dedicated to the Duke of Grafton, has also a spectacular heraldic display: 126 noble and genteel subscribers paid an extra half-guinea towards engraving their own arms. The cheaper version engraved by James Basire at half-scale and without heraldry followed in 1737. John Kirby died in 1753, and his sons Joshua and William published an enlarged *Suffolk Traveller* with frontispiece map (4 miles) in 1764.[7] They also republished the two wall maps. The larger, dated 1766, was re-engraved by John Ryland; it carried vignettes of twelve castles and religious houses, and the revised arms and names of estate owners.[8]

Joseph Hodskinson was the surveyor and William Faden the London publisher of the map of 1783, at one inch to the mile. It has almost as much detail as a modern survey, as well as an inset plan of Ipswich. Fortunately this rare map is accessible in facsimile.[9]

Of early-nineteenth-century maps the most important are those by C. and J. Greenwood (one mile, 1825) and A. Bryant (0.8 mile, 1826), both on six sheets. The first Ordnance Survey of the county took from 1805 to 1838 to complete. Thomas Moule's map of 1836 is highly decorative, with vignettes of Euston and Heveningham Halls; later editions show the course of the county's earliest railways.[10]

Further details on p.190

Further details on p.190

Opposite: The first printed map of Suffolk (1575), drawn by Christopher Saxton and engraved by Lenaert Terwoort. Saxton's Atlas of all the counties of England and Wales was commissioned by Thomas Seckford of Ipswich, whose arms feature on the bottom right. (Taken from a facsimile published by the British Library in 1936)

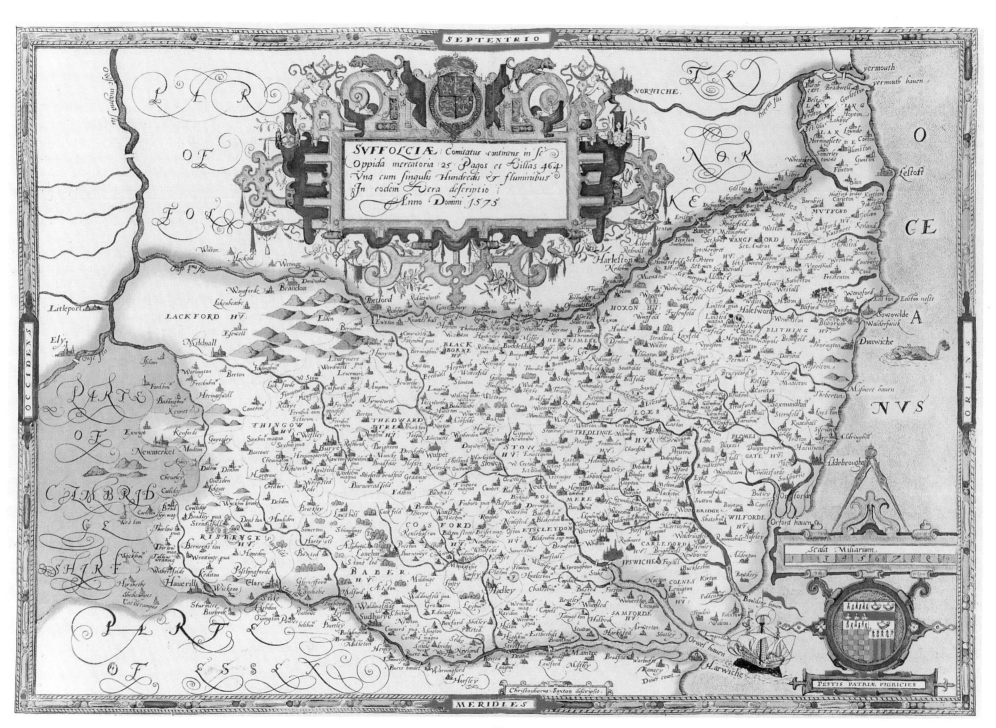

SEPTENTRIO

SVFFOLCIÆ Comitatus continens in se
Oppida mercatoria 25 Pagos et Villas 464
Una cum singulis Hundredis & fluminibus
In eodem Hera descriptio
Anno Domini 1575

Scala Miliarium

Christophorus Saxton descripsit.

PESTIS PATRIÆ PIGRICIES

MERIDIES

OCCIDENS

ORIENS

13

2. THE SHAPING OF SUFFOLK

John Wymer

During the earlier part of the Middle Pleistocene, some half a million years ago, the geography of the area now known as Suffolk had no resemblance to that of today. Britain was not an island but a peninsula to the north-west of the European continent. There was no English Channel or North Sea, but a precursor of the River Thames flowed north-eastwards along the axis (syncline) of the London Basin, far to the north of its present valley and over much of Suffolk. Ancient river gravels remaining at Waldringfield, Sproughton and Kesgrave belong to this period. They probably relate to the final stages of a long history of river development since the Crag sea receded. There was also a major tributary of this ancestral Thames, known as the Bytham River,[1] which flowed from the Midlands, across what is now the Fens and joined the main river near Bury St Edmunds. Remnants of its gravels are at Lakenheath, Eriswell, Mildenhall and Icklingham, containing numerous red quartzite pebbles derived from the Triassic Beds of the Midlands. It was a drainage pattern that was to be totally erased by the ice-sheet of the Anglian Glaciation, which started 470,000 years ago according to one estimate,[2] but rather more recently according to others.

The Anglian ice-sheet covered all of Suffolk except perhaps the very south-east. It similarly covered all the Midlands of Britain and reached to the south of Essex. It cannot be shown that ice ever reached so far south in Britain at any time before this, although there were certainly cold periods. Nor does it seem that ice ever covered Suffolk again, although it may have done around Mildenhall and parts of the Breckland.[3] The ice-sheet would have been hundreds of metres thick and obviously dammed all the river valleys. This was the time when the Thames was diverted from its course through the Vale of St Albans and eventually settled into its present valley through London. When the ice-sheet melted and gradually receded back towards the polar regions, it left behind a thick deposit of Boulder Clay (Lowestoft Till) and outwash gravels. Melt-waters drained east and south-east, producing the valleys now occupied by the major rivers of Suffolk: Waveney, Deben, Gipping and Stour. The basic landscape of Suffolk was established, although millenia of erosion, thawing, changing sea-levels and subsidence to the south-east have modified it to what is seen today.

Each time the climate warmed after the disappearance of the ice, the bare rock became clothed with vegetation. Initially a forest of birch and pine covered the land, gradually giving way to mixed oak forest as soils developed. However, these soils eventually became exhausted and the landscape became more open again. Cooler climate accentuated this openness, and long periods ensued of very cold or periglacial conditions. The warmer periods are known as interglacials. Sediments which settled into a lake at Hoxne, immediately after the Anglian ice disappeared, contain fossil pollen which enables us to interpret much of the history of the interglacial, and the site gives its name to the Hoxnian Stage of the British Quaternary sequence.[4] Contemporary lake sediments have also been found at South Elmham St Michael and Sicklesmere. However, other interglacial sediments, particularly in the Ipswich area (Stoke Tunnel and Maidenhall), at Brundon and along the Stour at Sutton and Harkstead, are clearly more recent geologically and represent another interglacial. Also at Ipswich, in the little valley of the Belstead Brook, are other sediments which are regarded as belonging to the last interglacial of this country; they give their name to the Ipswichian Stage of the British Quaternary sequence.

The last glaciation did not reach southwards beyond the north Norfolk coast. However, the effects of a periglacial climate at that time caused much contorting of soils, patterned ground caused by ice-wedges, and the sand which still blows about in the Breckland. On the evidence of radiocarbon dating, the maximum of this last glaciation was between 24,000 to 15,000 years ago. It was also a time of very low sea-level, a phenomenon always associated with glacial periods when rain-water is locked up as ice and does not return to the sea. It was certainly 60m. or more below the present level of the sea, and the coastline of Suffolk varied accordingly. The English Channel existed, probably having been first breached during the Anglian glaciation, and all the eastward-flowing rivers of Suffolk would have eventually joined the Rhine and the Thames, and flowed *westward* through the Channel. There was thus dry land between Suffolk and the Low Countries and Denmark. The coastline of the North Sea at about 10,000 years ago was north of the Dogger Bank. This had, of course, a profound effect on the migration of people and animals, but with the gradual rise in sea-level as our present interglacial progressed, the coastline receded until eventually, about 6500 BC, the land-bridge was broken and Britain became an island—probably not for the first time. Buried channels in the lower reaches of Suffolk valleys testify to these changes. The coastline would have been a few kilometres distant from the present one, but otherwise the land which would eventually be known as Suffolk had assumed its present shape.

Further details on p.190

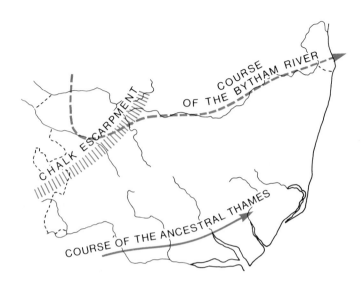

1. BEFORE THE ANGLIAN GLACIATION c. 500,000 BC

Within the map: COURSE OF THE BYTHAM RIVER · CHALK ESCARPMENT · COURSE OF THE ANCESTRAL THAMES

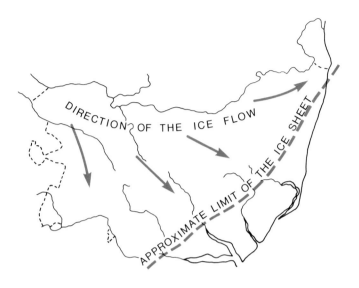

2. THE ANGLIAN GLACIATION

Within the map: DIRECTION OF THE ICE FLOW · APPROXIMATE LIMIT OF THE ICE SHEET

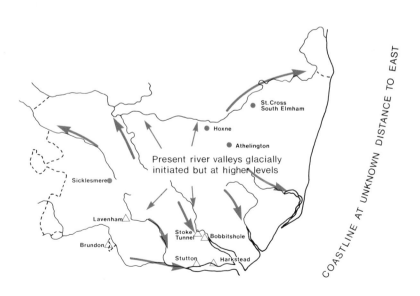

3. INTERGLACIAL SITES AFTER THE ANGLIAN

Within the map: St. Cross South Elmham · Hoxne · Athelington · Sicklesmere · Lavenham · Stoke Tunnel · Bobbitshole · Brundon · Stutton · Harkstead · Present river valleys glacially initiated but at higher levels · COASTLINE AT UNKNOWN DISTANCE TO EAST

- ● HOXNIAN INTERGLACIAL
- △ IPSWICHIAN & OTHER POST-HOXNIAN INTERGLACIALS

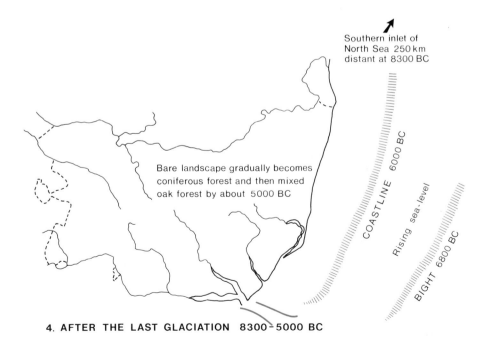

4. AFTER THE LAST GLACIATION 8300–5000 BC

Within the map: Southern inlet of North Sea 250 km distant at 8300 BC · Bare landscape gradually becomes coniferous forest and then mixed oak forest by about 5000 BC · COASTLINE 6000 BC · Rising sea-level · BIGHT 6800 BC

15

3. SOLID GEOLOGY

John Wymer

The solid geology of Suffolk has been modified and mantled by the effects of the Ice Age and the ever-continuous processes of natural erosion and deposition. The actual rocks are barely visible, except in commercial quarries and in cliffs, but they are reflected in the whole form and character of the landscape.

Chalk is the dominant underlying rock of Suffolk. Only in the very north-west of the county, on the edge of the Fens, do some of the older rocks rise to near the surface. The chalk is too soft to be used as a building stone except for a couple of bands, three to four metres thick, one in the Lower Division and the other between the Middle and Upper Divisions. Within the latter are seams of nodular or tabular flint which, eroded from the chalk and in the form of pebbles, are to be found everywhere in Suffolk.

The chalk was formed from the calcareous ooze of a sea-bed between 100 and 70 million years ago. As crustal movements gradually raised the chalk from the sea, so the flint formed from the silica of sponges and microscopic marine creatures. Later subsidence produced a thickness of sands and clays mainly offshore and eventually, as subsidence continued, the London Clay. These rocks of the Tertiary Period only remain in the southern part of the county, and the cross-section (opposite) shows that they lie unconformably on the tilted chalk. The earlier Tertiary rocks only outcrop where recent valleys have exposed them and they have had little effect on the landscape, although the sarsen stones scattered thinly on the ground in south-west Suffolk derive from them. The London Clay underlies most of south-east Suffolk and is to be seen along the lower reaches of the rivers Stour and Orwell.

A hiatus exists from this time (about 40 million years ago) as the land was lifted up and deposition ceased.

Not until the end of the Pliocene Period did submergence on the east side of the county cause the accumulation of estuarine or marine shelly sands known as Crags. These continued to be deposited during the earlier part of the Quaternary or Pleistocene Period, from about two million years ago. They contain fossils which indicate a gradual cooling of the climate, heralding the Ice Age.

Further details on p.191

Red Crag cliff and beach at Bawdsey

SOLID GEOLOGY

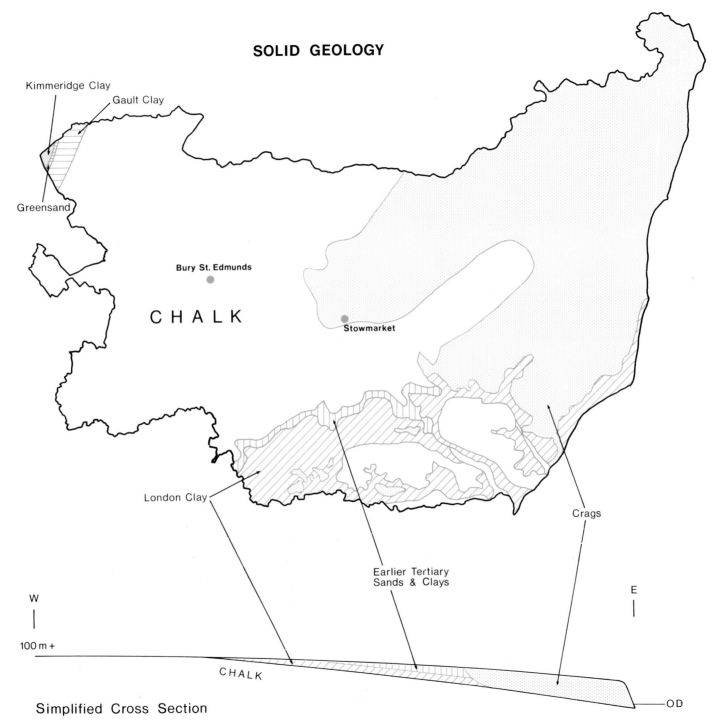

Kimmeridge Clay

Gault Clay

Greensand

Bury St. Edmunds

C H A L K

Stowmarket

London Clay

Crags

Earlier Tertiary
Sands & Clays

W

E

100 m +

CHALK

OD

Simplified Cross Section

4. SURFACE GEOLOGY

John Wymer

Further details on p.191

Suffolk is almost entirely covered by deposits of the Quaternary or Pleistocene Period, mainly resulting from the glaciations of its Middle and Late phases. Boulder Clay, or more accurately Till, covers all central and western Suffolk, except where it has been removed by the erosion of rivers. This till is the rocky debris left by ice-sheets. It is described as Lowestoft Till as it is exposed in the cliffs there.[1] Chalk is a relatively soft rock and, as the ice-sheets melted and receded, they left in their wake a great, flattish plain dotted with depressions that became lakes as the climate warmed up. This plain is mainly 30 to 40 metres above Ordnance Datum, but the till descends into some of the existing valleys and occupies buried channels or 'tunnel valleys'. Most of the till in Suffolk is a grey or brownish clay. It contains lumps of chalk, and sometimes great rafts of chalk 100 metres or more in length, as can be seen in the pits at Claydon. Outwash gravels occur in or under the till, often mixed with it as glaciers temporarily re-advanced.

Permafrost has also had a great effect on surface deposits, contorting layers to a considerable depth. It also left cracks in the form of polygons or stripes which, although now filled in, are often visible from the air as cropmarks: the so-called Patterned Ground.

Between different glacial episodes, sediments accumulated in lakes and rivers. For example, river gravels at various heights above the present floors of valleys indicate ancient flood plains.

By the end of the last major glaciation, about 15,000 years ago, Suffolk had assumed much of its present topography, except on its eastern side. Here in place of a coastline was a bridge of land extending to modern Denmark. The sea was at least 60 metres below its present level, and the coast was north of the Dogger Bank. Rivers flowing eastwards had much deeper channels than those of today, and would have joined the Rhine and Thames where the English Channel now flows.

Typical scene on the boulder-clay plateau or till plain of central Suffolk. In the middle is the isolated church of Little Finborough.

SURFACE GEOLOGY

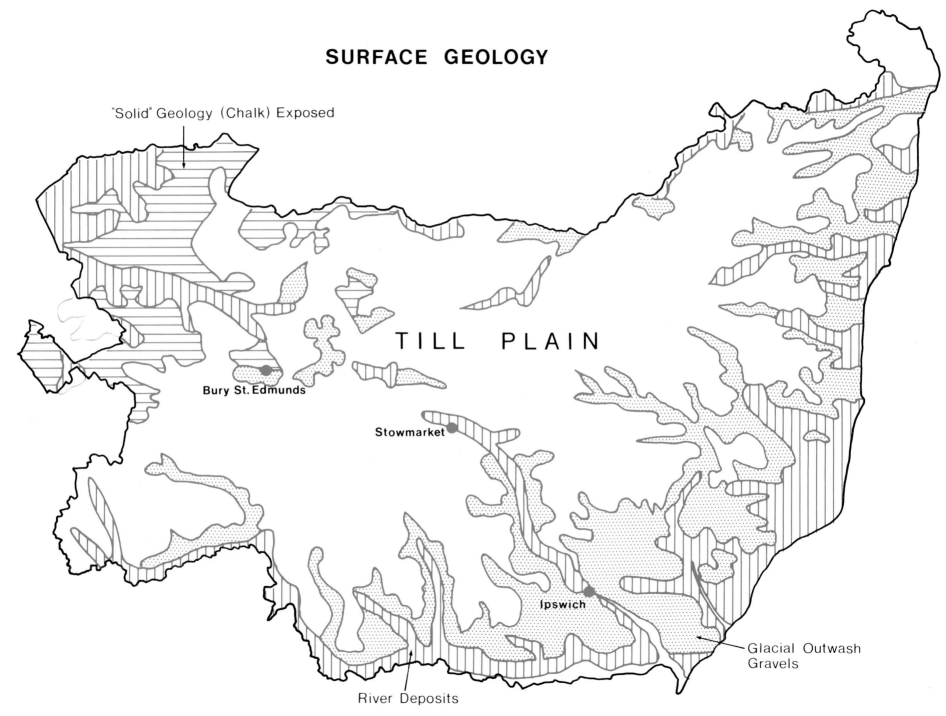

"Solid" Geology (Chalk) Exposed

TILL PLAIN

Bury St. Edmunds

Stowmarket

Ipswich

Glacial Outwash Gravels

River Deposits

19

5. SOIL REGIONS

Edward Martin

It has long been recognised that Suffolk contains several distinct regions and landscapes, which are largely the product of different soils. These soils are nearly all derived from the glacial 'drift' that effectively masks the solid geology (chalk in western and central Suffolk, crag in the east). About two-thirds of the county is covered by a great mantle of chalky boulder clay, which was dumped by retreating glaciers of the Anglian glaciation and is up to 226ft thick (at Wickhambrook). The clayland to the north of the A14 road is flat with wide interfluves, but to the south it is much more dissected by streams.[1] Flanking the clay are two large areas of sandy soils. In the west these cover chalk, the upper surface of which lies at varying depths, while in the extreme north-west the sands dip under the peats of the fen basin. In the east great expanses of sand overlie crag deposits, except in the Shotley and Felixstowe peninsulas, where the covering is a wind-blown loess called cover-loam.

The anonymous author of the *Chorography of Suffolk* (*c*.1600-05) identified three regions—the 'Woodlande & High Suffolcke' in the centre of the county, a coastal strip 'fitte for sheep and corne', and an area in the north-west that was 'mostly heathy and barren fit only for sheepe and conyes'.[2] In 1735 John Kirby of Woodbridge noted the same three divisions, and named them as the 'Woodlands' extending from the 'north-east corner of the Hundred of Blything, to the south-west corner of the county at Haverhill'; the 'Sandlands' which stretched along 'the sea coast, from Landguard Fort to Yarmouth'; and the 'Fielding' which comprised the Hundred of Lackford and parts of Blackbourn, Thedwastre and Thingoe. Kirby adds that the Woodland part was famed for its butter and cheese, and the Sandlands and Fielding were mainly used as sheepwalks, but with some good arable.[3]

In 1797 Arthur Young of Bradfield Combust, the noted writer on agricultural matters, identified five main soil zones in Suffolk — the Fen, the Sand of the north-west, the Strong Loam in the centre, the Rich Loam of the Shotley and Felixstowe peninsulas, and the Sand of the east coast. He also noted that the name 'Sandling' was given to the area 'south of a line of Woodbridge and Orford, where a large extent of poor, and even blowing sand is found'.[4]

Young's fivefold division of Suffolk was followed by most 19th-century writers. In 1849 W. and H. Raynbird gave the title of 'Heavy Land or Strong Loam' to the central clayland, but nevertheless this area, which includes the highest land in the county, was increasingly known by the older name of 'High Suffolk'. At the same time the equally venerable name of the 'Woodland(s)' fell into disuse, though the Raynbirds were still able to cite 'the number of hedges and hedge-row trees' as one of the bad practices of Suffolk farming.[5] The Sandlings became the accepted name for the eastern sand region.

Although the Raynbirds referred to the western sands as the Fielding, this term was probably going out of use. In 1866 Professor Alfred Newton referred to it as 'The Breck District'[6]—a 'breck' being a tract of heathland that was broken up for cultivation for a few years and then allowed to revert to its former condition.[7] The final form of the name of this highly distinctive region—Breckland—was coined in 1894 by the Thetford-bred journalist, W. G. Clarke.[8]

Today these regions are still discernible, but they have changed. The claylands of High Suffolk no longer bear a patchwork of small fields surrounded by dense hedges, but instead are characterised by enormous expanses of arable land, as a result of the bulldozing of hedges and the amalgamation of fields since the 1950s.

The huge open heaths, sheepwalks and rabbit-warrens of Breckland and the Sandlings have largely disappeared beneath the conifer plantations of the Forestry Commission (from 1922), or have been converted into arable land with the aid of modern fertilisers and irrigation. The Fens are now drained and intensively farmed. Since they were drained the peat has steadily dried and shrunk, so that the distinction between the Fens and Breckland is becoming ever less clear.

In the 1980s new impetus was given to the definition of natural regions by the designation of 'Environmentally Sensitive Areas' by the Ministry of Agriculture, three of which are partly in Suffolk.[9] In 1996 the Countryside Commission and English Nature produced a map entitled *The Countryside of England, landscape, wildlife and natural features,* which identified seven 'Character Areas' in Suffolk.[10] Based on this, English Nature has defined six 'Natural Areas'.[11]

Further details on p.191

KEY TO MAP OPPOSITE:

1. Wet peat-based soils of the Fens and river valleys
2. Soils derived from chalk
3. Mixtures of peat, chalk and sand in the Fen 'skirtland'
4. The sandy soils of Breckland and the Sandlings
5. Clay loams derived from chalky boulder clay, sandier in the east than in the west. Young's 'Strong Loam'
6. Loamy soils, mainly in river valleys
7. Loamy soils derived from loess, overlying sands and gravels. Young's 'Rich Loams'
8. Wet alluvial soils in coastal and river marshes

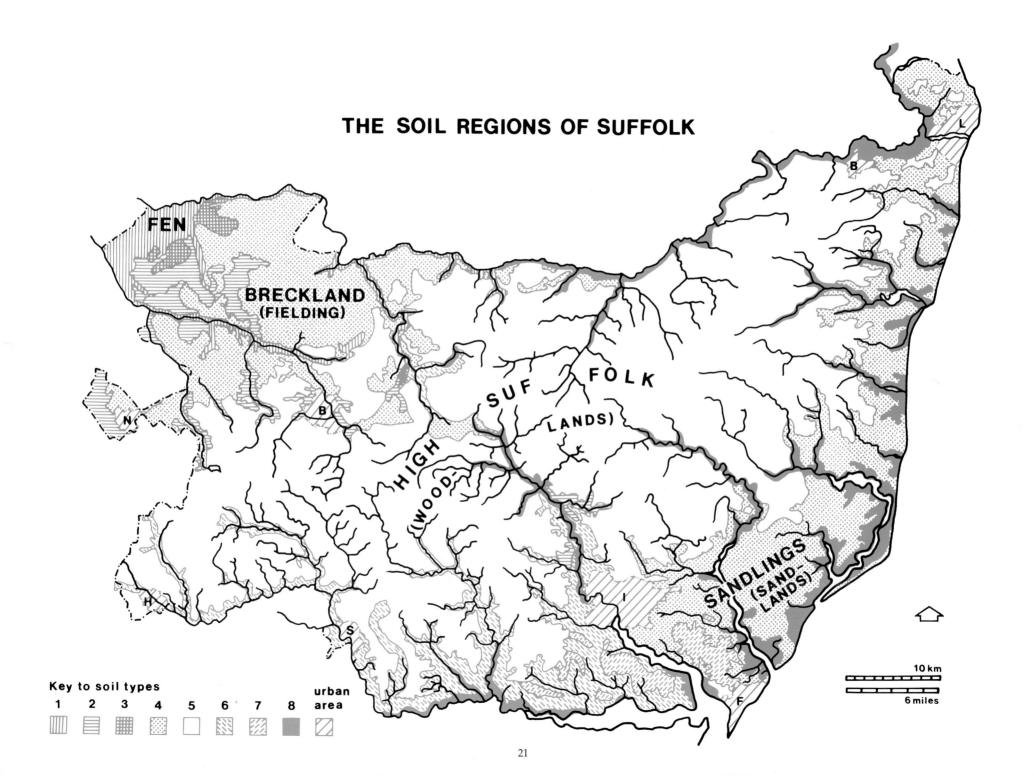

THE SOIL REGIONS OF SUFFOLK

FEN

BRECKLAND
(FIELDING)

HIGH

SUF FOLK

LANDS)

(WOOD-

SANDLINGS
(SAND-
LANDS)

B

N

H

S

F

I

L

B

Key to soil types

| 1 | 2 | 3 | 4 | 5 | 6 | 7 | 8 | urban area |

10 km

6 miles

6. SUFFOLK AND THE EAST ANGLIAN KINGDOM

Edward Martin

Suffolk and Norfolk are first recorded by name in the 1040s, in the will of a man called Thurstan.[1] Meaning the south and north folk, these names indicate that the two counties were once parts of a larger entity known as the kingdom of East Anglia, or the province of the eastern Angles. The *provincia Orientalium Anglorum* is mentioned by the Venerable Bede in his great history completed in AD 731. He also stated that the Angles were Germanic people who migrated to this region from a place called *Angulus* (now Angeln in Schleswig-Holstein, north Germany), an event that probably took place in the 5th century.[2] The Angles brought with them the English language, and the earliest known inscription in English is on a gold pendant of the late 5th century found at Lakenheath in 1981(see p. 7).[3]

The independent kingdom came to an end in 654, when King Anna was slain by King Penda of Mercia, and later kings were mostly subordinate to the Mercians. St Edmund, the last Anglo-Saxon king of East Anglia, was killed by Viking invaders in the winter of 869/870, but was quickly revered as a great Christian martyr, saint and patriot. Danish kings then ruled the region until 902 when King Eohric perished in battle against Edward the Elder of Wessex. Subsequently the region was ruled by ealdormen or earls, the earldom of East Anglia remaining undivided until after the Norman Conquest.[4]

It is not known when Suffolk and Norfolk were first distinguished: the division could reflect folk differences stemming back to the original migrations, but could also be a later administrative convenience. One possible context is the splitting of the East Anglian bishopric in or about 673. From then on there were two bishops, one seated at *Dommoc* and the other at Elmham, each presumably serving a part of East Anglia. The equation of *Dommoc* with Dunwich and Elmham with North Elmham would place one bishop in Suffolk and one in Norfolk, but this is by no means certain. If 'Elmham' at this period was South Elmham, both bishops would have been in Suffolk. This pattern was disrupted by the Vikings in 869/870. When the diocese was restored *c.*955 it was as the bishopric of Elmham. Although there was now only one East Anglian bishop, he had a seat in both counties: one at North Elmham for Norfolk and one at Hoxne for Suffolk.[5]

The North Sea provides an obvious boundary for East Anglia on the east and north, but the southern and western sides are more of a problem. The medieval diocese of Norwich covered Norfolk and Suffolk, but also extended a short distance into Cambridgeshire, its western boundary following the line of the Devil's Dyke. This strongly suggests that this was the boundary of East Anglia when the diocese was refounded in the mid-10th century. Bede, however, stated that Ely was part of the province of East Anglia, and that St Æthelthryth (Etheldreda) had founded a monastery there (in 673) because she belonged to the East Anglian royal family. The 11th-century Book of Ely gives a different story, that Ely was a marriage gift to Etheldreda from her husband Tondbert, a chieftain (*princeps*) of the South Gyrwe. This source also says that the Gyrwe (a name implying marsh-dwellers) were 'South Angles living in the great fen in which lies the Isle of Ely'.[6] A possible explanation of this confusion is that the Gyrwe were a semi-independent people who came under East Anglian control in the early 7th century, but were later grouped with the Middle Angles, their western neighbours, when they both fell under Mercian domination later that century.[7]

The southern boundary of East Anglia has been assumed to follow the River Stour, which for most of its course forms a natural boundary between the present counties of Suffolk and Essex. However in Iron Age and Roman times the Stour was not a boundary, and both south-east Suffolk and Essex lay within the territory of the Trinovantes (see Map 15). When then did it become a boundary? Could the East Saxon kingdom have once stretched into Suffolk? The distribution of typical artefacts confirms the predominant Anglian character of north-west Suffolk and Norfolk, but in south-east Suffolk the position is less clear.[8] This is surprising because in the 7th century the south-east was the heartland of the East Anglian royal dynasty, the Wuffingas. Bede refers to their royal residence at Rendlesham, and their bodies lie under the burial mounds at Sutton Hoo. Bede also records that they had friendly relations with the East Saxon Seaxneating dynasty, and the Wuffingas even seem to share naming patterns used by the Seaxneatings.[9] However they also had strong links with Sweden and could even have been of Swedish origin.[10] One explanation may be that the 7th-century English kingdoms were formed through the coalescing of smaller territorial units, each perhaps with a different folk history. South-east Suffolk could have been one of these units, perhaps with a population of mixed origin. It may originally have been loosely allied to the East Saxons but then, for unknown reasons, allied itself with, or conquered, its northern Anglian neighbours. In so doing a new boundary may have been formed.

Further details on p.192

LINCOLNSHIRE

GYRWE

FENS

HUNTS.

MIDDLE

ANGLES

Two Hundreds of
the Isle of Ely

Ely ★

Medieval
boundary of
Norwich Diocese

Devil's Dyke

CAMBRIDGESHIRE

CLAY

NORFOLK

★N. Elmham

EAST

ANGLIA

★S. Elmham

★Hoxne

Dunwich★

Bury St Edmunds ★

SUFFOLK

Rendlesham
★

★Sutton
Hoo

Ipswich ★

ESSEX

EAST SAXONS

LONDON

JUTES

5th-century folk
migrations

FRISIANS   SAXONS   ANGLES

0   500 km

SUFFOLK, EAST ANGLIA AND ENGLAND :

THE ANGLO-SAXON MIGRATIONS

AND

THE KINGDOM OF THE EAST ANGLES

0   30 miles

0   50 km

Joanna Martin

The whole of Suffolk comes under the jurisdiction of the Archbishop of Canterbury, and has done so since the conversion to Christianity in the 7th century AD.

The first East Anglian diocese was founded in the 630s when St Felix, a Burgundian, was sent by Archbishop Honorius to convert the East Angles. With the support of King Sigeberht, the first see was established at *Dommoc*, which has been variously identified as Dunwich or Walton Castle near Felixstowe. In the latter part of the 7th century, the diocese was split into two, with bishops at *Dommoc* and Elmham. Whether the latter was North Elmham in Norfolk or South Elmham in Suffolk has been the subject of much debate: both places have early ruined churches which have been claimed as cathedrals. In the second half of the 9th century, the Danish invasions swept away these East Anglian bishoprics.

In the 920s however, Bishop Theodred of London re-established episcopal rule in Suffolk. His will of *c*.942-51 mentions his 'episcopal demesne' at Hoxne. After his death the line of local bishops recommences. They called themselves 'Bishops of the East Angles' and had seats at Hoxne and Elmham (by this time almost certainly North Elmham), to respect the sensitivities of both the Northfolk and Southfolk. This situation continued until the 1070s when Bishop Herfast moved the see to Thetford in accordance with Archbishop Lanfranc's order that bishops should be based on major towns. It seems that Herfast's ultimate aim was to move the episcopal seat to the wealthy abbey of Bury St Edmunds, but the abbey successfully resisted his take-over. Finally, in the 1090s, Bishop Herbert Losinga settled on Norwich as the centre of the East Anglian diocese.

From 1094 until 1836, the whole of Suffolk, apart from a few parishes, lay within the Diocese of Norwich. The only exceptions were the parishes of Moulton, Hadleigh and Monks Eleigh which were in the Archbishop of Canterbury's Peculiar Deanery of Bocking, and Freckenham which was a Peculiar of the Bishop of Rochester.[1]

The chief administrative officers of bishops were the archdeacons, to whom they delegated much of the day-to-day work of the diocese. Therefore archdeacons exercised general disciplinary supervision over the clergy of their areas, and were also responsible for the administration of ecclesiastical property. Suffolk appears to have had one archdeacon down to about 1125. The county was then divided into two: the Archdeaconry of Sudbury covered the western half and the Archdeaconry of Suffolk the eastern half.

From at least the 11th century onwards, the archdeaconries of Suffolk were themselves divided into rural deaneries, the boundaries of which corresponded very closely to those of hundreds (see Map 8). Fifteen of the 23 deaneries, indeed, bore exactly the same names as the hundreds.[2] The duties of deans were not very precisely defined but, like archdeacons, they were expected to supervise the welfare and conduct of the parish clergy, and take some responsibility for parish churches and other ecclesiastical buildings. By the end of the Middle Ages, the duties of the rural dean often seem to have been carried out rather perfunctorily. After the Reformation the office was suspended, but deaneries continued to function to a limited extent as administrative divisions.[3] In 1842 the office of rural dean was revived by Bishop Stanley.

The traditional deaneries of Suffolk contained a total of over 500 parishes (501 in 1836), most of whose boundaries went back at least to the late Anglo-Saxon period. Recent work has suggested that ecclesiastical parishes founded in Middle or Late Saxon times merely took over earlier boundaries of a secular and economic kind.

Indeed, in one or two places, it has been shown that parish boundaries probably followed lines established in prehistoric times.[4] A small number of places in Suffolk, however, did not fall within the parochial system, and were classified as 'extra parochial'.[5]

In 1837 the Deaneries of Hartismere and Stow, together with the parishes of Rickinghall Inferior and Hinderclay in Blackbourn Deanery, were transferred to the Archdeaconry of Suffolk. Thus reduced, the Archdeaconry of Sudbury simultaneously became part of the Diocese of Ely. Some of the larger deaneries were subdivided in 1884, but otherwise the situation remained largely unchanged until 1914. In that year the new diocese of St Edmundsbury and Ipswich was created from the Archdeaconries of Sudbury and Suffolk, apart from the Deanery of Lothingland which remained in the Diocese of Norwich. Then, in 1932, the Archdeaconry of Ipswich was formed out of parts of the older two. There were also changes in the parish structure in the 19th and 20th centuries.[6]

Further details on p.192

Bronze seal of Bishop Æthelwold of *Dommoc c*.AD 850. 2¾ in long. Found at Eye before 1822.

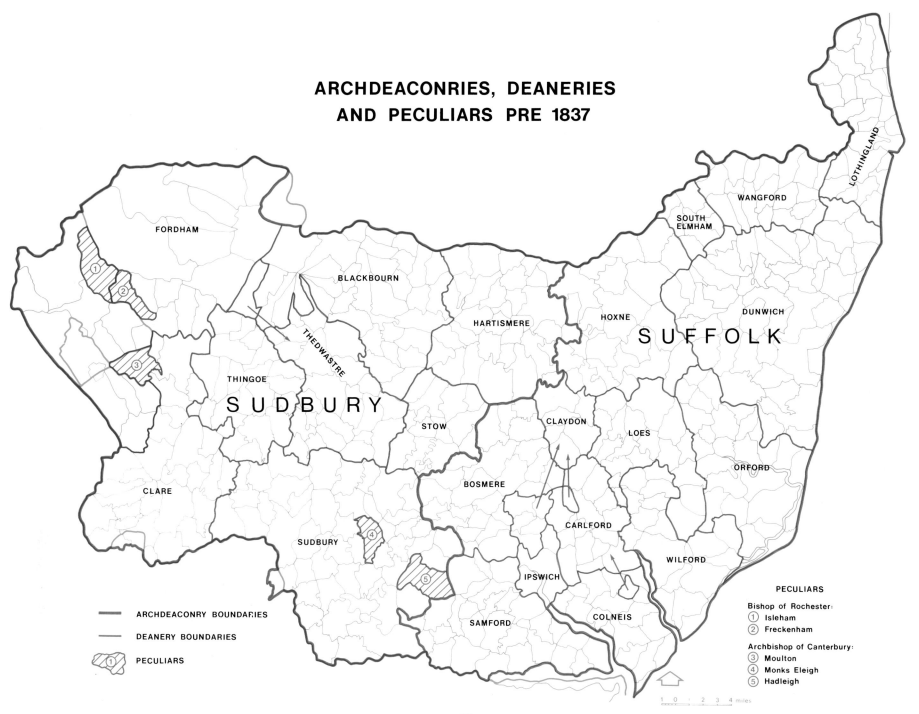

ARCHDEACONRIES, DEANERIES
AND PECULIARS PRE 1837

LOTHINGLAND

FORDHAM

WANGFORD

SOUTH ELMHAM

BLACKBOURN

DUNWICH

THEDWASTRE

HARTISMERE

HOXNE

SUFFOLK

THINGOE

SUDBURY

STOW

CLAYDON

LOES

CLARE

BOSMERE

ORFORD

CARLFORD

SUDBURY

WILFORD

IPSWICH

SAMFORD

COLNEIS

—— ARCHDEACONRY BOUNDARIES

—— DEANERY BOUNDARIES

① PECULIARS

PECULIARS

Bishop of Rochester:
① Isleham
② Freckenham

Archbishop of Canterbury:
③ Moulton
④ Monks Eleigh
⑤ Hadleigh

1 0 2 3 4 miles

8. HUNDREDS AND LIBERTIES

Edward Martin

The division of the county into Hundreds—perhaps originally representing a hundred *hides* or family holdings—dates back to at least the 10th century, and some may be based on even older land units. Above the level of each individual vill, the hundred was the basis of all public administration in medieval England, judicial, fiscal and military. Each hundred had its own court, second only to the county court, presided over by a hundred bailiff. These courts dealt mainly with public law (folk right) and were originally known as 'moots' or 'things'.[1]

From the 13th century onwards the rise of royal justice undermined hundred and county courts, and both were largely superseded by the establishment of Quarter Sessions in the later Middle Ages. However, Petty Sessions continued to be held within hundreds until the 19th century. In 1894 District Councils, the modern successors of the ancient hundreds, were set up and, until 1974, often bore the same names.

Most of the Suffolk hundreds take their names from the original open-air meeting-places of their Anglo-Saxon courts. These were held at prominent or well-known features in the landscape—such as fords, meres and mounds.[2] Some meeting-places were central to their hundreds but others, like Lackford and Wainford, were on the borders. By the 18th century many hundred courts were held in inns: for example the Blackbourn court was held in the Cock Inn at Stanton.

In 1086 the Domesday survey listed 25 hundreds in Suffolk, but by the 19th century the number had been reduced to 21 (see map). For largely fiscal reasons some hundreds like Babergh were rated as double hundreds, and others like Cosford as half hundreds; Samford was the only one regarded as a hundred and a half. The two hundreds of Blackbourn and Bradmere, already in-separable in 1086, were by 1100 united to form a double hundred. Claydon was dismembered in the 12th century when one third became the half hundred of Thredling; the remainder was united with Bosmere in the 15th century.[3] The half hundred of Parham was absorbed into Plomesgate by 1240.[4] The two small hundreds of Mutford and Lothingland were united in 1763.[5] Exning was part of Cambridgeshire in 1086, but was drawn into Suffolk in the 12th century as a half hundred, before becoming a detached portion of Lackford.[6]

The ancient boroughs were largely outside the hundredal organisation. In 1086 Ipswich was separately rated as a half hundred. Bury St Edmunds was also a distinct entity, unspecified, but it must once have been in Thingoe Hundred as the mound of Thingoe lay on the outskirts of the medieval town. Sudbury was a detached part of Thingoe in 1086, but was later assessed either with Babergh or separately.

Superimposed on the hundred system were two major Liberties or Franchises—areas where royal jurisdiction was delegated to a monastery. The Liberty of St Etheldreda, then called *Wicklaw*, was granted in 970 by King Edgar to St Etheldreda's abbey at Ely. When in 1109 the bishopric of Ely was founded, the Liberty was transferred to the Prior and monks. After the dissolution of the abbey in 1540, the Liberty was granted to the Dean and Chapter of the cathedral. The territory that comprised the Liberty of St Edmund had formed the dowry of Emma, wife of King Canute, and was granted by her son, Edward the Confessor, to St Edmund's abbey at Bury in the early 11th century. At the dissolution in 1540, the Liberty reverted to the Crown and was subsequently, in Elizabeth's reign, granted to Sir Nicholas Bacon. In 1889 the area of the Liberty became the county of West Suffolk, and survived as a distinct administrative unit until 1974.

The remainder of Suffolk, called the Geldable or 'taxable', remained under royal jurisdiction and, because of its small size, shared a sheriff with Norfolk. Suffolk did not have a sheriff of its own until 1576. The Geldable had a northern capital at Beccles and a southern one at Ipswich.[7] When royal taxes were due, the Geldable paid half while the two Liberties combined to pay the other half (Bury paying two parts to Ely's one).

Within these three major units were several smaller, often fragmented, feudal liberties: the Honours of Clare, Eye and Haughley, the Liberty of the Duke of Norfolk, and the Bishop of Norwich's Liberty of Elmham. The first was centred on Clare castle and extended into Essex.[8] The Honour of Eye was closely connected with the Earls and Dukes of Suffolk and had jurisdiction over scattered lands in east Suffolk. The Honour of Haughley was closely connected with the office of constable of Dover Castle, and was alternatively known as the Honour of the Constable; after the 12th century it was frequently held in conjunction with the Honour of Eye. The Duke of Norfolk's Liberty was created as late as 1468 and extended into Norfolk: it included Bungay but not the important castle at Framlingham. The Bishop's Liberty was based on ancient episcopal estates in South Elmham and lasted until 1536.

Further details on p.193

HUNDREDS AND LIBERTIES

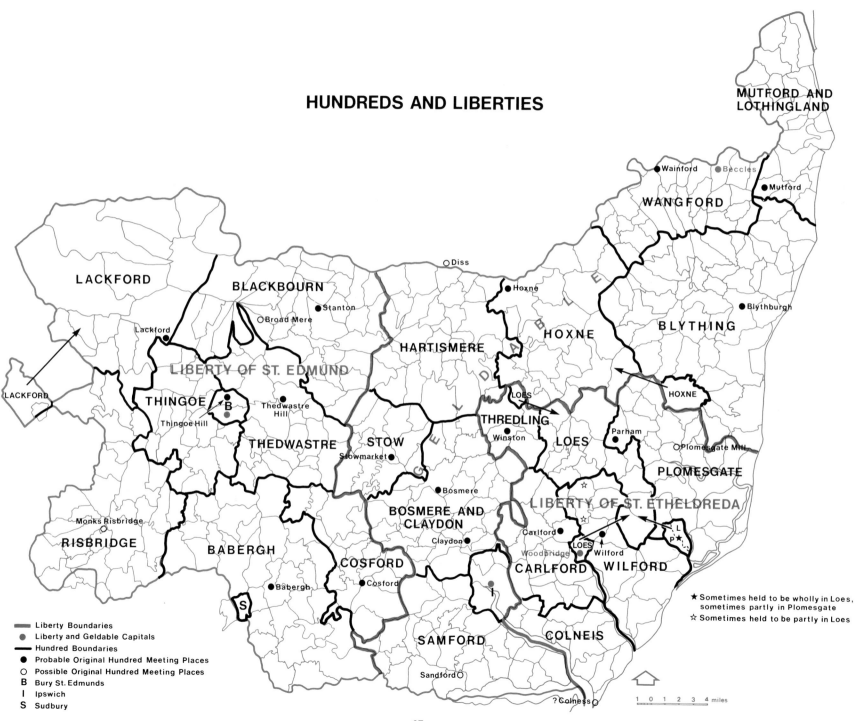

MUTFORD AND LOTHINGLAND

● Wainford   ● Beccles
● Mutford

WANGFORD

LACKFORD   BLACKBOURN   ○ Diss
● Hoxne   ● Blythburgh

● Stanton
○ Broad Mere   BLYTHING

Lackford ●
LIBERTY OF ST. EDMUND   HARTISMERE   HOXNE

THINGOE   B   ● Thedwastre Hill
LOES   HOXNE
LACKFORD   Thingoe Hill   THREDLING
THEDWASTRE   STOW   ● Winston   LOES   ● Parham
● Stowmarket   ○ Plomesgate Mill

● Bosmere   PLOMESGATE

Monks Risbridge ○   BOSMERE AND CLAYDON   LIBERTY OF ST. ETHELDREDA
RISBRIDGE   ● Claydon   ☆
Carlford ●   ☆   L
P★
COSFORD   LOES   Wilford   ☆
BABERGH   Woodbridge   ● Wilford
● Babergh   ● Cosford   CARLFORD   WILFORD
I
S   ★ Sometimes held to be wholly in Loes,
sometimes partly in Plomesgate
COLNEIS   ☆ Sometimes held to be partly in Loes
SAMFORD

Sandford ○

? Colness ○

── Liberty Boundaries
● Liberty and Geldable Capitals
── Hundred Boundaries
● Probable Original Hundred Meeting Places
○ Possible Original Hundred Meeting Places
B Bury St. Edmunds
I Ipswich
S Sudbury

1 0 1 2 3 4 miles

27

9. LOCAL GOVERNMENT SINCE 1872

Gwyn Thomas

THE COUNTY: Although Suffolk had been a single county for centuries, the western portion—the Liberty of Bury St Edmunds—had long enjoyed a degree of autonomy. During the second half of the 19th century, this status came under fire in the interests of efficiency: the police forces of East and West Suffolk were merged in 1872, and the desirability of a single court of Quarter Sessions was vigorously debated (already there was a single Clerk of the Peace).

The local Government Bill of 1888, designed to transfer the justices' administrative powers to elected County Councils, proposed a single County Council for Suffolk. Predictably West Suffolk campaigned hard for a separate administrative county and succeeded. The Boundary Commissioners had proposed that if West Suffolk became a separate county, it should contain the whole of Stow and Risbridge Unions, and that the whole of Newmarket Union should go to Cambridgeshire but, when the Bill became law, the traditional Anglo-Saxon boundaries of the Liberty were adopted. The Local Government Act allowed towns with a population of over 50,000 to become County Boroughs, carrying out all the functions of County Councils. Ipswich was just large enough to qualify, and therefore became totally independent of the administrative county of East Suffolk.

Various adjustments were made to the county boundaries between 1889 and 1896.[1] After 1896 they remained unchanged until 1974, except for minor extensions to Ipswich in 1934 and 1952. The Ministry of Health suggested in 1934 that efficiency might be improved by uniting the two counties. In 1965 the Local Government Commission for England discussed amalgamation, but did not propose it in view of strong antipathy in West Suffolk and little enthusiasm in the East. In 1966, however, the Redcliffe-Maud Commission was set up to review the whole of local government. Its proposals of

1969 would have obliterated the historic county of Suffolk. 'Unitary Area 44' was to include East Suffolk (less what was later to become the Waveney District), West Suffolk (less Haverhill and Newmarket and their hinterlands) and north-east Essex. Public outcry against these proposals led to their abandonment in the White Paper of 1971, which instead proposed to merge East and West Suffolk and Ipswich, while transferring Haverhill and Newmarket Urban Districts and parts of Clare and Mildenhall Rural Districts to Cambridgeshire. These areas were later returned to Suffolk, so that the new county which emerged on 1 April 1974 comprised the former East and West Suffolk counties, less six parishes north of Lowestoft which were transferred to Norfolk. The two county councils had to go, as both were too small, but the historic county of Suffolk survived reorganisation remarkably well.

SECOND-TIER UNITS OF LOCAL GOVERNMENT: The Public Health Act of 1848 allowed borough councils to become Local Boards of Health; if a town was not a borough, an *ad hoc* board could be established. In 1872 another Public Health Act rationalised previous piecemeal developments by creating a network of Sanitary Districts. Boroughs, local Boards and Improvement Commissioners automatically became Urban Sanitary Authorities;[2] Poor Law Unions, increasingly seen as useful administrative units for other purposes, became Rural Sanitary Authorities (Map 1, opposite).

The Local Government Act of 1894 attempted to rationalise the whole pattern: all urban Sanitary Authorities either remained boroughs or became Urban Districts;[3] all rural Sanitary Authorities became Rural Districts. Unions had been created as convenient areas based on urban centres, often with little reference to county boundaries; however all Rural Districts were required to lie wholly within one administrative county. As a

result Rural Districts of West Suffolk represented the Suffolk portions of unions which crossed county boundaries—Clare (part of Risbridge Union), Melford (Sudbury), Thedwastre (Stow), Moulton (Newmarket) and Brandon (Thetford) (Map 2, opposite).

The local Government Act of 1929 obliged County Councils to review district boundaries, in order to increase administrative efficiency. In East Suffolk changes took effect in 1934. Stowmarket, Halesworth and Leiston-cum-Sizewell Urban Districts were enlarged, as were Aldeburgh and Lowestoft Municipal Boroughs; the nine Rural Districts were reduced to seven. In West Suffolk, in 1935, Glemsford Urban District and the very small Rural Districts of Brandon and Moulton were abolished, and Bury St Edmunds Municipal Borough was enlarged (Map 3, opposite).

This remained the pattern until 1974. Despite the changes of 1934-5, the administrative map was still a patchwork with some very small authorities. The aim of the Local Government Act of 1972 was to create large counties and larger, stronger and more uniform second-tier authorities, reuniting urban centres with their rural hinterlands. The 31 districts, of four different types, were replaced in the 'new' Suffolk by seven much larger districts, two of which (Ipswich and St Edmundsbury) opted to be designated Boroughs (Map 4, opposite). The only concession to the past was that the new districts comprised groups of the former units. Even so, the eastern boundary of the Liberty of St Edmund was all but abandoned. Despite strong campaigns for unitary authority status by Ipswich and St Edmundsbury, the pattern created in 1974 survived the Local Government Review of the mid-1990s intact.

Further details on p.193

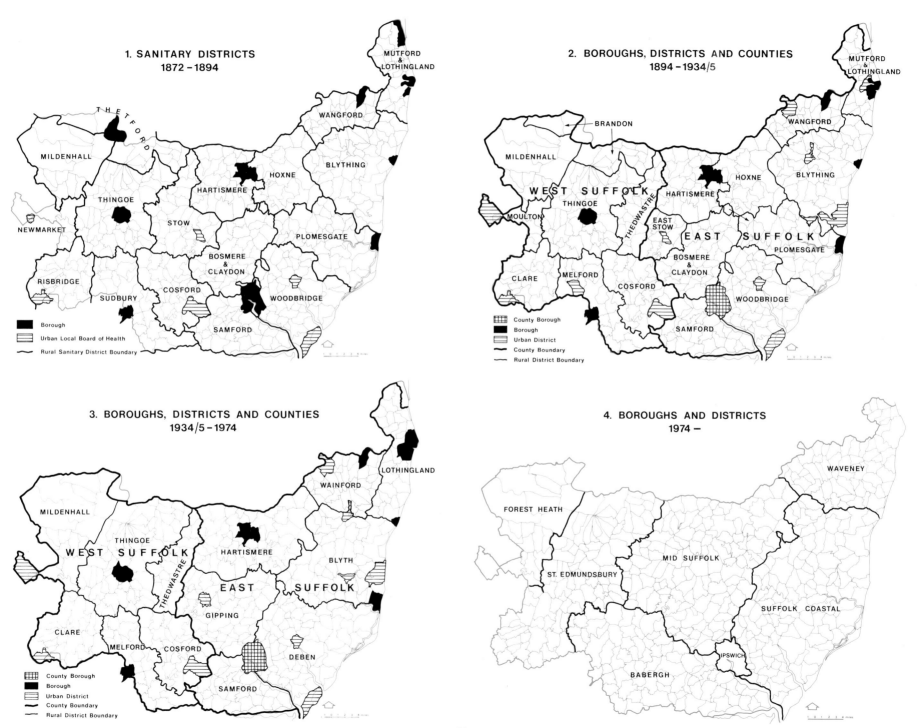

1. SANITARY DISTRICTS
1872–1894

THETFORD
MUTFORD & LOTHINGLAND
MILDENHALL
WANGFORD
BLYTHING
HOXNE
HARTISMERE
THINGOE
STOW
NEWMARKET
PLOMESGATE
BOSMERE & CLAYDON
RISBRIDGE
COSFORD
WOODBRIDGE
SUDBURY
SAMFORD

■ Borough
▤ Urban Local Board of Health
— Rural Sanitary District Boundary

2. BOROUGHS, DISTRICTS AND COUNTIES
1894–1934/5

MUTFORD & LOTHINGLAND
BRANDON
MILDENHALL
WANGFORD
WEST SUFFOLK
BLYTHING
THINGOE
HOXNE
MOULTON
THEDWASTRE
HARTISMERE
EAST STOW
EAST SUFFOLK
CLARE
MELFORD
BOSMERE & CLAYDON
PLOMESGATE
COSFORD
WOODBRIDGE
SAMFORD

▦ County Borough
■ Borough
▤ Urban District
— County Boundary
— Rural District Boundary

3. BOROUGHS, DISTRICTS AND COUNTIES
1934/5–1974

LOTHINGLAND
WAINFORD
MILDENHALL
THINGOE
WEST SUFFOLK
HARTISMERE
BLYTH
THEDWASTRE
EAST SUFFOLK
CLARE
GIPPING
MELFORD
COSFORD
DEBEN
SAMFORD

▦ County Borough
■ Borough
▤ Urban District
— County Boundary
— Rural District Boundary

4. BOROUGHS AND DISTRICTS
1974–

WAVENEY
FOREST HEATH
MID SUFFOLK
ST. EDMUNDSBURY
SUFFOLK COASTAL
IPSWICH
BABERGH

10. PARLIAMENTARY CONSTITUENCIES

Gwyn Thomas

Before Parliament was reformed in 1832, Suffolk returned sixteen members. In addition to the county constituency, where forty-shilling freeholders had returned two knights of the shire since 1290, seven parliamentary boroughs each returned two members. Dunwich and Ipswich were represented continuously from 1298; Orford also returned members in 1298, but did so regularly only from 1529. Sudbury was first represented in 1558, Aldeburgh and Eye from 1571, and Bury St Edmunds in 1621.

It is hard to give details of the size of the electorate before 1832. In the early 18th century, Suffolk probably had between 5000 and 6000 county electors, and about 1800 in the seven boroughs. While the county had a uniform franchise, the boroughs varied considerably. In Bury the 37 members of the Corporation alone returned two members; in the other boroughs the Corporation and freemen had the vote. On the eve of Reform, the county electorate was probably much the same in size—4849 men polled at the general election of 1790. The boroughs too remained the same size, except for Ipswich where wholesale creation of burgesses for political reasons had inflated in electorate in 1826 to over a thousand.

The Reform Act of 1832 removed many of the small 'rotten' and 'pocket' boroughs, and began to widen the franchise. It added various types of leaseholder and tenant to the freeholder in the county, and created a uniform qualification of £10 householder in the boroughs. As a result of the Act three Suffolk boroughs—Aldeburgh, Dunwich and Orford—were completely disfranchised (Map 1, opposite). Eye only survived by having its constituency extended to include ten surrounding parishes: even so it was reduced to one member. On the other hand, Bury, Ipswich and Sudbury each retained two members. The county was split into Eastern and Western Divisions, each with two members. After the Act, Suffolk returned eleven members to Parliament. This remained the arrangement until 1885, with one exception. In 1844 Sudbury was disfranchised because of spectacularly corrupt practices. The borough was merged into the Western Division and its two members removed from the county's total of eleven.

The franchise was extended in 1867 and again in 1884. After the latter date, any male householder or lodger who had resided for a year in the county, or in one of its boroughs, was normally entitled to vote. In 1885 the electoral map was tidied up by creating constituencies of roughly uniform population, and by reducing the number of constituencies returning two members. In Suffolk (Map 2, opposite) the two county divisions were rearranged into five, each with one member: Northern (Lowestoft), North-Eastern (Eye), North-Western (Stowmarket), South (Sudbury) and South-Eastern (Woodbridge). The borough seat at Eye was abolished and absorbed into the new Eye division; Bury St Edmunds was reduced to one member and only Ipswich retained two.[1]

These constituencies remained in existence until 1918, when the franchise was further extended and seats were again redistributed. The voting qualification for men was reduced to six months' residence, and for the first time women—those over the age of thirty—were given the parliamentary vote. Suffolk's parliamentary representation was now cut to six members (Map 3, opposite). Ipswich lost one of its MPs. Bury St Edmunds was so small that it could no longer continue as a separate seat, and became part of the North-Western Division, re-named the Bury St Edmunds Division. The area around Stowmarket was moved into the Eye Division, and minor alterations were made to the boundaries of the other constituencies which retained their former names.

In 1948 another redistribution of seats reduced the number of Suffolk's MPs still further (Map 4, opposite). Despite strong protests from east and west, and from all political parties, the geographical county of Suffolk was henceforth regarded as the 'Parliamentary County': seats would no longer have to fall entirely with East and West Suffolk. This allowed the abolition of the Sudbury and Woodbridge divisions, and the creation of a new Sudbury and Woodbridge County Constituency. The Bury, Eye and Lowestoft divisions were all enlarged and re-designated County Constituencies, while Ipswich became a Borough Constituency. With a few minor adjustments in the boundary of the Ipswich seat in 1953, this arrangement stood until 1983. Then, for the first time in 350 years, the number of Suffolk MPs was increased. Sudbury and Woodbridge was re-named South Suffolk; its eastern parishes and the huge Eye constituency were split to form Mid-Suffolk and Suffolk Coastal. Lowestoft became Waveney, while Ipswich and Bury St Edmunds retained their names. Yet another increase took effect in 1997 after the Bury St Edmunds seat was split into the two constituencies of Bury St Edmunds and West Suffolk.[2]

Further details on p.194

Hustings on Angel Hill, Bury St Emunds, general election of 1868. Such open voting was replaced by the secret ballot in 1872.

MAP 1 : 1832-1885

EYE

BURY ST. EDMUNDS

WESTERN   DIVISION

EASTERN   DIVISION

IPSWICH

SUDBURY

MAP 2 : 1885-1918

NORTHERN

NORTH – WESTERN

NORTH – EASTERN

BURY ST. EDMUNDS

SOUTH

SOUTH – EASTERN

IPSWICH

MAP 3 : 1918-1948

LOWESTOFT

BURY ST. EDMUNDS

EYE

SUDBURY

WOODBRIDGE

IPSWICH

MAP 4 : 1948-1983

LOWESTOFT

BURY ST. EDMUNDS

EYE

IPSWICH

SUDBURY AND WOODBRIDGE

11. THE PALAEOLITHIC

John Wymer

Our human ancestors were in existence for a vast span of time before they set foot in Europe, leave alone Britain. Certainly they lived in East Africa some two million years ago, but it would seem that they first explored the temperate zones of the northern hemisphere about one and a half million years later. We have evidence that they were in parts of Britain before the major glaciation of the Anglian Stage. At High Lodge, Mildenhall, is a remarkable site where a whole raft of interglacial river or lake deposits, containing palaeoliths (flint implements and waste flakes), was lifted by the glacial ice of the Anglian Stage into its till. Palaeoliths are also found in the gravels of the pre-Anglian Bytham River (see Map 2) at Lakenheath, Mildenhall and Icklingham. A recently excavated site at Barnham of the succeeding interglacial period has yielded many hundreds of flakes, cores and at least one hand-axe, found where they were originally discarded. No human skeletal remains have been found but they would presumably have been of *Homo sapiens*.

Suffolk is very rich in the number of places where worked flints of the Palaeolithic period have been found, mainly in river gravels that formed when, after the major glaciation, the drainage pattern and land-scape were assuming their present form. It also contains some very famous sites for archaeologists, especially Hoxne, where the great antiquity of these flint tools was first realised as early as 1797. Warren Hill at Mildenhall is one of the most prolific sites for the finding of hand-axes. These are heavy, pointed or ovate tools that are often very symmetrical and elegant, used for butchering and other purposes. In various forms, hand-axes dominate the period until the later part of the last glaciation. Some sites can be dated to stages of the British Pleistocene sequence, but the majority only very broadly within the long period involved, spanning 200 or even 300 thousand years. Particularly significant is

that the land was not only occupied during the warm interglacials, but also during the cool climates of the so-called Wolstonian Stage (see p.191). People had therefore adapted to difficult conditions, in which abundant game must have been a great attraction. Many of the animals which they hunted are no longer found in Britain or are extinct such as the lion, bear, mammoth and woolly rhinoceros. Horses, deer and bovids were the main source of meat. In order to survive they must have had shelter or clothing, but of these nothing has survived save for flint scrapers used for dressing hides.

The pattern of life remained very similar from millenium to millenium, though changes did slowly occur. We have little evidence in Suffolk for activity during the latter part of the last glaciation, some 30-35,000 years ago. This was a time when complex, highly organised hunting societies appeared in Europe, associated with our own species, *Homo sapiens sapiens*. This period is described as the Earlier Upper Palaeolithic, and some of the distinctive flints made at this time (long blades, leaf-shaped spearheads) were washed into low-lying gravels of the River Gipping at Bramford Road, Ipswich. They probably represent the casual losses of small hunting parties from what is now the Low Countries, using a land-bridge which existed across what is now the North Sea (see Map 2). It would have been very cold in Suffolk, and as ice came closer from the north the periglacial climate would have resembled that experienced in Siberia today. A few hunters may have braved the elements, but we have no clear evidence of any further human occupation until the ice retreated.

Further details on p.194

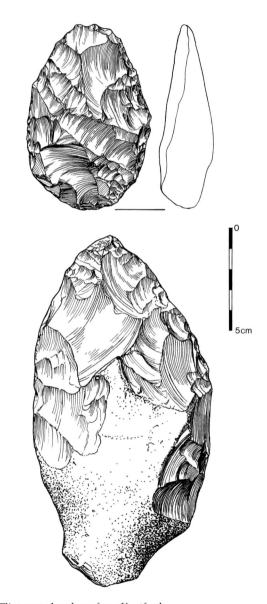

0

5cm

Top: Flint ovate hand-axe from Kentford.
Bottom: Flint hand-axe from Barnham.

THE PALAEOLITHIC PERIOD

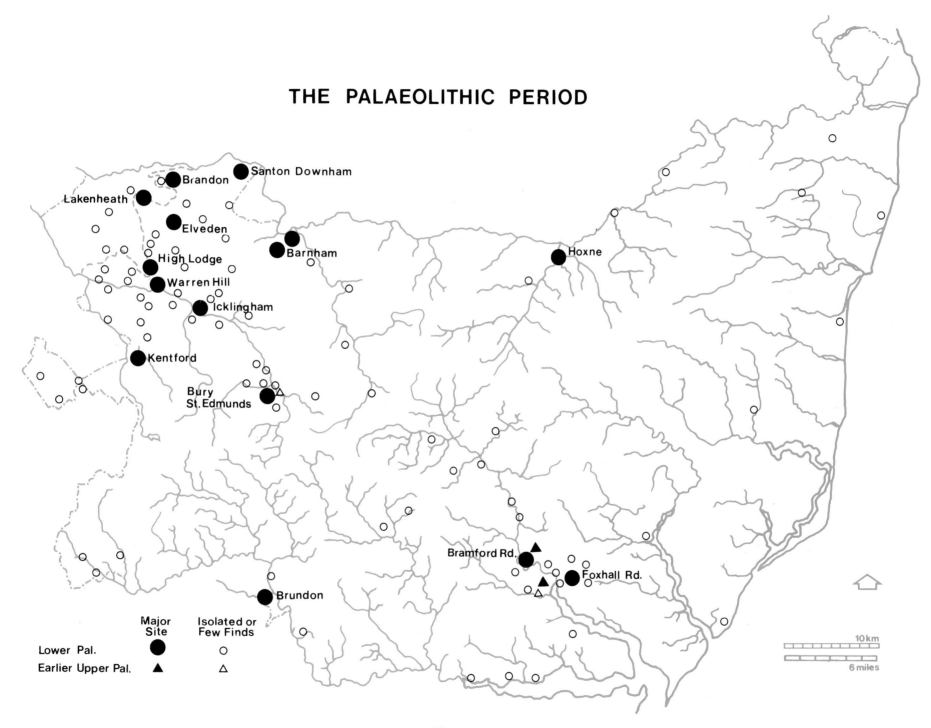

Santon Downham

Brandon

Lakenheath

Elveden

Barnham

High Lodge

Hoxne

Warren Hill

Icklingham

Kentford

Bury
St. Edmunds

Bramford Rd.

Foxhall Rd.

Brundon

Major
Site

Isolated or
Few Finds

Lower Pal.

Earlier Upper Pal.

10km

6 miles

12. LATE GLACIAL AND MESOLITHIC HUNTERS

John Wymer

By 11,000 BC glacial ice had almost disappeared from northern Britain, and the climate was warm enough to attract herds of animals, especially horse and deer. Small bands of hunters occupied parts of England, particularly the highland zone where caves gave natural shelter. Although hunting forays may have been made seasonally—even when much of the country was covered by ice—these people had probably spread from the continent, across a land bridge which existed between Britain and the Low Countries (see Map 2). Perhaps some had adapted to the climate, as Eskimos do today. Suffolk was not actually glaciated during this final episode of the Ice Age, but a glacier had previously reached as far as the North Norfolk coast. Nothing in Suffolk can definitely be dated to this time (11,000-9,000 BC), although it seems likely that it was occasionally visited.

Human movement was also influenced by a very cold period between 9000 and 8300 BC, called the Loch Lomond Stadial, when glaciers re-advanced into parts of Scotland. It is towards the end of this cold period that evidence can be found for the presence of such hunters in Suffolk: broken barbed points of antler and bone have come from Sproughton[1], in gravels of the River Gipping which at this time were filling a buried channel. Shortly afterwards, on the banks of the river, men found nodules of fine quality flint and produced distinctive artefacts from them: long, parallel-sided blades, scraping tools and stout chisel-like tools for working bone and antler. A few other discarded pieces of this time have been found elsewhere in Suffolk.

Mesolithic is a term used to describe the period after the final episode of glaciation in Britain (for convenience accepted as 8300 BC but obviously varying in different parts of the country), and lasting until an economy appeared which was not dependent on hunting, fishing and food-gathering. As the climate ameliorated, forests of pine and birch developed, until by about 5500 BC mixed oak forests dominated the landscape. Archaeologists prefer to divide the Mesolithic period into Early and Late Stages, the latter much affected by Britain becoming an island. The sea rose to a level similar to that of today, and broke through the final bridge of land by around 6500 BC. It is unlikely that the pattern of life was very different from that of the late Glacial hunters, but adapted to a more forested environment and a consequent change in the large game available. A vital factor in their food economy was the red deer. Flint tools and weapons which identify the presence of these resourceful people reflect the changes: the hafted axe appears, the arrows and spears were tipped with tiny barbs (microliths) in order to increase the efficiency of selective hunting and the conscious conservation of herds. To judge by ethnographical parallels, the barbs would have been coated with lethal poison.

A major site on Home Heath, Lackford, is of the Early Stage. Wangford, Lakenheath, West Stow and probably another site at Sproughton and Barham are of the Later Stage. In the absence of other evidence, these later sites can only be identified by subtle changes in their flintwork, such as a greater proportion of very minute microliths and geometric forms. Where only few of isolated finds are made, it is often impossible to know whether they are early or late. Sites clearly concentrate on the Breckland and along major rivers but finds, mainly axes, on the high Till plain show that most environments were exploited.

Further details on p.194

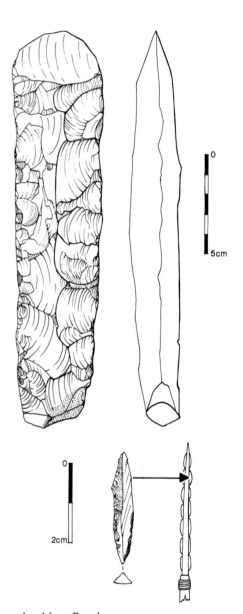

Top: Flint axe-head from Rougham.
Bottom: Flint microlith barb from West Row Fen.

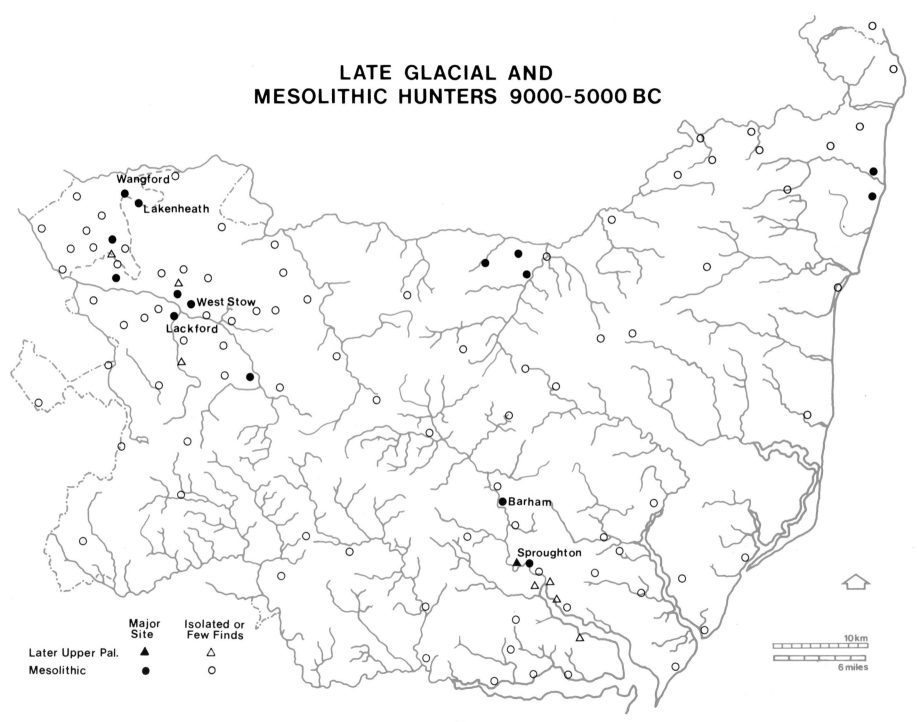

LATE GLACIAL AND
MESOLITHIC HUNTERS 9000-5000 BC

Wangford

Lakenheath

West Stow

Lackford

Barham

Sproughton

Major Site   **Isolated or Few Finds**

Later Upper Pal.   ▲   △

Mesolithic   ●   ○

10 km

6 miles

13. THE NEOLITHIC

Edward Martin

The origins of farming lie in the Near East around 7000 BC. From there the knowledge of how to grow crops and domesticate animals spread across Europe, reaching these islands sometime around 4500 BC. The new skills included not only the growing of wheat, barley, beans and flax, and the keeping of cattle, sheep, pigs and goats, but also the making of pottery vessels in which to store and cook cereals. New types of tool also appear: stone axes with ground edges, querns for grinding grain and leaf-shaped flint arrowheads. Although the original seeds and livestock must have been imported, the continent shows few precise parallels for the artefacts of the British Neolithic. Furthermore, the longhouses that are so characteristic of the period in Europe are curiously absent here. All this suggests that the actual number of colonists may have been quite small, and that they interacted with indigenous Mesolithic hunter groups to produce a Neolithic culture that was markedly insular in character.

The few Neolithic settlements that have been excavated in this region have merely revealed clusters of small pits, post-holes and the occasional ditch or gulley. Elsewhere in England, however, the ground-plans of a few rectangular houses have been found. In Suffolk, the distribution of Neolithic pottery strongly suggests that settlements were mainly on light soils—in the Breckland, Sandlings and river valleys—and within a mile of a watercourse. It was in these areas that the new farmers first cleared the natural woodland to provide themselves with fields and pastures. The distribution of axes, however, implies that they also penetrated the heavy claylands of central Suffolk, which were then probably densely wooded, if only to forage for fuel, timber, game and other natural resources.

By the 4th millennium BC these farming communities were sufficiently well-established and organised to embark on the building of large earthworks: causewayed enclosures, linear monuments called 'cursuses' and long barrows. Three causewayed enclosures are known in Suffolk at Fornham All Saints, Freston and Kedington, but are only visible from the air as cropmarks.[1] Various interpretations of these enclosures have been put forward, ranging from tribal centres or markets to religious sites where the dead were exposed or cremated.

Superimposed on the causewayed enclosure at Fornham is the cropmark of a cursus, over a mile long. A smaller cursus existed at Stratford St Mary, and probably another small one at Bures St Mary.[2] The purpose of these linear monuments is unknown, though they may have been ceremonial procession ways.

None of the large circular monuments called henges exist in Suffolk, but clusters of small hengi-form monuments are visible at the ends of the cursuses at Fornham and Stratford.[3] In addition, a Late Neolithic circular setting of post-holes, about 18m in diameter, has recently been found at Flixton, which suggests the timber equivalent of a stone circle.[4]

Although Norfolk has four of the large burial mounds called long barrows, no certain examples are known in Suffolk. However, several cropmarks of elongated oval enclosures have been recorded, which may represent long barrows that have been ploughed flat. These sites have also been interpreted as mortuary enclosures, where the dead were taken before burial. Smaller round barrows of Neolithic date have, however, been identified at West Stow and Worlington.

The society that built these large monuments was also capable of organising trade over long distances, as is shown by the evidence of stone axes. 'Factories' in northern and western Britain produced large numbers of ground and polished axes which were distributed all over the country, though not in a random way as the products of individual factories are more numerous in some areas than others. In north-west Suffolk, axes from the Lake District are commonest, while in south-east Suffolk axes of Cornish origin are dominant. This suggests that two quite separate trading networks served this region. It also hints at a division between the Neolithic peoples of Suffolk, perhaps foreshadowing the later tribal divisions of the Iron Age (see Map 15). If this interpretation is correct, it might explain why Suffolk has two major causewayed enclosures, one on each side of the county; they could be the centres of two major 'territories' or tribal groupings.

The local Neolithic population not only imported stone tools from distant parts of Britain, but also manufactured its own, of flint, at places like Grimes Graves in Norfolk. Here, the shafts, tunnels and spoil-heaps of flint mines dug in the Late Neolithic (c.2700-2200 BC) can still be seen. Over 430 shafts (some up to 12m deep) have been recorded in an area of about 10 ha, which is remarkable testimony to the scale and organisation of this, the earliest major industry in East Anglia.

Further details on p.194

Causewayed enclosures and cursus at Fornham All Saints.

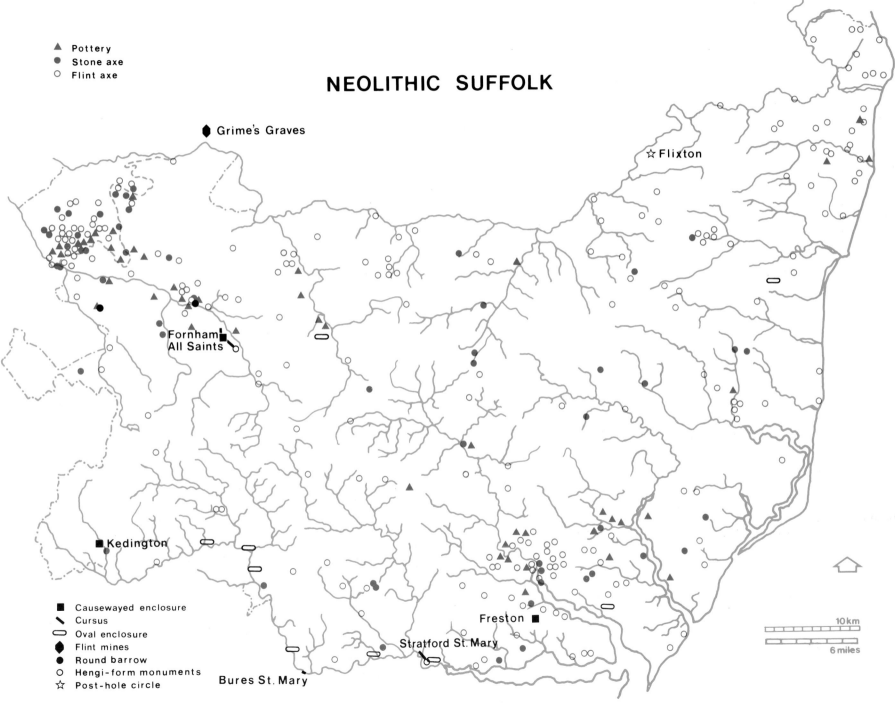

NEOLITHIC SUFFOLK

Pottery
Stone axe
Flint axe

Grime's Graves

☆ Flixton

Fornham
All Saints

■ Kedington

Freston ■

Stratford St. Mary

Bures St. Mary

■ Causewayed enclosure
╲ Cursus
▭ Oval enclosure
⬖ Flint mines
● Round barrow
○ Hengi-form monuments
☆ Post-hole circle

10km

6 miles

14. THE BRONZE AGE

Edward Martin

Around 2700-2500 BC the first metal tools—initially made of copper and then of bronze—were introduced into Britain. Their appearance appears to be linked with what has been termed the 'Beaker Phenomenon'. Beakers are distinctive pottery vessels, often richly decorated with geometric patterns, which are found across much of western Europe at this time. This has lead to speculation about an actual 'Beaker Folk', but more recently archaeologists have suggested that it may have been new ideas, rather than actual people, that moved around. Beakers, which may have been used for drinking alcoholic beverages, perhaps mead, are associated with a number of other prestigious items: metalwork, archery equipment, horses and an emphasis on burial under round mounds or barrows.

Round barrows are the earliest surviving man-made features in the Suffolk landscape. Although most seem to date from the Early Bronze Age (particularly the period around 1900 BC), a few belong to the earlier Neolithic. At least 825 barrows are known to have existed in Suffolk, but only 114 are visible on the ground today. The encircling ditches of many of the flattened barrows do, however, show up from the air as crop-marks which are known as ring-ditches. The distribution of barrows shows a close correspondence with areas of lighter soil—the Sandlings of south-east Suffolk, the Breckland in the north-west and major river valleys. The clayland of central Suffolk is virtually empty, which suggests that it was still heavily wooded, in contrast to areas like the Breckland which already had extensive tracts of open grassland.

In north-west Suffolk, both inhumation and cremation burials have been found, often in the same barrow, but so far only cremations are known from south Suffolk. This may indicate different folk or cultural groups, as has already been suggested for the Neolithic period.

The number of burials in a barrow can vary from one to fifteen. Study of the bones suggests that the average height of men then was 5ft 7½in, and of women 5ft 4in. The average age of death was 34 for men and 37½ for women.

In the later Bronze Age, flat cremation cemeteries came into fashion. Cremated bones were placed under inverted pots in small pits, possibly marked on the surface by small mounds. These cemeteries are mainly a feature of south-east Suffolk and north-east Essex. Within individual cemeteries, the number of burials can vary from one or two to over a hundred.

Settlements of the earlier part of the Bronze Age are very rare, but a group of sites dating from *c.*1700-1500 BC has been found on the low-lying fen-edge at West Row, Mildenhall. Excavation there has revealed the postholes of small round houses, 5m in diameter, with porches protecting the entrances. The inhabitants were farmers who kept cattle, sheep, goats, pigs, horses and dogs, and grew wheat, barley and flax.

Metal objects become much more numerous from the Middle Bronze Age onwards. The majority of finds have again been in areas of light soil, with a very marked concentration on the fen-edge. It has been argued that many of the finds from the fens were deliberate votive offerings to water spirits or deities, but this is probably too simplistic an interpretation. However it is worth noting that the bronze objects from West Row Fen are nearly all later than the known settlements, which appear to have been abandoned in the Middle Bronze Age as the climate deteriorated and the area became increasingly wet. A smaller group of metal finds cluster around Rymer Point on the high Breckland plateau. Here a series of ponds has always provided an invaluable source of water in an arid sandy area. Shepherds of

the Bronze Age doubtless exploited it in the same way as their successors did in historical times—its importance reflected by the fact that no fewer than ten medieval parishes converged on this spot. Another significant cluster of finds, this time of Late Bronze Age hoards, can be seen in the Eye-Thorndon area of the Dove valley. Bronze Age smiths may have been drawn to this area of heavy clay by a good supply of wood for their furnaces. In fact, about 40 per cent of the locatable bronze hoards in the county are within a kilometre of the edge of the clay.

Further details on p. 194

How Hill in Icklingham, an Early Bronze Age burial mound.

BRONZE AGE SUFFOLK

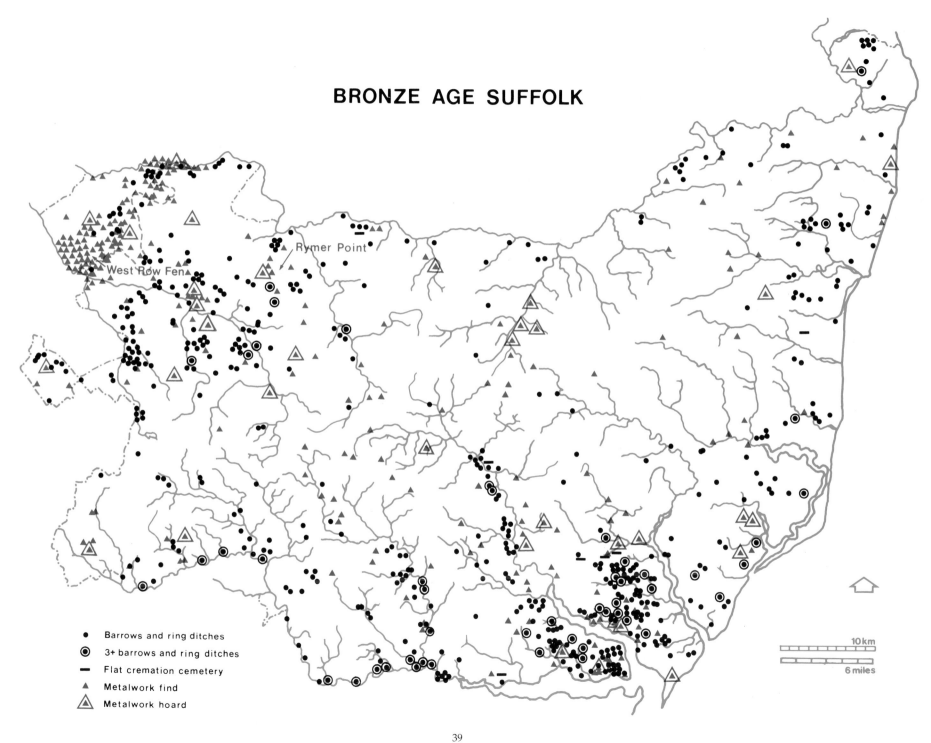

Rymer Point

West Row Fen

● Barrows and ring ditches
◉ 3+ barrows and ring ditches
— Flat cremation cemetery
▲ Metalwork find
△ Metalwork hoard

10 km

6 miles

15. THE IRON AGE

Edward Martin

Iron was introduced into Britain in the early part of the 1st millennium BC (a date around 700 BC is often suggested, though that may be too late). Although this technological advance led to the abandonment of bronze as the chief material for tools and weapons, very few other changes are detectable in the patterns of life established in the preceding Late Bronze Age. The pottery of the Early Iron Age forms a continuous sequence with that being made before, which strongly suggests that no major change of population took place at this time.

Settlements of the Iron Age are densest on the light-soil areas of the north-west and south-east, but they are also present on the heavy clay lands of central Suffolk. Proximity to a source of water was, however, a crucial factor in determining where people lived. Most sites are within one mile (1.6km) of a watercourse or mere—a distance which corresponds well with that recommended today by the Ministry of Agriculture as the maximum that should be walked by cows in milk. This suggests that the requirements of stock, particularly cattle, were an important factor in deciding which areas were suitable for settlement, though of course humans have a vital need for water as well. In some valleys, like that of the Fynn in south-east Suffolk, a regular pattern of sites about 700m-1km (approx. half a mile) apart has been identified. The interfluves, however, are noticeably bare of settlements, though the reasons vary with soil-type. On the free-draining sandy soils of the Breckland and Sandlings, the areas away from the main watercourses were probably too dry to support anything more than flocks of hardy sheep (in later times these areas were dominated by extensive sheepwalks and rabbit warrens). The Breckland meres provided isolated sources of water in otherwise dry locations and were certainly exploited. On the clay, areas away from watercourses were plagued more by poor drainage and their heavy wet soils were difficult to cultivate. This was probably particularly true of the very flat interfluves of north Suffolk, where settlement at this period appears particularly thin.

The majority of settlements appear to have been undefended, as seems to have been the case throughout East Anglia. Some were defined by ditches of field-boundary size but others seem to have been completely open. Scatters of pottery on arable fields suggest that some of the settlements were of considerable extent—one site recently found at Wyken covers 17ha (42 acres). Houses were built of timber and round, commonly 10-12m in diameter. The inhabitants were mostly engaged in farming—keeping cattle, sheep, goats, pigs and horses and growing wheat and barley. In recent years groups of roughly parallel longitudinal field boundaries and lanes, termed *co-axial systems*, have been identified on some of the clay interfluves, for which a Late Iron Age origin has been suggested (see Map 19). However, at present it is difficult to reconcile this evidence implying extensive and organised land management with the meagre indications of contemporary settlement in those same areas.

Fortified sites are rare, though there is a substantial one at Burgh, near Woodbridge. This enclosure with double ditches and banks covers 7ha (17 acres) and appears to have contained a rich settlement in the Late Iron Age, using imported pottery vessels and wine from continental Europe. Some aspects of the site suggest a ritual use, as is also thought to be case with a smaller (1ha) double-ditched enclosure at Barnham. This is similar to rectangular ritual enclosures on the Continent called *viereckschanzen*. A radiocarbon date from the ditch suggests that it was built between 180 BC and AD 20. A third fortified site, Clare Camp, is often claimed as Iron Age, but as yet no dating evidence has been found.

In the Late Iron Age, Suffolk was occupied by two major British tribes, the *Iceni* in the north and the *Trinovantes* in the south. The distributions of their coins suggests that the dividing line between them ran along the River Lark and then across the central clay lands towards Hacheston and the Alde estuary.

The most famous artefacts from Iron Age Suffolk are the six gold torcs that were found at Ipswich in 1968-70 and are now in the British Museum. These were made in the 1st century BC and each weighs about 2lbs (858-1044 gms). Their weight suggests that they were only worn on special occasions, or may even have been intended for the necks of idols in a religious sanctuary.

Further details on p. 195

Enamelled rein-ring from Weybread, 8.3cm high.

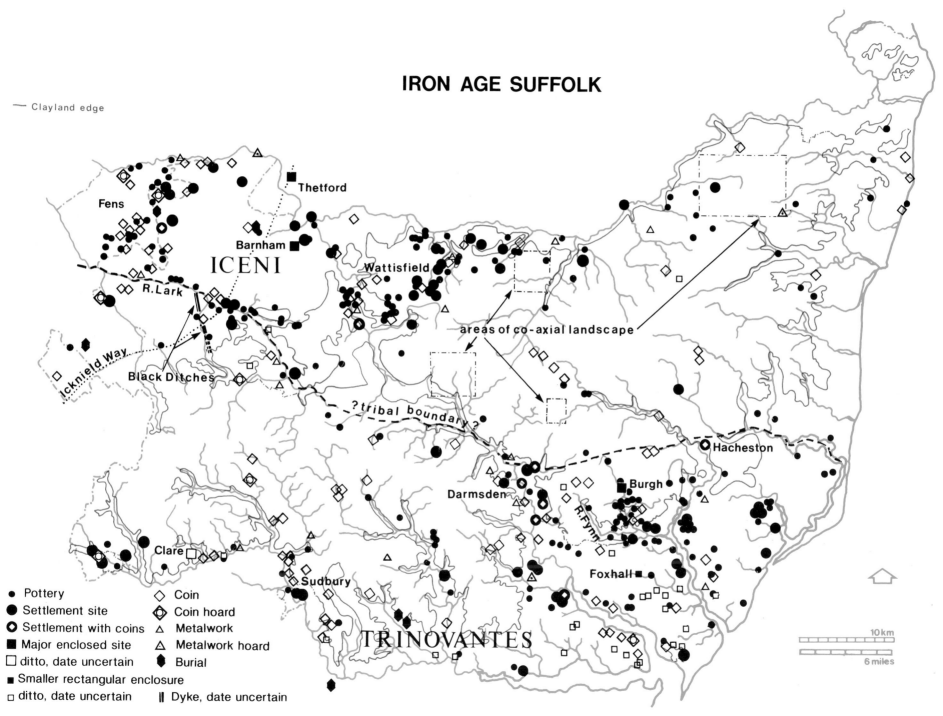

IRON AGE SUFFOLK

— Clayland edge

Fens

Thetford

Barnham

ICENI

Wattisfield

R.Lark

Icknield Way

Black Ditches

areas of co-axial landscape

?tribal boundary?

Hacheston

Darmsden

Burgh

R.Fynn

Clare

Foxhall

Sudbury

TRINOVANTES

- ● Pottery
- ● Settlement site
- ◉ Settlement with coins
- ■ Major enclosed site
- □ ditto, date uncertain
- ■ Smaller rectangular enclosure
- □ ditto, date uncertain
- ◇ Coin
- ◈ Coin hoard
- △ Metalwork
- △ Metalwork hoard
- ⬢ Burial
- ‖ Dyke, date uncertain

10km

6 miles

16. THE ROMAN PERIOD

Judith Plouviez

In later prehistoric times the population was increasing and the landscape was more thoroughly exploited than ever before. These trends were intensified when the area was incorporated into the Roman Empire after AD 43.

Roman administration was based on urban centres such as Caistor St Edmund in Norfolk and Colchester in Essex. In Suffolk the largest settlements are classifiable as small towns and are relatively unplanned; at least six of these were in existence by the end of the 1st century. The map shows that they are quite evenly distributed across the county and at focal points in the network of communications, presumably serving as market centres for the surrounding countryside. Excavations at Coddenham, Hacheston, Pakenham and Scole (on the Norfolk border) have revealed industrial activity such as potting, metalworking and brewing, while Icklingham was both a pagan religious centre and the site of a 4th-century Christian church.

The vast majority of Roman sites were individual farmsteads. These range from 'villas', often assumed to be the centres of large estates, to numerous small homesteads. The typical villa is a complex building with mortared flint foundations, tiled roof, tessellated floors, painted plaster on internal walls, and rooms heated by a hypocaust system (the latter either within the main house or in a separate bathhouse). These buildings are utterly different from the native tradition, and represent the thoroughly Romanised life of the wealthy. The distribution of the thirty-seven identifiable villas (using the evidence of excavations, aerial photography and surface finds) is uneven, with concentrations around some of the market centres and much sparser in the eastern half of the county. By contrast the distribution of hoards of coins or other objects, another indication of relative wealth, covers the county more evenly except for a large number in the north-west. Most of the known villas

seem to date from the mid-2nd century and later. Earlier occupation on these sites consisted of less substantial structures of timber and clay. Much less excavated evidence is available from the other rural settlements. However, systematic fieldwalking and metal-detecting in the last two decades has clearly shown that small farmsteads were extremely common in all parts of the county. Over 1000 sites are currently recorded, and it is possible that the true number may have been as high as 4000. The greatest density of settlement is, as previously, along the gravel terraces of river valleys, but the clay lands are also well populated except on the more inhospitable high plateaux.

Although agriculture dominated the economy, we also have evidence for several industries, of which the commonest is the manufacture of pottery. Kilns have been identified at many of the market centres and in rural locations. The largest concentration is around Wattisfield and Rickinghall, where potters were able to find both good clay and an abundance of fuel. This area saw a revival of pottery-making in the Middle Ages, and the industry still survives today at Wattisfield. Another industry identified on coastal estuaries is the extraction of salt, well known in the 'Red Hills' of Essex but less well preserved in Suffolk. Scatters of debris resulting from the evaporation of brine have been recognised at Trimley, Snape, Iken and Blythburgh.

In the modern landscape the best preserved features of the period are the roads, some of which are still in use today, while others can be traced as straight lengths of hedgerow or parish boundary. The main network probably results from military campaigns of the 1st century, and forts of that date have been identified at Coddenham and Pakenham. Military activity in Suffolk resumed in the late 3rd century when a coastal fort (part of the system known as the Saxon Shore) was built at

Felixstowe in an area now completely lost to coastal erosion. During the 4th century it seems that Roman activity, for example the use of coins, diminishes in the east of the county. This might have been the result of military dominance blighting the coastal zone or insecurity in the face of raids by pirates from beyond the Roman empire. In the early 5th century, probably around AD 410 when the British province was severed from the empire, insecurity is certainly illustrated by numerous coin hoards which were hidden and not recovered. The most spectacular of the late Roman hoards are 32 pieces of silver tableware from Mildenhall, and the golden jewellery, around 100 silver spoons and other objects with over 14,000 coins, found recently at Hoxne. These give us a glimpse of the luxurious lifestyle of the wealthiest inhabitants of the county who very probably owned further estates elsewhere in Britain and beyond.

Further details on p.195

Group of pottery and glass vessels from a Roman burial mound at Rougham. The glass jar contained cremated human bone; the bowls and flagons would have contained food and drink as offerings for the dead.

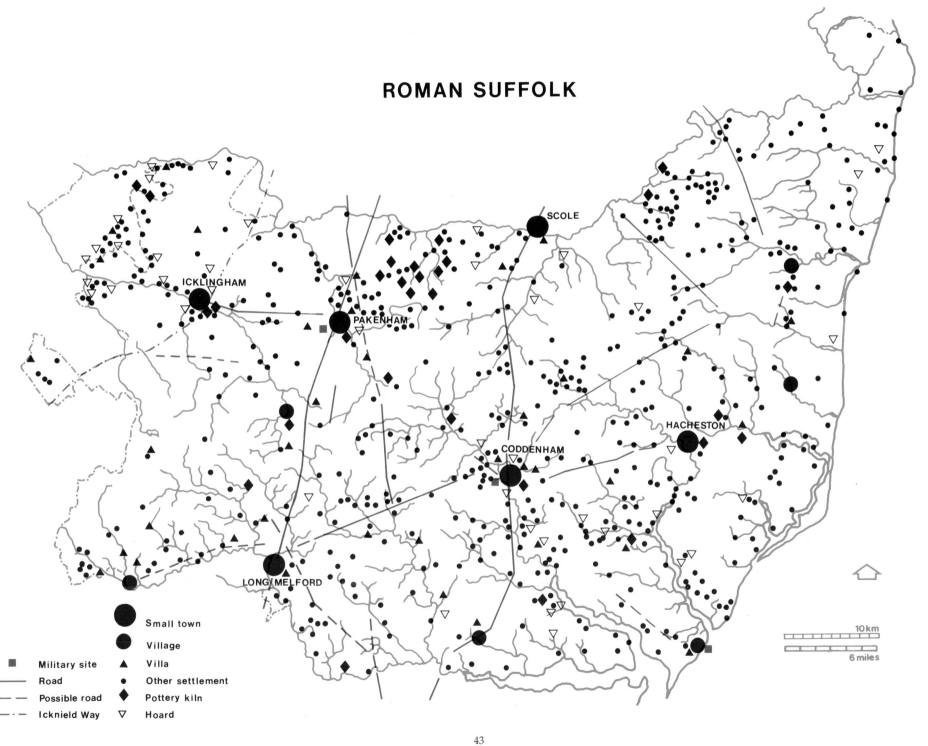

ROMAN SUFFOLK

SCOLE

ICKLINGHAM

PAKENHAM

HACHESTON

CODDENHAM

LONG MELFORD

● Small town

● Village

■ Military site   ▲ Villa

— Road   ● Other settlement

- - - Possible road   ◆ Pottery kiln

-·-·- Icknield Way   ▽ Hoard

10km

6 miles

17. THE EARLY ANGLO-SAXON PERIOD

Stanley West

The precise date and manner of the English settlement is still a matter of considerable debate. The traditional view is that invading Anglo-Saxons drove out or killed the Romanised inhabitants of Britain. However, at the end of the Roman period we have little archaeological evidence of violent destruction. Some Germanic people were in fact deliberately settled in Britain by the Romans to help defend the province against civil unrest and raiding barbarians. Late Roman metalwork of a type associated with these Germanic mercenaries has been found in Suffolk at Lakenheath, Icklingham, Hinderclay, Nacton, Ufford, Sweffling and Felixstowe.

By the mid-5th century the Lark, Blackbourn and Little Ouse valleys of west Suffolk had been settled by a mixed group of immigrants of Anglian, Saxon and Frisian origin. They used 'facetted-angled' pottery of a type that can be matched in the Elbe-Weser area of Germany. Objects of the early 5th century are also turning up now in the south-east of the county (except, for some reason, in the Shotley peninsula). It looks likely that the Anglo-Saxon colonists established themselves at the heads of the Orwell and Deben estuaries, and made use of the Gipping corridor through the central clay region to reach the valleys of the Lark and Blackbourn in the north-west. The recent discovery of cruciform brooches at Flixton and South Elmham in the Waveney valley hints at similar early settlement along that route as well. The extensive clay soils of central Suffolk show no traces of settlement, although we know that they were occupied in the Roman period. The fate of those Romano-British settlements and of their once substantial populations remains unknown. It therefore seems that the early Anglo-Saxon settlers of Suffolk, whether invited or invaders, moved into an already managed landscape, but for themselves preferred the more easily worked lighter soils and gravel terraces.

West Stow is the only settlement of the period to have been extensively examined, although fragments of others have been excavated at Honington, Grimston End in Pakenham, Little Bealings and Hacheston. The settlement at West Stow is, however, probably typical of communities of the period. It consisted of a number of family units, each with a hall and up to six other buildings for storage, workshops and living accommodation. Their mixed economy was based on the growing of wheat, barley, rye and peas, and keeping of sheep, cattle, pigs, horses and goats, supplemented by fishing, wildfowling and some hunting of red and roe deer. Settlement of this type seems to have been successful and largely self-sufficient, trading, by the late 6th century, in only luxury items such as jewellery, occasional glassware and some pottery.

Much of our information concerning the early Anglo-Saxons comes from cemeteries. Both inhumation and cremation burials are known and the distribution of the two rites is shown on the map opposite. Superficially it would appear that cemeteries with inhumations outnumber those with cremations by 2:1, but this could be misleading. Very few cemeteries have been extensively excavated and when they are, as recently at Snape, what is considered to be a cremation cemetery can in fact produce inhumations as well. The cemetery at Lackford with more than 390 cremations appears to have served a large area whereas the inhumation cemeteries probably served individual settlements. The extraordinary ship-burials at Snape and Sutton Hoo must surely be royal and demonstrate the wealth, power and wide-ranging contacts of the East Anglian dynasty, the Wuffingas.

The most prominent features of this period are the large dykes built across the Icknield Way. Only the most easterly of these, the Black Ditches, is in Suffolk. The largest is the Devil's Dyke, just west of Newmarket. The purpose and date of these earthworks is uncertain, but they appear to be late Roman or later, and were built against an enemy approaching from the west.

The 7th century was a period of great change. The consolidation of the kingdom of East Anglia, the advent of Christianity and the development of Ipswich as a town trading with the Rhineland, were reflected in the countryside by the abandonment of old settlements and the establishment of new. Whatever the causes of this shift of population, the move, if West Stow is typical, took place over several generations. Some of the new sites became the cores of late Saxon and medieval villages, while others were merely outlying farms.

Further details on p.195

A reconstructed Anglo-Saxon hall at West Stow.

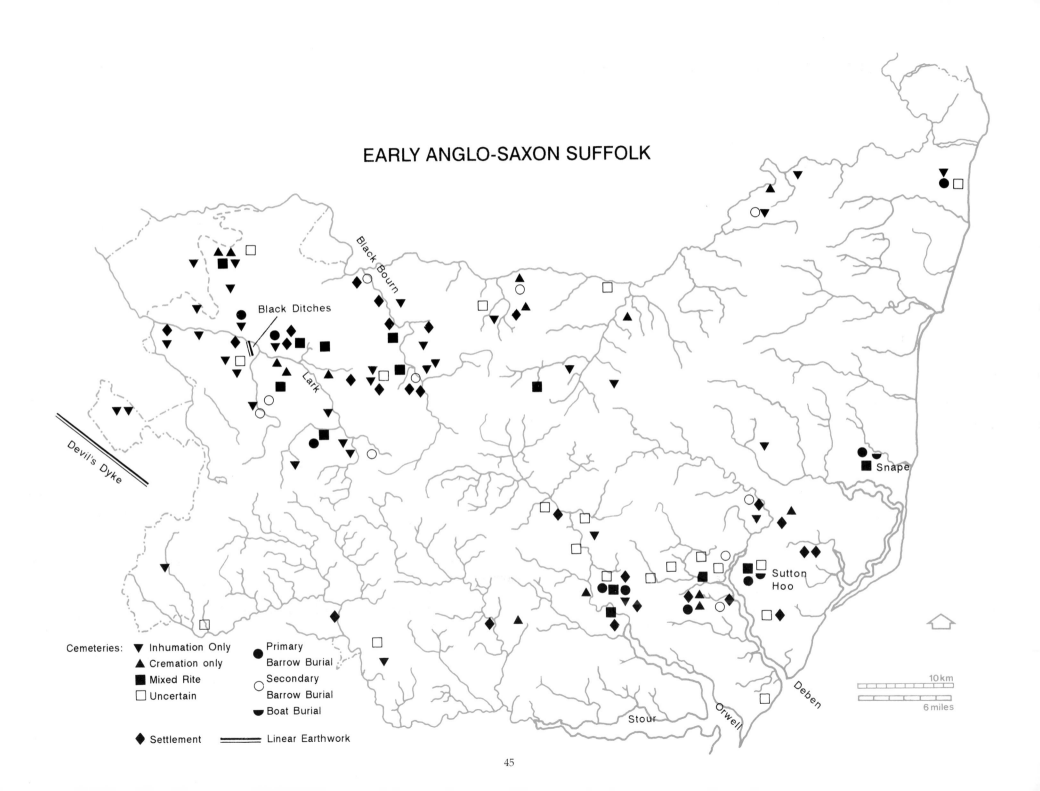

EARLY ANGLO-SAXON SUFFOLK

Black Bourn

Black Ditches

Devil's Dyke

Lark

Snape

Sutton Hoo

Stour

Orwell

Deben

Cemeteries:
▼ Inhumation Only
▲ Cremation only
■ Mixed Rite
□ Uncertain

● Primary Barrow Burial
○ Secondary Barrow Burial
⬗ Boat Burial

◆ Settlement
═ Linear Earthwork

10 km
6 miles

18. THE LATER ANGLO-SAXON PERIOD

Keith Wade

The existing framework of villages and towns in Suffolk was established in the four centuries before the Norman Conquest. At the beginning of this period, in the early 7th century, the East Anglian kingdom under the Wuffinga dynasty was independent, powerful and economically successful. However, it was increasingly threatened by its Mercian neighbours to the west. The linear earthworks of Devil's Dyke (just in Cambridgeshire) and the Black Ditches could well represent the East Anglian response to the threat of Mercian invasion. After the death of King Anna in 654, East Anglia was indeed dominated by Mercia, though it did retain its own kings until the late 9th century.

The Fens and extensive claylands of central Suffolk had been largely abandoned after the end of the Roman period, but they were re-occupied during the Middle Saxon period (c.AD 650-850). By the 9th century the majority of our villages had been founded, though not necessarily on the same sites as today. Systematic field-work in south-east Suffolk has provided the first comprehensive picture of the density of settlement in the Middle and Later Saxon periods.[1] Although few rural settlements have as yet been excavated, Middle Saxon sites have been investigated at Brandon and Butley. The settlement at Brandon lies on a small 'island' with the Little Ouse River on one side and marsh on the others. Over twenty rectangular timber buildings were excavated, including large halls and a church with a burial ground. Among the items found are glass vessels, window glass, bronze *styli* and a gold plaque depicting St John the Evangelist: collectively these indicate a high ranking settlement with a literate and devout Christian population.[2] At Burrow Hill, Butley, limited excavation revealed traces of buildings and a cemetery with predominantly male burials.[3]

The process of urbanisation began when Ipswich was founded in the late 6th or early 7th century (see Map 72).This town remained Suffolk's major industrial centre and trading port until the middle of the 9th century. Royal vills of the Middle Saxon period (the residences of peripatetic kings) probably provided a network for the distribution of Ipswich's products and imports, as well as points where exports could be collected. After the Danes had conquered and settled the region in the later 9th century, markets were functioning at Ipswich, Sudbury, Bury St Edmunds and Dunwich. By 1086, a further seven markets are recorded for Beccles, Blythburgh, Clare, Eye, Haverhill, Hoxne and Thorney (Stowmarket) (see Map 74).

The Great Army of the Danes arrived in 865, and began to settle the area from 879. Curiously, only five major place-names in Suffolk appear to be purely Danish in origin.[4] However, their influence is clearly greater at the level of minor place-names (see Map 20) and 'Viking' objects are being increasingly found in the county, especially at Ipswich where a significant Danish presence is likely in the late 9th and early 10th centuries.

Christianity was snuffed out at the end of the Roman period,[5] but re-introduced into East Anglia in the early 7th century. The first bishop, Felix, established his see at *Dommoc* (probably Dunwich, although Walton near Felixstowe is still a possibility) in the 630s, and the population of the kingdom seems to have been quickly converted, at least nominally. A second see was established later in the century, probably in the 680s, almost certainly at South Elmham. In the 10th century, after the Danish invasions, bishops were re-established at Hoxne and at North Elmham in Norfolk.

In the 630s monasteries were founded at Bury St Edmunds and Burgh Castle, and another at Iken in 654, but little is known of these early foundations. Excavations at Burgh Castle in 1960-1 revealed a possible church, cemetery and some curious oval structures interpreted as 'wattle and daub beehives'.[6] In 1977 excavations at St Botolph's church at Iken revealed traces of Middle Saxon occupation; built into the tower was a carved cross-shaft of the late 9th or early 10th century which had possibly been a memorial to Botolph, founder of the monastery.[7] It is possible that the excavated sites at Brandon and Butley, mentioned above, were also monasteries. Documents also reveal monastic foundations at Clare, Mendham, Rumburgh, Stoke-by-Nayland, Sudbury and perhaps Blythburgh (see Map 21).

From the late 7th century onwards, churches were constructed in almost all settlements, and over 400 are recorded in 1086. Architectural details of Saxon date only survive in thirteen Suffolk churches, and most of these could well be 11th-century.[8] However, most churches would originally have been built of timber, and it was probably not until the 11th century that stone came into widespread use. Significantly, Saxon details survive mainly in small churches which were not greatly enlarged or improved in later centuries. One early timber church has recently been excavated within the Middle Saxon settlement at Brandon.

Further details on p.195

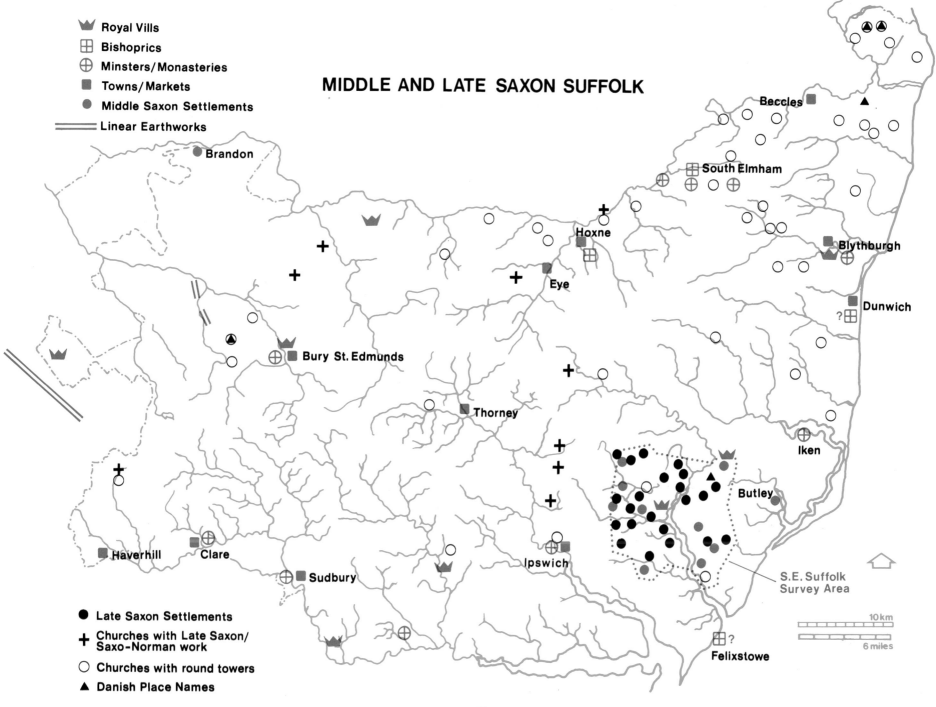

MIDDLE AND LATE SAXON SUFFOLK

Legend:
- ♛ Royal Vills
- ⊞ Bishoprics
- ⊕ Minsters/Monasteries
- ■ Towns/Markets
- ● Middle Saxon Settlements
- ═ Linear Earthworks

- ● Late Saxon Settlements
- ✚ Churches with Late Saxon/Saxo-Norman work
- ○ Churches with round towers
- ▲ Danish Place Names

Place names:
Brandon, Beccles, South Elmham, Hoxne, Blythburgh, Eye, Dunwich, Bury St. Edmunds, Thorney, Iken, Butley, Haverhill, Clare, Ipswich, Sudbury, S.E. Suffolk Survey Area, Felixstowe

10 km
6 miles

47

19. ANCIENT LANDSCAPES

Tom Williamson

The boulder-clay plateau of High Suffolk is an area of 'ancient countryside';[1] the essential framework of its field boundaries and roads does not derive from the planned general enclosure of open fields in the post-medieval period, though some commons were enclosed by Parliamentary Acts. Many boundaries result from the early piecemeal enclosure of irregular open fields, a process which has partially preserved the general lay-out of medieval strips and furlongs, but many surround fields which have probably always been under the control of individuals 'in severalty'.

According to the traditional view, the basic framework of this landscape results from the slow, unplanned and intermittent expansion of cultivation from the Saxon period onwards. Yet detailed examination of 19th-century and earlier maps suggests a more complex picture. In many areas the superficial irregularity of the clayland landscape disappears when features of medieval or post-medieval date are removed: they were, in fact, originally *planned*, and their irregular appearance results subsequently from centuries of piecemeal alter-ation.

These organized field systems are often of so-called *co-axial* form: that is, they are defined by parallel but slightly sinuous lanes and boundaries, and have few prominent, continuous features running in a transverse direction.[2] While the principal longitudinal boundaries provide the main axis of the system, they do not individually run uninterrupted from end to end. Such systems tend to be laid out with little regard to the subtleties of natural topography and drainage. Parallels are known from many parts of Britain in the form of cropmarks or earthworks, such as the Bronze Age 'reaves' and fields of Dartmoor. The latter usually cover between 2 and 5 square kilometres but occasionally extend over as much as 30 square kilometres. In Suffolk

these patterns on average fall into the range of 5 to 15 square kilometres; and they survive, or at least until recently survived, as upstanding and functional elements in the landscape, rather than as tumbled walls and earthworks.

Co-axial patterns of land-division occur in a wide range of prehistoric, Romano-British and post-Roman contexts. The Suffolk examples also appear to have a variety of dates, to judge from their relationships with other dated features, particularly Roman roads. Some appear to be of pre-Roman, perhaps late Iron Age, origin. Around Yaxley, for example, the Roman road called Pye Street cuts across an organized landscape rather like a modern by-pass (Fig. 1). Of course, not all the boundaries are original: centuries of alteration, including the division of fields into strips and their later piecemeal consolidation and enclosure, have preserved the general orientation of boundaries but rarely the boundaries themselves. Nevertheless, individual fields south of Yaxley church do appear to be cut by the road.[3] Pye Street was not the only continuous feature imposed on this landscape, however. At a later date, a linear ditch, now represented by sections of lane and parish boundary, was cut across the earlier pattern and may in origin have been the Grimms Ditch referred to in field-names and in a 13th-century charter relating to Thorn-ham Parva.[4] The area to its south was subsequently reorganized parallel with it on a rough grid pattern.

Some co-axial field systems appear to be later than the Roman roads which they abut. One example is the well-known, well-preserved and highly regular pattern which extends over some 35 square kilometres in the Ilketshalls and South Elmhams.[5] The orientation of these fields is shared by the Roman Stone Street, which strongly suggests that those laying out the fields used the road as a base-line. The system may be of Romano-

British origin, but a Saxon date and, perhaps, an association with the enigmatic minster at South Elmham remains a possibility.

When organized landscapes are situated away from Roman roads, they are difficult to date. Nevertheless, there seems little doubt that they are of pre-medieval origin: that is, they were created during the Saxon period, or earlier. They do not relate well to administrative or tenurial divisions known from the Middle Ages: parish and manorial boundaries appear to be imposed on them arbitrarily: field systems often extend into a number of early medieval estates or vills,[6] as in the area north of Crowfield (Fig. 2). Characteristic features of the medieval landscape—greens, lanes, estate boundaries and settlements—often appear to have been intruded into such systems, rather than being integral to, and contemporary with, them.

In the pattern of fields and minor routeways we can detect two millenia or more of planning and re-planning, expansion and contraction, and piecemeal alter-ation. The clayland fieldscape is a rich historical document, and no effort must be spared in preserving what remains from being further destroyed by modern agriculture.

Further details on p.195

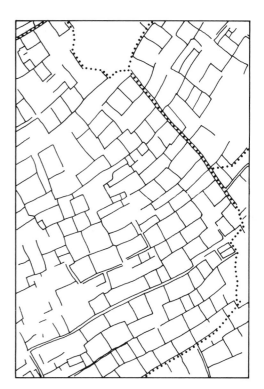

2. Part of the Stonham Aspal/Crowfield field system.
(Based on Tithe Award maps).
. . . . represents parish boundaries.

0   1km

0   1mile

ANCIENT LANDSCAPES

1. The Roman Pye Road (modern A140) cutting through an organised, co-axial landscape around Yaxley.
(Based on Tithe Award and early 19th century estate maps:
a - a represents the suggested line of Grimms Ditch, a possible early linear earthwork (after Scarfe 1986).

20. PLACE-NAME PATTERNS

Edward Martin

Place-names play an important part in local distinctiveness, for across Britain their changing patterns and sounds are as important as scenery in conveying impressions of familiarity or strangeness.

Eastern England has a noticeable concentration of Old English names that end in -ham, which means 'a village or group of houses', and names that end in, or incorporate, -ing. The latter denotes groups of people, either in the sense of 'the people of' a particular leader (Barking=Berica's people), or the inhabitants of a particular locality (Wratting=dwellers where crosswort grows).[1] In the past, both -ham and -ing names were thought to belong to the earliest phase of Anglo-Saxon settlement in England, but recent studies have cast doubt on this theory.[2] In Suffolk, instead of being concentrated in areas of known early settlement, like the Lark and Blackbourn valleys, the names show a closer relationship with the edges of the central clayland, as can be seen along the sides of the Gipping, Deben and Brett valleys. They are largely absent from the sandy soils of central Breckland[3] and also from the poorly-drained clay plateaux or interfluves (though several -ing- names do occur there). Curiously, the compound -ingham names only occur to the north-east of a line drawn diagonally from Ipswich to Mildenhall. They also have a tendency to occur deeper within the clayland, towards the heads of watercourses. The degree of penetration of the clayland probably has a chronological significance: the -hams and -ings along the edge are probably the earliest, the -inghams are further in and perhaps slightly later, while the occurence of some -ing- names on the clay interfluves suggests they may be even later.

Names ending in -ton (OE tun, 'a farmstead or village') are numerous across much of England, and are thought to represent a later Anglo-Saxon stratum, more frequent from the mid-8th century onwards. In Suffolk the -tons, like the -hams, appear to cluster along the edges of the clayland, but tend to be grouped further upstream (as in the Glem and Brett valleys). They also concentrate significantly around the Orwell estuary and in the Lowestoft area. They are rare in Breckland and in the claylands of north-east Suffolk. It is also noticeable that whereas -ham and -ing names are sometimes shared by two or more neighbouring settlements (e.g. the Stonhams and Creetings), no examples can be found of divided -tons.[4] Differences are also apparent in status: most settlements with -ham or -ing names became separate parishes, but quite a number of -tons occur as subsidiary settlements in other parishes.[5] This suggests that the -hams and -ings represent a relatively early stratum of substantial settlements that were capable of later subdivision, while the -tons in many cases seem to represent daughter settlements that were established in areas capable of supporting increased populations. This impression of secondary settlements is reinforced by names like Newton and Nowton, and also by names implying a relationship with a parent settlement, e.g. Easton, Weston, Norton and Sutton.[6]

Areas of cleared open land are signified by names ending in -field and -ley or -leigh (OE feld and leah). These terms were often used to imply a contrast with woodland, and it is therefore not surprising to find them almost confined to the clayland areas of Suffolk, where the Domesday record shows the greatest amount of woodland. Names containing these elements are likely to represent settlements established in marginal areas close to woodland. Evidence from elsewhere in England suggests that -fields refer to larger tracts of land than -leys. The Suffolk evidence tends to confirm this. Names ending in -field are more numerous in north-east Suffolk where they occur on the extensive flat interfluves; by contrast, -ley names are commoner in south-west Suffolk where the more dissected topography has given rise to smaller and narrower interfluves.

In the late 9th century and again in the 11th century, Suffolk came under Danish rule. The final map is therefore an attempt to plot the distribution of names showing Scandinavian influence. Most important are those ending in -by, an Old Norse term for a village.[7] Others elements include toft (ON topt, a plot of land containing a dwelling), thwait (ON thveit, a clearing), lound (ON lundr, a wood or grove), ellough (ON elgr, a heathen temple) and finally thorp (ON thorp, a secondary settlement, or dependent outlying farmstead or hamlet). In addition, the map also shows in red those names where a Scandinavian personal name is compounded with an English term for settlement, as at Flowton (Floki's tun) and Somerleyton (Sumarlithi's tun). The strongest evidence for Scandinavian settlement is clearly in the Lowestoft area of north-east Suffolk, which matches similar evidence in the adjoining part of Norfolk.[8] The pattern elsewhere is less distinct, but there appears to be significant groupings in the Felixstowe peninsula, and in the upper reaches of some valleys, notably those of the Dove, Brett and Glem.

The effect of the Norman Conquest can be seen in only a few names, notably Boulge (Old French bouge, heath or uncultivated land). In Essex many existing place-names acquired suffixes commemorating the surnames of their Norman lords, but these are rare in Suffolk.[9]

Further details on p.196

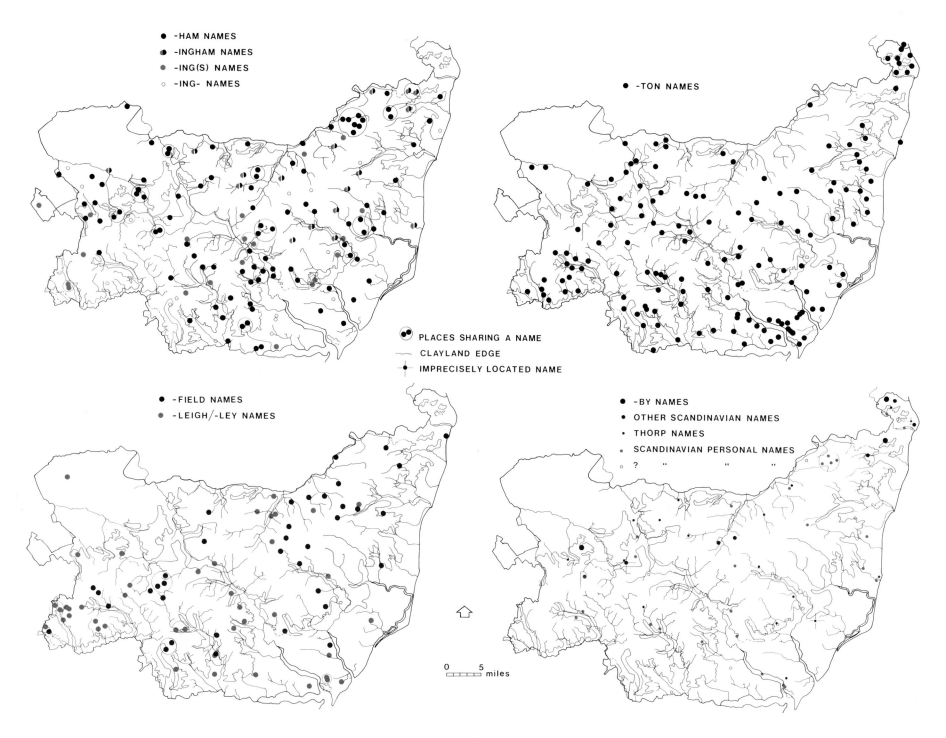

-HAM NAMES
-INGHAM NAMES
-ING(S) NAMES
-ING- NAMES

-TON NAMES

PLACES SHARING A NAME
CLAYLAND EDGE
IMPRECISELY LOCATED NAME

-FIELD NAMES
-LEIGH/-LEY NAMES

-BY NAMES
OTHER SCANDINAVIAN NAMES
THORP NAMES
SCANDINAVIAN PERSONAL NAMES
?   "   "   "

0   5 miles

Domesday Book presents an extraordinary record of Suffolk churches: it shows that about 418—four out of every five of our surviving medieval churches—were founded by 1086.[1] This total is by far the greatest of any county in England: the same source mentions only 274 churches in Norfolk and a mere 17 in Essex.

The list of Domesday churches is complicated by references to parts or fractions of churches (which were divisions of ownership rather than of fabric). Sometimes the fractions add up to convincing totals, as at Aspall which had two-thirds and one-third of a church, but elsewhere the situation is more complex. At Akenham, where a half and 'three parts' of a church were recorded, the surplus probably refers to the church at nearby Claydon, which contains Anglo-Saxon masonry but is not mentioned in Domesday.[2] Similarly two and a half churches listed for Worlingham probably represent the existing All Saints, the long-demolished St Peter's at Little Worlingham[3] and St Botolph's at North Cove (a place without separate mention in Domesday).

More problematic are the seven and a quarter churches listed for 'Stonham' (Earl Stonham, Stonham Aspal, Little Stonham and possibly Creeting St Olave, but where are the other three and a quarter?); the four and three-quarter churches in Coddenham (Coddenham, Crowfield and three others); and the two churches at Market Weston. In some cases, single fractions are recorded as at Old Newton (one-sixth of a church) and Pakefield (half a church). Sometimes the missing parts are recorded in assessments for neighbouring vills (as probably with the example at Old Newton), but others must be accidental omissions caused by the speed with which the Domesday survey was compiled.

In spite of the high total of recorded churches, some may have been omitted altogether. This is some-times suspected because of other documents (Exning, Brantham and Ixworth Thorpe[4]), because of an early fabric (Ufford), or because of an early dedication (St Ethelbert's at Falkenham). The absence of churches in the adjacent vills of Lavenham, Cockfield, Brent Eleigh, Bradfield Combust and Bradfield St Clare is noteworthy. By contrast, a number of churches existed in surprisingly small vills, as at Undley, Little Bricett and Little Fakenham, though several have since disappeared.

The relative scarcity of churches in north-east Suffolk (Mutford and Lothingland) may be the result of Norse settlement there (see Map 20). This thinner density is much closer to the general pattern for Norfolk, where only 217 country churches are recorded with a further 57 in the three major towns. However, the disparity between Norfolk and Suffolk is so striking that one must suspect that the assessors applied different criteria in the recording of churches.[5]

There is also a significant difference between the bishop's estates in the two counties: in Suffolk they are notably related to the Norfolk-Suffolk boundary, the Waveney valley. Apart from the church at Hoxne, described as 'the seat of the bishopric of Suffolk in the time of King Edward', he had at South Elmham all royal rights over 'the quarter-hundred of Elmham', a little palatinate.[6] The distribution of episcopal estates in Norfolk seems more deliberately organised: one in each of eleven western hundreds. (In the east, his acquisitions were late and irrelevant to this study).

In some parts of England it is possible to discern a framework of early large parishes (termed *parochiae* by modern historians to distinguish them from later parishes) that were served by teams of priests operating from important central churches known as *minsters*.[7] In East Anglia the pattern seems to have been disturbed by the period of Danish rule, for instance, the minster that was founded at Iken in 654 was probably destroyed by the Danes c.869.[8] However some minsters survived or were refounded, for wills of the 10th century indicate their presence at Bury St Edmunds, Hoxne, Mendham, Stoke by Nayland and Sudbury.[9] Domesday records two more recent foundations at Clare and Rumburgh.[10]

Several other minsters may be inferred from the Domesday record because of their large endowments (the average was 24.5 acres): St Peter's in Ipswich (720 acres), St Mary's in Thetford (712.5 acres and four dependent churches), Blythburgh (240 acres and two dependent churches), Eye (240 acres), Long Melford (240 acres), Oulton (120 acres),[11] Hadleigh (120 acres), Stowmarket (120 acres), and probably also Desning with Gazeley (two churches with 180 acres), Leiston (three churches with 100 acres), Reydon (two churches with 120 acres), Barking (83 acres), Bramford (two churches with 80 and 30 acres),[12] East Bergholt (two churches with 62 acres),[13] and perhaps even at Framlingham (60 acres), Hundon (60 acres),[14] Lakenheath (60 acres) and Shimpling (60 acres). The exceptional later values of churches at Exning and Mildenhall suggests that they may also have been minsters.[15] A minster must also have been at the centre of the ancient episcopal estate of South Elmham.[16] The five churches listed under Bungay may reflect an earlier *parochia* that extended into the Ilketshalls, where three of the churches were probably situated. The groupings of churches under Stonham and Coddenham may also reflect former large *parochiae*. In general the distribution of minsters seems to be related to the principal rivers, with strings lining the Waveney, Gipping and Stour valleys. In many cases they are also associated with important royal or ecclesiastical manors.

Further details on p.196

DOMESDAY CHURCHES

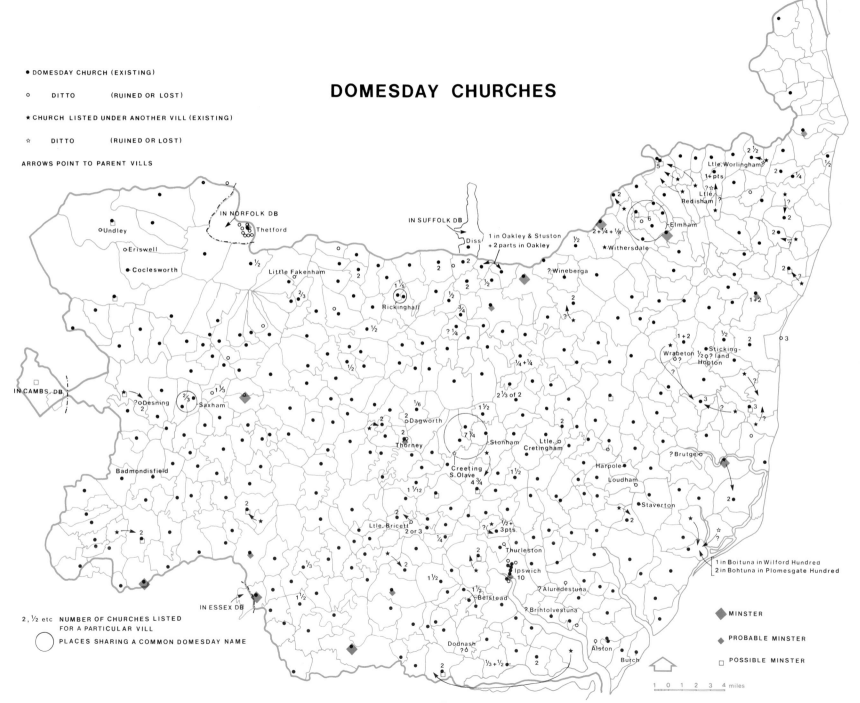

Legend:

● DOMESDAY CHURCH (EXISTING)

○   DITTO   (RUINED OR LOST)

★ CHURCH LISTED UNDER ANOTHER VILL (EXISTING)

☆   DITTO   (RUINED OR LOST)

ARROWS POINT TO PARENT VILLS

2, ½ etc NUMBER OF CHURCHES LISTED FOR A PARTICULAR VILL

◯ PLACES SHARING A COMMON DOMESDAY NAME

◆ MINSTER

◆ PROBABLE MINSTER

▢ POSSIBLE MINSTER

Map labels:

IN NORFOLK DB

IN SUFFOLK DB

IN CAMBS. DB

IN ESSEX DB

Undley, Eriswell, Coclesworth, Thetford

Little Fakenham, Rickinghall

Desning, Saxham, Badmondisfield

Thorney, Dagworth, Creeting S. Olave, Stonham, Ltle. Cretingham, Harpole, Loudham, Staverton

Ltle. Bricett, Thurleston, Ipswich, Belstead, Aluredestuna, Brihtolvestuna, Dodnash, Alston, Butch

Diss, 1 in Oakley & Stuston + 2 parts in Oakley, ?Wineberga, Withersdale, Elmham, Ltle. Worlingham, Ltle. Redisham, Wrabeton, Sticking-land, Hopton, ?Brutge

1 in Boituna in Wilford Hundred
2 in Bohtuna in Plomesgate Hundred

1 in Oakley & Stuston + 2 parts in Oakley

2 ⅓ of 2

Scale: 1 0 1 2 3 4 miles

53

22. CHURCHES AND CHURCHYARDS

David Dymond

The parish churches of Suffolk seem familiar and well-studied. Their architectural history has been summarised in several indispensable books,[1] and newer archaeological approaches to their fabric and sites are now yielding important results.[2] Meanwhile, ecclesiastical historians are dissecting 'popular religion' at local and parish level. As a result we now have a better understanding of late medieval piety, the physical and liturgical effects of the Reformation, and the evolving demands of Anglican worship.[3] In spite of all this accumulating knowledge, however, certain fundamental characteristics of local churches are still regularly neglected. This limited study of a single deanery attempts to demonstrate the value of comparing and contrasting churches within a selected area.

Thedwastre Deanery (and Hundred) traditionally contained 24 parishes. It covered an area about 12 miles long and 6 broad in the middle of west Suffolk, from sandy Breckland in the north to heavy boulder-clay in the south. Most of its 24 benefices were rectories; the three vicarages were, not surprisingly, among its best-endowed parishes (see Map 31). Twenty of its churches were already mentioned in Domesday Book.[4] In later centuries the most popular dedications were All Saints (5), St Peter (4), St Nicholas (3), St Mary (3) and St Andrew (2); other saints represented by single examples were Ethelbert, Genevieve, George, Holy Innocents, Martin, Mary Magdalen and Thomas à Becket.[5] Opposite are plans of all but one of the churches, with their surrounding churchyards, taken from 19th-century evidence.[6] Further background information for each parish is given in a Table (p.197). Out of a mass of detail, three characteristics seem worthy of special comment.

1. The highly variable plans and sizes of churches, even in adjacent parishes. The largest is at Thurston (145 ft long externally) while the smallest at Bradford Com-

bust is less than half that size (55 ft).[7] All have a nave and chancel (under separate roofs),[8] and all save two have western towers.[9] The occurrence of other features, however, is less predictable. For example, seven of the original 24 churches had two aisles, three had one aisle, and *fourteen had none*. This reminds us that the 'normal' Suffolk church is aisleless, and that we must not be misled by rarer and 'greater' examples like Blythburgh or Long Melford which are usually rebuildings of the 15th century. Another fact to emerge is the comparative modernity of vestries. In the early 19th century Davy recorded eight vestries in 24 parishes, but at least another six were added before 1904.

2. The inconsistent orientation of churches. Everyone knows that Christian churches normally lie with their chancels facing east, yet this 'orientation' is only approximate. Of 23 surviving churches, eight lie *south* of east and 15 *north* of east; only four are within 2 degrees either way.[10] The most aberrant are at Timworth (13 degrees south of east) and Fornham St Martin (21 degrees north of east). Future research may yet explain this inconsistency: among possible causes are seasonal differences of sunrise, the constant movements of magnetic north, and simple human rough-and-readiness.[11]

3. The variable shapes and sizes of churchyards. In the late 19th century two parishes (Gt Barton and Thurston) had yards of two acres or more, while three (Ampton, Beyton and Rushbrooke) had less than a third of an acre. Very few conformed strictly to 'God's Acre'. In shape most are roughly rectilinear, but Great Livermere's is trapezoidal and Rattlesden's is almost oval. It would be wrong, of course, to assume that the boundaries remained stable over the centuries: minor adjustments, straightenings and encroachments were obviously commonplace.[12] Several yards have rectangular 'cut-outs' which imply shrinkage, or had secular buildings

planted on them, while others have clearly expanded to some degree. For example, in the 19th century Woolpit's yard absorbed an adjacent meadow, while Bradfield Combust's contracted on two sides. So it is not surprising that at least five yards show evidence for both expansion *and* contraction, at different periods. At Gedding a building erected on the southern end of the churchyard may have been a medieval guildhall, and was certainly a workhouse and 'town house' in the early 19th century,[13] but a small meadow to the north was absorbed between 1838 and 1904. Bradfield St George, in an institutional cluster away from the village, has its church wedged between a parsonage on the south and a moated hall to the east: the outbuildings of the parsonage have obviously encroached on the churchyard, which was extended westward after 1843. The most dramatic evidence comes from Hessett, where a map of 1723 shows five houses lining the west side of the yard against the village street. None survives today, so the churchyard probably lost territory at some point in the Middle Ages, but regained it before 1838.[14]

The largest churches and churchyards tend to lie on the lighter soils on, or fringing, the Breckland, and the smallest on the heavier clays where parishes were on average smaller but populations denser. Nevertheless, exceptions are not hard to find—like Ampton in the north and Rattlesden in the south. Architectural and topographical variations of the sort discussed above can only be explained by the complicated interaction of many, as yet dimly understood, factors: geographical, chronological, demographic, economic, social *and* personal.

Further details on p.197

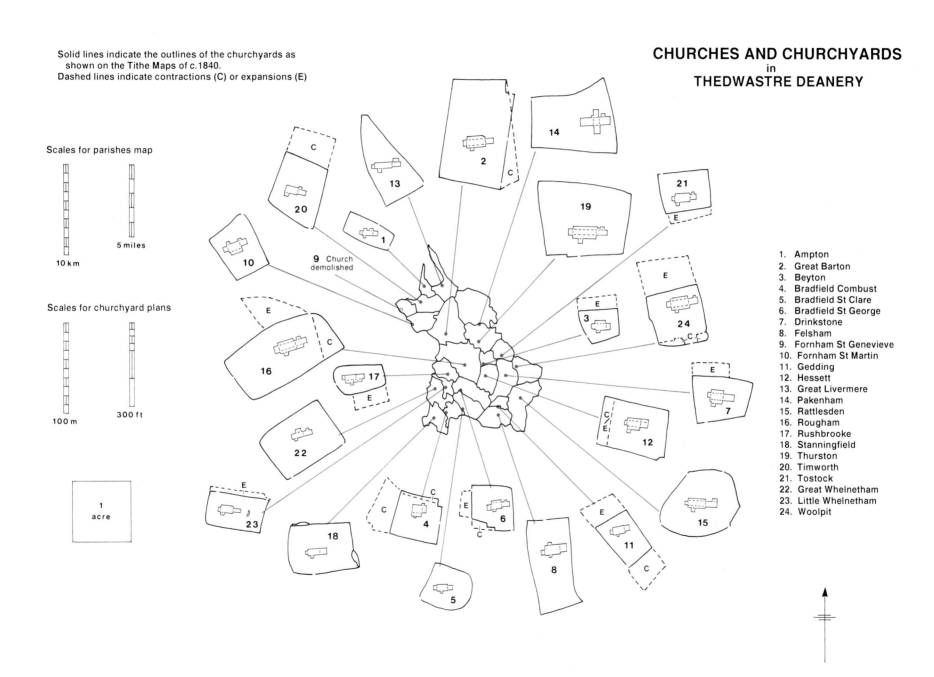

Solid lines indicate the outlines of the churchyards as
shown on the Tithe Maps of c.1840.
Dashed lines indicate contractions (C) or expansions (E)

CHURCHES AND CHURCHYARDS
in
THEDWASTRE DEANERY

Scales for parishes map

5 miles

10 km

Scales for churchyard plans

100 m   300 ft

1
acre

9 Church
demolished

1. Ampton
2. Great Barton
3. Beyton
4. Bradfield Combust
5. Bradfield St Clare
6. Bradfield St George
7. Drinkstone
8. Felsham
9. Fornham St Genevieve
10. Fornham St Martin
11. Gedding
12. Hessett
13. Great Livermere
14. Pakenham
15. Rattlesden
16. Rougham
17. Rushbrooke
18. Stanningfield
19. Thurston
20. Timworth
21. Tostock
22. Great Whelnetham
23. Little Whelnetham
24. Woolpit

Many people regard Suffolk as an area characterised by relatively small parishes and frequent parish churches. Over most of the county one expects to see a church tower looming up after every two or three miles. Compared, say, to a county like East Yorkshire where parishes were much larger and medieval chapels were considerably more numerous than churches,[1] the temptation is to assume that such chapels in Suffolk were quite rare. In fact, a surprisingly high number of medieval chapels existed, of various types. Many of them became redundant after the Reformation and were soon abandoned. In fact, the situation in the 16th century was not unlike that in the later 20th century when many *Nonconformist* chapels, which had been built since the Act of Toleration in 1690, have been abandoned, converted or demolished (see Map 50).

Many medieval chapels were component parts of large houses, as can still be seen today at Little Wenham Hall and Orford castle. By the time of the Reformation, virtually every large house contained its own private chapel. However, other categories of medieval chapel were also established as separate buildings, to meet some special purpose or to serve a set of people, and these are the ones which have been plotted on the map opposite. Five categories have been distinguished. It should be noted that the following groups of medieval chapels are *not* included in this survey: private chapels within houses;[2] chapels which subsequently became churches;[3] chapels which form part of other institutions such as religious houses, hospitals, gaols, etc.; and hermitages apparently without associated chapels. The map does not claim to be comprehensive, but represents our present state of knowledge.

1. Proto-churches and chapels of ease. Chapels of ease served communities or settlements which were at some distance from their parish churches (though such distances in Suffolk were miniscule compared with those in the north of England). In other words, they were places of worship to give 'ease' or convenience to specific groups who had some awareness of their separateness and own identity within the larger parish. In some instances they survived after the Reformation, at least for a time, as in the cases of the town chapels at Bildeston and Lowestoft. Proto-churches were those chapels apparently regarded almost as churches yet never achieving the status of ecclesiastical parish, like Botesdale, Mells (Wenhaston) and Dagworth (Old Newton). A reverse situation existed at Beccles, where what is thought to have been an original parish church became the chapel of St Peter when the grander St Michael's church was built nearby. It should be remembered that many medieval chapels grew into fully-developed parish churches by the end of the Middle Ages, and a few later. It seems almost an accident of history whether any particular chapel did, or did not, become a full parish church: Needham Market had to wait until 1901, while Botesdale never did achieve ecclesiastical independence.[4]

2. Churchyard chapels, where evidence suggests that they were physically separate from the parish church. Some like Long Melford, although regarded by their builders as a separate building 'in the churchyard', were attached to the church, or were later absorbed into it, as at Ampton. Bures had the unusual distinction of having two chapels in one churchyard, while Woolpit's became a great pilgrimage shrine visited by many notable people.[5]

3. Freestanding 'private' chapels. These were set up by individuals (now often unidentifiable), but were accessible to other parishioners. Some of them would have been chantry chapels, where prayers were offered for named people or families, like the Peyton or 'Neeling' chapel in Boxford. A fine example of such a private chapel, still surviving in a relatively isolated position, is St Stephen's at Bures.[6]

4. Roadside, bridge and gateway chapels. The sites included roadsides, bridges, gateways into towns (for example, Bury St Edmunds), or at major entries into the county (such as Beccles, Bungay and Cattawade). Some of these chapels had hermitages attached (as at Brandon and Beccles).

5. Other chapels, a miscellaneous group about which little or nothing is known. If we knew more of their nature and origins, many could undoubtedly be allotted to the other four categories discussed above. Some, we know from their dedications, were built for the veneration of specific saints: St Edmund at Hoxne,[7] St Albert (Ethelbert) near Boss Hall in Bramford, St Edmund Pountenay[8] and Our Lady of Grace at Ipswich, St Mildred at Exning and St Runwald at Wetherden. Our Lady of Grace at Ipswich, like Woolpit, became a major shrine, and its image earned the hatred of reformers in the 16th century.[9]

Those working on any aspect of Suffolk's past are urged to keep their eyes open for further examples of this largely overlooked aspect of the county's religious history.

Further details on p.198

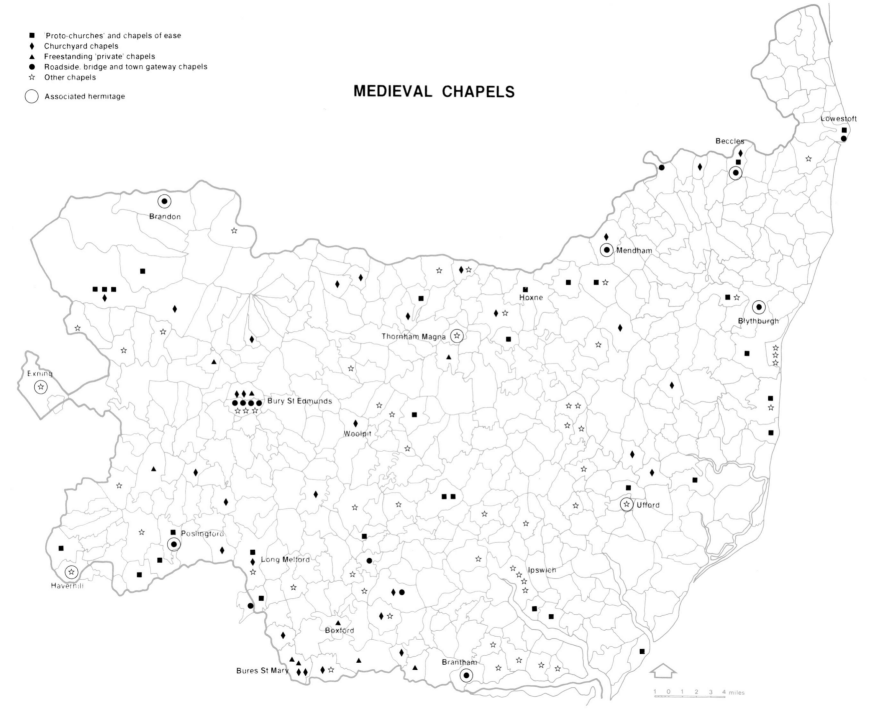

MEDIEVAL CHAPELS

■ 'Proto-churches' and chapels of ease
♦ Churchyard chapels
▲ Freestanding 'private' chapels
● Roadside. bridge and town gateway chapels
☆ Other chapels
◯ Associated hermitage

Lowestoft

Beccles

Brandon

Mendham

Hoxne

Blythburgh

Thornham Magna

Exning

Bury St Edmunds

Woolpit

Ufford

Poslingford

Long Melford

Ipswich

Haverhill

Boxford

Bures St Mary

Brantham

1 0 1 2 3 4 miles

Castles first appeared in England in the mid 11th century, having been imported as a new and still developing idea from Normandy. After the Norman Conquest in 1066 hundreds of castles were built by the new Norman lords to consolidate and defend their new landholdings. These castles served not only as the defended residences of their lords, but also as the administrative centres of their feudal estates. As such, they were powerful and very visible symbols of power and status. Their defensive qualities were often secondary to their symbolic role.

Domesday Book only gives incidental references to castles and cannot be taken as a reliable record of those that existed in 1086. The only castle in Suffolk that is actually mentioned was erected by William Malet at Eye. It formed the *caput* or administrative centre of his great feudal estate known as the Honour of Eye. Castles were probably built around the same time at the *caputs* of the two other honours in Suffolk: that of Richard Fitz-Gilbert at Clare (in existence by 1090) and that of Hugh de Montfort at Haughley. Eye, Clare and Haughley all have typical Norman motte-and-bailey castles (large earthen mounds that served as the bases for towers, attached to banked enclosures).

The civil war in the reign of King Stephen (1136-53) caused a spate of new castles to be built. A castle had appeared at Bungay by 1140, built by the powerful Bigod family, soon to be made Earls of Norfolk. Their first castle at Framlingham had been erected by 1157,[1] and they also re-fortified the old Roman fort at Walton. A now lost castle at Ipswich was beseiged by Stephen in 1153.

The dating of many of the smaller earthwork castles is problematic and the best that can be suggested at present is that they were probably built between the late 11th century and the mid 12th century, often by *mesne* lords (i.e manorial lords who did not hold their lands directly from the king, but from an intermediate magnate). William of Diss, writing *c*.1200,[2] states that in the time of King Stephen, the abbey of Bury St. Edmunds granted the vills of Groton and Semer for life to Adam de Cokefeld (one of the principal knights of the abbey) because he had a castle close by at Lindsey and could defend the vills against 'W. de Mildinges and W. de Ambli', who had castles a few miles away at Milden and Offton.

Also probably of a similar date are the earthen castles at Great Ashfield, Denham, Freckenham, Ilketshall St John, Lidgate and Otley[3] and the ringwork fortifications (enclosures without mottes) at Burgate, Fakenham Magna, Nayland (and perhaps at Cavendish, Great Cornard and Wissington) and the proto-moats at Bramfield and Creeting St Peter.[4]

In the late 12th century castle building was resumed: Henry II erected a major royal stronghold at Orford in the years 1165-73, and Hugh Bigod probably built the stone keep at Bungay soon after the castle was restored to him in 1165. Earl Hugh joined the revolt of the Earl of Leicester in 1173, when Walton Castle was besieged, Haughley Castle was captured after a short seige and Eye Castle was attacked. In the aftermath of the revolt, Henry II ordered the destruction of the castles at Walton, Bungay and Framlingham. Earl Hugh managed to ransom Bungay, but only after its destruction had been started. Framlingham was restored to the Bigods in 1189 and Earl Roger soon afterwards built a new castle there in the latest style, with a curtain wall linking a series of towers. Yet, despite its advanced design, it fell after only two days siege by King John in 1216.

The final spate of castle building came in the 14th century. In 1342 Sir John de Norwich, a veteran of the wars in France and Scotland, had a licence to build a castle at Mettingham and in 1385 Michael de la Pole (created Earl of Suffolk in the same year) was similarly given permission to create a castle at Wingfield. Neither man belonged to the old aristocracy and neither had extensive landed estates; their castles were personal statements of status by men who owed their advancement to royal service and patronage. Both castles are more notable for their visual impressiveness than their military effectiveness.

In addition to the castles, there are also some semi-fortified houses, as at Little Wenham. This innovative brick house was built *c*.1270-80, perhaps for Master Roger de Holbroke,[5] and is not so much a castle as a high-class chamber block that probably once stood next to a now-vanished timber hall. Walton Old Hall, the remains of a stone house built by the Bigods, may have been a similar structure. Token defences were also present on numerous moated sites (see Map 25)[6]. The abbot of Bury's moated country retreat at Chevington has an internal bank as well as a deep moat, suggesting a more determined attempt at defence. This may have resulted from Abbot Richard de Draughton's experience in 1327, when he was captured there by the rioting townsfolk of Bury.

Further details on p.198

MEDIEVAL CASTLES

MOTTE AND BAILEY CASTLE

MOTTE AND BAILEY WITH STONEWORK

STONE CASTLE

STONE CASTLE WITH WET MOAT

REUSED ROMAN FORT

Great Yarmouth

Burgh Castle

Raveningham

Weeting

BUNGAY

METTINGHAM

Denton

Ilketshall St John

THETFORD
Red Castle

South Elmham Hall

Great Fakenham

Burgate

WINGFIELD

EYE

Bramfield

Freckenham

Great Ashfield

Burwell

Denham

HAUGHLEY

FRAMLINGHAM

Chevington Hall

Kirtling

Lidgate

Creeting St Peter

Otley

Offton

ORFORD

Cavendish

Milden

? Ipswich

Haverhill

CLARE

Lindsey

Castle Camps

Groton

Pond Hall

DITCHED MOUND

Great Cornard

Little Wenham Hall

RINGWORK

Walton

PROTO-MOAT

Grange Wood

Court Knoll

FORTIFIED HOUSE

Nayland

Mount Bures

1 0 1 2 3 4 miles

59

25. MEDIEVAL MOATS

Edward Martin

Suffolk's moated houses are amongst the most evocative and impressive survivals of its medieval landscape. Over 850 moated sites are known in the county, a total that only Essex can match in the whole of England. The defining aspect of these sites is a broad water-filled moat surrounding a central platform or 'island'. Although inspired by castles, moated sites differ from them in one crucial respect: they lack defensive banks and walls. Castles had actual defences and were controlled by the need to obtain a 'licence to crenellate' from the king, but moated sites had only token defences and their construction was uncontrolled. In the medieval mind the possession of a defended residence was closely linked with concepts of lordship and social status: great lords had their castles, while lesser members of the free classes (knights, esquires, clergy and some farmers) had, where conditions were suitable, moated houses.

Most moats function like ponds, relying on an imperious base or lining, though some are connected to water-courses or ground-water supplies. As the map opposite shows, the distribution of moats is clearly related to the natural occurrence of water-holding boulder clay. A clay subsoil made the construction of a moat relatively simple and cheap, as no special lining was needed.

Nationally, the earliest moated sites date from the later 12th century. They continued to be dug and constructed until about 1550, but the majority belong to the period 1200-1325. The mid-12th-century adulterine 'castle' at Offton may be regarded as a prototype, in that it has a broad rectangular moat surrounding, unusually, a platform of 0.9 acre which is 2.4m high.[1] Castle Yard, Bramfield, may be another proto-moat. It has the circular ditch (partly wet) of a ringwork castle, but lacks the internal bank, having only a slightly raised circular

platform of one acre.[2]

Some of the earliest true moats are circular. Nunnery Mount in Great Bricett has a circular platform (0.7 acre), attached to a polygonal 'bailey' of the same size.[3] Wattisham Hall has a circular house-moat (0.8 acre), set within a ditched rectangular enclosure (7.3 acres), which contains barns as well as the parish church.[4]

Most moats, however, are rectangular. A good example is at Brockley Hall, where the moat (1.2 acres) is probably contemporary with the timber-framed aisled hall of c.1400 on the island.[5] A hierarchy is apparent in the size of moats: those that are an acre or more in extent tend to be manorial in status (as at Brockley) or monastic (e.g. Flixton Priory). Moats of about half an acre in size are much more likely to be associated with parsonages (The Old Rectory, Whatfield) or farms that are ancient free tenements (Oak Tree Farm, Hitcham). At the lower end of the scale it is often difficult to distinguish clearly between true moated sites and farmsteads that are merely ditched, especially when complicated by ponds and green-edge ditches. However the broadness of the ditch (5m. or more), or the status of the site, is often the key indicator.

The normal position for the original house was roughly central to the moated platform, facing the main entrance across an open forecourt, with a garden or orchard at the rear. Access to the platform was by either an earthen causeway or a bridge. However from the late 14th century it became more fashionable to have the buildings on the edge of the moat, inspired by a new wave of visually dramatic castles with walls rising sheer from the water and with imposing gatehouses. To do this it was necessary to strengthen the soft edges of the earthen platforms with expensive mortared-flint or brick revetting. This can be seen at Columbyne Hall,

Stowupland, where flint walls rise from the moat and bear a timber-framed superstructure of c.1400, and the front range incorporates a gatehouse.[6] A contemporary but smaller timber-framed gatehouse exists at Burgate Hall.[7] In the 15th and 16th centuries the increasing use of brick gave further opportunities for developing these themes: perfectly rectangular brick-revetted platforms (Hawstead Place), impressive gatehouses (Gedding Hall)[8] and completely brick-walled buildings (Rushbrook Hall).[9]

Barns and other agricultural buildings are rarely sited on a house-moat; they are usually situated just outside, flanking the approach to the entrance. Sometimes they are within their own moated or ditched enclosure. Moats can also surround banqueting houses or 'gloriets' (Letheringham Lodge), deer-park lodges (Rishangles Lodge, Thorndon), gardens (Shelley Hall), fishponds (Balsdon Hall, Acton) and dovecotes (Otley Hall).

Further details on p.199

Denham Hall Farm: a typical moated site, with the house on the 'island', barns outside, flanking the approach.

MEDIEVAL MOATED SITES

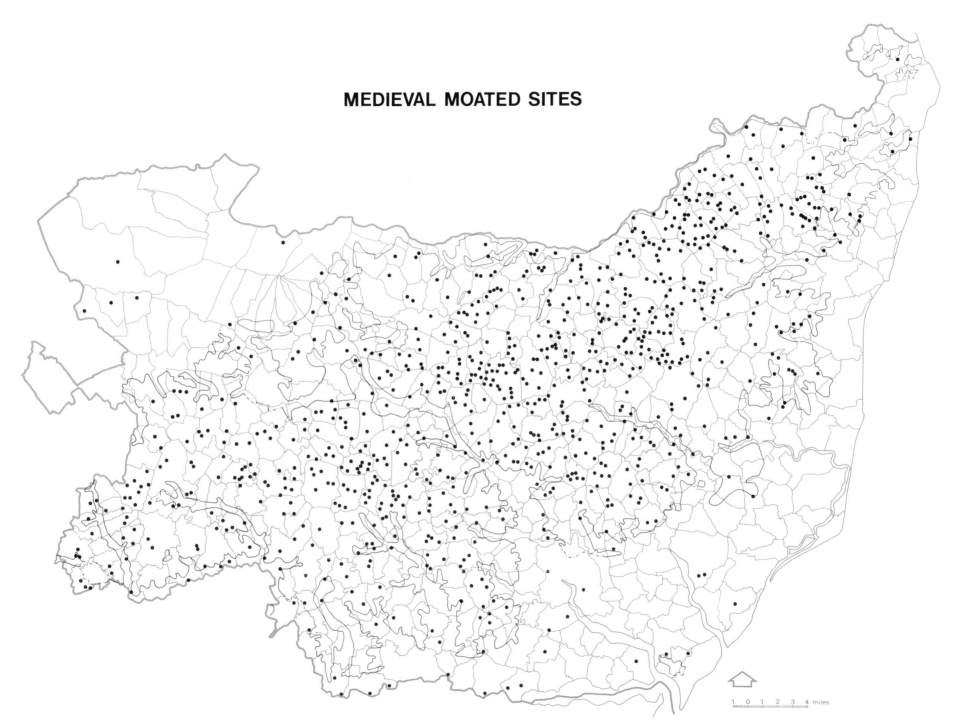

26. GREENS, COMMONS AND TYES

Edward Martin

Green, common and *tye* are all terms used in Suffolk for areas of common pasture—in that order of frequency. Until recently the terms have, to a certain extent, been interchangeable.[1] *Green* is derived from Old English *grene* meaning the colour green and, by extension, a grassy area, in particular a piece of public or common grazing land. In the latter sense it is not documented much before 1200, though it occurs in a few place-names of the 11th century, such as Mangreen in Norfolk (*Manegrena* 1086). *Common* comes from Latin *communa* or *communia*, meaning something held in common, and by the 12th century was applied to pieces of unenclosed land or 'waste' belonging to local manors. *Tye* is derived from Old English *teag*, meaning a small enclosure, but in Suffolk, Essex and Kent it developed, from at least the 13th century, the local meaning of a common pasture.

The occurrence, as place-names, of these terms has been mapped, giving the totals in each 5km. square (about 9.5 square miles). Although the three terms have similar meanings, it can be seen that they have different distribution patterns. *Greens* are concentrated in diagonal band running from Cowlinge in the south-west to the South Elmhams in the north-east, a distribution that closely matches that of boulder clay. *Commons* however are to be found mainly in the north-east of Suffolk, in the South Elmhams and Ilketshalls (where they overlap with greens) and along the east coast. *Tyes* have a very restricted distribution in south Suffolk (overlapping with greens), which suggests that this area had close links with Essex where tyes occur frequently.

Physically, greens and tyes are usually to be found on clay soils and have farmsteads and houses around their margins. This is also true of commons in areas like the South Elmhams. However, along the coast and in Breckland, commons are found on light sandy soils and are often heathlike, with edges that have few houses.

Greens can range in size and shape from just an acre or two to a large compact block in the region of 900 acres.[2] Large greens were a particular feature of north Suffolk, occurring mostly on the wide and flat interfluves that are typical of that area.[3] In the more dissected landscape of south Suffolk, narrow strip greens alongside roads were more usual.[4] J. Hodskinson's map of Suffolk, published in 1783, shows extensive heath commons in Breckland and the Sandlings which contained thousands of acres (Lakenheath Warren had 2,328 acres), as well as huge fen commons in the parishes of Lakenheath and Mildenhall. However the largest surviving common is probably at Sutton (661 acres). By contrast, the largest tye, at Battisford, contained only 157 acres (enclosed 1810).

The present archaeological evidence from Suffolk suggests a 12th-century origin for many of the settlements around greens, which is consistent with place-name evidence. Greens tend to be located on the high, heavy land with poor natural drainage, often on the periphery of their parishes, suggesting that they are secondary features in the medieval landscape. This view is supported by the distribution of churches (mostly in existence by 1086) which are rarely associated with greens.[5] Greens tend to share the same topographical locations as woods, and quite a number actually have 'wood' names, e.g. Norwood Green, Cratfield. This suggests that some greens, at least, arose from the felling of woods or the over-grazing of wood-pasture.

Rights of pasturing were normally attached to individual land-holdings (usually those bordering the pasture), and the number and types of animals that could be grazed were carefully regulated. The rights were variously termed 'beast-goings', 'shares', 'stints' or 'gates'. In some places 'intercommoning' existed, where two or more communities had rights on the same piece of land.[6]

Many pieces of common land were encroached upon, or totally enclosed, from medieval times onwards. Nevertheless, a large acreage, as demonstrated by Hodskinson's map of 1783, remained to be enclosed by Parliamentary Acts in the late 18th and 19th centuries. Enclosure tended to produce a highly distinctive landscape—a straight road running down the centre of the old green, with new brick houses beside it, while long tracks lead to the older timber-framed houses set back around the original edge. Good examples of this can be seen at Battisford Tye and to the north of Elmswell (Buttonhaugh Green).

Further details on p. 199

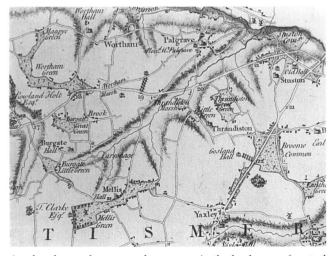

An abundance of greens and commons in the landscape of central Suffolk, as mapped by Joseph Hodskinson in 1783.

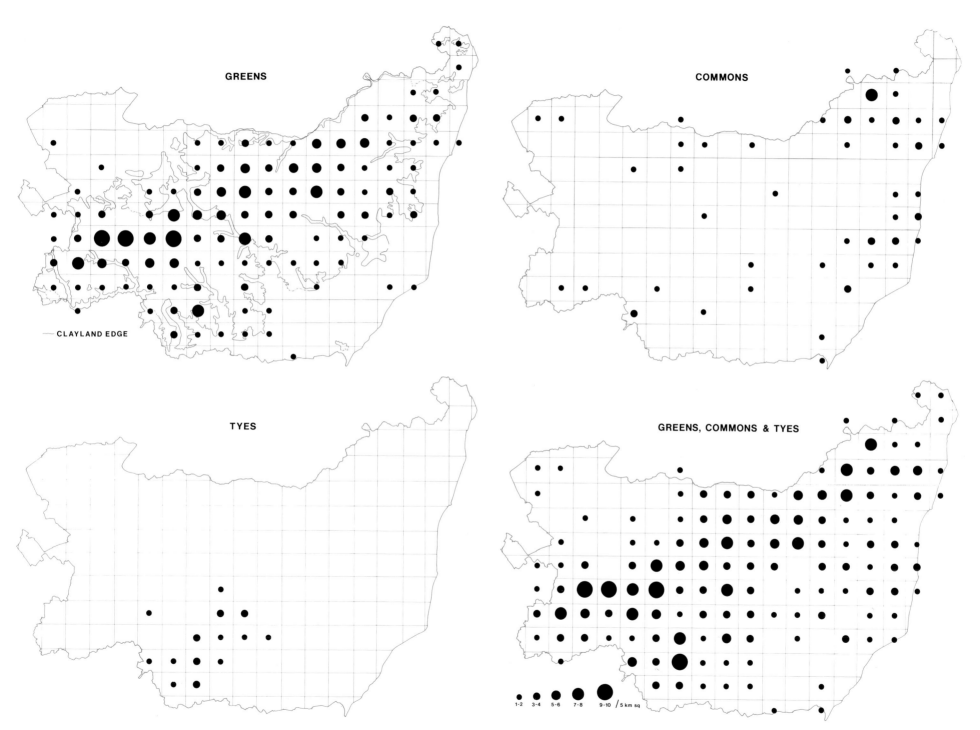

GREENS

COMMONS

CLAYLAND EDGE

TYES

GREENS, COMMONS & TYES

1-2 3-4 5-6 7-8 9-10 / 5 km sq

63

Oliver Rackham

Medieval England was not a very wooded land, and Suffolk was less wooded than most counties. The whole country had once been covered by wildwood, but most of this was destroyed in prehistoric times to make farmland or heath. What remained in the Middle Ages was regularly managed and conserved, either as woodland or as wood-pasture.

Domesday Book, unfortunately, lists Suffolk woodlands in terms not of their areas but of the numbers of pigs that were supposed to fatten on their acorns. This was not a realistic way of enumerating woodland, but I have tried to give meaning to the figures by comparing the swine-assessments of particular woods with their acreages as known from other sources. The map based on Domesday Book, therefore, indicates roughly how woodland was distributed, but its details should not be pressed. Much of the woodland then was in north-east Suffolk; the Breckland and Sandlings had almost none. The total adds up to 9% of the area of Suffolk. For a few places, Domesday says that the swine-assessment had been greater in 1066 than in 1086; this is indicated by an outer circle around the point.

At least half of that 9% of woodland was grubbed out in the next two-and-a-half centuries, a time of great pressure on land. Such woods as remained by 1350 were usually to persist for the next 500 years; some of them are extant today. The main map gives the distribution of woodland as it was after 1350. It is a summary of the separate histories of some hundreds of individual woods. It includes (1) woods directly documented; (2) woods inferred to be medieval on archaeological or botanical grounds; (3) medieval woods whose extent is known (e.g. from early maps) but which have since been destroyed.

The map is not exhaustive. I have taken a more rigorous view of what to include than the Nature Conservancy Council's *Inventory of Ancient Woodland*. There are undoubtedly surviving woods, and records of destroyed woods, waiting to be discovered. Nevertheless, the map gives a reasonably accurate general distribution of late-medieval woodland. By 1350 the big woods of the north-east no longer existed; most of the surviving woods were in the south-west.

These woods were natural woods, not plantations. They were intensively managed as a renewable resource. Suffolk woods consisted (as they still do) of many different kinds of trees. Every five to twenty years the wood was cut down and allowed to grow again from the stools to yield *underwood*—poles and rods used for fuel, fencing, wattle-and-daub, etc. Scattered among the underwood were oaks, allowed to stand for 25 to 100 years and then felled for *timber*—for beams and planks.

Woodland was scarce and valuable, although it was not the only source of trees for Suffolk had plenty of hedges. Woods were protected by great banks and ditches around them. The average medieval Suffolk house contains some 200 small oaks, representing a year's growth of the *timber* component of about 200 acres of woodland. Only the better-wooded districts can have been self-sufficient in timber and wood, even for rural uses. Most towns, woodless areas, and especially the Breckland which lacked both hedges and woods, would have relied on imported timber, peat (where available) and probably coal.

Both during and after the Middle Ages, new woods sometimes sprang up on land that went out of cultivation. From the late 17th century onwards, landowners also deliberately created plantations by planting trees. The modern plantations of the Forestry Commission in the Breckland and Sandlings now much exceed the area of ancient woodland.

Medieval woods still extant include the Suffolk Wildlife Trust's reserves of the Bradfield Woods, Bull's Wood at Cockfield, Combs Wood and (in part) Groton Wood. Here one can see coppice management in operation, boundary banks, giant underwood stools, and the characteristic plants of ancient woodland.

Further details on p.200

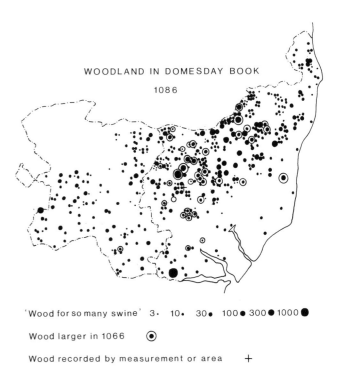

WOODLAND IN DOMESDAY BOOK

1086

'Wood for so many swine'   3·   10·   30●   100●   300●   1000●

Wood larger in 1066   ⊙

Wood recorded by measurement or area   +

MEDIEVAL WOODS

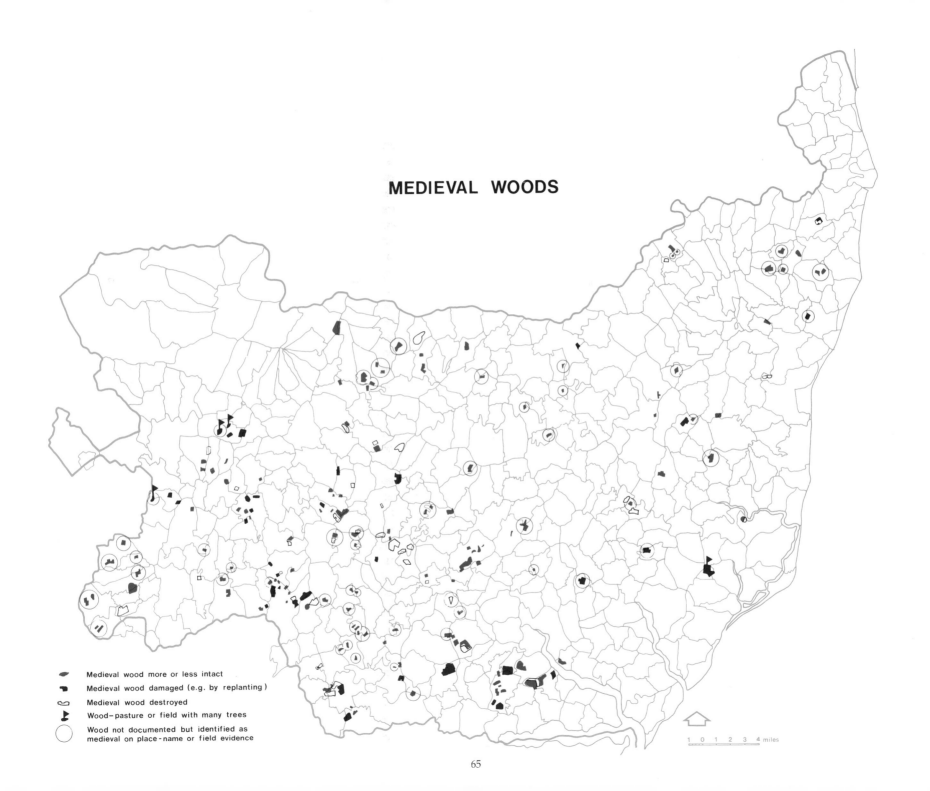

Medieval wood more or less intact

Medieval wood damaged (e.g. by replanting)

Medieval wood destroyed

Wood-pasture or field with many trees

Wood not documented but identified as
medieval on place-name or field evidence

1 0 1 2 3 4 miles

28. DEER PARKS, 1086-*c*.1600

Rosemary Hoppitt

Deer parks fulfilled a number of roles in the medieval economy and landscape. They were status-symbols, places of leisure and recreation, stores of venison and sources of a wide range of other produce for surrounding manors and estates. In England parks were probably a Norman development coinciding with the introduction from the continent of fallow deer.[1]

In the early medieval period parks shared a number of features. Usually covering 200 or more acres, they included areas of wood-pasture and coppiced woodland. Boundaries were usually defined by combinations of banks, ditches, hedges and/or fences or pales. At intervals the boundary was punctuated by a small number of gates, beside which there may have been lodges. The main lodge was usually located fairly centrally, or on a site with a commanding view over the park.[2] Parks also provided secure locations for fishponds and warrens.[3] While the main purpose of a park was to breed and keep deer, which were hunted or culled for the table, it was in reality a multi-purpose land-unit. The relatively high costs of wages and maintenance (repairing fences, hedges, gates and lodges) were offset by income generated from the production of timber, wood, fuel, fodder and bedding, from the lease of grazing (agistment) and, where it occurred, pannage in the form of acorns. Towards the end of the medieval period the role of parks was to change. They continued to be important status-symbols but their utilitarian purpose was superseded by aesthetic considerations.

In Suffolk the physical evidence for the existence of early parks is limited. Traces of former boundary banks do occur, but most, if they ever existed, have long since been ploughed out. The location and extent of parks are gleaned mainly from historical maps, place-names and field-names, with Park Farm and Park Wood being among the best indicators. The shapes of former parks often emerge as long, usually curving lines which other boundaries abut but do not generally cross. Some parks survive in a more subtle way as discrete land-holdings, for example at Wetheringsett where Lodge Farm was probably coincident with the former park. Other indications may come from 19th-century tithe apportionments, or from the records of tithe disputes: this is because some parks were partially exempt from the payment of tithes.[4]

The map opposite shows the distribution of parks between 1086 and *c*.1602.[5] Each circle shows the position of a park but not its extent. Where the actual location within a parish is uncertain, the symbol has been placed centrally. The dates given against each example are based on documentary or cartographic evidence. Some parks are poorly documented and may have continued in use beyond the dates indicated on the map.

The documentary record suggests an upsurge in the creation of parks during the period 1200-1400, but this may be simply reflecting an increase in the number of documents which survive. Topographical evidence, coupled with detailed investigation at a manorial level, shows that parks were created from an earlier date, certainly by the mid-12th century. Parks at Semer and Chelsworth, belonging to the abbot of Bury St Edmunds, were recorded in 1130. In 1200 Jocelin of Brakelond commented that the abbot had 'made a number of parks which he filled with beasts and kept huntsmen and hounds'.[6]

Lay magnates also made parks in Suffolk. Already by 1086 Robert Malet had three, and by 1306-07 Roger Bigod had as many as nine.[7] Parks were the prerogative of wealthy landowners, and often located near their major seat (*caput*), along with other major investments such as a market or castle. Later in the period, lesser landowners are documented as holding parks. For example William de Boville, who held the manor of Badingham, had a park there in 1324.[8] The total number of parks declined in the 15th century, but recovered in Tudor times as newly affluent landowners drawn from trading and legal backgrounds invested in rural estates.

Early parks were distributed in a broad band running across the county from south-west to north-east. By contrast, the Breckland had none. Locally, early parks were on higher land near parish boundaries, and associated with areas of woodland and common; they were therefore at a distance from the manor house and village. By contrast later parks were closely associated with manor houses, and formed part of an overall design intended to enhance the setting of the house. At Hoxne, where he already owned a wooded park, the bishop of Norwich created a second park in the 15th century, nearer the church and village and probably to set off a new palace. By the 16th century the majority of early parks had been 'disparked' and the land brought under cultivation. A number of late, aesthetically conceived parks still survive as at Long Melford and Hengrave, but only at places like Bradfield, Holbrook and Staverton do landscapes exist which would have been familiar to a medieval park-keeper.

Further details on p.200

DEER PARKS 1086-c.1602

PARK RECORDED IN DOMESDAY BOOK

PARK RECORDED 1086 – 1200

PARK RECORDED 1200 – 1400

PARK RECORDED 1400 – c.1602

1 0 1 2 3 4 miles

29. RABBIT WARRENS

Rosemary Hoppitt

Warrens were areas of land, often fully or partly enclosed, dedicated to the keeping and breeding of rabbits. As a term, 'warren' must be distinguished from 'free warren'. The latter is a legal right which the crown granted to a manorial lord enabling him to hunt 'beasts of the warren' (pheasant, partridge, hare and rabbit) anywhere over his property; such rights were granted for nearly every vill in Suffolk from the 13th century onwards.[1] However, this privilege tells us little about the existence, or not, of a physical enclosure reserved specifically for rabbits. The maps opposite relate only to this latter category and ignore the notion of 'free warren'.

The rabbit, or more correctly the 'coney', originated in the Mediterranean region and appears to have been brought to Britain during the early Norman period. Warrens were first recorded in documents in the first half of the 12th century.[2] Rabbits were bred for their fur, both for warmth and decoration on clothing, and of course for food. As an exotic species, they initially needed cosseting to survive and breed. Thereafter they adapted rapidly, tolerating a widening range of climates, until they eventually became a major pest capable of destroying crops and, in some places, of damaging the environment.[3] Numbers rose greatly in the 19th century because of agricultural improvement and the removal of natural predators. The introduction of myxomatosis in the 1950s reduced the population of rabbits dramatically and led to a decline in the demand for, and consumption of, rabbit meat.[4]

In the Middle Ages manorial lords established large numbers of warrens. The most successful and productive examples in Suffolk were associated with sandy heathland, and made major contributions to manorial revenues.[5] Landlords continued to create and run warrens in later periods, right through to the 19th century when they often formed parts of sporting estates, and rabbit farming was still regarded as a form of agricultural improvement.[6] The evidence for warrens comes from a variety of sources: maps and place-names, documents such as manorial accounts and court rolls, and a range of topographical features such as banks, mounds and special buildings.

Enclosure banks served a number of purposes by defining boundaries, keeping the rabbits out of farmland and, conversely, protecting them from predators. Some warrens on the Breckland have substantial banks enclosing hundreds of hectares.[7] The interior of the warren gave a combination of cover and grazing. There may also have been internal enclosures for the growing of supplementary fodder. In some cases the rabbits were provided with elongated mounds into which they could burrow and where they could breed. Such 'pillow mounds' exist at Sutton Common and Covehithe in the east of the county, and at Knettishall Heath on the Breckland.[8] Each warren was in the charge of a skilled employee or lessee called the warrener. On the Breckland, where large medieval warrens produced rabbits on a commercial scale, substantial 'lodges' of wood and stone were constructed within the enclosures. Here the warrener and his family lived, and equipment, rabbit pelts and carcasses were kept secure from theft. Rabbits were a valuable commodity, and poaching, which could be highly organised, became a major nuisance.[9] Located at high points, the lodges also provided excellent lookouts. The best surviving example is at Thetford Warren, but other remains exists at a number of Breckland sites.[10]

Map A shows the location of place-names incorporating the words 'warren' and 'coney'.[11] Two main clusters emerge: one in the Breckland at the north-western end of the county, the other in the east on the Sandlings.

Both these areas are characterised by dry sandy soils of poor quality, and traditionally had similar farming systems based on 'sheep and corn'.[12] By introducing and nurturing rabbits on these heathland pastures alongside their sheep flocks, landlords could supplement and enhance their income from otherwise unproductive land. It was here that commercial warrens of the later 14th century produced large numbers of rabbits each year. For example, at Lakenheath the output of the warren varied from around 380 rabbits per year in the 1360s to over 3600 in the 1390s, most of which were sold off the manor.[13] However, these figures pale into insignificance when compared to the 'bags' of the 18th and 19th century which were measured in tens of thousands per year.[14]

Map B shows the location of former warrens. However, neither the survival of evidence across the county nor the amount of scholarly research into the surviving evidence is consistent, and the map must be read with this in mind. For example, detailed research on the Breckland has produced a reliable and clear picture of the number, extent and significance of the warrens there since Norman times.[15] In contrast, our knowledge of the rest of the county, particularly the central and southern areas, is much less complete. Some of the evidence results from detailed research in particular areas, and some through looking at documents from a particular period over a more extensive area; other information is topographical and of unknown date. Thus, the distribution must be interpreted with caution because of considerable diversity in the nature, extent and chronology of the warrens shown. Only through further research will the full picture become clearer.

Further details on p.200

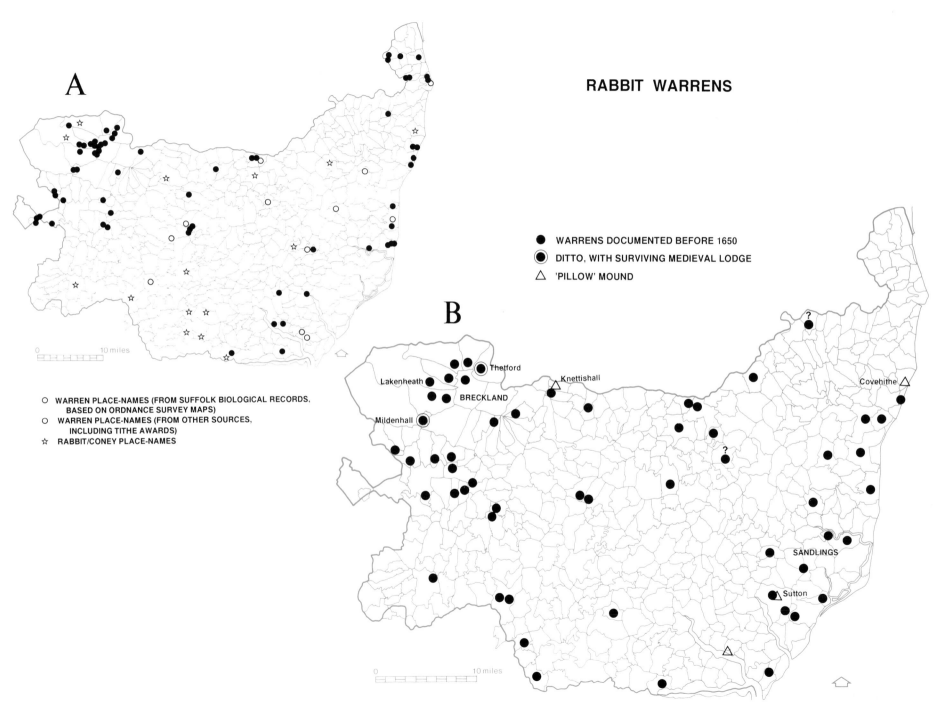

RABBIT WARRENS

A

- ● WARRENS DOCUMENTED BEFORE 1650
- ⊙ DITTO, WITH SURVIVING MEDIEVAL LODGE
- △ 'PILLOW' MOUND

○ WARREN PLACE-NAMES (FROM SUFFOLK BIOLOGICAL RECORDS, BASED ON ORDNANCE SURVEY MAPS)

○ WARREN PLACE-NAMES (FROM OTHER SOURCES, INCLUDING TITHE AWARDS)

☆ RABBIT/CONEY PLACE-NAMES

10 miles

B

Thetford

Lakenheath

BRECKLAND

Knettishall

Covehithe

Mildenhall

?

?

SANDLINGS

Sutton

10 miles

69

30. RELIGIOUS HOUSES

Peter Northeast

The map opposite illustrates the distribution of religious or monastic houses founded in Suffolk during the Middle Ages. It covers the whole range of such institutions including abbeys, priories, friaries, nunneries, colleges, hospitals and small cells. A marked imbalance is immediately visible between the west and east of the county. This must, without any doubt, be attributed to the power and influence of the great Benedictine abbey of Bury St Edmunds. The imbalance was even greater than appears on the map because the Cluniacs at Thetford moved over the river into Norfolk in 1114, the monks at Clare had been removed to Stoke in 1124 (to become a college three centuries later), and of the houses at Sudbury, Thetford, Whelnetham and Chipley, only the nunnery at Thetford and the friary at Sudbury contained inmates numbered in double figures.

In fact, the numbers of 'religious' making up individual monastic communities were much smaller than is generally imagined. Apart from the huge abbey of Bury, which at times had up to 80 monks, the only monastic houses regularly to have more than dozen inmates were Butley, Ixworth, Leiston and Sibton, and only the last of these exceeded twenty. Similarly, the only nunnery to have over a dozen inmates was Campsey. Several establishments, such as Snape and Sudbury (both Benedictine) were often down to two monks. In general, friaries had higher numbers. The majority had over twenty friars while the large ones, such as the Black Friars (Dominican) in Ipswich and the Grey Friars (Franciscan) at Babwell near Bury, had over forty.[1]

In the later Middle Ages the friars were the best known and most popular of the religious orders. This is partly because of their greater numbers, but principally because of their philosophy summed up in the oft-quoted, albeit simplistic, definition: 'a monk stayed in a monastery to save his soul, and a friar went into the world to save the souls of others'. This is reflected in numerous requests by testators for prayers to be said for their souls by friars; only rarely are monks so commissioned. The parish clergy also were only too ready to invoke the assistance of friars in this respect, despite the alleged animosity between the two groups.

The greatest impact that religious houses had upon the countryside was in their ownership of land and manors.[2] The map shows that many parishes contained manors of which the lords were religious establishments—with whom, or their stewards, the tenants had to deal. This was in addition to the overall jurisdiction that the two great abbeys of Bury and Ely had over their respective liberties (see Map 8). Towards the end of the Middle Ages, however, religious houses frequently lost direct contact with their tenants because they commonly rented their manors to lessees or 'farmers'.

In the spiritual field, religious houses controlled many parish churches. They did this as patrons having the right to appoint incumbents, as rectors receiving a proportion of the tithes, and as impropriators responsible for the appointment of vicars or curates (see Map 31). However, in the case of Augustinian or Austin Canons, whose main *raison d'être* was the provision of priests for churches, canons from the houses actually served the cures without being technically appointed to them. They were regarded locally as parish priests, but they never appeared in 'lists of incumbents' and the written record of such arrangements is very thin.

The extent to which religious institutions held land and manors is best appreciated when they were finally dissolved. Several houses had disappeared from Suffolk in earlier centuries, and five were among the score confiscated in the 1520s by Cardinal Wolsey to support his great educational schemes at Oxford and Ipswich.

Nevertheless, about forty establishments survived in Suffolk to be dissolved under the two Acts of 1536 and 1539. The Court of Augmentations, established in 1536 to dispose of land formerly held by the church, was presented with over 200 manors in Suffolk to sell for the king. (It is a total misjudgement to imagine his *giving* them away.) This presented golden opportunities for county families to expand their holdings.[3] The map shows all those parishes where manors had been held by religious institutions, including a few wealthy chantries.[4]

Of some 35 hospitals in the county, about a dozen, which by then had become little more than almshouses, survived the main dissolution, but only a small handful managed to continue beyond the middle of the 16th century. The colleges of priests also managed to escape the general dissolution but they too, all fell by 1550.

Further details on p.201

KEY TO ABBREVIATIONS ON MAP OPPOSITE

A	Augustinian Canons/Canonesses
AF	Augustinian Friars
B	Benedictine Monks/Nuns
C	Cistercian Monks
CF	Carmelite (White) Friars
CN	Cluniac Monks
CR	Crutched Friars
D	Dominican (Black) Friars
F	Franciscan (Grey) Friars/Nuns
H	Hospital
KH	Knights Hospitallers
KT	Knights Templars
P	Premonstratensian Canons

MEDIEVAL RELIGIOUS HOUSES

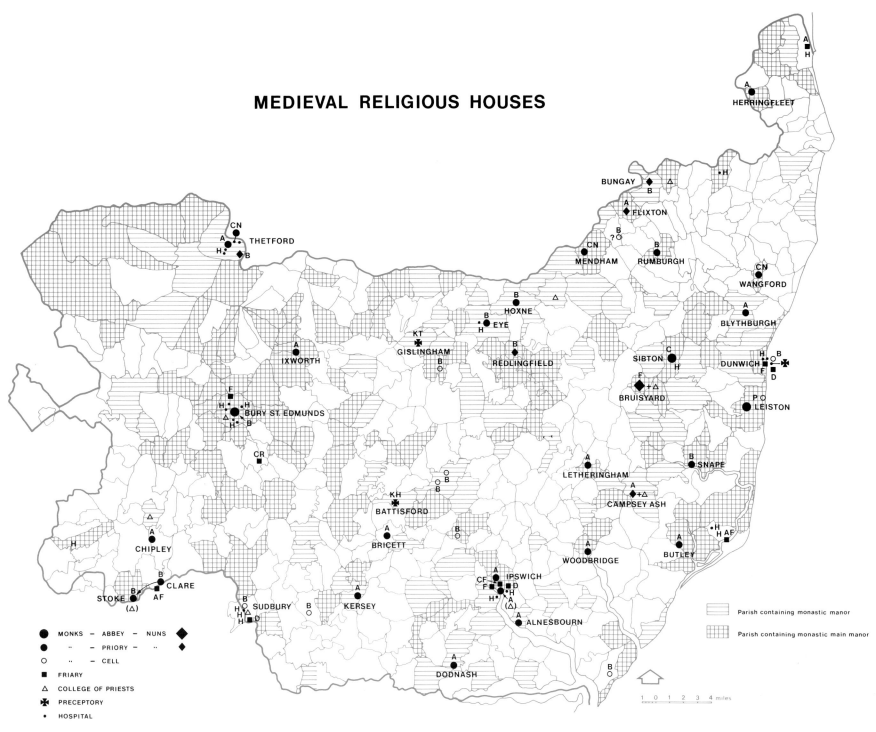

HERRINGFLEET

BUNGAY
FLIXTON
THETFORD
CN
A
H·
B
MENDHAM
CN
RUMBURGH
B
WANGFORD
CN

HOXNE
B
EYE
B
H
BLYTHBURGH
A

IXWORTH
A
GISLINGHAM
KT
B
REDLINGFIELD
B
SIBTON
C
H
DUNWICH
H
B
O
F
D

BRUISYARD
F
+△
LEISTON
P
O

BURY ST EDMUNDS
F
H·
H
△
H
B
CR
SNAPE
B

LETHERINGHAM
A
CAMPSEY ASH
A
+△

CHIPLEY
H
A
BRICETT
A
B
O
BUTLEY
H A F
H·

BATTISFORD
KH
B
O
B

WOODBRIDGE
A

CLARE
B
STOKE
B
AF
(△)
SUDBURY
B
H
O△
A
H H
D
B
O
KERSEY
A
IPSWICH
A
CF
F
B
D
H·
H
A
(△)
ALNESBOURN
A

DODNASH
A
B
O

● MONKS – ABBEY – NUNS ◆		
● " – PRIORY – ◆		
○ " – CELL		
■ FRIARY		
△ COLLEGE OF PRIESTS		
✠ PRECEPTORY		
· HOSPITAL		

Parish containing monastic manor

Parish containing monastic main manor

0 1 2 3 4 miles

31. VICARAGES AND APPROPRIATED CHURCH LIVINGS

David Dymond

In the Anglo-Saxon period, churches of all types were endowed by law with customary payments such as churchscot and waxscot, and their founders gave them houses (parsonages) and land (glebe). They were also entitled, from at least the 11th century, to receive tithe, a valuable tenth share of the produce of each parish. Other forms of income included donations, known as oblations, and fees. A *vicarage* was an ecclesiastical living in which, during the Middle Ages, the original endowments were 'impropriated' by a religious house—which thereby became the legal rector. Some of the endowments were then officially re-allotted to support a *vicar* (meaning a 'substitute' for the rector).[1] Normally the impropriating institution received the 'greater' tithes levied on the principal crops and animals, and the greater part of the glebe, while the vicar was given the 'lesser' tithes, alterage (offerings in money or in kind) and the rest of the glebe.[2] Other livings were impropriated but *not* converted into vicarages. Instead, the religious house appointed and removed stipendiary priests, at will, while they either swallowed the endowments directly, or 'farmed' them out in return for rents.[3]

Impropriations were therefore livings which had been carved up, leaving the incumbent with a substantially reduced income—often no more than a quarter of the original. In about 1730, Thomas Cox listed the livings of Suffolk, distinguishing those which paid the ancient levy of First Fruits and Tenths, and those which were exempt or 'discharged' because they were worth less than £50 a year. Of all the vicarages listed, no fewer than 66% were in the exempt category.[4] Impropriations may seem legalised piracy, but we must remember that many parishes were originally well-endowed, while religious houses were often short of money—particularly in their early days.[5] Vicarages and impropriations together constituted about a third of all livings in

Suffolk.[6] About sixty religious houses, of which slightly more than half lay *outside* the county, were impropriators of Suffolk parishes.

In practice, the difference between rectories and vicarages was less than might appear.[7] Though never impropriated, rectories were not necessarily rich and they, too, frequently lost parts of their endowments in the form of 'pensions' and 'portions' payable to religious houses, lay lords and other parishes.[8]

Although the religious houses were destroyed by Henry VIII, impropriations survived because they were sold or granted to laymen ('lay rectors') or to institutions such as Cambridge colleges.[9] Nevertheless, the totals of rectories, vicarages and curacies did not remain static. In the 17th and 18th centuries, about fourteen vicarages in Suffolk were once again given the status of rectory when the rectorial income was given back to the incumbent.[10] In the 19th century, over sixty perpetual curacies were re-styled as vicarages.[11] In addition, a few totally new parishes were created as vicarages in modern times.[12]

The map shows impropriations in most parts of Suffolk. Nevertheless, they were noticeably rarer in the Breckland and around Bury St Edmunds where the great majority of livings remained rectories. Conversely, impropriations were relatively common in the north-east quarter of Suffolk, especially in a belt of country from Eye to Southwold. A high proportion of market towns was also impropriated, for example Mildenhall, Stowmarket and Bungay. Finally, areas of influence are clearly discernible around certain religious houses such as Ixworth, Bungay and Butley.

What does this distribution mean historically? To some extent the clustering of impropriated parishes reflects

the greater concentration of religious houses in eastern Suffolk (see Map 30). In parishes which surrounded them, religious communities were often given patronage and control by their founders and other benefactors. However, they also gained control in parishes which were more scattered and distant. Any of these impropriations, local or distant, might have been the result of quite unsolicited gifts, but they could also have been 'engineered' by religious houses for their own benefit, in parishes where the pickings were particularly good. The relative absence of impropriations in west Suffolk can be partly explained by the policies of Bury abbey. Although it acquired the patronage of many parishes (over 60 by 1200), it chose, in most cases, not to impropriate them. It did, however, take many pensions and portions from them.

By the 12th and 13th centuries, the full agricultural potential of the heavy clay lands of north-east Suffolk was being exploited by a large and growing population, and many wealthy parishes were impropriated.[13] Out of 40 vicarages in Suffolk which were listed in 1291, 32 (or 80%) had previously received total incomes of £15 or more a year. As Suffolk's parishes then had total endowments averaging £14 15s 6d, these high values demonstrate that religious houses preferred, where possible, to exploit those parishes which had above-average endowments.[14]

Further details on p.201

APPROPRIATED CHURCH LIVINGS

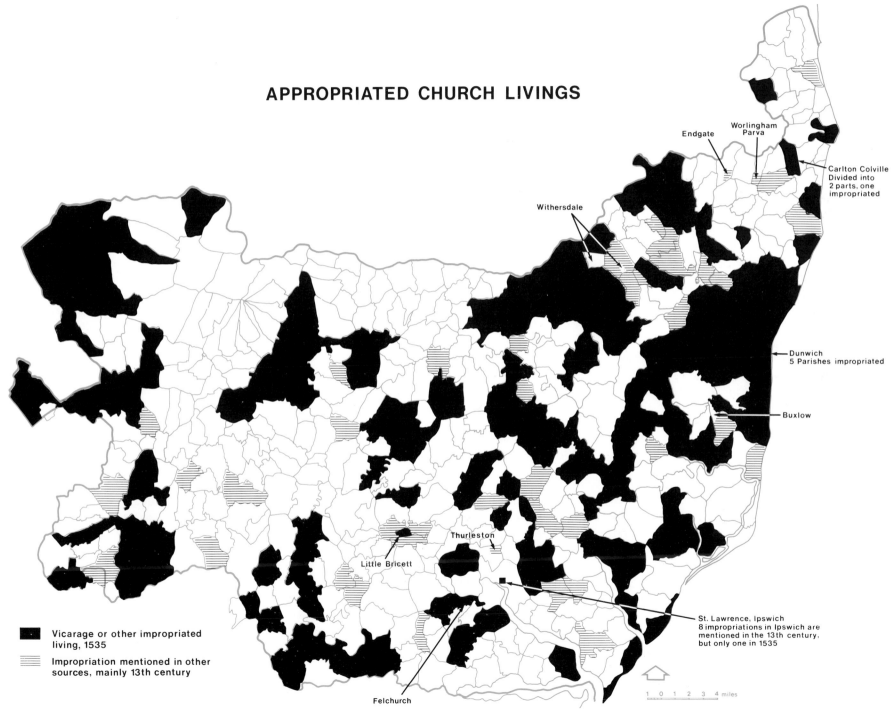

Worlingham Parva

Endgate

Carlton Colville
Divided into
2 parts, one
impropriated

Withersdale

Dunwich
5 Parishes impropriated

Buxlow

Thurleston

Little Bricett

St. Lawrence, Ipswich
8 impropriations in Ipswich are
mentioned in the 13th century,
but only one in 1535

Felchurch

■ Vicarage or other impropriated
living, 1535

Impropriation mentioned in other
sources, mainly 13th century

1 0 1 2 3 4 miles

Gilds played an important part in the social and religious life of the medieval parish.[1] By being a member of a gild, a man or woman earned the right to be helped in adversity during life, and to be prayed for by gild members after death. In addition, the individual member could join in general activities such as dinners, plays and celebrations on the day of the gild's dedication.

The study of these institutions has long been bedevilled by confusion with craft gilds and civic gilds. Rural Suffolk had no craft or trade gilds, while even in the towns of Bury St Edmunds and Ipswich, at least in the period for which documentary evidence survives, they were the exception rather than the rule. Civic gilds seem to have been confined to those of Corpus Christi in Ipswich and Candlemas at Bury St Edmunds, although the gild of the Holy Ghost at Beccles also seems to have become a civic gild and survived the Reformation in modified form.[2]

The existence of individual parish gilds is often known only through incidental references in contemporary documents, especially in wills and tax-lists, so that their identification today involves an element of chance.[3] A national survey was conducted in 1389, but returns survive for only thirteen places in Suffolk, describing about 40 gilds.[4] Another official list was made in 1548 when gilds were suppressed, but by then many had ceased to function or, having little or no property, went unrecorded.

Altogether, approaching 500 gilds have now been identified in the county, which sounds like approximately one to each parish. However the map shows that this is far from the true picture. The majority of parishes in the western half of Suffolk certainly had gilds; most parishes in the north-east of the county also had gilds, but conspicuously few in the south-east. In this latter area, most parishes seem to have depended on certain centrally-placed gilds, principally at Framlingham, Kelsale and Woodbridge.

It is difficult to give an adequate explanation for this distribution. We might be tempted to attribute the prevalence of gilds in the west to the influence of Bury Abbey, but have no evidence to substantiate this. Similarly, it seems unlikely to be mere coincidence that the two strongest gilds in the eastern part of the county, at Framlingham and Kelsale, were on two important manors of the most powerful lords in the area, the Dukes of Norfolk (the Howard family, and previously the Mowbrays and Bigods); but here again we have no documentary evidence.

Few gilds seem to have been wealthy enough to employ their own priests: presumably unbeneficed local clergy were used as required for gild services. Sometimes a concerted effort, no doubt associated with an 'appeal', was made to provide an endowment for a gild priest: this was done at Eye, for instance, at the end of the 15th century.

Gild chapels were also a rarity, although gilds appear to have held their services at particular altars in their respective parish churches. Kelsale was distinctive in this respect, as the south aisle there, in which the gild of St John the Baptist was held, was known as the St John's aisle.

The social activities of gilds, in addition to services, were originally held inside churches, but popular opinion steadily moved against this and special gild-halls were built, sometimes a single hall being used by more than one gild. Fressingfield gildhall (still noted for its good food) must have been one of the later ones, having been established in the last years of Henry VII's reign. Its setting up was designed specifically to remove all 'church ales, gilds, yeardays, buryings and other drinkings' from the church.

Few records of Suffolk gilds have survived, perhaps the best being the accounts of the Bardwell gild, which have been printed. They show the gild owning sheep and cows to be rented out, and appointing an official cook and minstrel.[5]

Like many other parochial organisations, gilds waxed and waned. Old ones disappeared and new ones were established; some parishes, not always the largest, had several gilds, while others had none. By the time they were dissolved under an Act of 1547, many had run down or ceased to function. Under the Act, their property including the gildhalls was confiscated by the crown, although some enterprising individuals attempted to 'conceal' both funds and property from the crown's commissioners. Only rarely were they successful: Nayland with its considerable charitable holdings could well be a rare example of such a concealment. Sometimes a parish was able to buy back its gildhall, and so some continued as parish property and later appear as schools or workhouses. Physically, many gildhalls still survive today, like the fine timber-framed examples at Laxfield and Eye. In addition, former gildhalls or their sites are occasionally re-discovered by documentary and architectural research, as happened recently at Hitcham and Stowlangtoft.

Further details on p. 202

MEDIEVAL GILDS

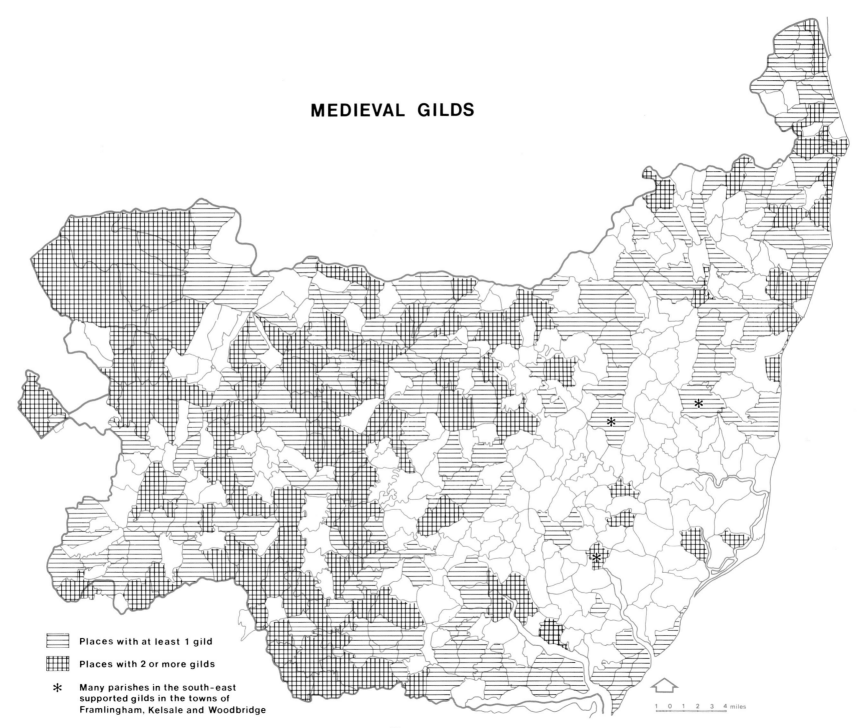

Places with at least 1 gild

Places with 2 or more gilds

* Many parishes in the south-east supported gilds in the towns of Framlingham, Kelsale and Woodbridge

1 0 1 2 3 4 miles

33. MEDIEVAL AND LATER MARKETS

Norman Scarfe

This map shows, fairly completely, how the Crown granted market-rights to various lords of manors in medieval Suffolk. It is based on my provisional list of 1965[1] and its first revision in 1972,[2] checked first against the Calendar of Grants of Markets and Fairs of 1888[3] and then, in the Public Record Office, against its card-index and the chancery rolls themselves.[4]

The map indicates the dates of grant, or very occasionally the earliest recorded use so far determined, and the day of the week on which the market was held. There are surprisingly close clusters, which suggest that markets may have succeeded one another, or may have co-existed by being held, in adjacent manors, on different days of the week. For instance, no grant earlier than 1582 has been found for Wickham Market, yet the market-place is medieval. The nuns of Campsey Ash apparently acquired the manors of both Pettistree and Wickham in 1383, and one might suppose that they transferred Pettistree's market to Wickham. But the transfer clearly came about earlier, for the name of *Wickhammarket* appeared in a parliamentary appeal of 1377.[5]

In its account of the bishop's manor at Hoxne, Domesday Book tellingly illustrates the relative value of Saturday as market-day and the effect of having markets close together:

> In this manor there was a market, and it continued after King William came a It was a Saturday market. William Malet built his castle at Eye and, on the same day as the bishop's market at Hoxne, William Malet established another market in his castle [*probably outside its gate, since 25 burgesses dwelt there*]. So the bishop's market is spoilt, worth little. Now it is held on Friday, but the market at Eye is on Saturday.[6]

A charter of 1227 shows Hoxne's market-day moved again: in view perhaps of Eye's success with Saturday, Hoxne shifted further away, from Friday to Wednesday. That year (October 1226-October 1227), Henry III, aged

nineteen, declared that he was of full age and that all grants made during his minority needed chartered confirmation (at considerable cost!). The lords of nearby Stradbroke and Laxfield obtained grants at the same time: Stradbroke on Friday, Laxfield on Saturday. One sees why at Hoxne the bishop might want to shift to Wednesday. Later in Henry III's uneasy reign, in 1267, Richard de Brewse secured a Tuesday market for his Whittingham manor in Fressingfield, adjoining both Stradbroke and Laxfield. Some such experience can be presumed a few miles further east. Blythburgh had its market already in 1066 and Halesworth's grant of a Tuesday market in 1223 was confirmed in 1227. In the Close Rolls of 1226-7, Hubert de Burgh was allowed to switch his Thursday market at Sotherton to Wednesday, but three years later he had to move it to his adjacent manor at Westhall.

Some general conclusions emerge from the map. Many markets were clearly related to coastal and riverine traffic, and to main roads (though the latter have been omitted from the map). Chronologically, markets developed most significantly in the course of the 13th century. Between 1201 and 1300, forty-seven new markets were recorded in Suffolk, no fewer than thirty-three of them in the years 1250-1300. This contrasts with the fifteen noted between 1066 and 1200, and the eleven from 1300 to 1349. In the two centuries from 1350 to 1550, only six new names appear, and we know little of how far market trading survived in the 73 places named before 1350.

Thick though some of these clusters look on the map, the density seems less than in neighbouring Essex where 67 grants were made between 1200 and 1350 (as against 58 in Suffolk). Perhaps the chief explanation of Suffolk's *relative* shortage is the jealousy with which St Edmund's abbey preserved its own markets in Bury,

stifling wherever possible the few other markets granted within its Liberty of West Suffolk.

Further details on p.202

Cornhill, Ipswich, as drawn by George Frost before 1794. The Market Cross was erected *c.*1628 and demolished in 1812.

MEDIEVAL MARKETS

SHOWING DATES OF GRANTS & MARKET DAYS

Belton
1270 M

Flixton
1253 W

Oulton
1307 M

Lowestoft
1308 W

Beccles
D.B. S

Carlton Colville
1267 F 1295 Th

Bungay
1199/1200
in use 1228
Th

Kessingland
1251 T

Brandon Ferry
1319/20 Th

Brampton
1271 M

West hall
1229

Covehithe
1298 M

Lakenheath
1201 Th 1309 W

Wissett
1267 F

Sotherton
1226 Th
then W

Easton
Bavents
1330 W

Botesdale
1220 Th

Market Weston
1263 S

Whittingham
(Fressingfield)
1267 T

Halesworth
1223 T

Southwold
1221 Th

Mildenhall
1220 T 1412 S

Hoxne
D.B. S then F
1227 W

Blythburgh
DB Th ?
1324 M

Burgate
1272 M

Eye
D.B. S

Stradbroke
1227 F

Bramfield
1270 Th

Freckenham
1218

Worlington
1270 W

Laxfield
1226 S

Dunwich
12th cent
? Daily

Ixworth
1384 T

Walsham le
Willows in
use 1384

Westhorpe
1372 T

Middleton
1270 F

Exning
1257 M

Wyverstone
1231 F

Kelsale
DB ?

Leiston
1312 F 1391 T

Moulton
1298 W

Barrow
1267 S

Bury St. Edmunds
DB, W, S & ?

Mendlesham
1280 T

Earl Soham
1302 Th

Framlingham
in use by 1270
T F S

Saxmundham
1272 Th

Sizewell
? 1237

Newmarket
c.1200 T

Haughley
1231 S

Debenham
1221 F

Kelton(Benhall)
1292 T

Woolpit

Ousden
1254 W

Kettleburgh
1265 W

Aldeburgh
1547 W
1568 S

Felsham
1268 F

Stowmarket
D.B. 1338 T

Earl Stonham
1327 W

Wickham Market
in use 1377

Lidgate
in use 1279
Th

Thurston
(Hawkedon)
1290 T

Needham Market
1226 W

Clopton
1304 T

Pettistree
1253 Th

Orford
c.1154 M
1256

Lavenham
1257 T

Ringshall
1270 S

Grundisburgh
1284 T

Great Thurlow
1272 T

Great Bricett
c 1135-54 T

Witnesham
1227 Th

Great Bealings
1227 T

Woodbridge
1227 W

Haverhill
DB, W

Clare
D.B. F

Long Melford
1235 Th

Bildeston
in use 1348 W

Brent Eleigh
1260 Th

Stoke by Clare
c.1247-52 T

Kersey
1252 M

Toppesfield
(Hadleigh) 1252 M

Ipswich
D.B. perhaps daily
after 1200

Bawdsey
1283 F

Sudbury
DB S & ?

Croxton
(Kirton)
1270 W

RED —MARKETS STILL IN USE IN THE 17TH CENTURY

Raydon
1310 S

Shotley
1303 F

BLACK—MARKETS OUT OF USE BY THE 17TH CENTURY

Stoke by Nayland F
1303 W

Stratford
St Mary
? 1384

East Bergholt
? pre 1495

Erwarton
1254 F

⬡ —MARKETS RECORDED IN DOMESDAY BOOK 1086

Bures St Mary
1271

Nayland
1227/8

Cattawade
(Brantham)
1247

1 0 1 2 3 4 miles

In the Middle Ages, the right to hold a fair, usually once a year, was often given in the same charter as the grant of a weekly market. The years when medieval fairs were officially granted have been indicated on the map opposite, and can be compared with those for markets (see Map 33). It is now fashionable to relate the precise days when fairs were held to the seasons, as though the weather mainly determined the choice. Summer and autumn were certainly the most popular seasons; only three 'cold' or 'frost' fairs are known for the winter months. In any case, this obscures the fact that a fair often coincided with the patronal festival of the parish church: thus the fair granted in 1235 to the abbot of Bury, lord of the principal manor of Long Melford, was to be held at the feast of the Holy Trinity—to whom Melford church is dedicated. Most fairs lasted for three days, centring on a saint's day or other feast of the church, with the day before (the vigil) and the day after (the morrow), but a few lasted longer—in fact, for several weeks. At present, we know of the existence of about 90 medieval fairs in Suffolk. They were scattered quite widely but were much thinner around Bury, on the central Breckland, in the southern Sandlings and, to a lesser extent, around Ipswich. Some places like Newmarket and Dunwich had two annual fairs, while Stoke-by-Nayland and Sudbury had three. Nevertheless, it must be admitted that, as with markets, our information is probably incomplete. What chasms of omission are suggested by the Domesday reference to 'one-third of a fair' at Aspall, where no other record of a fair has ever come to light!

In 1603 Robert Reyce listed 25 places in Suffolk which still had markets, and 69 with fairs.[1] Although his list, too, is probably incomplete, it does suggest that annual fairs survived the economic changes of the later Middle Ages and Reformation more successfully than weekly markets. Reyce continued the medieval practice of relating fairs to ecclesiastical feasts, so one presumes that many pre-Reformation grants survived without any later legal confirmation or modification. When Reyce's ecclesiastical dates are translated into the modern calendar, we see that June and September were still the favourite months.

To give a wide chronological coverage to this map, however, the fairs listed by Reyce have been omitted in favour of those listed by William Owen in 1759 and 1805.[2] His work shows that a large number of medieval fairs had dropped out of use, but that the loss had been more than counterbalanced by the creation of many new ones, some in totally new places and others giving a second, third or even sixth fair in already established venues. In 1759 Owen's total of fairs in the county was 92 in 65 different towns and villages; by 1805 the number had risen to 105 fairs in 69 different places.[3] So, by the end of the 18th century, Suffolk had a large number of rural and urban fairs, scattered throughout the year and over most parts of the county. Again, the Breckland had conspicuously few, and so did the southern end of the Sandlings, but across the rest of the county most people were within striking distance of an annual fair in a not-too-distant village or town. The largest number of fairs seems to have been held in Ipswich with its suburb Handford, and in the populous industrial districts of south-western Suffolk from Haverhill downstream to East Bergholt.

A substantial number of these 18th-century fairs were of small consequence, being merely for 'toys' and 'small peddling'. Others, however, were much more specialised and economically significant. For example, Hacheston was known for its 'boots, shoes, upholstery and joyners'. Woolpit fair in mid-September had long been noted for the sale of horses: Thetford Priory bought horses there in the early 16th century, and in 1577 William Harrison mentioned Woolpit as one of four English places 'wherein great plenty of horses and colts is bought and sold'.[4] In the 19th century E.R. Smythe painted the same fair with its lively gathering of people and horses.

Another factor of interest is the precise site used for a fair. Occasionally a suggestive place-name survives: for instance St Mary's Square at Newmarket was once known as the 'Fairstead', while the October fair at Halesworth, celebrated for the sale of Scotch or northern bullocks, took place at Fairstead Farm, formerly Bullock Fair Farm, actually in the parish of *Spexhall* but only one mile from the town of Halesworth.[5] However, a fair may not have been held in exactly the same place across the centuries.

The number of fairs was sharply reduced after the Fairs Act of 1871 which argued that they were unnecessary, injurious and the cause of 'grievous immorality'. Local justices or owners had merely to petition the Home Secretary to effect closure: thus in 1872 W. S. Calvert, lord of four manors in East Bergholt duly petitioned, and the local fair was immediately abolished. In 1885 William White listed only 33 fairs, and Kelly a mere 13 in 1912.

Further details on p.202

FAIRS

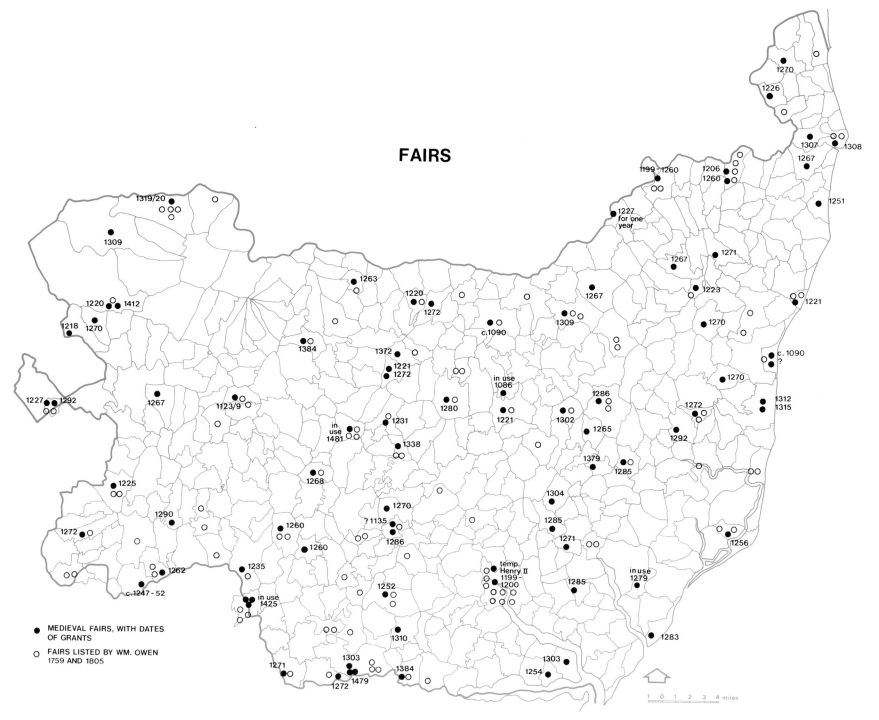

1270
1226
1307 1308
1267
1251
1319/20
1199 - 1260
1206
1260
1227
for one
year
1309
1271
1267
1267
1263
1223
1220
1220 1412
1272
1270
1221
1218
1270
1309
c.1090
c. 1090
?
1384
1372
1270
1221
1272
in use
1086
1267
1312
1315
1227 1292
1123/9
1280
1286
1272
1221
1302
1280
in
use
1481
1231
1292
1338
1265
1268
1379
1285
1225
1304
1290
1285
1272
1271
1256
1260
1270
1262
?1135
1286
1285
c.1247-52
1260
1235
in use
1425
1252
temp.
Henry II
1199 -
1200
1285
in use
1279
1283
1310
1303
1271
1303
1254
1272 1479
1384

● MEDIEVAL FAIRS, WITH DATES
   OF GRANTS

○ FAIRS LISTED BY WM. OWEN
   1759 AND 1805

1 0 1 2 3 4 miles

35. POPULATION DENSITIES, 1327 AND 1524   Hilary Todd & David Dymond

The next three maps summarise the distribution of tax-payers as recorded in returns for the Lay Subsidies of 1327 and 1524.[1] Both come at useful periods. In 1327, shortly before the Black Death swept the nation so devastatingly, Suffolk was one of the most densely populated, intensively farmed and economically advanced counties of England. Nearly two centuries later, in 1524, the shape of agriculture and landholding had changed profoundly, and the local economy had been complicated by the rise of a thriving cloth industry.

The map opposite concentrates on those parishes where one individual contributed 30% or more of the total tax paid. In 1327 fewer than thirty parishes showed this kind of social differentiation, and they were almost entirely restricted to the west or south-west of the county. In 1524, this personal dominance was clearly much more common, and occurred over 180 times in different parts of the county. Since the mid 14th century, the general level of population had been reduced and many vills were reckoned as impoverished and deserving of tax-relief;[2] in such conditions it was probably easier for wealthy and enterprising individuals to emerge. Some were lords of manors like Sir Edward Echyngham of Barsham or Robert Crane of Chilton; but others were successful manorial lessees, farmers and business men like Thomas Smyth of Long Melford or Thomas Coo of Boxford.

Individuals tended to dominate where parishes were small in acreage (though there are notable exceptions like Icklingham, Long Melford and Blythburgh) and where tax-relief in the mid 15th century was highest.[3] A good example can be seen in the north-east (in Wangford and the northern end of Blything) where over thirty parishes, some quite small in area and population, were dominated by one or two principal tax-payers in 1524 and lay in an area which had received major tax-relief in the 15th century. Similar trends can be seen in rural areas within the influence of large towns, for instance, around Bury St Edmunds and to the north of Ipswich. The hundred of Samford, however, behaved differently: most of its parishes were economically polarised in 1524, but only Erwarton had received tax-relief of more than 25% in 1449. Clearly, these trends cannot be given the status of an historical law: while by 1524 some parishes were already displaying the characteristics of 'closed' communities, destined to be overshadowed by a 'great house' (as at Heveningham and Rushbrooke), the majority of parishes were to experience other kinds of development. Furthermore, the early dominance of a resident individual or family could decline or disappear, especially if the Hall later became a tenant farmhouse, as happened at Ubbeston and Pettaugh.

In the two maps overleaf, the numbers of taxpayers have been related to the acreages of parishes: the darker the shading, the more taxpayers per acre.[4] These figures do not of course represent total population, nor even heads of households. The taxation of 1327 was on moveable wealth only, and several categories of people were exempted; by contrast the 1524 Lay Subsidy was paid by nearly all households, and was a graduated tax on either land, moveables or wages. Thus, direct comparisons between the two sources, in terms of tax paid and numbers of taxpayers, are dangerous and we should look primarily at relative levels within each set of returns.

The distribution of taxpayers clearly reflects Suffolk's basic soil divisions (see Map 5). At both dates, the light soils of the Breckland in the north-west and of the Sandlings in the south-east showed sparser tax-paying populations and raised less tax than the more fertile wood-pasture region of central or High Suffolk. A more subtle difference can be seen in 1327 between the south-western and north-eastern parts of High Suffolk, the latter having more taxpayers per acre; this may reflect some diversity of soils and of agricultural practices. By 1524, the position is reversed and the south-west had the higher density, mainly because the woollen cloth industry had flourished there (see Map 63). Along the Stour valley, from Stoke-by-Clare in the west to East Bergholt in the east, is a string of parishes with high densities and high wealth in 1524.[5] Nevertheless, the north-east still has a large tax-paying population, which was to be increasingly dominated by its emergent yeomanry who specialised in dairy farming.[6]

Also noticeable is the Suffolk coast where foreign and coastal trade, fishing and boat-building produced larger concentrations of taxpayers in various ports, especially from Dunwich in the south to Gorleston in the north; by 1524 the relative densities of these parishes is even clearer. Finally, the major inland towns, as might be expected, produce the highest densities of taxpayers and of tax paid. In 1327 the largest were Ipswich, Bury St Edmunds, Sudbury and Beccles. Two centuries later, the rise of the cloth-making towns like Lavenham and Hadleigh had dramatically improved their positions in the urban hierarchy, not only locally but nationally.[7]

Further details on p.203

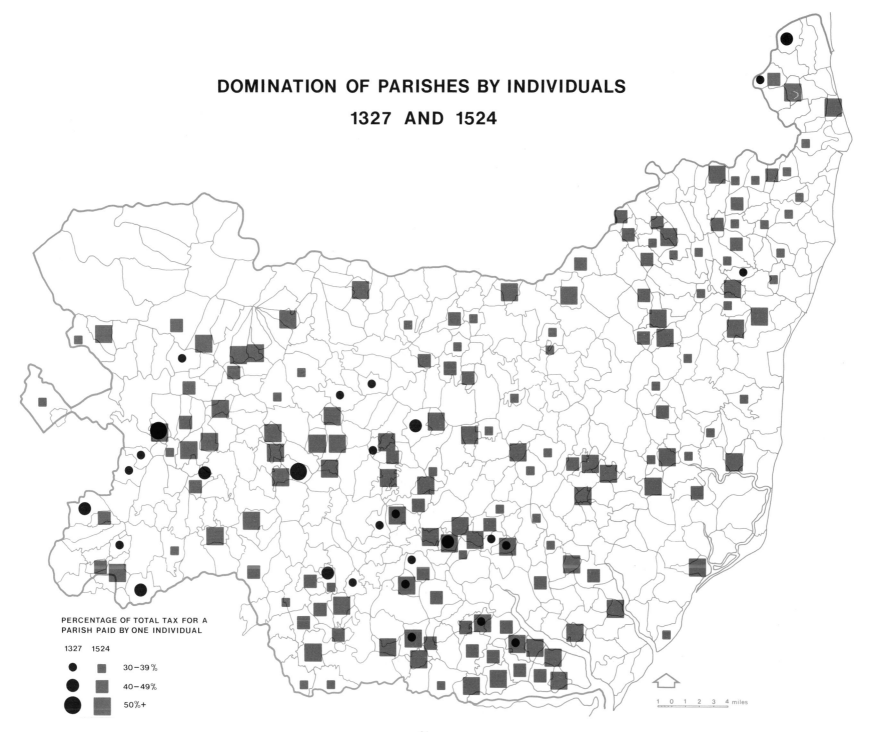

DOMINATION OF PARISHES BY INDIVIDUALS

1327 AND 1524

PERCENTAGE OF TOTAL TAX FOR A
PARISH PAID BY ONE INDIVIDUAL

1327	1524	
●	■	30-39%
●	■	40-49%
●	■	50%+

1 0 1 2 3 4 miles

ACRES PER TAXPAYER 1327

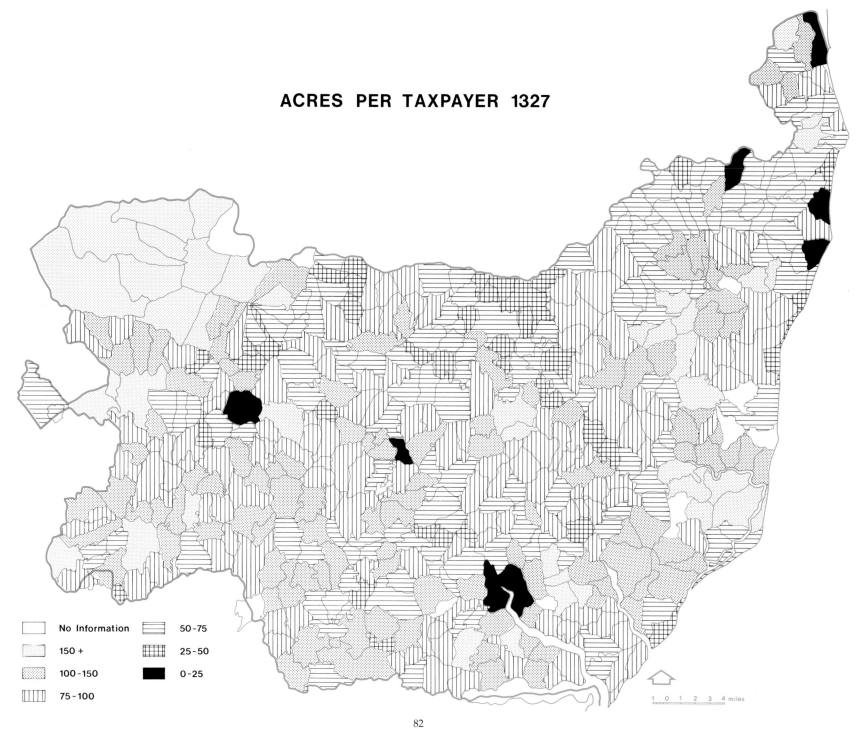

	No Information		50-75
	150 +		25-50
	100-150		0-25
	75-100		

1 0 1 2 3 4 miles

ACRES PER TAXPAYER 1524

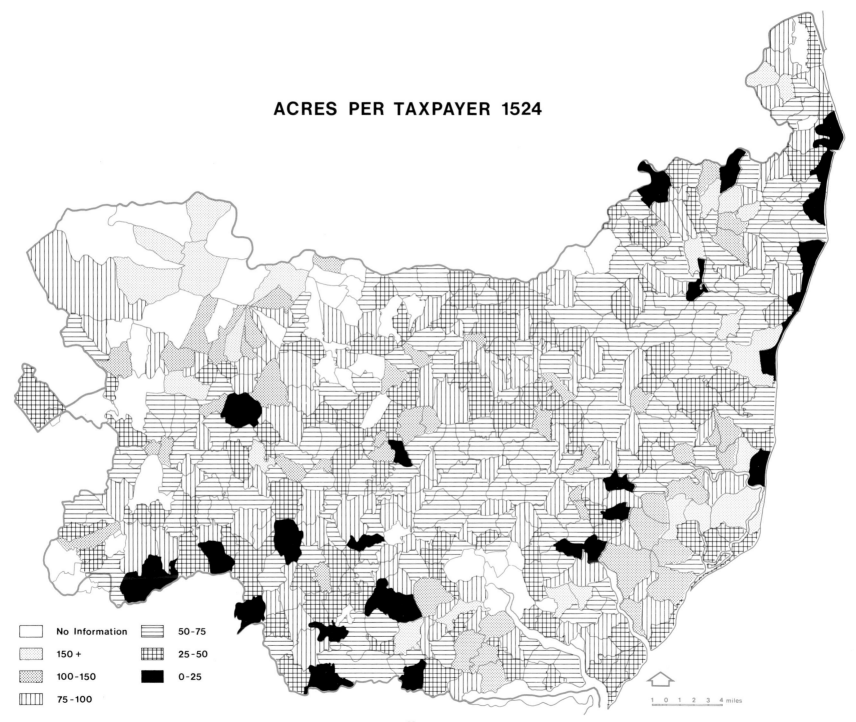

☐	No Information	☰	50-75
▦	150 +	▦	25-50
▦	100-150	■	0-25
▥	75-100		

1 0 1 2 3 4 miles

36. MOBILITY AND SURNAMES

David Dymond

During the later 12th and 13th centuries, when a limited number of Christian names was in use, nearly everyone in East Anglia adopted or acquired a surname, and sometimes more than one. Within a few generations, thousands of new names were coined, far more numerous, varied and informative than those still in use today. Many of the names recorded in medieval documents we would regard today as typically 'Suffolk', such as Baldry, Cobbold, Kemball and Stannard. However, many others have since disappeared, principally because families have died out or only survive in the female line.

In their rich abundance, medieval surnames are important historical evidence in their own right, and they divide into several different categories.[1] Some referred to the Christian names of parents (patronymics like *Edmond* and *Jackessone*, and metronymics like *Edeth* and *Milcent*), some were comments on a person's appearance or character (like *le Long* or *le Fool*); many others were occupational (like *le Parmenter* or *le Webbestere*). In addition, a significant number of surnames referred to two kinds of place. 'Topographical' names show where an individual lived within a parish, with the help of English, French or Latin prepositions (such as *atte* Church or *del* Ford). The so-called 'locative' names indicate that an individual or family had moved into a village or town from elsewhere; usually, though not invariably, they incorporate the French proposition *de*, meaning 'of'. For example, in 1327 the village of Mutford near Lowestoft had inhabitants who were called *de Hemgrave* (Hengrave near Bury St Edmunds), *de Feltewelle* (Feltwell in west Norfolk) and *de Blofelde* (Blofield near Norwich).[2]

Locative names were particularly prominent in towns, because in the early Middle Ages, as in later periods, they were constantly attracting new immigrants. The map opposite analyses the locative names recorded in the Lay Subsidy returns of 1327 for the two most important towns in Suffolk, Bury St Edmunds and Ipswich.[3] The proportion of such names was 24% in Ipswich and as much as 49% in Bury. It must be remembered that the movement implied by the surname may not have occurred in the lifetime of the individual paying tax that year. By 1300 surnames were becoming hereditary, and being passed from generation to generation, so it could have been that individual's father or grandfather who was the actual immigrant.

Not surprisingly, many migrants were drawn from the nearby rural area, up to a radius of about 15 miles. There was some overlap between the 'pull' of these two towns, but not much: Bury drew heavily from western Suffolk, and Ipswich from the south-eastern corner of the county. Some migrants came from more distant sources, and here the two towns differed. Bury had two families from Essex, three from Cambridgeshire, and at least 14 from Norfolk. One family called *Houeden* may have come from Howden in Yorkshire (or Hoveden in Norfolk), but another possibly Yorkshire name, *Holdernesse*, is in fact from a farm called Holderness on the north-east side of Bury.[4] There were also three families of French origin, from Amiens and Cambrai, and a third with the more general name of *Fraunceys* meaning 'French'. Ipswich by contrast seems to have had less attraction for those living in adjoining counties. It drew only one certain immigrant from Essex, which at its closest lies only eight miles away, and perhaps two from Norfolk. However, being a port, it did produce a handful of surnames which implied more distant connections: *de Hasting* (?Sussex), *Doubeney* (Aubigny in France), *Fraunche* (French), *de Bruges* (in Belgium), *Brytoun* (Breton), *le Waleys* (Welsh or Breton). Both Bury and Ipswich produced a family called *Skot* or *Scut* which is probably a genuine link with Scotland.[5]

The map shows those places which can be tied to surnames with some certainty. Naturally where places share the same name, the nearest is assumed to be the one referred to (for example, either of the two Draytons in Cambridgeshire is nearer Bury St Edmunds than Drayton near Norwich). Names that cannot be identified with certainty have not been mapped, but have been listed in the notes.

Finally, it must be remembered that this kind of evidence is no more than impressionistic, and that we cannot estimate the numbers involved. Those with locative surnames were certainly not the only people to move, and the movement was not only from countryside to major town. An *Albred de Gippeswico* appears in Burgate and Cotton, and a *Margaret de Sancto Edmundo* is listed in Sudbury. Moreover many Suffolk people moved out of the county altogether, to live, for example, in London.[6]

Further details on p.203

MOBILITY AND SURNAMES 1327

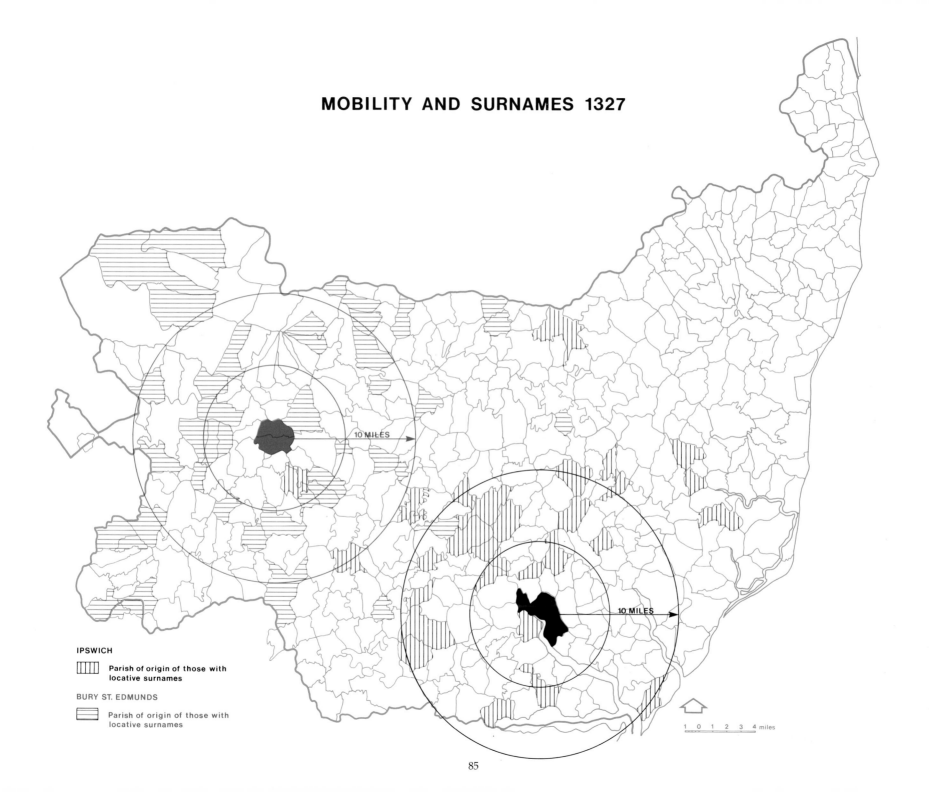

10 MILES

10 MILES

IPSWICH

Parish of origin of those with
locative surnames

BURY ST. EDMUNDS

Parish of origin of those with
locative surnames

1 0 1 2 3 4 miles

37. THE STRUCTURE OF A MEDIEVAL MANOR

John Ridgard

At Worlingworth, the survival of a very early and unusually detailed map of the manor (*c.*1606) coincides with the preservation of an excellent manorial archive. Because manor and parish were co-terminous, the map covers virtually the whole village. Although such a windfall seems unlikely elsewhere in Suffolk, other parishes do possess good combinations of manorial records, written surveys of the 16th or 17th centuries, and maps of the 18th and 19th centuries.

The combined evidence of these records shows medieval Worlingworth to have been unlike the arche-typical villages of midland England. At first sight, certainly, it had a traditional 'nucleus' which included parish church, rectory, manor house and, later, a gildhall. However, the great majority of its domestic houses and, more curiously, a building called *le letecote* in which manorial courts supposedly met, were situated some distance away. The ordinary population lived either around the greens, near the commercial nucleus which included a smithy and at least one of the more permanent beer-retailers, or along any of the roads outside the perimeter of the demesne. The manor farm and the glebe (both manor and advowson belonged to St Edmund's Abbey) thus formed a strikingly compact block enveloping the administrative 'nucleus', but quite separated from tenants' land and facilities.

Certainly Worlingworth had 'open fields', blocks of land in strips such as *Crowchfeld* or *Carrfeld*.[1] These lay, not around the administrative nucleus, but incon-veniently towards the edges of the parish. Moreover, it is clear that for most established tenants their strips were secondary in size and importance to the land which actually adjoined their dwellings. This applied particularly to those tenants whose houses and 'allot-ments' abutted the Great Green.

Part of the common meadowland of medieval Worling-worth (*Tunmanmedewe*) has survived in the form a sloe thicket near Stanway Hill. The last remnant of its ancient woodland (Beggars Wood) was recently destroyed, although the distribution of primroses and dog's mercury within the parish indicate where the 14th-century woods were situated. Despite its enclosure in the 19th century, part of the Great Green has never been converted to arable, and an impression of its character can still be obtained west of Paradise Farm.

As in later centuries, tenancy did not necessarily mean occupancy. Nevertheless, the map can be used with manor-court rolls to explore territorial and social re-lationships between medieval inhabitants, for example, murders committed by neighbours, or the co-operative production of cloth by 14th-century tenants living on Stanway Green. The abbey's documents yield supple-mentary information of a similar kind: such as an account of the sexual expectations and appetites of monks on summer holiday from Bury, and extremely useful, comprehensive lists of tenants swearing fealty to a newly elected abbot.

Taken together, the records throw light on the age and development of the village plan. Medieval surveys group the free and customary tenements according to services they owed to the manor. Analysis of these groups suggest that the two largest and earliest clusters of customary tenants were identical in number to those held by the villeins and bordars recorded in Domesday Book (1086). The map indicates where these older tene-ments were situated and, because their totals were not changed by the Norman Conquest, it suggests which roads and which house-sites were late-Saxon or earlier. Both the greens and free tenements were the products of later reorganisations and expansion. The development of free tenements undoubtedly began in earnest in the

12th century and was still continuing, though at a much reduced rate, in the 14th century, whereas the greens with tenements of mixed tenurial class around them appear to have been created from the mid-13th century until the first quarter of the 14th century.

Most of the Roman artefacts so far recovered in Wor-lingworth were on the demesne or on Stanway Green. This and the compact nature of the demesne, sub-divided into various closes and crofts, prompt the speculation that Iron Age or even earlier field-systems were still in use throughout the Middle Ages.[2] The next step in tackling these possibilities is undoubtedly a sys-tematic search for surface finds.

Perhaps the greatest single factor to change the face of Worlingworth was the Black Death of 1348-9. A mortal-ity rate of about 38% seems certain. The consequent depopulation is most in evidence around the Great Green. On its south side, with one exception, the medieval tenements were all abandoned. Other sub-stantial alterations to the landscape cannot, however, be discounted. The establishment of the Great Green may not have been a simple process.[3] Similarly, the concen-tration of the abbey's residential properties and admin-istrative nucleus in the east of the parish may indicate that the village centre underwent a radical reshaping in the 11th or early 12th century. It is possible that the original location of the church was on the site of one of the parish's five crosses, the White Cross,[4] by the medieval village's commercial centre.

Further details on p.203

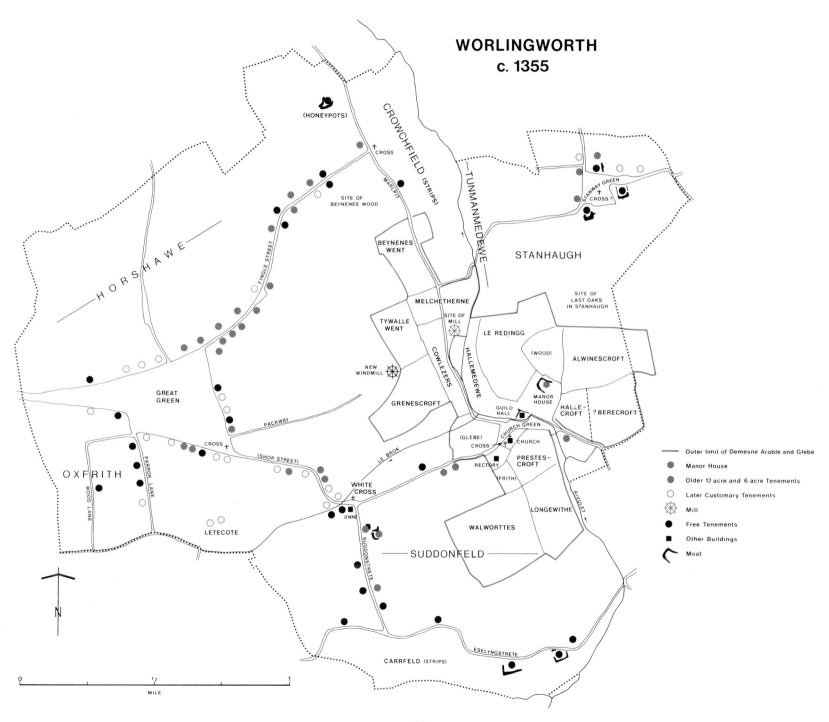

WORLINGWORTH
c. 1355

(HONEYPOTS)

CROWCHFIELD (STRIPS)

TUNMANMEDEWE

+ CROSS

MARLPIT

SITE OF
BEYNENES WOOD

STANWAY GREEN
+ CROSS ?

STANHAUGH

HORSHAWE

FINGLE STREET

BEYNENES
WENT

MELCHETHERNE

SITE OF
LAST OAKS
IN STANHAUGH

TYWALLE
WENT

SITE OF
MILL

LE REDINGG

(WOOD)

ALWINESCROFT

NEW
WINDMILL

COWLEZERS

HALLEMEDEWE

MANOR
HOUSE

HALLE-
CROFT

? BERECROFT

GREAT
GREEN

GRENESCROFT

GUILD
HALL

CHURCH GREEN

PACKWAY

(GLEBE)
CROSS

CHURCH

CROSS +

(SHOP STREET)

LE BROK

RECTORY

PRESTES-
CROFT

OXFRITH

PARROX LANE

WOOD LANE

WHITE
CROSS

(FRITH)

LONGEWITHE

(INN)

LETECOTE

SUDDONSTRETE

WALWORTTES

SUDDONFELD

RIVULET

N

CARRFELD (STRIPS)

ESELYNGSTRETE

Outer limit of Demesne Arable and Glebe

Manor House

Older 12 acre and 6 acre Tenements

Later Customary Tenements

Mill

Free Tenements

Other Buildings

Moat

0   ½   1
MILE

87

38. DESERTED, DISPERSED AND SMALL SETTLEMENTS

Edward Martin

The archetypal deserted medieval villages of the English Midlands, with their well-preserved earthworks and associated fields of ridge-and-furrow, are not a feature of Suffolk. It is certainly true that the highly arable nature of Suffolk over the last two hundred years has resulted in a general scarcity of earthworks,[1] but this is not the sole explanation. Much more important is the original settlement pattern and the nature of the deserted settlements that do occur.

The classic medieval arrangement of three large open fields, subdivided into hundreds of strips, around a nucleated village is largely absent from Suffolk. Open fields did exist, particularly in Breckland and the Sandlings, but were more irregular: being more numerous (twelve at Brandon), of varying sizes and with more complex cropping regimes.[2] Examples of medieval ridge-and-furrow are also very rare in Suffolk.[3] In the claylands of High Suffolk, some open fields of an irregular kind did exist. However, the evidence is also strong, stretching back to the 13th century, for farmsteads that were either dispersed across the landscape or arranged around greens, in both cases with groups of their own hedged fields.[4] Recent work by Brian Roberts on national settlement patterns in the mid-19th century has shown that Suffolk had medium to high densities of dispersed settlements, in contrast to the Midlands where nucleated settlements were dominant.[5]

A picture is now emerging, especially in the clayland, of a medieval landscape in which farmsteads were either isolated or in small groups. As a result, when desertion occurred, they tended to be of individual farmsteads rather than whole villages. As the buildings were normally all of timber, they have left little trace above ground. Until the 1950s, many of the former farmsteads were still discernible as small enclosures or yards, either on the edges of greens or in isolated positions with tracks or driftways leading to them. Many of these have since been obliterated by the removal of hedges and the enlargement of fields, and now the sites only show as scatters of pottery, brick and tile on arable fields. Field-walking has revealed the locations of large numbers of these vanished medieval farmsteads.[6] Their sheer number has prevented them being shown on the map opposite. Green-edge settlements more commonly experienced shrinkage than complete desertion, even after the green itself was enclosed, but a few deserted examples are known (e.g. Hunger Green in Earl Soham).

Another important feature of the medieval landscape of Suffolk is the occurrence of parish churches and manorial halls in paired isolation. As the majority of the churches existed by 1086, this is likely to reflect a Late Saxon pattern of thegnly halls with dependent churches. The disappearance or moving of the hall could leave the church completely isolated, as seems to have happened at Ixworth Thorpe. A scatter of Saxo-Norman pottery near this isolated Norman church probably indicates the site of the original hall, but in the 12th century the hall was moved to a moated site on the edge of a newly-established green, 750m. to the north. Shifts of settlement associated with the creation of greens have also been demonstrated in Norfolk.[7] At present it is unclear to what extent these original 'hall and church' complexes included the houses of ordinary villagers. At All Saints, South Elmham, an isolated church was flanked by a hall and parsonage (both moated), but fieldwalking has failed to reveal evidence of a deserted village.

Even the supposedly marginal Breckland yields only limited evidence for villages deserted in the Middle Ages (with more in the Norfolk part than in Suffolk).[8] An exception may be Little Fakenham: always small, it had under ten households in 1428, by 1668 had only one family and no church, and was incorporated into Euston Park in 1671. Wordwell was likewise small in 1428 and was reduced to a church, hall and shepherd's house by 1757, with earthworks of a row of deserted tenements that survived until the 1960s.[9] The settlement around Timworth church appears to have been in steady decline until its extinction earlier this century. Slightly more desertions resulted from the creation of parks around large houses in the 16th to 18th centuries: Hengrave after 1588, Euston after 1666, Little Livermere in 1735-50, Fornham St Genevieve in the 1770s, Elveden c.1816, and Culford in 1825-8. In all cases the actual number of houses moved was small.

Post-medieval emparking also affected some settlements elsewhere in the county: Ixworth after 1701, Boulge c.1790, possibly Somerleyton by 1652, Little Glemham c.1720, Sotterley after 1746, Assington c.1750, and Nacton c.1805-26, but in all cases the numbers of houses cleared was again small, sometimes only two or three as at Boulge.

Several places on the east coast suffered depopulation as a result of coastal erosion, most notably the town of Dunwich. One of the largest ports in England in the late 12th century, it was badly damaged by violent storms in the 13th and 14th centuries. It has grown smaller every year since, and now is just a small estate village.[10] Other places that suffered include Corton, Newton, Easton Bavents, Covehithe and Walberswick.

Further details on p. 204

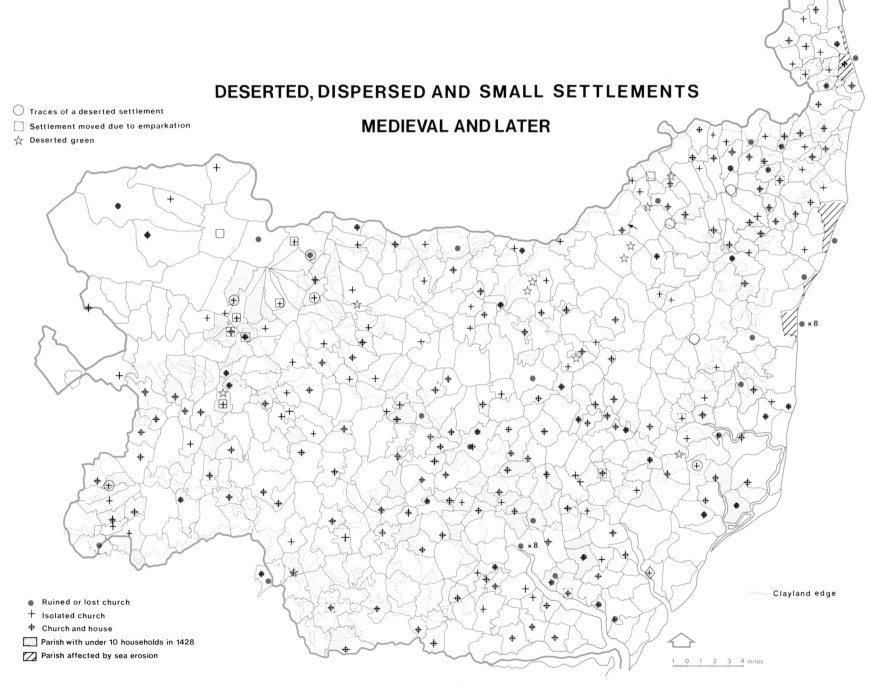

DESERTED, DISPERSED AND SMALL SETTLEMENTS

MEDIEVAL AND LATER

○ Traces of a deserted settlement
□ Settlement moved due to emparkation
☆ Deserted green

● Ruined or lost church
+ Isolated church
⊕ Church and house
▦ Parish with under 10 households in 1428
▨ Parish affected by sea erosion

····· Clayland edge

×8

×8

1 0 1 2 3 4 miles

39. THE UPRISING OF 1381

John Ridgard

Known as the Peasants' Revolt, this insurrection exposed a variety of grievances affecting virtually all social and economic groups within the population. For more than a decade, Suffolk was in a state of reformist ferment. Although the issues provoking outright rebellion seem to have varied from place to place, certain common factors can be identified.

Manorial records were often targeted because they contained written proof of the unfree tenants' onerous position. This applied particularly to 'villeins by blood', the least free members of society. Public burnings of manorial documents, as happened at Hollesley, were clearly part of a campaign to end villeinage. Wherever manor court-rolls begin after 1381, rebel activity may be strongly suspected.

Tax-collectors, especially those gathering the infamous poll-taxes, attracted much public vilification. Their methods also antagonised many 'middle-class' figures. For example, Thomas Sampson, a local businessman, became a prominent rebel leader in the Ipswich area.[1] The involvement, perhaps sometimes under duress, of men like Sampson helps to explain why remarkably few tax collectors were killed or injured—they were from the same social group as some rebel leaders.[2]

One professional group in peril were lawyers. The execution at Lakenheath of Sir John de Cavendish, then Chief Justice of England, was one of the most serious incidents seen anywhere in England. Long marked for his zealous enforcement of the Statute of Labourers, which severely disadvantaged working people, Cavendish epitomised the lawyer made wealthy by serving the establishment.

The church was heavily involved on both 'sides' of the revolt. On the one hand, the property and muniments of wealthier monasteries as at Bury and Butley were a major source of contention, while a major target for the Ipswich insurgents was diocesan property.[3] On the other hand, the overall leader of the Suffolk rebels was a chaplain, John Wrawe of Sudbury, and other lowly paid clergy were noticeably active on the popular side. It may be no accident that several rebels in the Waveney and Stour valleys had surnames later associated with the heretical Lollard movement.

The map is based on lists of rebels recorded by the medieval equivalent of top-ranking civil servants. It marks the parish of residence of only those who took *direct* action, and is not definitive. The scale and distribution of the rebellion is only broadly indicated, although the sampling is probably as representative as any that could be constructed from surviving sources. Because of the apparent loss of one document which identified rebels active within the Liberty of St Edmund,[4] the map better describes the rebellion in East Suffolk than in the West. The list of rebels at present contains about 1500 names, of which about 70 were of women. The map does not reveal the very considerable, perhaps crucial, part played by men from other shires, especially from northern Essex.[5] Suffolk men similarly crossed county boundaries, notably into Norfolk.[6]

The rebellion in its most intense phase lasted eight days, from the 12th to the 18th June, 1381. It was very carefully timed to coincide with the riot-inducing feast of Corpus Christi on the 13th. Two days later a large assembly in Bury's market-place saw Robert Westbrom crowned King of Suffolk.[7] They also witnessed a macabre conversation between the severed heads of Sir John de Cavendish and another eminent victim, John de Cambridge, prior and acting head of Bury Abbey.[8]

Present evidence indicates that about twenty people from both 'sides' were killed in Suffolk.[9] With the possible exception of an incident at Sudbury, we have no evidence for a bloodbath perpetrated by either party. Practically all available documentation was produced by those who had a strong interest in playing down what had happened. This applies both to chroniclers,[10] and to the equally important writers and editors of manor court rolls. The main act of suppression was the arrival in Bury St Edmunds under the command of the Earl of Suffolk of 500 royal lancers. Despite this, on 25 July when show-trials of selected rebels began in Bury, a new rebellion was launched at one of the Earl's own manors at Hollesley. During the summer of 1381 a panel of justices conducted trials and executions in townships which had been particularly rebellious.[11]

Despite the tendency to suppress information, the evidence for revolt *after* 1381 continues to grow. In October 1381, Michael de la Pole in addressing Parliament referred to 'acts of disobedience and rebellion. . . which continue from one day to another'.[12] A 'new rebellion' was launched from the Hollesley/Bawdsey area also in 1383, targeting property of the Earl of Norfolk.[13] Lowestoft was still in a state of rebellion in 1385, expelling the king's ministers and putting them in fear of their lives. In this year reference was also made to 'outlaws in Suffolk lying in wait to kill the sheriff and his bailiffs in the execution of their duties'. The continuing despair of villeins-by-blood was the obvious motive behind rebellions in 1386 at Norton and Tostock. In 1391, Needham Market erected barricades against a sheriff's posse.[14] In 1397 Robert Westbrom, no less, was charged with breaking the peace[15] 'from the time of the Rumor until this very day'. He had accused jurors of giving 'false' verdicts and had been levying 'fines' on individuals, a fund-raising device earlier used by John Wrawe.[16] It appears that Westbrom had, until very recently, still been in a position of influence.[17]

Further details on p.204

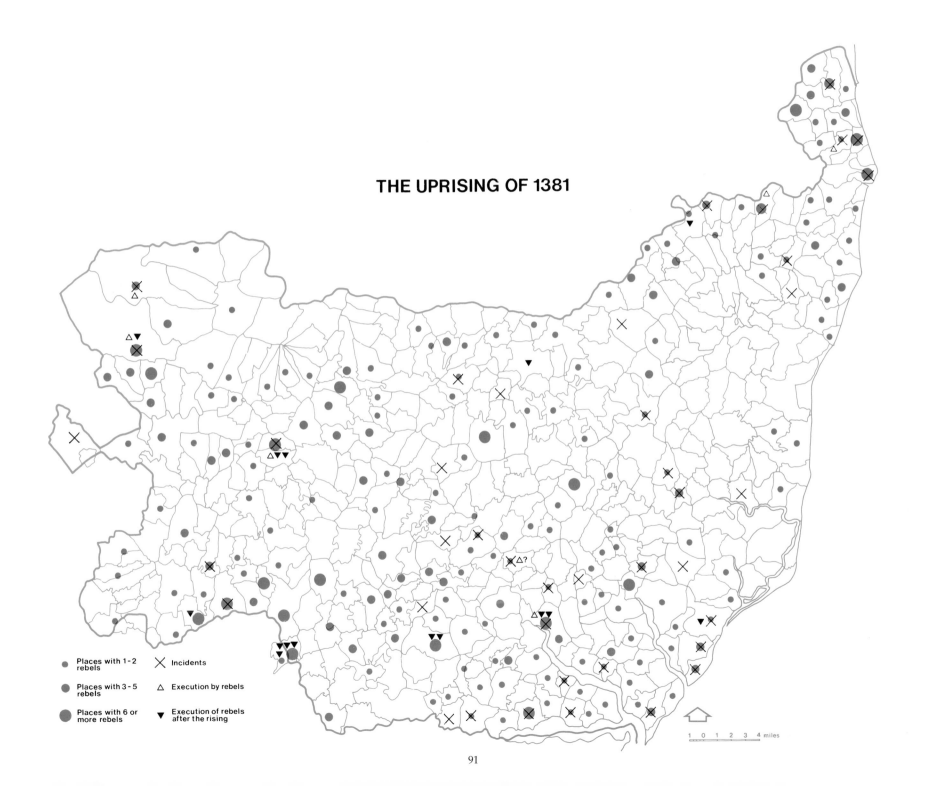

THE UPRISING OF 1381

Legend:

- ● Places with 1-2 rebels
- ● Places with 3-5 rebels
- ● Places with 6 or more rebels
- ✕ Incidents
- △ Execution by rebels
- ▼ Execution of rebels after the rising

1 0 1 2 3 4 miles

40. GREAT HOUSES OF THE 16th AND 17th CENTURIES

Edward Martin

Although many houses of this period have now disappeared, the Hearth Tax returns of 1674 provide a valuable indication of what once existed. They list 29,125 households, of which 453 (1.55%) had ten or more hearths. Most of the latter (80%) belonged to people who bore a title,[1] and 36% of the owners can be found in a list of 'Suffolk Nobility and Gentry' compiled by Richard Blome in 1673.[2] Of those identified from Blome's list, 66% had 10+ hearths, which suggests that this figure is a reasonably reliable indicator of a large gentry house.

The large houses tend to cluster in the two chief towns, Bury St Edmunds and Ipswich, and at the junctions between sand and clay soils—along the eastern edge of the Fielding in west Suffolk and along the line of the A12 in the east (see Map 5). This bears out Blome's contemporary observation that 'In the great towns, the mixt soil, the fielding by Bury and the Sand-lands, the gentry are commonly seated'. Conversely, he noted that the claylands of central Suffolk were 'chiefly the seat of the yeomanry'. Concentrations of large houses can also be seen in major river valleys.

Anomalies do of course exist. At Barton Mills the 33 hearths of Mrs Kempe, widow of a vintner, were almost certainly in the Bull Inn, and make it the largest inn in the county. The 20 hearths of Mrs Dimbleby in Ipswich (St Mary-le-Tower) also probably represent an inn, perhaps The White Horse, as she was an inn-holder's widow. Two inns, each with 10 hearths, are named in Bury St Edmunds (the 'Bushell' and the 'Half Moone').

Analysis of the 55 houses with 20 or more hearths reveals that 24% still exist, 14% are fragmentary, 18% have been rebuilt, a massive 40% have been demolished and 4% cannot be located. Most of these large houses seem to have been relatively old by 1674: of the 39 date-able houses, 85% were 16th-century in date (some with medieval parts) while only 15% belonged to the 17th century. Only three houses, the halls of Boxted, Euston and Helmingham, are still occupied by descendants of their owners in 1674.[3]

The largest house, with 51 hearths, was Hengrave Hall. With a typical early Tudor plan of four ranges around a central courtyard, it was built 1525-c.1540 by the London merchant Sir Thomas Kytson (see p. 9). He precociously used white bricks to imitate limestone, yet retained the medieval status-symbol of a moat. Although well short of the 70 hearths of a 'prodigy' house like Burghley, this was still a very large house. Melford Hall was nearly as big with 49 hearths. Sir William Cordell, Master of the Rolls, progressively enlarged this red brick house in the mid-16th century until it surrounded a courtyard (though later reduced to an E-shape) within a narrow but extensive moat. Other large courtyard-houses of the early-16th century existed at Hawstead Place (35 hearths), Henham Hall (31 hearths),Badley Hall (30 hearths), Gifford's Hall at Stoke-by-Nayland (27 hearths) and Helmingham Hall (20 hearths). At Westhorpe the great moated courtyard-house built in the 1520s by Charles Brandon, Duke of Suffolk, with its lavish terracotta ornaments, was partly abandoned by 1674 and can probably be identified with the 16 hearths held by a 'Mr Raineburd'.

A new style of house, U- or E-shaped with symmetrical fronts and flanking wings, started to appear towards the middle of the 16th century. Amongst the earliest were Redgrave Hall built in 1545-54 for Sir Nicholas Bacon, Lord Keeper, and Christchurch Mansion at Ipswich built in 1548-50 by the merchant Edmund Withipoll. Some of the same masons worked on both houses. A number of these new-style houses were provided with traditional moats: Rushbrook Hall (33 hearths), Playford Hall (25 hearths) and Kentwell Hall in Long Melford (24 hearths).

In the 17th century only a few large houses seem to have been built in Suffolk. Erected early in the century were Letheringham Abbey (37 hearths), Flixton Hall (24 hearths), Barningham Hall (33 hearths) and the White House at Easton (21 hearths). Whittingham Hall in Fressingfield (11 hearths) was one of the rare houses of the Commonwealth period, built in 1653 for Thomas Baker, a cultured parliamentarian.[4] One of the most enigmatic houses was at Fakenham Magna. It had 40 hearths in 1662 and 34 in 1674, and seems to have been a high-class hunting lodge occupied, and perhaps built, by Sir Lionel Tollemache between the 1620s and mid-1660s.[5]

Two notable houses were built shortly after the Restoration. At Brightwell the wealthy merchant Sir Samuel Barnardiston built a magnificent new house on an H-plan (26 hearths), that eclipsed his father's home at Kedington Hall (19 hearths). In 1666 Henry Bennet, Earl of Arlington and secretary of state to Charles II, acquired Euston Hall with its 30 hearths, and enlarged it to 42 hearths by 1674. Roger North, the contemporary architectural writer, criticized Arlington for being 'frugally profuse' in building himself an imposing seat in the latest French style, and thought 'it had bin much better to have bin contented with the plainess of the old design, than to vamp it to no porpose'.[6]

Further details on p.204

GREAT HOUSES IN 1674

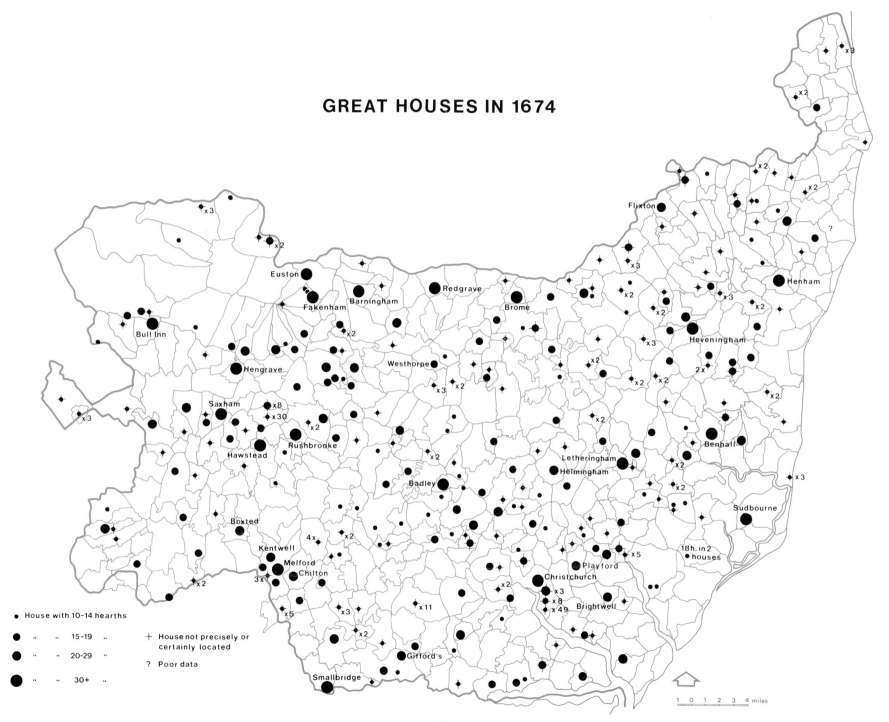

Euston · Redgrave · Barningham · Brome · Henham · Flixton

Bull Inn · Hengrave · Westhorpe · Heveningham

Saxham x8 · x30 · Rushbrooke · Hawstead · Badley · Letheringham · Helmingham · Benhall

Boxted · Kentwell · Melford · Chilton · Playford · Christchurch · Brightwell · Sudbourne · 18 h. in 2 houses

Gifford's · Smallbridge

Legend:

- • House with 10-14 hearths
- ● " " 15-19 "
- ● " " 20-29 "
- ● " " 30+ "
- + House not precisely or certainly located
- ? Poor data

Scale: 1 0 1 2 3 4 miles

41. THE GENTRY OF SUFFOLK DURING THE CIVIL WAR Gordon Blackwood

The gentry of Suffolk is here defined as those land-owners who were *consistently* described in official documents as baronets, knights, esquires and gentle-men, and recognized as such by their contemporaries. Were they predominantly Royalist or Parliamentarian during the Civil War of 1642-6? They were neither, and probably mainly neutral. Of 689 gentry families in Suffolk in 1642, only 182 (26%) participated in the war. That is, of course, a conservative estimate, yet many of the other 507 families (74%) must have been neutral because Suffolk was not one of the major theatres of war, and most gentlemen were not forced to choose sides.

Two other general points must be mentioned. First, unlike the situation in Lancashire, the allegiance of local gentry owed little to the influence of nobles. The three peers named on the map—the Earl of Cleveland and Lord Windsor who were royalist, and Lord Willoughby of Parham who was parliamentarian—were neither influential nor resident in the county. Secondly, very few gentry families in Suffolk were 'by the sword divided'. The thirteen families who did split, or whose members changed sides (symbolized on the map by two-coloured symbols) formed only 7% of the com-batant families.

The map opposite shows those gentry families of Suffolk who, between 1642 and 1646, served either Charles I or Parliament in a military or civil capacity. At first sight the two sides appear very uneven, with 105 gentry families supporting Parliament and just 64 the king. However, it was only in eastern Suffolk that the parliamentarians had an overwhelming majority: 80 families as against 42. In western Suffolk, on the other hand, the two sides were more evenly matched: 25 par-liamentarian families and 22 royalist. Perhaps it was riots in the Stour valley during August-September 1642 which helped to drive some of the western gentry into the arms of the king.

In Suffolk, in contrast to south-west England, the par-liamentary gentry were numerically superior in each of the three main agricultural regions.[1] In the sheep-corn area of the 'Fielding' (consisting of Lackford hundred, western Blackbourn and the northern parts of Thingoe and Thedwastre[2]) five royalist families were just out-numbered by six parliamentarian. In the Sandlings, another sheep-corn area (embracing roughly the coastal hundreds of Samford, Colneis, Wilford, Plomesgate, Mutford and Lothingland, plus eastern Blything), ten royalist families stood against 16 parliamentarian. In the large wood-pasture zone of High Suffolk, which had much higher numbers of resident gentry, the propor-tions were roughly similar: Roundhead gentry outnum-bered Cavaliers by 71 families to 45.

The parliamentarians were particularly strong, and the royalists weak, in the textile manufacturing regions. In the south-western district where woollen cloth was made—which included the hundreds of Risbridge,[3] Babergh and Cosford—there were 12 parliamentarian families and as many as seven royalist. But in the linen-producing areas of the north—including the hundreds of Hartismere, Hoxne, Wangford and eastern Black-bourn—the Roundhead families numbered a stagger-ing 39 and the royalist families a mere six.

Again, the parliamentarian gentry were far more numerous than the Cavaliers in urban centres, except in Bury St Edmunds where the two sides were evenly matched. But in Eye Roundheads outnumbered Cava-liers by two families to one, in Beccles by three to one, and in Ipswich by five to one.

Finally, political divisions roughly coincided with religious divisions. A small majority of parliamentarian gentry families were Puritan, whereas most of the Cavalier families were sincere or lukewarm Anglicans. Of the 64 royalist families, only five (8%) were Puritan, and six (9%) were Roman Catholic. Here Suffolk contrasts with Lancashire where at least 65% of Cavalier families were Papist. But Suffolk resembled Lancashire in having a high proportion of Puritans among the par-liamentarians. Of the 105 Roundhead gentry families, at least 60 (57%) were Puritans—the kind of people whom Percival Wiburn called 'the hotter sort of protestants'. Puritans were particularly numerous in the woollen-manufacturing district of the south-west, where they comprised ten out of twelve Roundhead gentry fami-lies, and in the port of Ipswich where they accounted for seven out of ten such families. The map alone suggests that Puritanism was the main driving force among the Roundhead gentry of Suffolk, and that it was religion which primarily caused the rift between them and the Cavaliers.

Further details on p.205

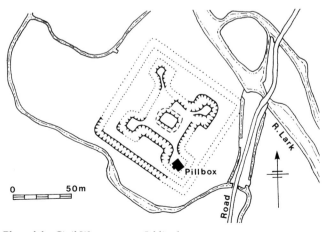

Plan of the Civil War sconce at Icklingham

THE SUFFOLK GENTRY DURING THE CIVIL WAR

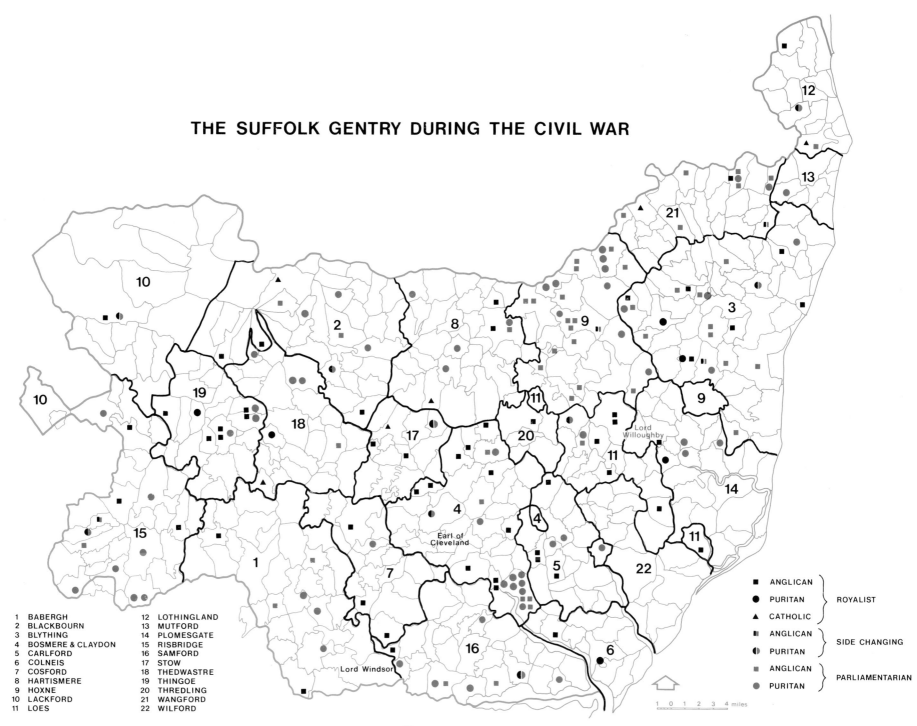

1 BABERGH	12 LOTHINGLAND
2 BLACKBOURN	13 MUTFORD
3 BLYTHING	14 PLOMESGATE
4 BOSMERE & CLAYDON	15 RISBRIDGE
5 CARLFORD	16 SAMFORD
6 COLNEIS	17 STOW
7 COSFORD	18 THEDWASTRE
8 HARTISMERE	19 THINGOE
9 HOXNE	20 THREDLING
10 LACKFORD	21 WANGFORD
11 LOES	22 WILFORD

■ ANGLICAN ⎫
● PURITAN ⎬ ROYALIST
▲ CATHOLIC ⎭

◧ ANGLICAN ⎫
◑ PURITAN ⎬ SIDE CHANGING

▪ ANGLICAN ⎫
● PURITAN ⎬ PARLIAMENTARIAN

Lord Willoughby

Earl of Cleveland

Lord Windsor

1 0 1 2 3 4 miles

42. PEOPLE AND POOR IN 1674

Nesta Evans

The Hearth Tax returns of 1674 have been in print for Suffolk since 1905.[1] Spot checks with the original manuscript have shown that the published version is accurate and reliable. The tax was levied from 1662 to 1689 at the rate of two shillings a year for every hearth, and was paid by occupiers and not by landlords.

The map shows the total number of persons (that is, heads of households) listed in each parish. The totals have been arrived at by adding together the taxpayers and those who were exempted from the tax. Where an entry records that an almshouse or a bracketed group of people had a certain number of hearths, each hearth has been taken to represent one household. Some historians have used these returns to calculate total populations, but this can be a rash exercise and there is no firm agreement on the best multiplier to convert households into people. Many of those excused payment of the tax are described as widows, and the possibility is strong that a number of them were living in single-person households. Detailed studies of a few parishes suggest that the listings may not be as comprehensive as is often believed.[2] Recent work on hearth-tax documents shows that they are far more complex than had been realised, and that their interpretation is fraught with problems.[3] For these reasons it seems best to present readers with the totals given in the returns, and leave them to make their own calculations. What the map does show is the *relative* density of population.

Those exempted and too poor to pay were described as 'certified for' (meaning that they had received a certificate of exemption) or as 'those that take collection' (meaning that they were supported from the poor-rates). The map shows their numbers as a percentage of the total number of households listed for each parish. The editor of the published transcript frequently bracketed names in groups of two, three or more households with a total of hearths.[4] This grouping appears to represent houses subdivided into tenements, another well-known manifestation of poverty which certainly existed in 17th-century Suffolk.[5]

Many places in Babergh, Cosford and Samford hundreds apparently had no inhabitants exempted from payment, so the suspicion arises that either the returns for these three hundreds are defective, or that for some reason the officials adopted a deliberate policy of omitting the non-taxpayers. However, where small parishes were dominated by single landlords, they may well have had no poor, and were similar to the 'closed' villages of the 19th century. Several of these places, for instance Euston, Hengrave and Flixton by Bungay, contained large houses of resident aristocracy or gentry (see Map 40).

The distribution of poverty throws light on the economic situation of Suffolk in the late-17th century. Many places on the coast were clearly impoverished by the decline of herring fishing and boat building, and special circumstances influenced decayed ports such as Dunwich where the proportion exempted from tax was the highest in the county (73%). More empty houses were to be found in ports than elsewhere, as is shown in the list below of the eight worst-affected communities in Suffolk. The inland exceptions were East Bergholt and Hadleigh where the cloth industry was in decline, and Botesdale which had recently suffered a serious fire. At Newmarket the six empty but 'newe erected' houses reflect the prosperity being brought to the town by horse racing. On the whole, the rural parishes of central Suffolk seem to have fewer poor than the towns or industrial districts of the south-west and the border with Norfolk. With the exception of Brandon and Debenham, all the towns which have more than 50% of listed persons excused payment of tax, are either ports or in the clothing district. Poverty was clearly much more of an urban problem and Suffolk was not peculiar in this respect. Towns attracted the poor because they offered anonymity as well as appearing, often falsely, to be easier places in which to find employment. In towns it was more difficult to control the subdivision of houses into poorer tenements, though that was clearly a rural phenomenon as well. Furthermore, some towns such as Beccles and Mildenhall offered the advantage of large commons open to all residents.

Further details on p.205

PLACES WITH MORE THAN TEN EMPTY HOUSES IN 1674

Name	No. of empty houses
Aldeburgh	38
Woodbridge	23
Botesdale	16 (burnt)
Southwold	15
Gorleston	14
East Bergholt	13
Hadleigh	11

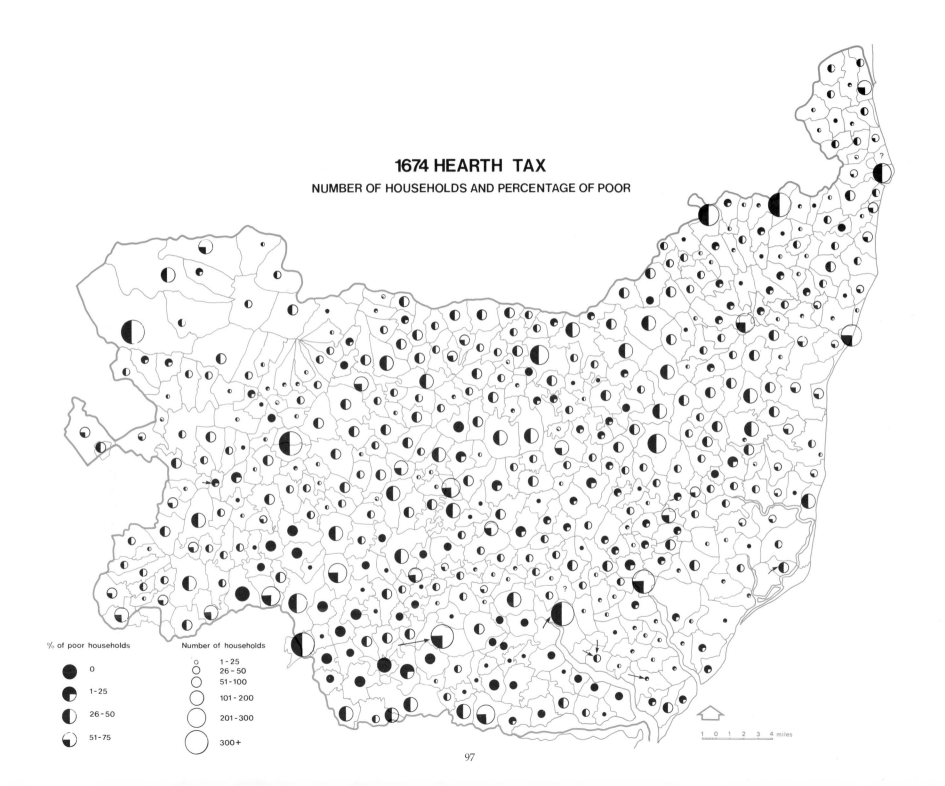

1674 HEARTH TAX

NUMBER OF HOUSEHOLDS AND PERCENTAGE OF POOR

% of poor households

- 0
- 1 - 25
- 26 - 50
- 51 - 75

Number of households

- 1 - 25
- 26 - 50
- 51 - 100
- 101 - 200
- 201 - 300
- 300 +

1 0 1 2 3 4 miles

By national standards Suffolk is not a county of great estates or the grandest houses, though it does have a rich legacy of medieval and early-modern domestic buildings. The map opposite shows the location and building history of seats whose owners had estates of more than 1000 acres in 1873.[1] Such houses reflected the political value and social status of landownership, after two centuries of estate enlargement and consolidation based on post-Restoration political stability, economic growth and agricultural improvement.

Nearly a quarter of these landowners lived in houses which were built before 1660 but subsequently altered to meet changing needs and new ideas of comfort, privacy and fashion. This choice, to renovate rather than rebuild, may have reflected personal preference, but may also have been forced upon landowners for whom financing a new house from landed income alone was always difficult. For example, in 1784 Francois de la Rochefoucauld noted that the cost of restoring their 16th-century house at Hengrave had obliged the Gage family to economize.[2] There is therefore an important association between country-house building and non-landed wealth.

The distribution of country houses corresponds to long-established patterns. There are two main groups, one centred on Bury St Edmunds, and the other along the inner edge of the Sandlings. They reflect lines of communication, tenurial structures that determined the ease with which an estate could be built up, the social pull of Bury, and perhaps desirable combinations of slope, drainage and aspect.[3]

Houses of the early-18th century are scarce, but if they did not involve known architects, and had short lives, they may be unrecorded. The new century saw the building of Dalham—an early Classical model—and

Great Livermere; both properties changed hands soon after. A new house at Heveningham was also sold, before being embraced by the much larger house, Suffolk's only major Palladian essay, built for the London banker Sir Gerard Vanneck. There are no Whig palaces to match Norfolk's Houghton and Holkham. Typical of Suffolk is the remodelling of Hintlesham Hall, with sashes and fashionable stucco, but on its Elizabethan plan.

Building by new owners at Sotterley in the 1740s and at Benacre in the 1760s presaged a surge of activity peaking in the 1790s. In the 1750s the Duke of Grafton had employed Matthew Brettingham, who was to design Benacre, to transform Euston Hall—an Elizabethan house that had been remodelled once before, in the 1660s, by the Earl of Arlington. Nationally-renowned architects were at work elsewhere, including James Paine at Shrubland Park (Barham), Sir John Soane at Tendring Hall (Stoke-by-Nayland), James Wyatt at Fornham, Henham, Heveningham and Sudbourne, and Samuel Wyatt at Culford. It is tempting to link this new building simply with improved agricultural fortunes from the 1760s, and with the boom during the French Wars after 1793. The truth however is more complex. Wealth from commerce, office, inheritance and marriage was also of great significance. The bishop of Derry, for example, funded idiosyncratic Ickworth from the income of his Irish see, and John Rous rebuilt burnt-out Henham, after a long delay, from the proceeds of two advantageous marriages and the sale of inherited land.[4]

House-building in the 19th century was dominated by new owners. They built at least nine of the sixteen precisely-dated houses on estates of over 2000 acres. Five of the sixteen replaced houses destroyed by fire. The Classical style was superseded by the Victorian taste for neo-Tudor and Jacobean, and for increasingly large and specialised mansions. Non-landed fortunes

built Flixton, Oakley Park (Hoxne), Somerleyton and Thornham, in the north of the county, away from the traditional concentrations of Suffolk estates. West Indian money contributed to Stowlangtoft, and South African gold to Cavenham. Lord Rendlesham built his hall (at Rendlesham) using proceeds from the bizarre will of his ancestor Peter Thellusson, an 18th-century financier. Mammoth additions transformed Culford, Orwell Park (Nacton), and Shrubland Park. Elveden, where in the 1780s the Earl of Albemarle began to create an agricultural and sporting estate from a sandy waste, was metamorphosed into an Indian-Gothic extravaganza for Maharajah Duleep Singh, and subsequently enlarged still further by the Earl of Iveagh. The fantastic Bawdsey Manor exemplifies even more clearly the 19th-century desire for a residence which also gave rural and seaside recreation.

When one estate was absorbed by another, the redundant seat sometimes declined in status to a farmhouse or was even divided into tenements. More often than not it remained a gentry house used by family or staff, or it was let or sold. A spectacular example is the growth of the de Saumarez estate centred on Shrubland Park. In two hundred years, by marriage and descent, the seats of the Acton, Broke, Fowle, Lee and Middleton families were acquired, at Bramford, Broke Hall (Nacton) and Livermere. These are shown on the map, but many 'houses in the country', associated with small estates, are not. They include medieval and Elizabethan survivals, and houses of the 18th and 19th centuries. Their history parallels that of the larger houses, with the same pressures determining the choice between alteration and rebuilding. But the smaller the estate, the more restricted was access to non-landed wealth, and the more pressing were economic constraints. The survival of many early houses is therefore as much a consequence of relative poverty as of affluence.

Further details on p.206

COUNTRY- HOUSE BUILDING IN SUFFOLK 1700 - 1900

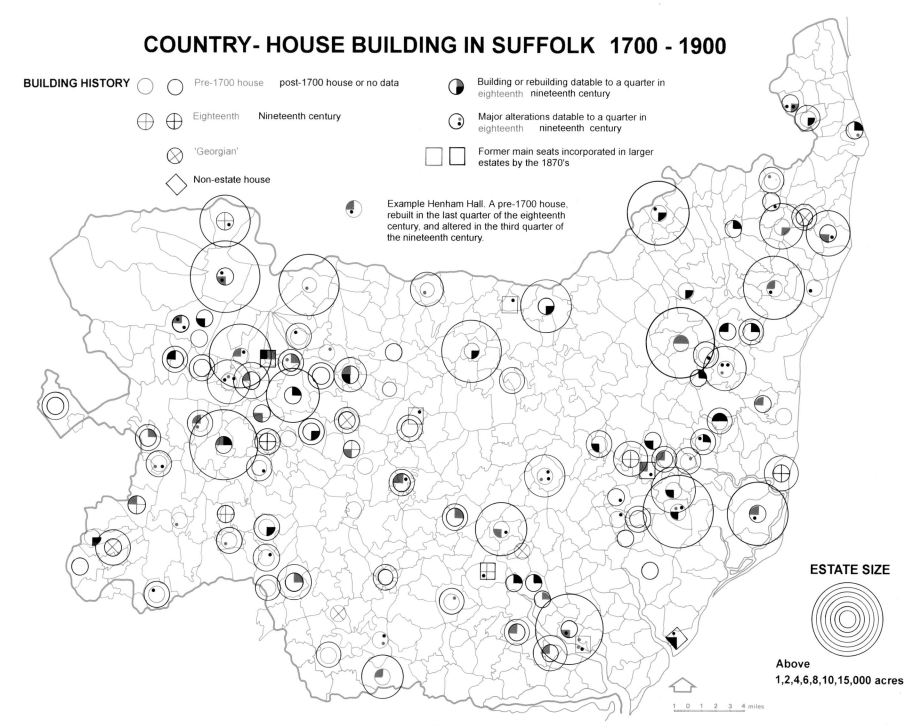

BUILDING HISTORY   Pre-1700 house   post-1700 house or no data

Eighteenth   Nineteenth century

'Georgian'

Non-estate house

Building or rebuilding datable to a quarter in eighteenth nineteenth century

Major alterations datable to a quarter in eighteenth nineteenth century

Former main seats incorporated in larger estates by the 1870's

Example Henham Hall. A pre-1700 house, rebuilt in the last quarter of the eighteenth century, and altered in the third quarter of the nineteenth century.

ESTATE SIZE

**Above
1,2,4,6,8,10,15,000 acres**

1 0 1 2 3 4 miles

44. PARKS OF THE 18TH CENTURY

Tom Williamson

These two maps show the changing distribution of parks in Suffolk during the 18th century. Both must be treated with caution for they do not necessarily show every park which existed at the time. Hodskinson's map, for example, fails to show Thornham Park, although contemporary estate maps reveal that it certainly existed. In part, such omissions reflect the difficulties experienced by surveyors and map-makers in defining precisely what was meant by a 'park'; problems exacerbated by the fact that the definition was changing. At the start of the century the word 'park' retained much of its ancient meaning, of an area where beasts of the chase were kept for hunting, although by this time parks were usually attached to residences and were already being considered and treated as aesthetic landscapes. By the end of the century, however, the hunting connotations were less important, and a park was primarily an aesthetic landscape: an irregular, 'naturalistic' setting of grass, trees and woodland around a big house. In the middle of the century some of these new landscapes might not have been considered true parks by surveyors more familiar with the older definition. And in all periods there were problems at the lower end of the scale: how small could a 'park' be, before it became a mere paddock?

Some of Suffolk's 18th-century parks, like that at Hengrave, developed directly out of deer parks with medieval or 16th-century origins. But within individual parishes most examples of apparent continuity are illusory, because early hunting parks and landscaped parks were not on the same sites. Most of the examples shown on Kirby's map of 1736 originated, in fact, in the 17th and early-18th centuries. They were created out of agricultural land, as were all of those established subsequently.

As the two maps suggest, the half-century from 1736 to 1783 saw a significant increase in the number of parks. It also witnessed the slow development of a more structured distribution: by 1783 parks were concentrated on both sides of the clay plateau running through the centre of Suffolk (a distribution rather different from that of medieval deer parks: see Map 28). This principally reflects the distribution of those who possessed a park—the gentry and larger landowners. The central claylands were not characterised by great landed estates, but rather by the holdings of smaller landowners. The largest estates were located to the west and east, in the Fielding, Breckland and Sandlings. Yet it is noticeable that many parks were located asymmetrically within their estates, so that they actually lay in anciently enclosed ground, on the heavier soils. They were thus established at the expense, not of unenclosed or recently enclosed open-fields, heaths or sheepwalks, but of landscapes anciently hedged. They therefore generally incorporated and adapted large chunks of the previous agricultural landscape in the form of woods, copses and (in particular) ancient hedgerow trees. Fine examples of ancient oak pollards, much older than the parks in which they stand, can thus be found at Sotterley, Lt Glemham and elsewhere.

Within this broad clayland-edge distribution, a subsidiary pattern is evident by the end of the 18th century. Parks clustered in the vicinity of Bury St Edmunds and, less distinctly, around Ipswich. This presumably reflects the residential preferences of the gentry, keen to live in the country but also to be near large towns which offered facilities and entertainments such as assemblies, balls and, above all, shops.

Some of Suffolk's parks—and especially the larger ones, around the homes of the greatest landowners—were designed by leading designers of national importance. Lancelot 'Capability' Brown worked at several places within the county (Branches, Euston, Heveningham, Ickworth, Redgrave and possibly Fornham St Genevieve); Richard Woods re-designed the park at Hengrave; and Nathaniel Richmond may have worked at Woolverstone. Humphry Repton, a little after Hodskinson's map was surveyed, worked on a dozen commissions in the county, including some of his earliest, most notably at Shrubland Park (1789). The majority of Suffolk's parks, however, seem to have been created by local practitioners, or by the owner himself working with his estate gardener.

Parks were expressions of status and wealth, marking out the owner as a member of the landed elite. In an increasingly polarised society, they acted as a barrier between 'polite society' and the outside world of the working agricultural countryside. And we must not forget that parks were *used* by their owners. Not only did they have a variety of economic functions—like grazing and the production of timber—but they were also arenas for élite entertainment. Parks continued to be used for hunting (their woods were laid out as pheasant reserves) and their lakes for fishing and boating.

The first half of the 19th century witnessed many additions to the pattern shown by Hodskinson. Indeed, some of the finest landscape parks in Suffolk (as at Gt Glemham) are of this date. However, the agricultural recession which set in from the late 1870s effectively stopped the creation of parks, and the 20th century has seen the progressive loss of these landscapes. Many have been largely or completely destroyed, and although much restoration is currently in progress many of the survivors are now in an over-mature and degraded condition.

Further details on p.206

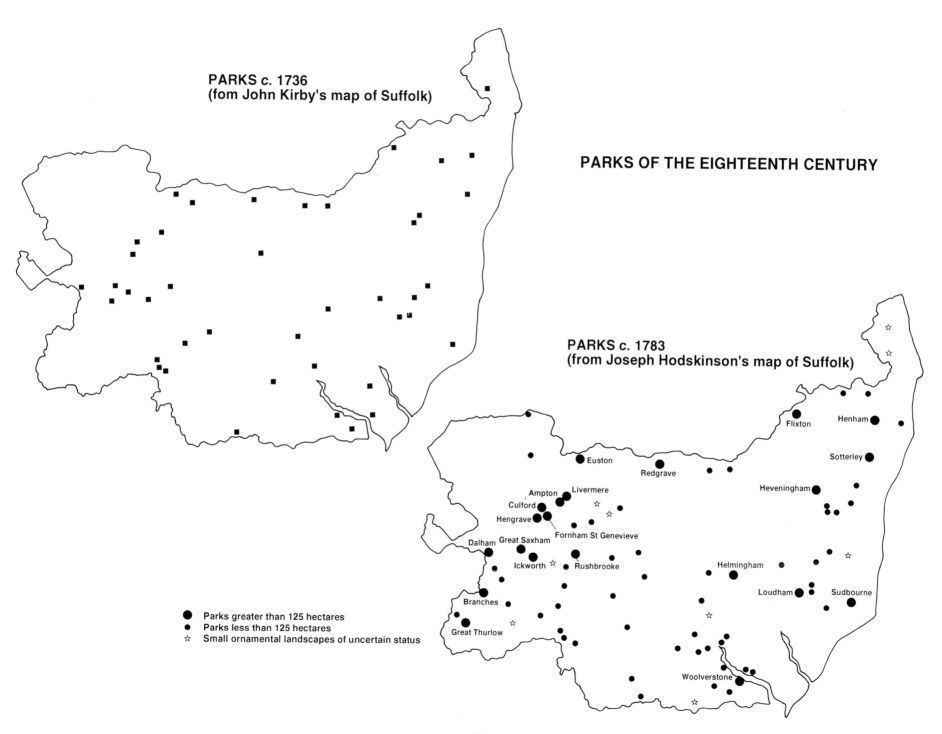

PARKS c. 1736
(fom John Kirby's map of Suffolk)

PARKS OF THE EIGHTEENTH CENTURY

PARKS c. 1783
(from Joseph Hodskinson's map of Suffolk)

Flixton
Henham
Euston
Redgrave
Sotterley
Ampton
Livermere
Heveningham
Culford
Hengrave
Fornham St Genevieve
Great Saxham
Dalham
Helmingham
Ickworth
Rushbrooke
Loudham
Sudbourne
Branches
Great Thurlow
Woolverstone

● Parks greater than 125 hectares
● Parks less than 125 hectares
☆ Small ornamental landscapes of uncertain status

In the 18th century, Suffolk returned sixteen Members of Parliament. Fourteen represented the seven boroughs of Aldeburgh, Bury St Edmunds, Dunwich, Eye, Ipswich, Orford and Sudbury. The two remaining members, termed 'Knights of the Shire', sat for the prestigious county constituency, in which the franchise was vested in all adult males with freeholds worth at least 40 shillings a year. During Queen Anne's reign, the county electorate stood at around 6,500, out of an estimated total population of about 155,000.[1]

Under the later Stuarts, Suffolk's freeholders, like those of other counties, had an unprecedented number of opportunities to vote. Sixteen general elections and one by-election were called for this county between 1679 and 1715.[2] No less than eight were contested and drew large numbers of freeholders to the polling booths at Ipswich. Of these contests, the general election of 1705 was one of the most fiercely fought.[3]

Events in Parliament in the previous autumn had ensured that religion became the dominant issue. In November 1704, 134 Tory MPs who were zealously High Church attempted to get a bill against Occasional Conformity through the House of Lords by 'tacking' it to another concerned with the Land Tax.[4] Although the move proved abortive, it fanned the flames of religious and political conflict. With some of its MPs among the 'tackers', and a substantial number of nonconformists in its midst, Suffolk was one of the nation's first constituencies to take fire, soon affording 'little news but the furious wrangle of parties'.[5] The campaign got underway in February 1705. By early spring, four candidates had been named: the two Tories were Sir Robert Davers Bt and Sir Lionel Tollemache Earl of Dysart— both 'tackers' in 1704—opposed by two Whigs who were Sir Dudley Cullum Bt and the octogenarian Sir Samuel Barnardiston Bt.[6] Over the ensuing weeks, these

principal protagonists and their supporters fought 'such a Trial of the Strength of Parties, that the like has hardly been known'.[7] On polling day, 9th May, a phenomenal total of 5,323 voters was recorded. The two High Church Tories, Davers and Dysart, finally emerged victorious with a margin of some 500 votes each.[8]

The map opposite, shows the geographical distribution of the 5,323 freeholders who voted; it also shows the final balance of the parties in 435 or so parishes for which a turnout is recorded.[9] The table below gives supporting figures. At a county level, it is clear that electioneering did not merely involve canvassing the larger, more densely populated parishes and towns. In fact two-thirds of all the voters came from 411 markedly rural parishes dotted all over Suffolk, each with a turnout of less than 30. Against such a background, it was obviously vital for party organisers to flush out and secure not just the urban voter but his rural counterpart as well; in this aim, however, the two parties had differing levels of success.

The Whigs obtained a majority in no less than 17 of the 24 parishes whose turnout exceeded 30 voters: 53.6%

voted for one or both of the Whig candidates only, while 46.4% did the same for the two Tories. In these larger, more urban communities, dissenters furnished invaluable support for the Whigs, at an election in which the main issue was Occasional Conformity.[10] However, in the smaller villages and hamlets the Tories were in a decidedly stronger position, for they had the support of most of the country gentry and Anglican clergy—two groups ideally placed to influence the rural voter.[11] In addition, these Tory supporters were well distributed across the county, while those few who favoured the Whigs were concentrated overwhelmingly in the western half of the shire. The Whigs managed to find some support in at least 320 of the 411 parishes which polled less than 30 voters, but in only 122 of these did they achieve total or majority turnouts. By contrast, the Tories won the entire support of voters from 81 rural parishes and the majority from a further 160. This county election fully endorses Speck's comment that 'the remotest freeholders could influence the outcome of an election, and the candidate ignored them at his peril'.[12]

Further details on p.206

THE 1705 ELECTION RESULTS

No. of voters per parish	No. of parishes	No. of voters per group	Tory voters only	Tory majority	Whig voters only	Whig majority	No majority
1-9	275	1,296	76	84	19	57	39
10-19	104	1,436	4	55	-	36	9
20-29	32	772	12	1	-	10	-
30-99	20	903	-	6	-	14	-
100+	4	916	-	1	-	3	-
	435 min.	5,323	81	167	19	120	48

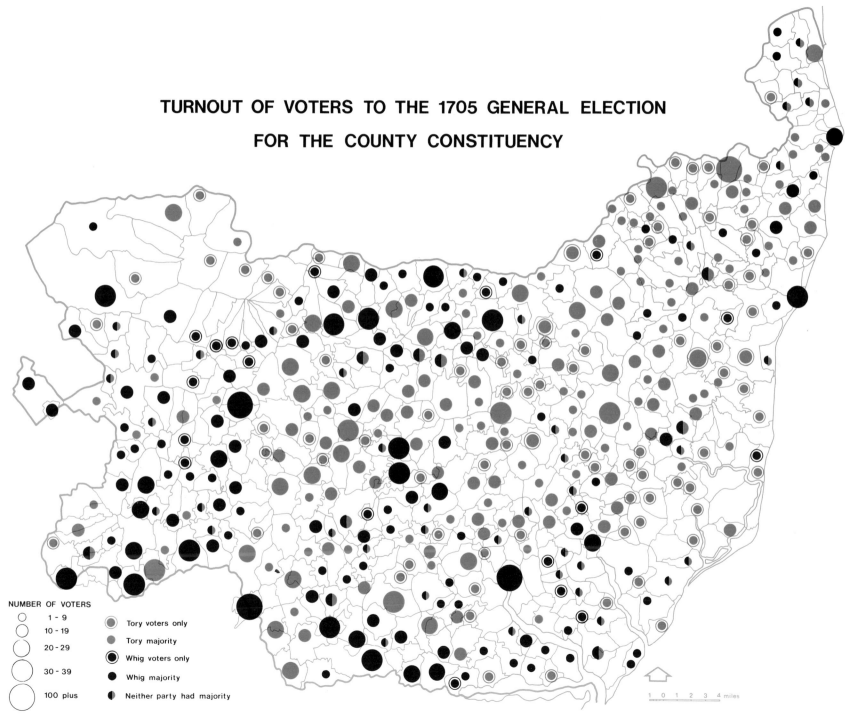

TURNOUT OF VOTERS TO THE 1705 GENERAL ELECTION

FOR THE COUNTY CONSTITUENCY

NUMBER OF VOTERS

○ 1 - 9
○ 10 - 19
○ 20 - 29
○ 30 - 39
○ 100 plus

⬤ Tory voters only
● Tory majority
◉ Whig voters only
● Whig majority
◑ Neither party had majority

1 0 1 2 3 4 miles

46. ENCLOSURE AND RECLAMATION

David Dymond

'Enclosure' is normally defined as the creation of hedged (or walled) fields on land which had previously been open: either as large arable open-fields or as some form of common land or 'waste' such as greens, heaths, moors, fens and marshes.[1] Although often associated with the recent past, enclosure can in fact be of many different dates. In Suffolk, we can point to extensive landscapes which were completely or substantially redesigned as the result of local or general Parliamentary Acts passed in the 18th or 19th centuries. Over an even larger area, we have abundant evidence to show that open-fields, commons and marshland were enclosed, mostly piecemeal, by landowners, yeomen and peasant farmers at any time from the Middle Ages until the 17th century. Finally, new research is strongly suggesting that large chunks of High Suffolk were planned and enclosed in Roman and even prehistoric times (see Map 19).

It is vital to recognise that physical enclosure is usually associated with much more important economic trends such as the exchanging of land, the consolidation of small, scattered parcels, the enlarging of holdings and changes in land-use and agricultural methods. Enclosure was achieved by various methods, for example by the dictate of landowners, by the simple agreement of those concerned, by registration with a legal court, or by Parliamentary Act.

We can broadly measure the relative importance of different methods of enclosure and the different periods involved, by mapping the details recorded in the *Domesday of Enclosures*.[2] This book deals exclusively with Parliamentary enclosure, giving acreages and distinguishing when arable open-fields were, or were not, involved. The map opposite shows that the great majority of Parliamentary Acts, passed in the period from 1790 to 1840, refer to the north-west of the county,

that is, to the Breckland and the chalk downland around Newmarket. Here, very large acreages of open-field and heathland were redesigned into large rectangular fields, with straight roads and tracks and formal tree-belts and plantations. In that same area, some of the enclosures were purely private because major landlords had almost total control and therefore no need of Acts, for example on the Euston and Hengrave estates.[3] In the extreme north-western corner of the county, a large area of fen in the parishes of Mildenhall and Lakenheath was reclaimed after a Drainage Act of 1759 and was converted into a similarly rectilinear landscape.

It will also be seen that Acts of enclosure were passed for a wide scatter of parishes elsewhere in the county, most obviously across the north. Most of these, however, dealt with relatively small acreages and were not concerned with former open-fields. Indeed, the heavy clayland landscape of High Suffolk had been largely enclosed centuries earlier, and the Acts were merely tidying up a few surviving anomalies like greens, commons and sometimes no more than wide road-verges.[4] This area is an example of what Joan Thirsk calls 'wood pasture' and Oliver Rackham 'ancient countryside', where a numerous yeomanry and peasantry had for many generations, from at least the 15th to the 18th centuries, put their main efforts into dairying and grassland. Although Arthur Young wrote in 1786 that the heartland of the dairying industry was in the north-east of the county, it should be remembered that this kind of farming was also commonplace in the south-western half of High Suffolk.[5]

Two other smaller districts within the county deserve mention. The extreme north-east clearly had a larger number of Acts of enclosure than most of central Suffolk, and some of them in Lothingland did affect open-fields. However, the acreages involved are

relatively small—except for the three parishes of Worlingham, Ellough and North Cove where nearly 4000 acres were enclosed, and Barnby and Mutford where 2529 acres were enclosed. Finally, it is not surprising to see a different pattern on the lighter soils of the south-east, the district known as the Sandlings. Here a few enclosure Acts were passed, but again for only small acreages. Many of the extensive local commons, heaths and marshes have been enclosed or reclaimed quite recently, in fact since the Second World War—for instance 607 acres at Iken Hall and 512 acres at Wantisden Hall were reclaimed between 1949 and 1952.[6] This work was undertaken privately by landlords and tenant farmers, often on individual estates.

Further details on p.207

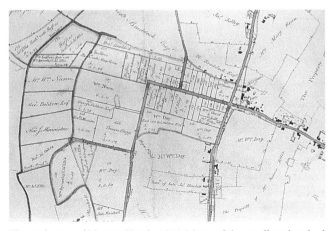

The enclosure of Norton Heath, 1814. Many of the smaller plots had houses built on them shortly afterwards.

ENCLOSURE AND RECLAMATION

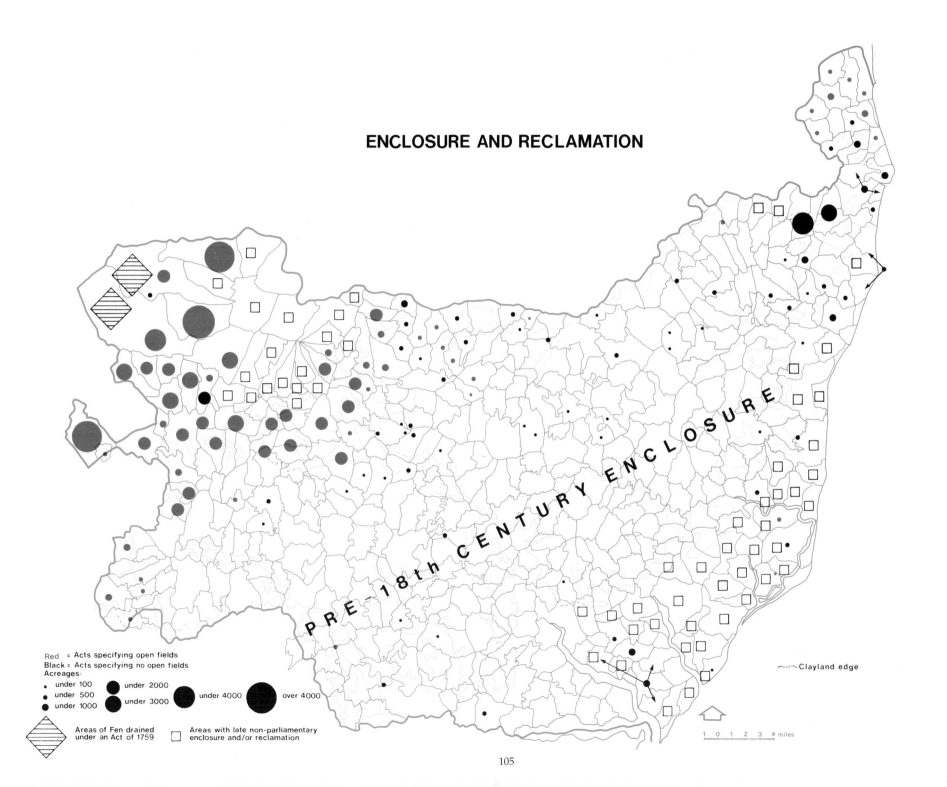

PRE-18th CENTURY ENCLOSURE

Red = Acts specifying open fields
Black = Acts specifying no open fields
Acreages:

- under 100
- under 500
- under 1000
- under 2000
- under 3000
- under 4000
- over 4000

Areas of Fen drained under an Act of 1759

Areas with late non-parliamentary enclosure and/or reclamation

----- Clayland edge

1 0 1 2 3 4 miles

47. POPULATION TRENDS, 1811-1981

Frank Grace

When the Census of 1811 was taken, the population of Suffolk stood at just over a quarter of a million (233,875). By 1981 it had risen to 598,355. This underlying upward trend can be paralleled in other mainly rural counties of England and Wales, but such overall figures conceal important and fundamental variations. The population grew strongly in the first half of the 19th century, with an increase of 44.2% between 1811 and 1851; it then stagnated or grew very slowly between 1851 and 1891, and recovered slightly up to 1914; stagnation set in again between the two World Wars when, for instance, the 1920s saw a growth of only 0.3%; finally rapid growth since the Second World War, especially in the 1960s and '70s, has given Suffolk one of the fastest growing populations in Britain. Between 1951 and 1981 the increase has been over 35%. Each of these periods shows important variations in the geographical pattern of distribution and growth.

1811-51 (MAP I):

The outstanding feature of this period is a rapid growth of population in most parishes, mainly caused by the natural excess of births over deaths. Rural parishes all over the county grew steadily, including those on the Breckland in the north-west and of the Sandlings in the south-east which started from very low levels at the beginning of the century. However, in major towns and the parishes which surrounded them, it is also clear that inward migration was a potent factor.[1] Only 16 parishes in the entire county actually declined during this period, and it is significant that they were usually dominated by major landlords as at Henham, Sotterley and Fornham St Genevieve.

1851-1951 (MAP II):

This span of a hundred years, in marked contrast with the first period, is characterised by widespread rural depopulation over huge areas of the county—a fact of

fundamental importance for the history of rural Suffolk. Especially affected were the heavy clays of north and central Suffolk where many communities declined by over one-third and some by over one-half (for instance, Stradbroke by 54% and Southolt by 59%). The same pattern of rural decline is clearly evident in south-west Suffolk. Indeed, between 1891 and 1931 the population of West Suffolk as a whole dropped by over 15,000.

The basic reason for this decline was the movement of people from rural parishes, leaving to seek a living in local towns, or in the growing industrial regions of England, or to emigrate to America and the colonies. This exodus from the countryside had begun in the later 18th century, but the outflow did not overtake the natural growth of population until after 1850. The outflow was further stimulated by bad harvests and by long years of agricultural depression in the 1870s and '80s, and again in the 1920s and '30s.

However, this rural decline is offset, especially in East Suffolk, by clear evidence of urban growth and development: Ipswich increased by 236% and Lowestoft, as a major fishing port and holiday resort, by 471%. Both these major towns also began to suburbanise their surrounding parishes. The fastest growing town, though, was the seaside resort of Felixstowe with its neighbour Walton, which had a combined population of only 1588 in 1851 and leapt to 15,081 by 1951.[2] By contrast, many of the smaller market and industrial centres of earlier centuries like Hadleigh, Eye, Framlingham and Halesworth decayed with their rural neighbours.[3]

1951-81 (MAP III):

Over these thirty years the population of Suffolk entered another new and important phase. Modest growth immediately after the Second World War became a boom in the 1960s when the population rose

by 15.2%—the highest for any decade since 1811-21 when the increase was 16.1%. Much of this was due to inward migration stimulated by county planning policies, especially in the west, and by the flow of retired middle-class newcomers. Certainly towns such as Brandon, Hadleigh, Mildenhall and, above all, Haverhill which grew by over 300%, were deliberately expanded to take new industrial developments and 'overspill' population from London.

The growth of Ipswich's population was much slower (12%). However, surrounding parishes like Capel St Mary and Martlesham were transformed into commuter villages, and with the town itself form a major conurbation. Similar developments near other towns, but on a smaller scale, led to the growth of places like Horringer, Holton St Peter and Great Barton; other villages like Rougham, Stanton and Elmswell expanded in connection with industrial estates. The smaller market towns, too, like Clare, Debenham and Saxmundham all revived after a century of decline.

By contrast, many rural parishes in north-east and central Suffolk still lost population, as a result of fewer agricultural jobs and planning policies which discouraged new building. Some, indeed, were referred to as 'dying' villages. Wordwell, Ampton, Benacre and Thorington all declined by over 60% in those thirty years.

Further details on p.207

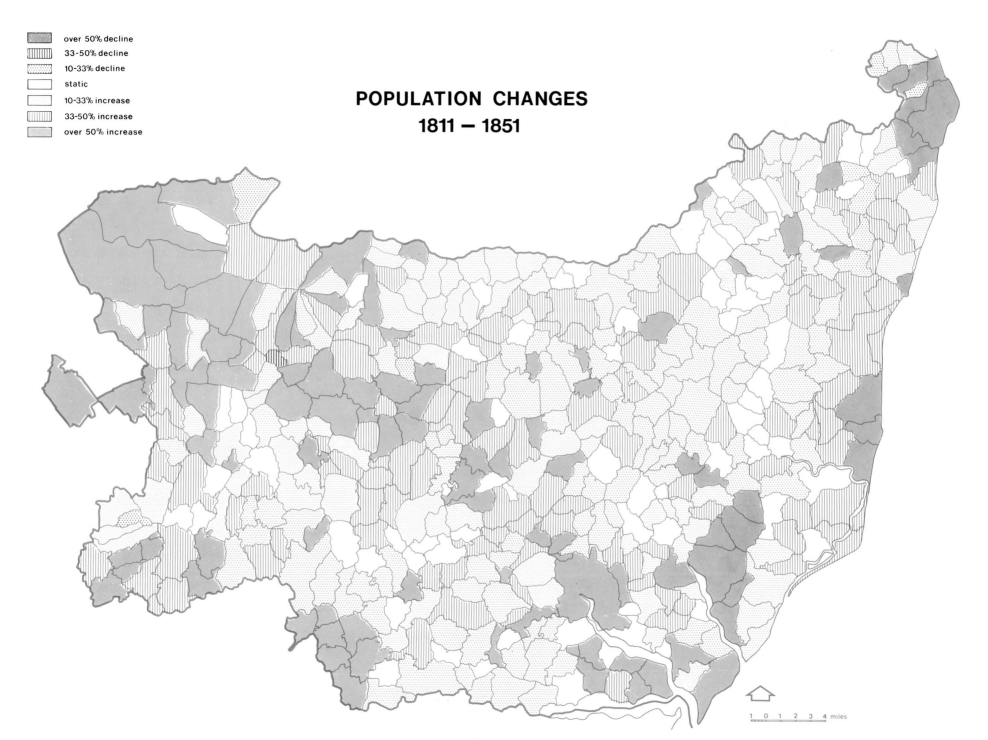

POPULATION CHANGES
1811 – 1851

over 50% decline
33-50% decline
10-33% decline
static
10-33% increase
33-50% increase
over 50% increase

1 0 1 2 3 4 miles

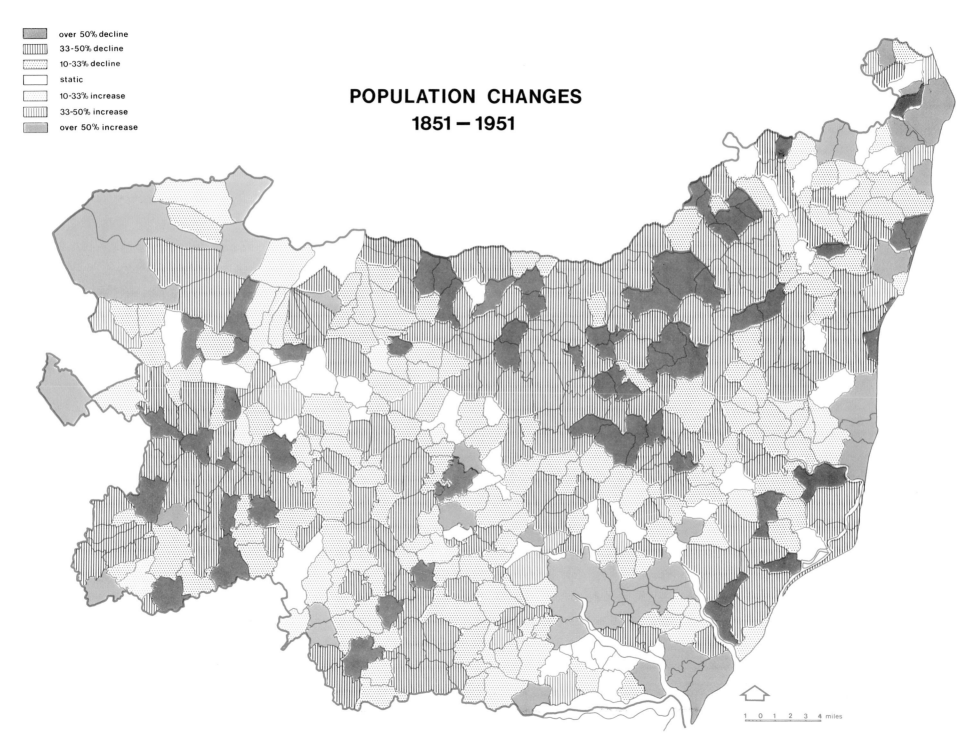

POPULATION CHANGES
1851 – 1951

over 50% decline
33-50% decline
10-33% decline
static
10-33% increase
33-50% increase
over 50% increase

1 0 1 2 3 4 miles

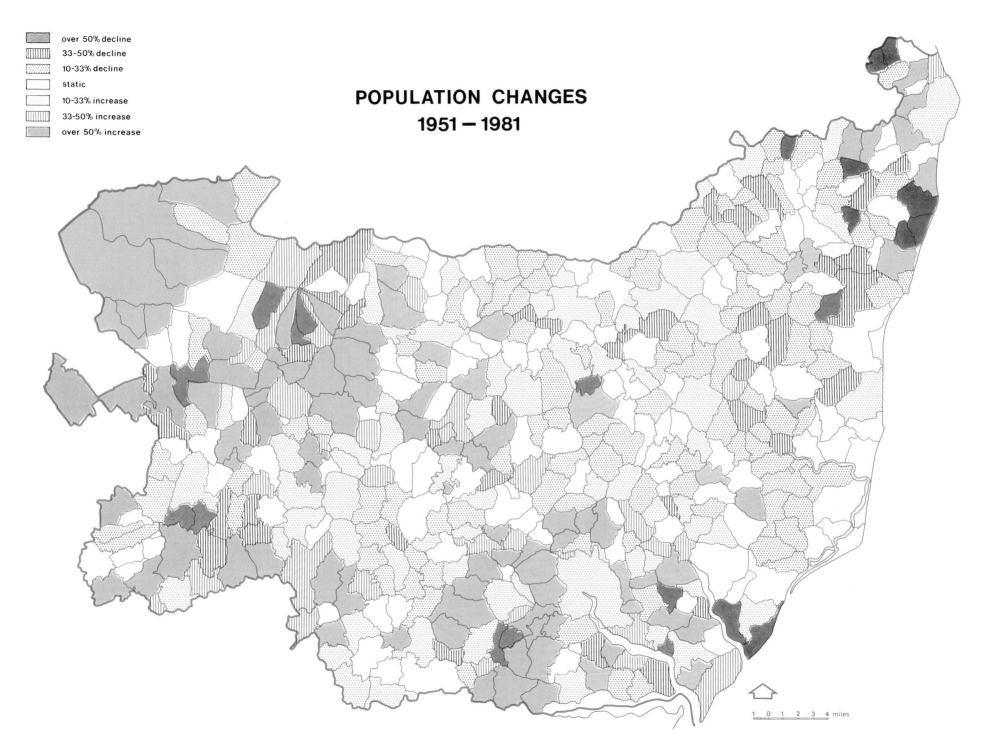

POPULATION CHANGES
1951 — 1981

Legend:
- over 50% decline
- 33-50% decline
- 10-33% decline
- static
- 10-33% increase
- 33-50% increase
- over 50% increase

1 0 1 2 3 4 miles

48. RURAL SETTLEMENT IN THE MID-19th CENTURY — Brian Roberts

Map B, opposite, presents the reader with an immediate challenge. It can only be compared with other maps in this atlas when studied with great care, for it has been cut out of a national map of mid-19th-century rural settlement currently being prepared by the author for English Heritage, as part of their Monument Protection Programme. This national map was originally drafted at a scale of 1:250,000 (a quarter of an inch to one mile) but the version used here was compiled in a graphics computer for reproduction at a scale of 1:3 million, so that it will fit comfortably on an A4 page. At this scale Suffolk appears little larger than a thumbnail.[1]

The source was the Ordnance Survey's first edition of maps at a scale of one inch to the mile, which for Suffolk appeared between 1805 and 1837.[2] In fact Map B consists of two layers: the upper one deals with nucleations, while the lower carries shading to suggest the extent of dispersion. Nucleations comprise major and minor towns, villages of varied size and hamlets, all of which are recorded as simple circles graded by size. Of course, nucleations in Suffolk could be mapped much more precisely, but the ten thousand or so recorded nationally demand this simplicity of treatment. The national map (A) resembles the sky seen on a clear night from a dark location: the massed pattern of simple symbols is dramatic and exciting, and reflects a thousand or more years of development. This broad pattern of three distinct settlement provinces was already present by 1086. Generalising at a county scale—perhaps based upon the Ordnance Survey's 1:10,560 maps (six inches to a mile)—might be expected to reveal more of the smaller hamlets than appear in this version. Such limitations are inevitable. No criteria have been agreed for mapping nucleations, although the author has in fact devised a system for recording the shape and general size of settlements. It is worth reflecting that

even the census of 1851, the first detailed census, does not allow us to estimate with any accuracy the population of individual nucleations within parishes or townships, and therefore its figures cannot be used to 'scale' the circles.[3]

The mapping of dispersed farmsteads and the smallest hamlets presents an even greater problem. Not only do the earlier Ordnance Survey maps vary considerably in cartographic style, but individual farmsteads are not identified by a specific symbol. Indeed it is not absolutely clear that they are named in all cases, so that in practical terms one cannot distinguish between a single large farmstead with many outbuildings and cottages, and a group of two, three or even more small farmsteads. While these can be mapped at a county scale, a national approach necessitates generalisation; the shading depicting dispersed settlement nationally is based upon approximately five and a half thousand scores counted within sample squares each of 2 by 2 kilometres. The detail of the method need not concern us here: suffice to say that the darker the shading in Map B, the more scattered in the actual landscape are dwellings, farmsteads, cottages, houses and industrial sites. The key, with two columns, has been devised to translate the technical jargon of the counting procedure into plain language: it is a reminder of the complexity which exists on the ground. Suffolk, with areas of medium, high and very high densities, is characteristic of eastern England, and can be contrasted with other regions which have 'very low' and 'extremely low' degrees of dispersion.

Local regional boundaries pose yet another problem. The best analogy is to be found in isobars on daily weather maps: no one imagines lines in the atmosphere, but lines are nevertheless drawn on maps—on the basis of surprisingly few measurements—to show where high pressure and low pressure lie. In the case of this settlement map, the measures available for both nucleation and dispersion were taken into account in defining local regions, and the end product approximately depicts local variations in the density of dispersion. No reference has been made to divisions made by other scholars.[4] As part of a national picture, the contrasts to be seen in Suffolk have a wider significance, but they will surely be qualified and corrected by local work—indeed this must happen if we are gradually to refine the national map. It is a paradox that some of the material needed to create a more refined view are in this atlas but were not available at the time of writing. On the other hand, the national map must be sufficiently sound to withstand rigorous criticism at a county level, and tests undertaken so far suggest that this is the case. Using the maps opposite the reader should be able to undertake a more detailed evaluation for Suffolk. For that reason, no descriptive analysis of this settlement map has been attempted: it is an image, a metaphor, created from a relatively homogenous source spread over several decades. It is not definitive, and now requires testing, refinement and evaluation. That is the challenge.

Further details on p.207

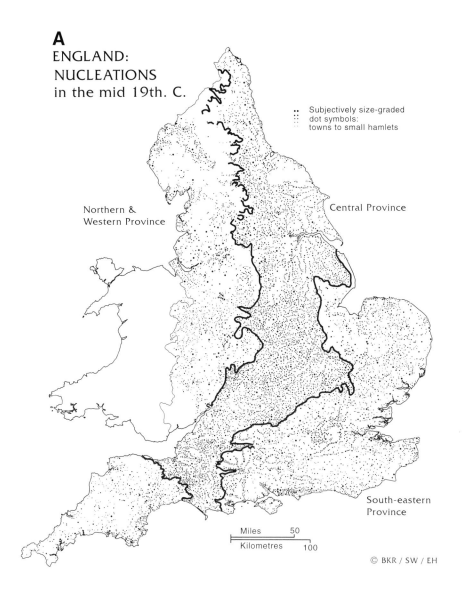

A
ENGLAND: NUCLEATIONS
in the mid 19th. C.

Subjectively size-graded
dot symbols:
towns to small hamlets

Northern &
Western Province

Central Province

South-eastern
Province

Miles   50
Kilometres   100

© BKR / SW / EH

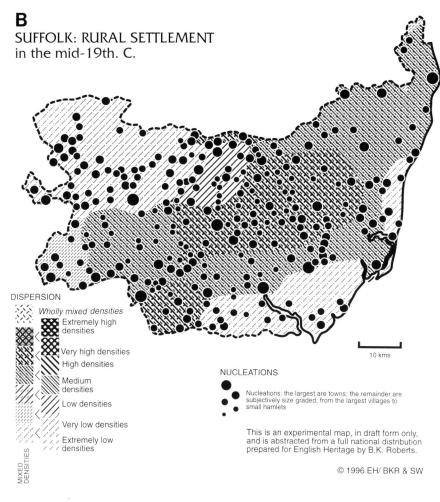

B
SUFFOLK: RURAL SETTLEMENT
in the mid-19th. C.

10 kms

DISPERSION

Wholly mixed densities

Extremely high
densities

Very high densities

High densities

Medium
densities

Low densities

Very low densities

Extremely low
densities

MIXED
DENSITIES

NUCLEATIONS

Nucleations: the largest are towns; the remainder are
subjectively size graded, from the largest villages to
small hamlets

This is an experimental map, in draft form only,
and is abstracted from a full national distribution
prepared for English Heritage by B.K. Roberts.

© 1996 EH/ BKR & SW

49. ROMAN CATHOLIC RECUSANCY

Joy Rowe

A 'recusant' was one who refused to conform to the Church of England as established by the Acts of Supremacy and Uniformity in 1558-9. Early in Elizabeth's reign, the term applied to Protestant as well as Roman Catholic nonconformists, and in some early presentments the two groups can only be differentiated when additional evidence is available. Here it is taken to apply to Roman Catholics who were later singled out for heavier penalties than the fine of one shilling imposed for non-attendance at the parish church. For the Catholic, the Mass rather than the Holy Communion was the touchstone of faith, and so the priest was all-important. The role of the laity was to shelter and provide for him, and so make the sacraments available to neighbouring Catholics. Statutes in 1581 and 1585 raised the penalty for non-attendance to 20 shillings a month, brought in the death penalty for all priests ordained abroad, and threatened all those who helped priests with imprisonment, the confiscation of goods and two-thirds of their estates and, in some cases, death. Although Catholics repeatedly declared that they were loyal subjects who owed only spiritual allegiance to the Pope, the excommunication of Elizabeth, plots to replace her by Mary Queen of Scots and finally the threat of the Armada, provoked an even more severe statute in 1593. Recusants nevertheless provided chapels where priests could say mass (for example, at Melford Place); built hiding places and escapes into chimney stacks and under floors (Coldham Hall, Stanningfield, 1574); and set up a network of communications to guide priests and pass on news.[1] Sometimes a priest lived in a substantial household as a servant.[2]

Up to 1574 when the first 'seminary' priests trained in English colleges abroad arrived in England, Catholicism had been kept alive by 'old' priests ordained in the reigns of Henry VIII and Mary who had not conformed to the Church of England.[3] The seminaries were staffed by exiles who taught and wrote for an English audience.[4] In 1580 a small number of English Jesuit priests arrived in England. Their influence was so great in strengthening the recusant community and in making converts that their numbers have been greatly overestimated. John Gerard, well known for his autobiography, wrote about a long stay with Henry Drury at Lawshall.

The predominantly Jesuit organisation of Catholics in Suffolk was set up in 1625 and formalised as the College of the Holy Apostles in 1633. The recusants of East Anglia subscribed to the support of 35 priests who met as a college most often at Bury St Edmunds, and occasionally at Ipswich and Lowestoft. A school was openly established in the monastic ruins at Bury St Edmunds. During the Civil War the majority of Catholics adopted the same neutralist position as their Protestant neighbours. After the Restoration, Catholics took a more prominent part in public life. Under a Catholic mayor, they helped to pack the Corporation at Bury St Edmunds to advance the policies of James II. As a result, the last large-scale anti-popery riot in Suffolk attacked the Jesuits and their property, forcing them to take refuge in a Catholic gentleman's house at Great Barton.

The most productive sources for recusancy are presentments and indictments before Quarter Sessions and the Consistory Court at Norwich, lists of fines in the Pipe Rolls, and after 1592 the Recusant Rolls. However, these do not give a complete picture of the numbers of recusants or of their financial penalties. Some recusants were very heavily fined (Michael Hare of Bruisyard), or had their estates confiscated (Nicholas Timperley of Hintlesham), but others, equally wealthy, escaped comparatively lightly. Returns of recusants, whether local gentry or less well-off, made by clergy and church-wardens do not correspond with Catholics recognised from other sources. The records of Gaol Delivery often provide names unknown elsewhere. The map shows known centres where a priest worked consistently throughout the penal period; it indicates the perdurable character of Suffolk recusancy, and the places where changes and expansion took place. Most Catholics were to be found either in Bury St Edmunds, or scattered about the countryside around the houses of known Catholic gentry, especially in the villages of High Suffolk and along the Norfolk border. Elizabethan Lothingland was a particular stronghold but did not last long, which suggests political rather than religious fervour. The lists of those unwilling to take the Oath of Allegiance in 1689 and the Register of Papists' Estates of 1715, although neither is complete for the whole county, indicate that Catholicism was to be found among the landed gentry, yeomen and artisans.

A collation of the Ecclesiastical Census of 1767 with existing Catholic registers in the Suffolk Missions shows substantial groupings of Catholics sufficiently strong to be organised into a system of parishes subsuming the old mass centres. The Roman Catholic Relief Act of 1781, the Places of Worship Act of 1789 and the Catholic Emancipation Act of 1829 removed the penalties for recusancy which had been increasingly laxly applied. The arrival of emigrant priests from revolutionary France solved the problem of providing sufficient priests and enabled parishes to be set up at Bury St Edmunds, Coldham, Ipswich, and at Thetford, which included the mass centres of the old Border Mission in High Suffolk.

Further details on p.207

ROMAN CATHOLIC RECUSANCY

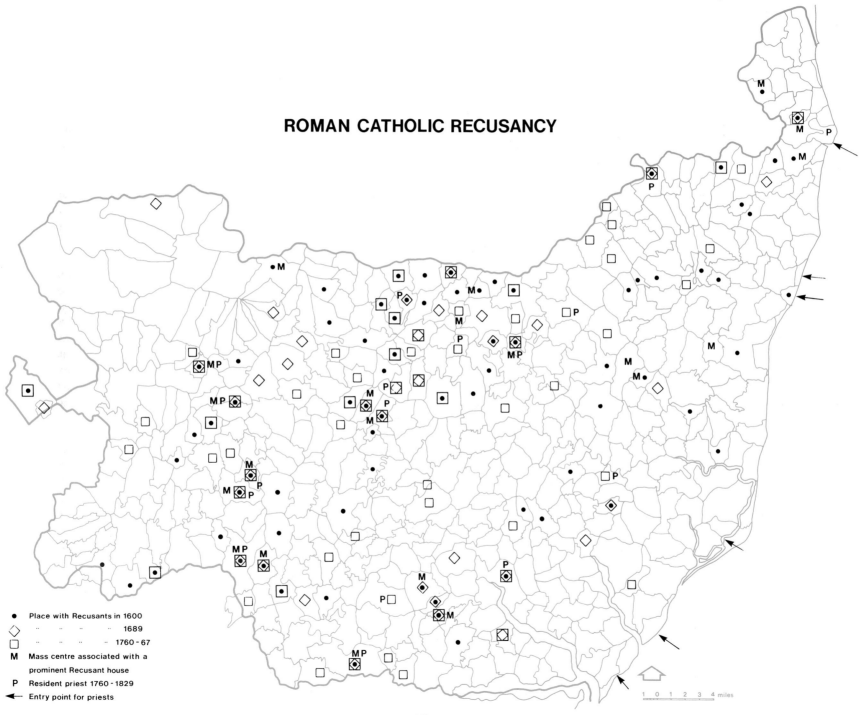

Place with Recusants in 1600
      "   "   "   " 1689
      "   "   "   " 1760 - 67

M Mass centre associated with a prominent Recusant house

P Resident priest 1760 - 1829

← Entry point for priests

1 0 1 2 3 4 miles

50. PROTESTANT NONCONFORMITY

Clive Paine

Religious dissent in Suffolk has a long history, reaching back to Lollardy in the late 14th century. After the break with Rome, the new Church of England was soon wracked by differences of opinion, and small groups began to break away before 1600. The mould was not really broken, however, until 1640-60 when the national church became nominally Presbyterian and numerous groups struck out on their own. In Suffolk the most important separatists were Independents who believed that each congregation should be entirely self-governing, and Quakers who saw no need of a ministry between the believer and God. After 1660, the Church of England was fully restored and 'nonconformity' was again persecuted.[1]

In 1672, however, Charles II's Declaration of Indulgence allowed the official licensing of nonconformist ministers and places of worship. Surviving licences enable us to see where different denominations held meetings,[2] but give no indication of the numbers attending.[3] Over 75 per cent of Independent meetings lay across the north of Suffolk, from the Blackbourne valley in the west to the coast in the east; 39 villages and towns contained at least 55 places of worship. The main concentration of Presbyterian meetings lay, by contrast, in the south-west of the county, with a thin scattering in north Suffolk east of Hunston; 37 communities held at least 47 places of worship. The Baptists were represented only by two meetings at Bungay, one of which was shared with Independents.[4] As Quaker meetings were not licensed in 1672, their location has to be derived from other sources.[5] By the nature of Quaker organisation, a monthly meeting might rotate among three or four venues; hence their distribution appears in scattered clusters. In total there were 42 Quaker meetings. To sum up, at least 98 towns and villages in Suffolk contained nonconformist congregations in the 1670s, and 27 had more than one.[7]

In 1674 the Declaration was revoked, and it again became illegal to be a nonconformist until a second indulgence was issued in 1687. Final recognition of the rift between Church and Dissent came with the Toleration Act of 1689, which gave nonconformists the permanent freedom to worship separately. So, soon after 1689, purpose-built chapels were erected by various denominations, like the two famous early examples which survive in Ipswich and Bury St Edmunds. In the 18th century a great religious revival, associated with John Wesley above all, caused nonconformity to grow spectacularly.[8] New denominations were founded, especially Methodism in its various guises, which are known collectively as 'New Dissent' to distinguish them from the older sects founded in the 17th century. A new series of 2060 licences issued in Suffolk during the period 1688-1852 shows that most congregations continued to use secular buildings for their meetings, and that many were short-lived.[9] Even as late as 1829, Suffolk had 659 licenced meetings, of which only 123 were in proper chapels.[10]

The Census of Religious Worship made in 1851 is the most detailed survey ever undertaken.[11] It showed that the largest group representing 'Old Dissent' were the Independents, also known as Congregationalists, who were now strongest in the south and south-west of the county: they had at least 100 meetings in 91 places, of which 23 per cent were in towns. The two groups of Baptists—the earlier General and the newer Calvinistic, Strict or Particular—were strongest from Stowmarket to the coast. They had at least 94 meetings in 88 places, of which 23 per cent were in towns. The Presbyterians were reduced to a single chapel in Cavendish. Three former groups at Bury, Framlingham and Ipswich had, in common with most of the denomination in England, denied the divinity of Christ and become Unitarian. In

1851 seven of the eight Quaker meetings used the same centres as in the 17th century.

In 1851 the largest form of New Dissent was the two branches of Methodism, with at least 193 meetings. The Wesleyans had 94 meetings in 89 places, of which 18 per cent were in towns. The other main group were the Primitive Methodists who aimed their message particularly at rural labourers. They had at least 87 meetings in 82 places, with 14 per cent in towns. The smaller Wesleyan Association had three meetings, and the Reformed Methodists nine. These two groups had broken away from the Wesleyans over matters of organisation rather than doctrine. Methodism came to Suffolk from Norfolk, and this is reflected by its greater strength in the north and north-east of the county.

Newer dissenting groups were also recorded in 1851. The Latter Day Saints or Mormons opened their first chapel in Boxford in 1842, only five years after arriving in England. By 1851 they had five meetings in Suffolk. The evangelical Plymouth Brethren held their first meeting in a barn at Tostock in 1837, only two years after they started at Plymouth.[12] By 1851 they had at least seven meetings around Stowmarket, Ipswich and Woodbridge.

The 1851 census shows that an estimated 5 per cent of Suffolk's population attended nonconformist meetings in 50 per cent of its parishes. Of these places, 94 had more than one meeting, and 87 had more than one denomination. Conversely, nonconformist worship was not recorded in over 200 parishes.[13]

Further details on p.208

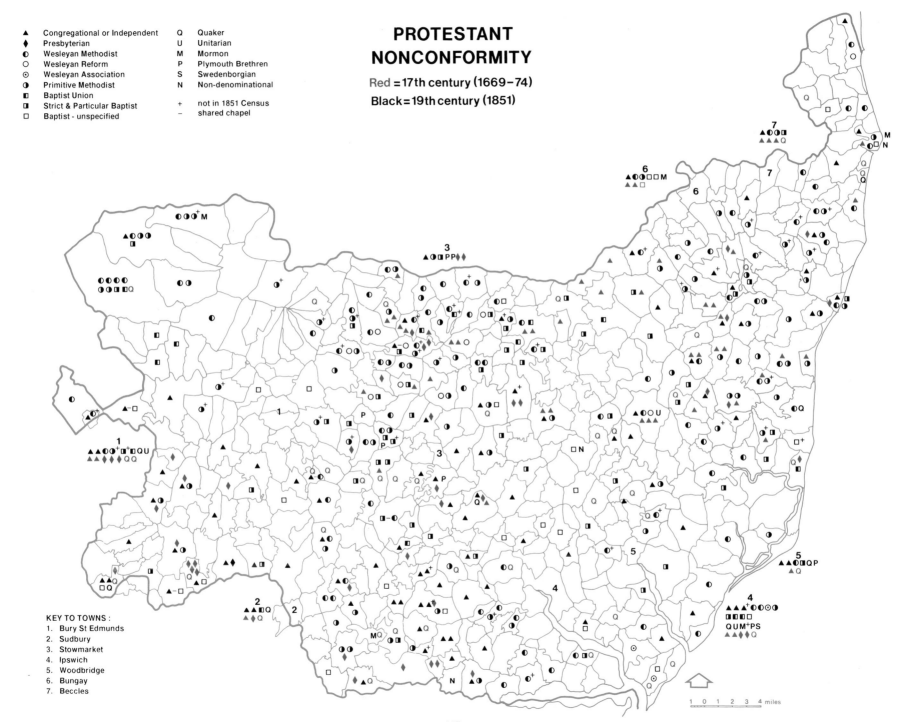

PROTESTANT NONCONFORMITY

Red = 17th century (1669–74)

Black = 19th century (1851)

Key (legend):

Symbol	Denomination	Symbol	Denomination
▲	Congregational or Independent	Q	Quaker
♦	Presbyterian	U	Unitarian
◐	Wesleyan Methodist	M	Mormon
○	Wesleyan Reform	P	Plymouth Brethren
⊙	Wesleyan Association	S	Swedenborgian
◑	Primitive Methodist	N	Non-denominational
▣	Baptist Union		
▤	Strict & Particular Baptist	+	not in 1851 Census
□	Baptist - unspecified	−	shared chapel

KEY TO TOWNS :
1. Bury St Edmunds
2. Sudbury
3. Stowmarket
4. Ipswich
5. Woodbridge
6. Bungay
7. Beccles

1 0 1 2 3 4 miles

115

51. EDUCATION BEFORE 1750

Peter Northeast

Like Macaulay's schoolboy, everyone knows that no government money was provided for education in this country before the famous grant of £20,000 in 1833. Prior to that, education had to be paid for by the pupil's family, or by a benefactor, live or dead. The relatively few exceptions were those boys who, before the Reformation, were lucky enough to be taken into the school of a religious house, or instructed by a conscientious parish priest.

Until well into the 17th century, the aim of almost all endowed education was to send boys to university, seen in the then general use of the word 'school' to signify university. Thus, schools founded before that date were almost always 'grammar' schools—in fact if not in name—concentrating on the classical subjects of Latin and Greek. Pupils were expected to be proficient in the reading and writing of English before they attended school, and the 'casting of accounts' (later called 'arithmetic') was of secondary consideration. The teaching of basic English was carried on in numerous small schools in towns and villages, occasionally glimpsed in the laconic 'he teacheth school' in presentments to ecclesiastical courts.

The fact that schools were endowed or called 'free schools' does not mean that all children attended them without paying, although there were exceptions like Thurlow, founded in about 1618, where instruction was given 'without any payment'. The endowment normally paid for only a small number of free pupils, but did provide a guaranteed income, if small, for a master, on which he could build by taking fee-paying pupils. The free provision varied greatly from the 40 or more children at Beccles and Framlingham, down to the 40s. a year for a schoolmaster at Kersey. In the case of all grammar schools and about two-thirds of the other endowed schools, the endowment also provided an actual school-building. Elsewhere, the individual master had to find a suitable room for himself.

In general, grammar school foundations were of an earlier date than other endowed schools. Those at Ipswich and Sudbury were founded before the Reformation, and the rest were Elizabethan except for Brandon (1646), Cavendish (1696) and Gislingham (1636). Lavenham grammar school is first mentioned in 1647, but the actual date of its foundation is unknown. Since their survival depended largely on their ability to attract fee-paying pupils, the great majority of grammar schools were, significantly, within the agriculturally prosperous clay-belt of central Suffolk. Private schools preparing boys for university were obviously much more ephemeral, being affected by the coming and going of individual masters. Nevertheless, certain places like Halesworth did build up a continuing tradition of sending boys to university.

In the 17th century, the need to educate poor children was more generally recognised, and most of the other endowed schools were then founded.[1] It was at this period also that we see the first signs of instruction being fitted to the ability of the child, irrespective of social class. At Thurlow, for instance, it was instructed that pupils should be taught 'according to their capacities', and as a result some local boys were sent up to university.

Education in these early years clearly depended upon the sympathy and charity of the wealthier members of local society. Nevertheless, some people saw a danger in providing too much education. In the early 1600s Sir Francis Bacon had warned James I of the over-provision of grammar schools, alleging that they caused a shortage 'both of servants in husbandry and apprentices for trade'. The fear of 'educating them above their stations' was the chief obstacle encountered by the supporters of charity schools in the early 18th century.

The establishment of charity schools was largely due to the encouragement of the Society for the Promotion of Christian Knowledge (SPCK). This was founded in 1698 principally to promote the spreading of the gospel 'in the plantations', but quickly became involved with education at home. The society provided no funds for setting up schools, but it ran a system of correspondents throughout the country whose task was to persuade benefactors to support new schools, and to keep the SPCK informed. The society, in turn, supported correspondents and schools with appropriate literature, and published annually their 'Account of Charity Schools Lately Erected. . .' Much depended on the enthusiasm of local correspondents. The two most active in this area appear to have been Dr Samuel Knight of Chippenham in Cambridgeshire and James Oldfield of Brome, and this could well account for such schools concentrating in the west of Suffolk and in the Eye area. Other charity schools were set up independently of the SPCK as at Ampton (1692, augmented in 1715), Blundeston (1726) and Benhall (1731), while some of the endowed schools, like Laxfield (1718) were really charity schools.

Many of these schools were short-lived and few survived after 1800. The exceptions were in Ipswich and Bury, and two late foundations at Holton St Mary (1746) and Blundeston. It remained for the great crusade of the British and National Societies in the 19th century to get popular education in this country fully under way (see Map 52).[2]

Further details on p.209

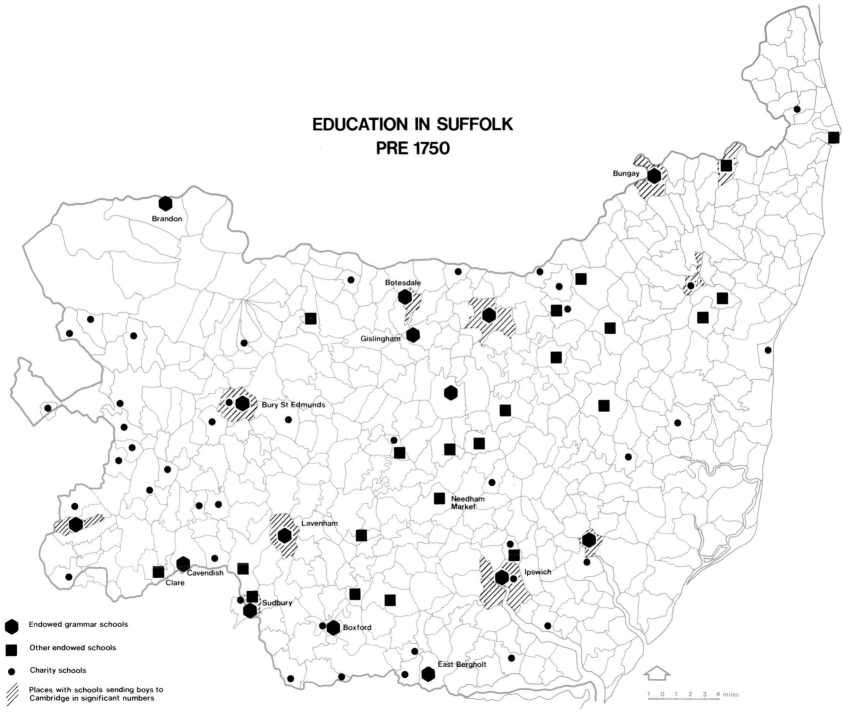

EDUCATION IN SUFFOLK
PRE 1750

Bungay

Brandon

Botesdale

Gislingham

Bury St Edmunds

Needham Market

Lavenham

Cavendish

Clare

Sudbury

Boxford

Ipswich

East Bergholt

⬡ Endowed grammar schools

■ Other endowed schools

● Charity schools

/// Places with schools sending boys to
Cambridge in significant numbers

1 0 1 2 3 4 miles

117

52. ELEMENTARY EDUCATION IN THE 19th CENTURY

Peter Northeast

At the beginning of the 19th century, the state neither supported education financially, nor controlled it. Such schools as existed operated as commercial ventures. They were either dependent on pupils' fees, or they benefited from the generosity of public-spirited individuals, in the form of endowments from the past or of donations by the living. In those first years of the century, under 5 per cent of Suffolk children had access to free education.[1]

In the country as a whole, however, the problem of providing education for the children of those unable to pay for it was attracting growing interest. This resulted in the setting up of two societies within a few years of each other. The British and Foreign School Society was begun (as the Royal Lancasterian Society) in 1808: it was mainly supported by Nonconformists and encouraged the foundation of 'British' schools. The National Society for the Education of the Poor in the Principles of the Established Church, set up in 1811, was entirely Anglican and set up 'National' schools.

When in 1833 government approved a grant towards the building of schools, these two societies were nominated to administer it, so schools seeking assistance were virtually obliged to become affiliated to one or other of the two societies. Schools not prepared to affiliate (mostly Anglican, but some of 'no-religion') have been designated 'parochial' for the purpose of this map. From 1853 grants became payable for each child in attendance, but applicant schools had to accept annual inspection as the price of receiving a grant—a deterrent to any school able to survive independently. With the introduction of the 'New Code' of 1862—the notorious 'payment by results' system whereby the size of a school's grant depended upon the pupils being able to pass tests in certain subjects—inspections became more stringent.

Under the great 'Forster' Education Act of 1870, the provision of elementary education over the whole country was surveyed. Inspectors compared the number of school places in existence with the number deemed necessary. Where there was a deficiency, the current providers were required to extend and upgrade their provision to comply with the inspector's estimate, or a school board would be formed to take responsibility for making adequate provision, with the cost falling on local ratepayers. As a result, most of the management of church schools did their best to meet the inspectors' requirements and so avoid the formation of Boards. A spate of building and extension took place in the two or three years after 1870. Supporters of the Nonconformist cause, on the other hand, did their best to have Boards formed in order to wrest control from Anglican hands.

Extreme examples of this manoeuvring can be seen in Ipswich and Bury St Edmunds. Ipswich Corporation was at the time dominated by nonconformists who had completed a detailed survey of all the town's schools ready for the inspector. A Board was formed by January 1871, the first in the county by far, and fourteeen Board schools were built by the end of the century. Bury, on the other hand, was an Anglican preserve where the church-dominated Guildhall Feoffees had helped to ensure that the provision of school places always outstripped demand. Consequently no School Board was ever formed, and in 1903 the LEA inherited an explosive situation in which many nonconformist townsmen were supporting the Passive Resistance League.[2]

School Boards were not all formed immediately after 1871. In several instances voluntary schools attempted to meet the inspectors' requirements but had to admit defeat a few years later. At Woolpit, for instance, the National school was enlarged in 1875, but a Board was formed in 1877 and took over control. Having 'made do'

with the old building for nearly 20 years, the Board built a new school in 1895. Hadleigh was the last Board to be formed in the county, in 1901, when it took over the failing British school; it did not have time to erect a new building before the new educational authority was formed two years later.

Something of the achievement of the 19th century can be seen from statistics in several government returns spanning almost the whole century. The first of these was for 1818 when nearly 6000 Suffolk children were receiving education freely or at a very small cost.[3] By 1833 the number had risen to about 9500.[4] By the time of the 1851 census, the figure was nearly 27,000.[5] The assessment of school places made in accordance with the 1870 Act showed accommodation for nearly 42,000.[6] By the time that the LEAs took over in 1903, under the Balfour Act of 1902, more than 450 elementary schools accommodated over 80,000 children.[7]

Note: All the schools shown on the map did not, of course, exist throughout the whole century, but at least each survived for a significant period. Where boys' and girls' departments in the same place were referred to as separate schools in the 19th century, they have been mapped as single establishments. Schools classed as 'infants' have not been mapped.

Further details on p.209

19TH-CENTURY ELEMENTARY EDUCATION

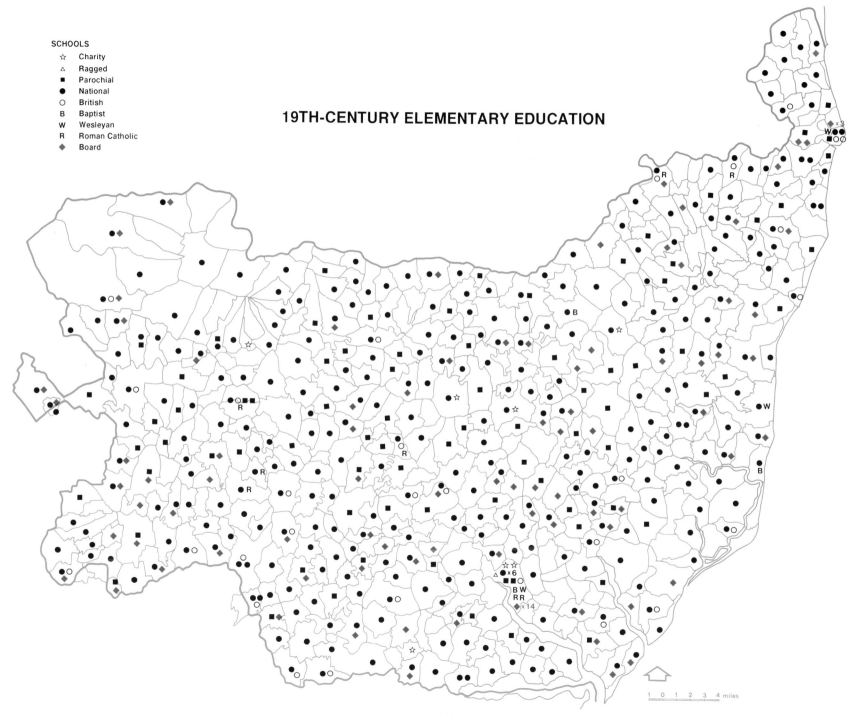

SCHOOLS

☆ Charity
△ Ragged
■ Parochial
● National
○ British
B Baptist
W Wesleyan
R Roman Catholic
◆ Board

53. PARISH AND HUNDRED WORKHOUSES, BEFORE 1834 David Dymond

During the 16th century, the problem of poverty increased so dramatically that the government of Elizabeth I was forced to devise a new system based on the compulsory payment of rates and the election of special officers in every parish. This new system was finally enshrined in the famous Act of 1601 which lasted, with modifications, until 1834.

In their own homes the poor were given 'out-relief', which consisted of money, clothing, fuel and medical assistance. Because a major cause of poverty was clearly the lack of work, the 1601 Act also empowered parishes to provide a stock of raw materials 'to set the poor on work'. (Market towns had been encouraged to invest in such stocks by an earlier Act of 1576.) A further option given by an Act of 1597 was to provide 'Abiding and Working Houses for the Poor'. Thus, Bury St Edmunds had a 'working house' as early as 1597 while East Bergholt was left a legacy for a similar building in 1624.[1]

The Workhouse Test Act of 1722 positively encouraged the foundation of parish workhouses, and stipulated that anyone refusing to enter such an institution was ineligible for relief. It also allowed two or more parishes to combine in running a workhouse. Thus, in 1747 James Vernon left Weathercock Farm at Great Wratting to be used as a workhouse by three contiguous parishes.[2] It should be noted that genuine workhouses, where the poor were both accommodated and put to work, can easily be confused with 'town houses' and Houses of Correction.[3]

Returns sent to Parliament in 1776[4] reveal, for the first time, the number and distribution of parish workhouses (see map opposite). Suffolk had 89 such institutions, scattered fairly widely but showing two major concentrations. The first was a group of twelve workhouses in Ipswich, the largest town in the county. The second was in the south-west of Suffolk—roughly from Haverhill to Hadleigh. This area had specialised in the making of woollen cloth since the 13th century, but by 1776 was in serious economic decline while its population was again growing. Faced with accumulating problems, most parishes in the manufacturing district had decided, at varying dates before 1776, to provide a workhouse. Another return in 1803 shows that 46 more parishes had created workhouses since 1776, noticeably in the middle and north-east of the county.[5] Another ten parishes followed suit between 1803 and 1815.[6]

These trends, however, were overtaken by another major development. Since the late 17th century, major towns had tended to establish Corporations of the Poor by unifying their parishes and running single workhouses: thus Sudbury was incorporated in 1702 and Bury in 1747. However from the 1750s onwards, the magistrates and principal inhabitants of a wide rural area in eastern Suffolk decided to set up Incorporated Hundreds to run large 'Houses of Industry', each capable of accommodating paupers from a large area.[7] The first House of Industry was opened at Nacton in 1757, to serve the hundreds of Colneis and Carlford. By 1766, similar institutions had appeared at six other places (see map). The purpose of this enterprising new system, well before Gilbert's Act of 1782 officially encouraged larger administrative units, was to make relief more efficient and less costly.[8]

The competing of two systems, one parochial and the other hundredal, led to a curious anomaly visible on the map. Although most of eastern Suffolk had followed the lead of Colneis-cum-Carlford, the hundred of Plomesgate did not. Indeed, its parishes were still busy creating their own new workhouses between 1776 and 1803, while their neighbours in Blything and Wilford-cum-Loes were building larger Houses of Industry, and abandoning the parish workhouses which had previously existed.

In the rest of Suffolk, where Houses of Industry were not being built, about fifteen parishes apparently abandoned their workhouses between 1803 and 1815. This surprising fact may be connected with the adoption of other radical policies—such as supplementing labourers' wages, giving allowances of flour or paying subsidies to employers.

Henry Stuart, whose report on poor-relief in East Anglia was published in 1834,[9] thought the smaller parish workhouses were often 'abodes of misery, depravity and filth', but conceded that those in larger parishes, for example at Saxmundham and Framlingham, were 'most comfortable places of abode' (meaning *too* comfortable). He found three main groups of inmates: the old and infirm, orphaned and illegitimate children, and unmarried pregnant women. Much more research is needed on individual parish workhouses, before the quality of their relief can be estimated. Finally, we must not forget that over two thirds of Suffolk's parishes, particularly the smaller ones, never did establish their own workhouses, but relied on other methods of relief.

Further details on p.209

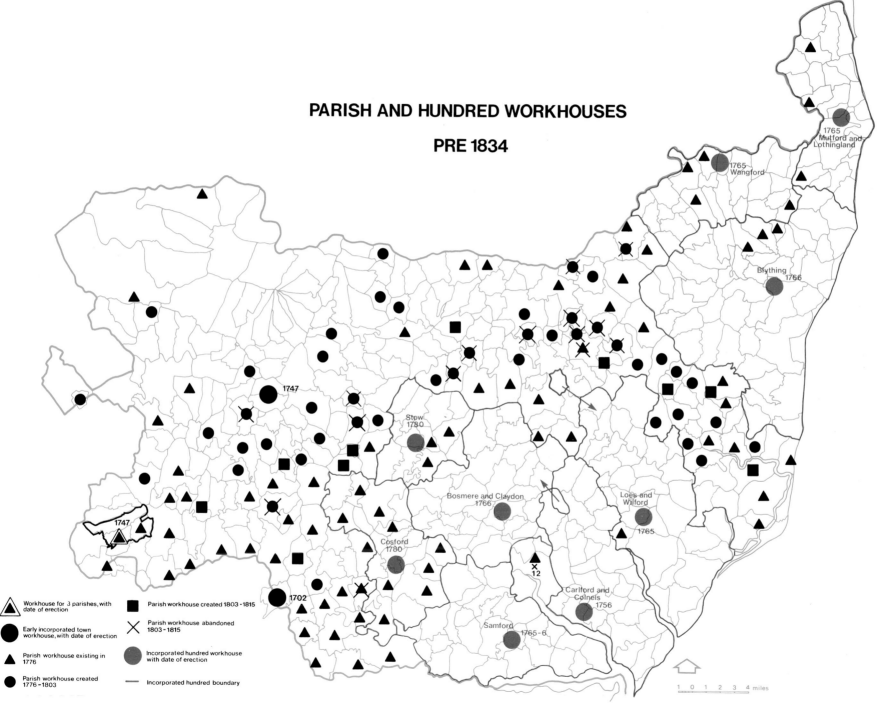

PARISH AND HUNDRED WORKHOUSES

PRE 1834

1765
Mutford and
Lothingland

1765
Wangford

Blything
1766

1747

Stow
1780

X
12

Bosmere and Claydon
1766

Loes and
Wilford
1765

1747

Cosford
1780

Carlford and
Colneis
1756

1702

Samford
1765-6

△ Workhouse for 3 parishes, with date of erection

● Early incorporated town workhouse, with date of erection

▲ Parish workhouse existing in 1776

● Parish workhouse created 1776–1803

■ Parish workhouse created 1803–1815

✕ Parish workhouse abandoned 1803–1815

● Incorporated hundred workhouse with date of erection

— Incorporated hundred boundary

1 0 1 2 3 4 miles

In February 1832 the Whig government appointed the famous Royal Commission into the 'operation of the laws for the relief of the poor in England and Wales'. The Report of 1834 and the consequent passing of the Poor Law Amendment Act constituted an unprecedented revolution in the government of local communities, and massive intervention by the State. Central to the thinking of the reformers was the desire for economy. Population increase, redundant labour especially in the rural areas of south-east England, and economic depression after the Napoleonic Wars, had led to massively increased expenditure on the poor and consequent pressure on the rates. The old parochial system was clearly inadequate to deal with the problem, as was indicated in the Report which compared the expenditure of nine Incorporated Hundreds in Suffolk with that of eight unincorporated hundreds. During the period 1824-31 the Incorporations were 54% more economical than those areas where relief was still in the hands of individual parishes. The Report also quoted Mr Meadow White's argument that for less than £10 a year each parish in the Incorporated Hundred of Blything obtained for the poor the services of a chaplain, governor and matron, schoolmistress, superintendant, clerk, visiting guardians and house surgeon —which individual parishes could never have afforded for themselves. The evidence from Suffolk of both the financial and administrative benefits of incorporation was thus an important factor in establishing the Union system as a universal one after 1834.

However, when the Unions were officially created in Suffolk in the late 1830s, only three of the existing rural Incorporations remained unaltered. Two of them, Mutford-and-Lothingland and Samford were regarded as efficient enough, under the rigorous terms of the Act, to remain independent of the central Poor Law Board for some years after 1834. The third, Wangford, kept its boundaries as before. Elsewhere in the county, totally new units were set up which cut across the ancient hundred boundaries. Carlford-cum-Colneis was now grouped with Wilford (excluding Wickham Market) to form the new Woodbridge Union; Cosford was enlarged to take in ten parishes from Babergh which was previously unincorporated; Stow was increased by eleven parishes form Blackbourn Hundred and nine from Thedwastre; Blything now included Kelsale-cum-Carlton (outlying parishes of Hoxne Hundred) and Dunwich, previously excluded. In the west of Suffolk, hundred boundaries were largely ignored. Risbridge, for instance, was decimated when its parishes were divided between Mildenhall, Newmarket, Thingoe and Sudbury Unions; Blackbourn was similarly split between Thingoe, Stow and the new Thetford Union. In fact, the only unincorporated hundred that remained intact was Hartismere.

As well as making the old hundreds irrelevant, the Act cut across the even more fundamentally important boundaries of the counties. Sudbury Union included 18 parishes in Essex; Risbridge another six; Newmarket Union included 22 parishes in Cambridgeshire, and Thetford Union 18 in Norfolk.

Ipswich, which had suffered from an influx of rural paupers, from corrupt parochial administration and from the manipulation of rates by small proprietors, had discussed the incorporation of its twelve parishes in 1815, in 1817, and again in 1822-23. Nothing, however, was done until after 1834 when, despite political manoeuvrings, the opposition of ratepayers and serious rioting, the union finally took place. The town was divided into five wards for general administration of the rates, and a large workhouse built in Great Whip Street in St Peter's parish. By the 1860s this house was inadequate, and the Poor Law Board pressed the Guardians to replace it, but it was not until 1899 that a new workhouse was opened on the town's perimeter in the Woodbridge Road.

Large workhouses were of course built for the new Unions: for Plomesgate Union at Wickham Market in 1836-37; for Hoxne Union at Stradbroke in 1834-35, and for Thingoe Union in Bury St Edmunds in 1835-36. Mildenhall Union adapted and enlarged an existing house in 1836, as did Risbridge at Haverhill in the same year. This latter was replaced by a new building at Kedington in 1856. Hartismere Union was unique in Suffolk in having two workhouses: at Eye a pre-19th century building housed adult and infant paupers, and was later enlarged in 1854, while at Wortham a former parish workhouse was enlarged to receive and educate boys and girls. By the 1840s Suffolk was served by twenty Union workhouses, one of which at Thetford was just outside the county boundary.

Further details on p.210

Designed by Thomas Fulcher of Ipswich, the House of Industry at Onehouse was built 1779-80, for the Incorporated Hundred of Stow, at a cost of £12,150. It became the Union Workhouse in 1835 and later became a hospital. To Arthur Young (1797), such buildings seemed more like the mansions of the gentry than poor-houses.

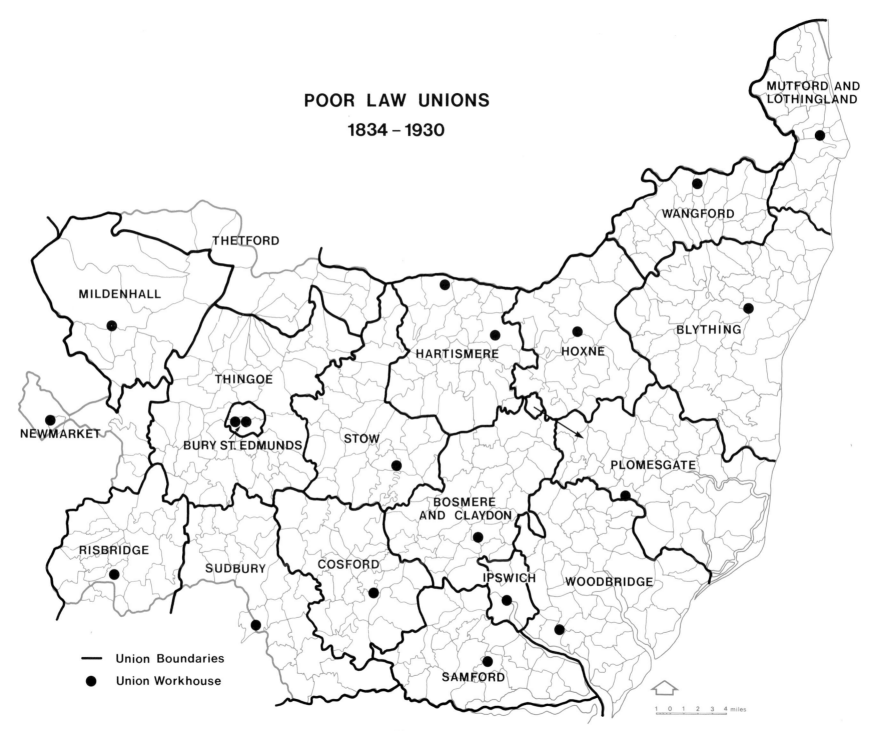

POOR LAW UNIONS

1834 – 1930

MUTFORD AND LOTHINGLAND

WANGFORD

THETFORD

MILDENHALL

BLYTHING

THINGOE

HARTISMERE

HOXNE

NEWMARKET

BURY ST. EDMUNDS

STOW

PLOMESGATE

BOSMERE AND CLAYDON

RISBRIDGE

SUDBURY

COSFORD

IPSWICH

WOODBRIDGE

SAMFORD

— Union Boundaries

● Union Workhouse

1 0 1 2 3 4 miles

55. RURAL PROTEST, 1815-51

John E. Archer

In 1815 the restoration of international peace marked the beginning of a protracted rural war in Suffolk. Between that year and the ending of the mid-century agrarian depression in 1851 Suffolk earned the unenviable reputation of being one of the most disturbed counties in England.

Many factors conspired to impoverish and demoralize labourers, not least the growing social gulf between them and farmers, population growth which rooted them to their parishes, and a long-term fall in wages. The latter fell as low as six shillings a week in the southwest of the county, particularly in the neighbourhood of Withersfield which John Glyde in the late 1840s believed to be the most criminal parish in the county. In addition unemployment and under-employment became routine experiences for many young and single farm-workers who no longer 'lived in' with their employers. This section of the workforce, more than any other, embarked on rural terrorism, especially after the New Poor Law was introduced in 1835-6.

Between 1815 and 1851 the entire arsenal of rural warfare—from open demonstrations, riots and machine-breaking to the more covert and individualistic activities of arson, animal maiming and the sending of threatening letters—was deployed against landowners, farmers, clergy and poor-law officials. Trouble first began in 1815 when threshing machines were destroyed at Gosbeck and Holbrook. In 1816, more widespread disturbances arose to the south and east of Bury St Edmunds and further north at Brandon, known as the 'Bread or Blood' riots; the causes were a complex series of inter-related grievances concerned not only with the use of agricultural machinery but also low wages and high food prices.

A combination of bad weather and agricultural depression meant that 1822 was a desperate year both for farmers, many of whom were facing bankruptcy, and the unemployed labour force. Enormous incendiary fires in the first six weeks of the year warned the authorities of impending troubles which eventually spread south from the Norfolk border to the Eye neighbourhood where threshing machines were destroyed. As the map indicates, these disturbances were mainly confined to northern parishes where they continued sporadically between the spring and autumn. In following years farmers appeared reluctant to reintroduce threshing machines, which suggests that the work of rioters and arsonists (there were 45 fires in 1822) was effective. This was borne out in 1830 when agrarian riots, known as Captain Swing, swept the nation. In this year Suffolk did not follow the experience of Norfolk closely since only two threshing machines were destroyed, both in Withersfield where Col. Brotherton reported that 'the excesses of the peasantry were greater than we have heard'.[1] More common were wage and tithe demonstrations, again in north Suffolk, which suggested a degree of collusion between masters and men. The riots ended with the arrest of Suffolk's Captain Swing, a travelling straw-plait manufacturer from Cambridgeshire who, at the time of his capture, had a parcel of anonymous and as yet undelivered letters.

The final wave of mass demonstrations occurred with the introduction of the New Poor Law. Protests began peacefully enough with a mass meeting at Horham in May 1835, but later that year many workhouses in the eastern division came under attack from labourers armed with pickaxes and crowbars. Arson yet again proved the most effective weapon when in November 1836 the workhouse at Sudbury, still under construction, was burnt down. Thereafter demonstrations and riots ceased, and arson became the endemic hallmark of rural protest in the county. Incendiarism, directed mainly at stacks and farmyards, reached epidemic proportions in 1843-4 when 180 fires occurred, and in 1849-51 when a further 131 fires were lit. As a weapon of intimidation, vengeance and terror, arson had many advantages. It was a cheap and effective form of protest which could be carried out with relative impunity since most of the perpetrators escaped conviction. In fact only 50 were successfully convicted during these years. Furthermore arson caused considerable alarm among farmers who found it increasingly difficult to insure their property. Underlying grievances are difficult to discern, but the scenes of jubilation which attended these conflagrations showed that arsonists were supported by the bulk of the labouring class. As in earlier years a catalogue of grievances relating to low wages, unemployment and poor-law practices, particularly the notorious 'ticket system', acted as catalysts. However, the map shows that the epicentre of protest in Suffolk had moved both west and south to the more densely populated parishes lying on heavier soils. In this region Thomas Campbell Foster reported in 1844 on the appalling poverty and oppression experienced by rural workers who told him 'that when the harvest is ripe, the fields will be fired'.[2] The situation had scarcely improved when five years later the *Morning Chronicle* sent in their reporter. He found that south-west Suffolk had the highest unemployment and the lowest wages in the county. The frequency of arson attacks in this area appears to support his findings.

Although arson remained a problem until the coming of trade unionism in the 1870s, migration from rural areas and the subsequent rise in wages, and more frequent employment opportunities for those left behind, meant that it declined in volume and frequency.

Further details on p.210

RURAL PROTEST 1815-1851

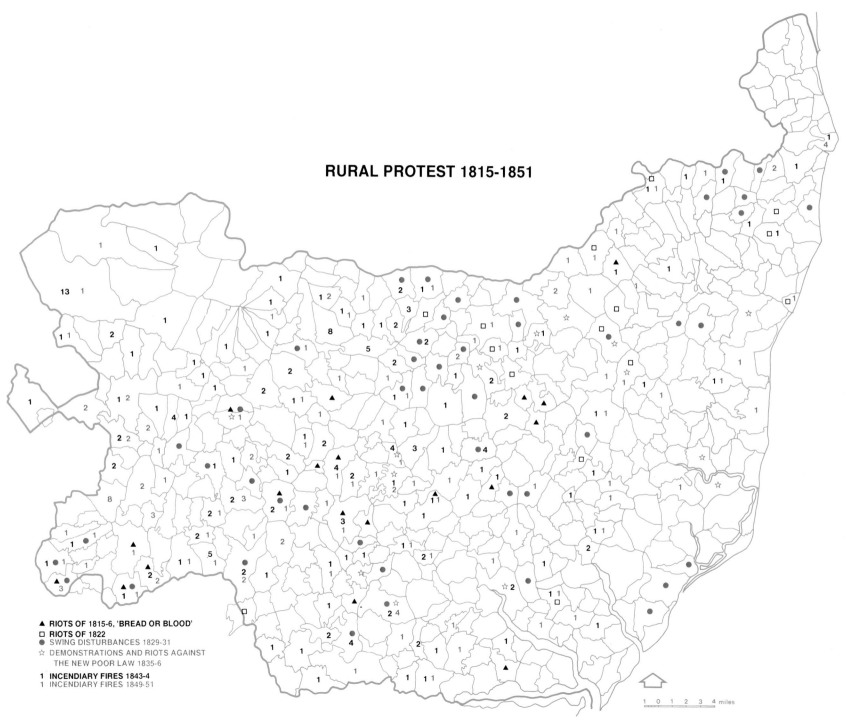

RIOTS OF 1815-6, 'BREAD OR BLOOD'
□ RIOTS OF 1822
● SWING DISTURBANCES 1829-31
☆ DEMONSTRATIONS AND RIOTS AGAINST
   THE NEW POOR LAW 1835-6
1 INCENDIARY FIRES 1843-4
1 INCENDIARY FIRES 1849-51

1 0 1 2 3 4 miles

56. TURNPIKES AND STAGECOACHES

Alistair Robertson

By an Act of Parliament of 1555 the maintenance of roads was placed in the hands of parishes. Each vestry was responsible for major and minor roads which passed through its territory. However, many parishes were unwilling or unable to maintain their roads in a reasonable state, and complaints were frequently made by local people and travellers. Many roads deteriorated as the amount of traffic and the size of vehicles increased, so it was proposed that the travellers themselves, as users, should contribute to the costs of maintainance and improvement. In 1663 the first turnpike authority was set up by Act of Parliament to maintain a stretch of the Great North Road. Under this and other early Acts, turnpikes were administered by local magistrates, but from 1706 separate Turnpike Trusts were regularly established.[1] Trustees were given the power to erect tollgates, collect tolls, appoint surveyors and undertake repairs. The first Turnpike Trust in Suffolk was authorised in 1711-12 and covered the road from Ipswich to Scole with some side-branches. Often these Acts were renewed or extended at a later date, so it is not easy to say when any length of road was actually 'turnpiked'. In one case, at least, the road from Bury to Thetford and Brandon, the Act was allowed to lapse and the work was never completed.

Under the Highways Act of 1862 the roads in the Liberty of St Edmund in west Suffolk were placed under the control of four Highway Boards: Blackbourne, Lavenham, Mildenhall and Wickhambrook. In the east of the county one board was set up for Hartismere; the remaining roads staying under parish control. However, these Boards were not popular and all, except Mildenhall, were dissolved and the roads returned to the parishes.[2] In 1889 the two newly established county councils took over responsibility for 188 miles of main roads and 232 bridges, and in 1930 the remaining country roads passed to the county authorities.[3]

As roads were slowly improved by Turnpike Trusts, a network of stagecoach services was built up over the whole country. These reached their peak in the 1830s and then declined rapidly with the spread of railways (Map 57). Alan Bates' list of coach services in 1836 shows that even a rural county like Suffolk had quite a comprehensive network. The 'expresses' were the Royal Mail coaches which were first introduced in 1784. The services from London to Norwich was started in 1785, and from London to Ipswich in 1791. By 1836, three Royal Mail routes crossed Suffolk: London to Norwich *via* Newmarket, Bury and Thetford; London to Norwich

Toll-house on the Sudbury to Bury turnpike at Sicklesmere.

via Ipswich and Scole; and London to Yarmouth *via* Ipswich and Lowestoft. Other services followed slightly different routes, and included two which went right through Norfolk to Holt and Wells. Complementing these services were cross-country and local coaches.

The coming of the railways swept away the stagecoach, leaving the private carriage and the carrier's cart as the main users of roads in rural areas. However, in the early years of the 20th century it was the railway companies who first saw the advantages of using the motor-bus—as a feeder service. The Great Eastern Railway, following in the steps of the Great Western Railway, started a service from Lowestoft to Kessingland and Southwold in 1904. The following year saw the introduction of further services in the Lowestoft and Ipswich areas. In 1908-9 a short-lived service ran in the Bury St Edmunds area. Most of these routes passed out of railway hands and eventually became part of the Eastern Counties Omnibus network.

Further details on p.210

Note: the map opposite is based on the road network shown on C. & J. Greenwood's *Map of the County of Suffolk* (London, 1825). Patrick Taylor supplied additional information on toll-houses.

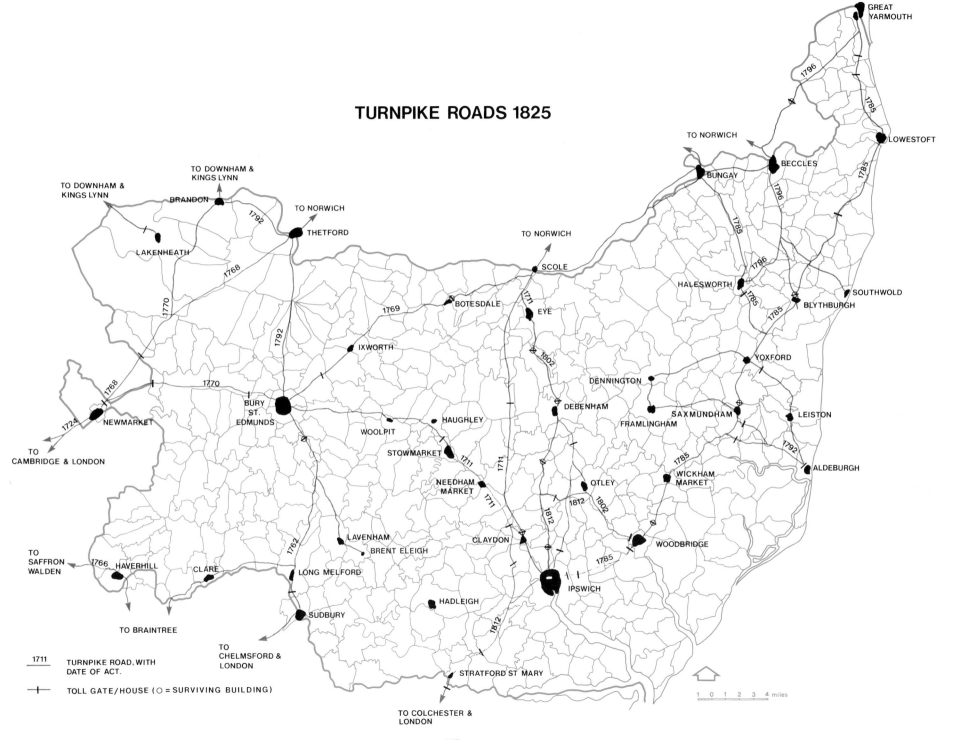

TURNPIKE ROADS 1825

TO DOWNHAM &
KINGS LYNN

TO DOWNHAM &
KINGS LYNN

BRANDON

1792

TO NORWICH

THETFORD

LAKENHEATH

1768

1770

1792

TO NORWICH

SCOLE

TO NORWICH

1768

1770

1769

BOTESDALE

1771

EYE

IXWORTH

1724

NEWMARKET

BURY
ST.
EDMUNDS

WOOLPIT

HAUGHLEY

1802

DEBENHAM

DENNINGTON

SAXMUNDHAM

FRAMLINGHAM

TO
CAMBRIDGE & LONDON

STOWMARKET

1711

OTLEY

WICKHAM
MARKET

1785

TO
SAFFRON
WALDEN

1766

HAVERHILL

CLARE

1762

NEEDHAM
MARKET

1711

LAVENHAM

BRENT ELEIGH

CLAYDON

1812

1802

WOODBRIDGE

LONG MELFORD

1785

TO BRAINTREE

HADLEIGH

IPSWICH

SUDBURY

1812

TO
CHELMSFORD &
LONDON

GREAT
YARMOUTH

1796

1785

LOWESTOFT

TO NORWICH

BECCLES

BUNGAY

1785

1796

HALESWORTH

1785

SOUTHWOLD

BLYTHBURGH

1785

YOXFORD

LEISTON

1792

ALDEBURGH

1711 ___ TURNPIKE ROAD, WITH
DATE OF ACT.

—|— TOLL GATE/HOUSE (O = SURVIVING BUILDING)

STRATFORD ST MARY

1 0 1 2 3 4 miles

TO COLCHESTER &
LONDON

57. RAILWAYS

Alistair Robertson

Not surprisingly, the railways came late to the agricultural county of Suffolk. It was twenty years after the opening of the Stockton and Darlington Railway in 1825 that a steam locomotive first crossed Suffolk soil. In 1836 the Grand Eastern Counties Railway was formed to link London with Norwich and Yarmouth *via* Colchester. Seven years later, the Eastern Counties Railway (no longer Grand) reached Colchester and there stopped. So Norfolk and Suffolk had to build their own lines, and the first to open was the Yarmouth and Norwich Railway in 1844. When it was decided to extend that line to get access to London, the company, instead of looking to the ECR at Colchester, turned to the Northern and Eastern Railway which was working towards Cambridge. The two companies agreed to meet at Brandon, and in 1845 it was at last possible to travel by train from the capital to Norwich and Yarmouth. Thus, the first two places in Suffolk to be served by railway were Brandon and Lakenheath.

Under the leadership of J. C. Cobbold of Ipswich, the Eastern Union Railway was formed in 1844 to extend the ECR from Colchester. It was opened to Ipswich in June 1846, and to Bury St Edmunds in December of that year. The main line was further extended from Haughley Junction to Norwich in November 1849. The Ipswich architect Frederick Barnes produced some fine stations and bridges for the EUR, and the Bury terminus was designed by Sancton Wood. The original Ipswich terminus was south of Stoke Hill, and so a tunnel had to be bored when the line was extended. The present station at Ipswich was opened in 1860 and enlarged in 1883.

A railway reached Newmarket from Great Chesterford in January 1848, but the company was soon in difficulty and closed down for two months in 1850. In October 1851, the line was extended to Cambridge, and the original line to Great Chesterford closed. The link between Bury and Newmarket was opened in April 1854, allowing traffic to pass from Ipswich to Cambridge, and on to the Midlands and North. The present through-route to Ely was opened in 1879, and a new station built at Newmarket in 1902.

Lowestoft was connected to the Norwich-Yarmouth line at Reedham in May 1847, and a branch from Haddiscoe to Beccles and Halesworth opened in December 1854. This line became part of the East Suffolk Railway which opened in June 1859, connecting Ipswich with Lowestoft and Yarmouth.

In 1862 most of the companies in East Anglia were amalgamated to form the Great Eastern Railway, but the Colne Valley and Southwold Railways were excluded. The latter was the only narrow-guage line (3 ft) in East Anglia, and had been opened in 1879. In 1922 the GER, together with the CVR and Mid-Suffolk Light Railway, became part of the London and North Eastern Railway, and in 1948 they were absorbed into British Railways.

The old companies were quite prepared to close stations and lines if they were unprofitable. It was, however, the coming of the motor-bus, car and lorry which led to permanent decline. Branch lines with no through services were the first to lose their trains in the early 1930s. More closure would probably have followed, had it not been for World War II which gave a respite until the early 1950s. In 1959 the main line between Beccles and Yarmouth Southtown was abandoned because of the cost of maintaining bridges. Following the Beeching Report of 1963 a whole series of branch lines was closed (see list on p. 210).[1]

By 1963 steam locomotives had been replaced by diesel locomotives and multiple-units. In the late 1960s paytrains with conductor-guards were introduced, and many stations became unmanned halts. However, stations have been re-opened as halts at Needham Market in 1971 and at Melton in 1984. In 1985 electrification reached Ipswich, and was extended to Norwich in 1987. Container trains or 'Freightliners' regularly connect the ports of Harwich, Ipswich and Felixstowe with London and the North of England. A link from Trimley to a new container terminal in Felixstowe Docks opened in 1986, and was the first new line in Suffolk for over 80 years.

When Parkeston Quay at Harwich was opened in 1882, the GER introduced 'The North Country Continental' through-train to the North of England *via* Ipswich, Bury, Ely and March. This continued under BR and later became 'The European'. In 1994, as part of the preparations for privatisation, the train was cut back to Peterborough. Three years later, with the introduction of Stena Line's High-Speed Sea Service between Harwich and the Hook of Holland, the service was replaced by a Harwich-Cambridge run.[2]

In 1997 British Railways was privatised. Railtrack became responsible for track, stations and signalling, while passenger services provided by train-operating companies under franchise. Anglia Railways provide the Inter City service between Norwich and London *via* Diss, Stowmarket, Ipswich and Colchester, together with most of the local services in East Anglia. Central Trains provide the service between Norwich and Ely (and onward to the Midlands and North), which calls at Brandon and Lakenheath. Great Eastern Railway also runs trains between Ipswich and London, and on the Sudbury branch. Freight services are provided by companies such as English, Welsh and Scottish Railway, Freightliner and Rail Freight Distribution.

Further details on p.210

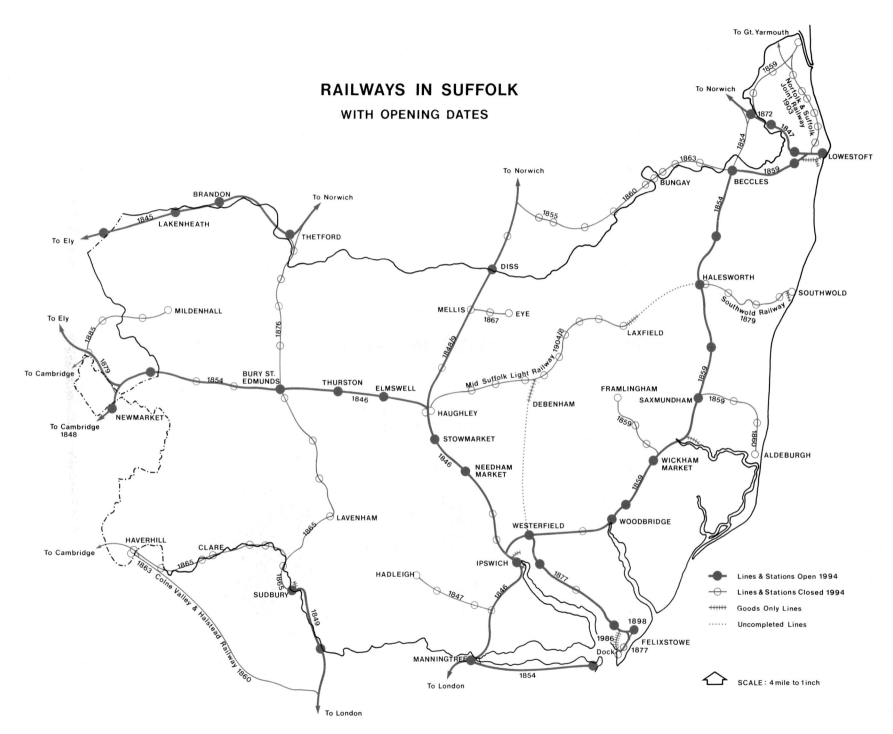

RAILWAYS IN SUFFOLK

WITH OPENING DATES

To Gt. Yarmouth

To Norwich

1859

Norfolk & Suffolk Joint Railway

1872

1847

LOWESTOFT

1854

1859

1863

BUNGAY

BECCLES

1860

1854

To Norwich

1855

DISS

HALESWORTH

SOUTHWOLD

Southwold Railway 1879

BRANDON

1845

LAKENHEATH

To Ely

THETFORD

To Norwich

MELLIS

EYE

1867

LAXFIELD

MILDENHALL

To Ely

1885

1876

1848/9

Mid Suffolk Light Railway 1904/8

1859

To Cambridge

1879

BURY ST. EDMUNDS

1854

THURSTON

ELMSWELL

1846

HAUGHLEY

DEBENHAM

FRAMLINGHAM

SAXMUNDHAM

1859

1859

To Cambridge 1848

NEWMARKET

STOWMARKET

1846

NEEDHAM MARKET

WICKHAM MARKET

1859

ALDEBURGH

1860

LAVENHAM

1865

WESTERFIELD

WOODBRIDGE

To Cambridge

HAVERHILL

CLARE

1865

1863 Colne Valley & Halstead Railway 1860

1865

IPSWICH

1877

HADLEIGH

1847

1846

SUDBURY

1849

1898

1986

FELIXSTOWE

Dock

1877

MANNINGTREE

To London

1854

To London

● Lines & Stations Open 1994

○ Lines & Stations Closed 1994

⊬⊬⊬⊬ Goods Only Lines

········ Uncompleted Lines

SCALE : 4 mile to 1 inch

129

58. RIVERS AND NAVIGATIONS

Alistair Robertson

The geography of East Anglia, together with its reliance on agriculture, led to the improvement of natural waterways which were then known as 'navigations', rather than to the creation of completely artificial canals. The rivers flowing westwards, in spite of their use for drainage and reclamation, had always been navigable and led across the Fens to the Great Ouse and Wash. The rivers flowing eastwards into the North Sea tend to have deep estuaries, and therefore provide ready-made highways along which quays or 'hithes' were built. To allow larger vessels to reach further inland, rivers had to be deepened and widened, and the flow of water controlled by locks or staunches. However, medieval bridges at the lowest crossing points of rivers were often a hindrance to navigation, and limited the size of vessels. Some, as at Blythburgh, were rebuilt by navigation companies, but many remained obstacles for years. For instance, the bridge at Beccles was not rebuilt until 1884. The Waveney and Blyth navigations were used by sailing wherries, but the others had tow-paths for horses to draw barges—until, that is, the advent of steam-powered barges or tugs. The use of waterways declined with the coming of the railways, and was virtually extinguished in the early 20th century when motor lorries were introduced and the surfaces of roads greatly improved.[1]

One of the earliest schemes to improve the rivers of East Anglia was put forward by Frances Mathew in the 17th century. His plan was to connect the Little Ouse with the Waveney and so provide a 'Mediterranean Passage' between Gt Yarmouth and King's Lynn. An Act of Parliament of 1670 'for making navigable the Rivers Brandon and Waveney' referred only to the stretches between Brandon and Thetford and between Beccles and Bungay, so the through-route was never achieved. The lower part of the Waveney (together with the Yare and Bure) was improved under an Act of 1722.

Under an Act of 1700 the Lark was made navigable from Mildenhall to Fornham St Martin. In the early 1890s the navigation was extended into the town of Bury St Edmunds, but soon fell into disuse. The Stour is easily the most famous of Suffolk's navigations because its locks and barges were frequently depicted in the drawings and paintings of John Constable; it had been created by an Act of 1705. After Southwold harbour had been improved, a project to make the Blyth navigable up to Halesworth was completed in 1761. The Ipswich and Stowmarket navigation was opened in 1793; it was leased by the Ipswich and Bury Railway Company in 1846, and returned to its trustees in 1888.

Because Yarmouth had a stranglehold on traffic using Breydon Water, the users of the Yare and Waveney began to look for an alternative outlet to the sea at Lowestoft. Proposals were made to deepen the Yare between Norwich and Reedham; to construct a canal from there to the Waveney at Haddiscoe; to enlarge Oulton Dyke; to provide a channel through Lake Lothing; to cut through the shingle bank to the sea; and finally to make a new harbour in Lowestoft. In spite of much opposition, an Act was passed in 1827 and work commenced soon afterwards. The new harbour was opened in 1831. The New Cut, as it was called, between Reedham and Lowestoft, was completed in 1832, and the whole system was opened on 30 September 1833. At about the same time, the Waveney was improved from Oulton Dyke to Beccles. Though Lowestoft became a thriving fishing port, the new waterway saw little commercial traffic.

Although the region's waterways are now controlled by the Anglia Water Authority, and many were abandoned in the early 20th century, certain lengths have remained navigable and today are used by leisure craft. In fact, because an increasing number of people wish to own or hire motor-launches and sailing craft, the Inland Waterways Association are advocating that some of the former waterways be restored and brought back into regular use. The River Stour Trust (founded in 1968) has restored the locks at Flatford, Dedham and Cornard, and the Quay Basin, Gasworks Cut and the Granary at Sudbury.

Further details on p.210

A billy-boy ketch on the Waveney near Oulton Dyke, on its way upriver to Beccles. Photograph by George Christopher Davies, 1884.

RIVERS AND NAVIGATIONS

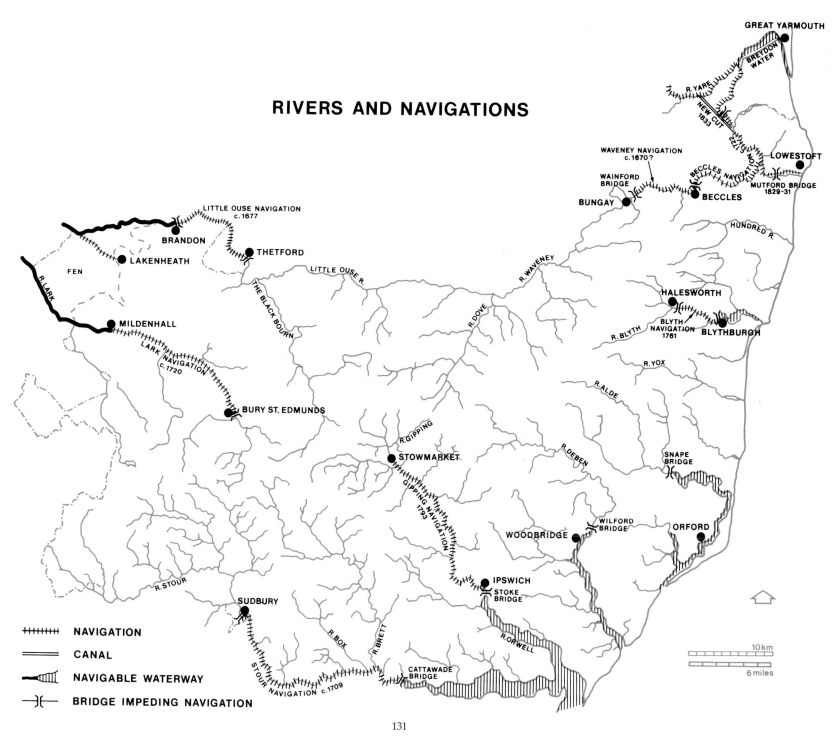

GREAT YARMOUTH

BREYDON WATER

R. YARE

NEW CUT 1833

LOWESTOFT

WAVENEY NAVIGATION c.1670?

WAINFORD BRIDGE

BECCLES NAVIGATION 1831

MUTFORD BRIDGE 1829-31

BUNGAY

BECCLES

HUNDRED R.

LITTLE OUSE NAVIGATION c.1677

BRANDON

THETFORD

LAKENHEATH

FEN

R. LARK

LITTLE OUSE R.

THE BLACK BOURN

R. WAVENEY

HALESWORTH

R. DOVE

R. BLYTH

BLYTH NAVIGATION 1761

BLYTHBURGH

R. YOX

MILDENHALL

LARK NAVIGATION c.1720

R. ALDE

BURY ST. EDMUNDS

R. GIPPING

SNAPE BRIDGE

STOWMARKET

R. DEBEN

GIPPING NAVIGATION 1793

WILFORD BRIDGE

WOODBRIDGE

ORFORD

R. STOUR

SUDBURY

IPSWICH

STOKE BRIDGE

R. BOX

R. BRETT

R. ORWELL

CATTAWADE BRIDGE

STOUR NAVIGATION c.1709

┼┼┼┼┼┼ NAVIGATION

═══════ CANAL

▬▬◤ NAVIGABLE WATERWAY

┤├ BRIDGE IMPEDING NAVIGATION

10 km

6 miles

131

59. NAVIGATION, PORTS AND TRADE

Robert Malster

Suffolk has a long seafaring tradition which goes back at least to the late 4th and early 5th centuries when pagan Anglo-Saxon immigrants from northern Europe invaded and carved out the kingdom of East Anglia. Several members of their royal family, the Wuffingas, were elaborately buried at Sutton Hoo, two of them with long wooden boats. In the early 7th century the Wuffingas encouraged the growth of Ipswich as a trading centre with links to the continent; it has remained a significant town and port ever since (see Maps 72 & 73). Subsequent fluctuations in its prosperity were closely linked with the state of the River Orwell, where mudbanks seriously restricted trade from time to time. Other ports such as Woodbridge, Orford, Aldeburgh and Southwold have also suffered from river approaches of varying difficulty, while Dunwich was destroyed by violent storms and coastal erosion. Offshore, the shipping channels were bounded by sandbanks which, while giving shelter from storms, also provided traps for the unwary and unlucky.[1] Not only was navigation difficult, particularly in bad weather and poor visibility, but the sands and the channels between them were (and are) constantly changing.[2] Lighthouses were established along the coast to aid navigation, the earliest being a pair of lights set up at Lowestoft by Trinity House in 1609.[3] These were crowded waters and wrecks were frequent. The most famous tragedy, described by Defoe, was in 1692 when a single storm led to the loss of more than 200 ships and 1000 men.[4]

The dominant trade, in coal from north-eastern England, led to an astonishing development of coasting in the 16th century. Shipping from Norfolk and Suffolk carried most of the coal supplied to London, as well as having a considerable share in the export trade from Newcastle to foreign markets.[5] In the 17th century Ipswich played a leading role in the coal trade and had a healthy reputation for shipbuilding, launching vessels

'so prodigious strong, that it was an ordinary thing for an Ipswich collier, if no disaster happen'd to him, to reign (as seamen call it) forty or fifty years and more'.[6] In Tudor times the merchants of Ipswich had sent ships to Iceland for dried cod and to Bordeaux for Gascon wine, but by the 18th and 19th centuries the trade of Ipswich, Woodbridge, Southwold and Lowestoft was predominantly coastwise. As the size of ships grew the smaller ports found themselves at a disadvantage. Increasingly their trade was confined to coasting vessels, which by the early 20th century were distributing cargoes imported into larger havens such as the Port of London.

Ipswich, like Woodbridge, Orford, Aldeburgh and Southwold, had the advantage of sheltered up-river quays, but the disadvantage of approaches that were both tortuous and liable to silting. Until the 1830s Lowestoft, without a river frontage, still managed to trade in small vessels that unloaded on the beach during the summer months; some of them were even built on the beach. In the 19th century other places, Dunwich and Sizewell among them, received their coal supplies in the same fashion.[7]

Grain, flour, malt and other agricultural produce, including cheese, were among the most common outward cargoes from Suffolk's ports. In the 19th century, bricks and agricultural implements also featured as exports. Inward cargoes included timber from the Baltic, raw materials for local industries such as pig-iron from South Wales, salt from Liverpool and, of course, coal.

At Ipswich moves to improve the navigation of the Orwell and to provide better facilities for shipping were under consideration in the later 18th century. However, it was not until 1805 that an Act was obtained to

improve the port, and not until 1837 that a further Act authorised the building of a wet dock of the kind first proposed 40 years earlier. In 1842 the opening of the dock, then the largest in Britain, if not in the world, equipped the town to meet the challenges of the Victorian era.[8] Seven years later, no fewer than 1312 coasting vessels of 97,350 tons were recorded inwards and 718 totalling 38,320 tons outwards (the remainder left in ballast, that is, without cargo).

Lowestoft gained a harbour in the 1830s when a scheme was implemented for bringing sea-going vessels to Norwich by a ship canal and river navigation. The project failed and the harbour fell into disuse until it was acquired by Samuel Morton Peto, the railway entrepreneur, who added an outer harbour and connected the port to the railway system. A steamer service to Denmark run by one of Peto's companies flourished in the short term; Danish cattle were landed at Lowestoft and sent off to Smithfield Market by rail. The long-term role of Lowestoft, however, was as a fishing port rather than a trading centre.[9] Other dock schemes were proposed in the River Ore in 1814[10] and at Felixstowe in the 1880s. The former did not materialise and the latter failed to meet the hopes of its promoter, George Tomline.[11]

In the 20th century Southwold, Aldeburgh and Woodbridge have ceased to be trading ports, but Ipswich continues and has shipping links to various parts of the world. Since 1960 Felixstowe has blossomed in a way that Tomline could hardly have foreseen, and is now the country's foremost container port.

Further details on p.211

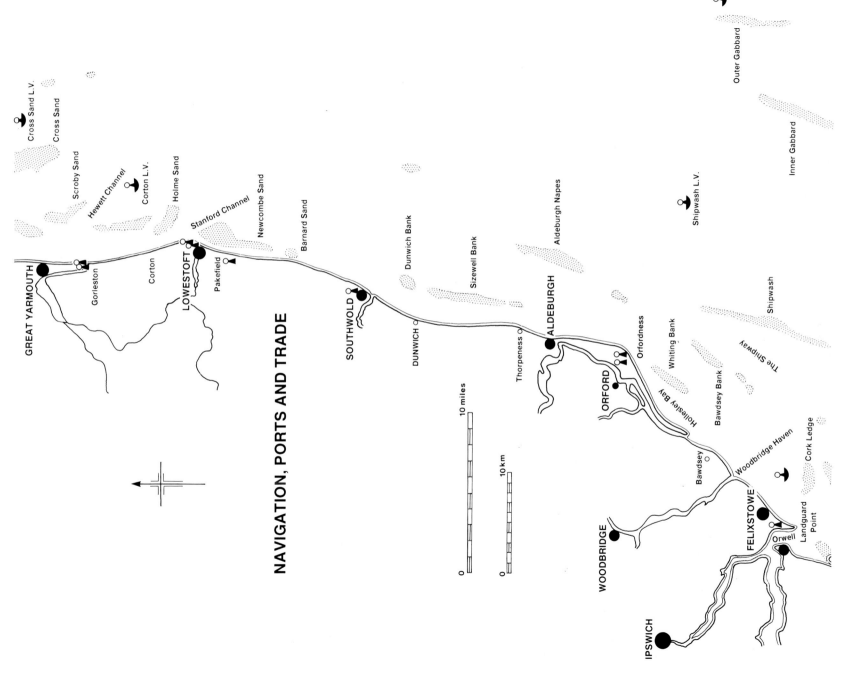

NAVIGATION, PORTS AND TRADE

Cross Sand L.V.

Cross Sand

Scroby Sand

Hewett Channel

Corton L.V.

Holme Sand

Stanford Channel

Newcombe Sand

Barnard Sand

Dunwich Bank

Sizewell Bank

Aldeburgh Napes

Shipwash L.V.

Inner Gabbard

Outer Gabbard

GREAT YARMOUTH

Gorleston

Corton

LOWESTOFT

Pakefield

SOUTHWOLD

DUNWICH

Thorpeness

ALDEBURGH

Orfordness

Whiting Bank

Shipwash

The Shipway

ORFORD

Hollesley Bay

Bawdsey Bank

Bawdsey

Woodbridge Haven

Cork Ledge

WOODBRIDGE

FELIXSTOWE

Landguard Point

Orwell

IPSWICH

10 miles

10 km

0

0

60. CHANGING AGRICULTURE IN HIGH SUFFOLK, 1650-1850 — John Theobald

Although intensively arable today, High Suffolk was a pastoral region in the 17th and 18th centuries. Within it, Arthur Young in the 1780s delineated a district which he called 'the great dairying region' of the county, to which one could add the Elmhams and Ilketshalls in the east and a cluster of parishes around Walsham-le-Willows to the west (Map A).[1] Together these parishes cover the north-eastern part of Suffolk's central boulder-clay plateau.

Because of low corn prices and the absence of effective drainage, much of the enclosed heavy clay lands of England were under grass between 1650 and 1750. On these soils dairy farming seemed a sounder option: cheese and butter paid better than corn, and less labour was needed. In High Suffolk some holdings were completely devoted to pasture, such as the Chevallier farms at Aspall and Bedingfield, and Hill Farm in Cotton, during the 1730s.[2] However, more common was a mixed system of 'plough and pail', with the second as the more important. Typically, farmers had between 15-30 per cent of their land under the plough. Examples include the Grimston estate at Thorndon and Rishangles c.1660, the Heveningham Hall estate c.1700, and Ulveston Hall, Debenham, in 1723 (Map B).[3] Most farmers had between fourteen and sixteen cows for each hundred acres, and the native breed was the polled Suffolk Dun.[4]

The second half of the 18th century saw gradual rises in population, grain prices and land rents, which encouraged farmers to convert some of their grass into arable. In the 1780s Young acknowledged that many farms had one-third in tilth, though holdings on valley soils, as at Stoke Ash and Finningham, had a higher proportion. He believed that farmers were increasingly turning to arable so that they could meet increased rents.[5] By the final years of the century many parishes in the region were half arable and half grass. Examples of such 50:50 ratios include Saxtead in 1785, Mickfield in 1795, Fressingfield in 1797 and Mendlesham in 1801.[6] Individual farms include Towranna Farm in Huntingfield, Home Farm in Crowfield and Ulveston Hall in Debenham (Map C).[7] The total shift to arable in the second half of the century was around 25 per cent. However, this move did not signal a fundamental change in the farming economy. Much of the increased arable acreage was sown with fodder crops such as turnips, cabbages, clovers and pulses. These not only helped to maintain the dairy, but also boosted the numbers of pigs and horses.

The gradualness of this process was shattered by the Napoleonic Wars. Dramatic surges in the price of corn between 1800 and 1812 provided an irresistible temptation for tenants and landlords to plough up old grassland. Just a cursory glance at contemporary farm leases, for example on the Tollemache and Henniker estates, will show the extent of this 'rush for corn'. The 'mischievous variations' in grain prices were caused by increasing demand, a succession of bad harvests and the cutting off of European imports during the war. By 1815 most holdings had two-thirds of their land under the plough. The shift to arable since the turn of the century was therefore between 15 and 20 per cent. For example, the proportion of arable land at Mickfield had risen from 49 per cent in 1795 to 65 per cent in 1813.[8]

This more rapid conversion to arable had a significant impact on the economy of the region. Between the mid 1790s, when parishes like Crowfield were described as still keeping 'many cows', and 1804, the number of dairy cattle was considerably reduced. In the area around Debenham and Earl Soham, for example, it was believed that the number of cows had gone down by about one thousand.[9] An analysis of probate inventories suggests that stocking densities fell from sixteen dairy cows per hundred acres in the 1780s to ten in 1803. This process continued so that by 1819 many of the region's farms had 'entirely declined' their dairy herds. Farmers who wanted to abandon dairying could sell their stock *en masse* at Michaelmas sales. The local press contained five examples of this between 1814 and 1819, including Hestley Hall in Thorndon, and Denham College Farm and Cousens Farm in Mickfield.[10] Furthermore the post-war depression between 1819 and 1823 did not tempt farmers to revert to dairying.[11] By the early 1820s the region's economy had been fundamentally and irrevocably altered.

From tithe apportionments of around 1840, it can be seen that land-use in this region had been reversed since the mid-17th century: the amount of pasture on most holdings, instead of being 70-85 per cent of the total, was now only 15-30 per cent (Map D).[12] The new maxim in stock management was 'cows, bullocks and sheep—some of each and too many of neither'. The tilling of the heavy clays had become easier and more profitable, mainly because of improvements in drainage, the making of better implements and the availability of manure from stock increasingly fed in yards and stalls. The new system of relating crops and animals came to be known as 'High Farming'.

Further details on p.211

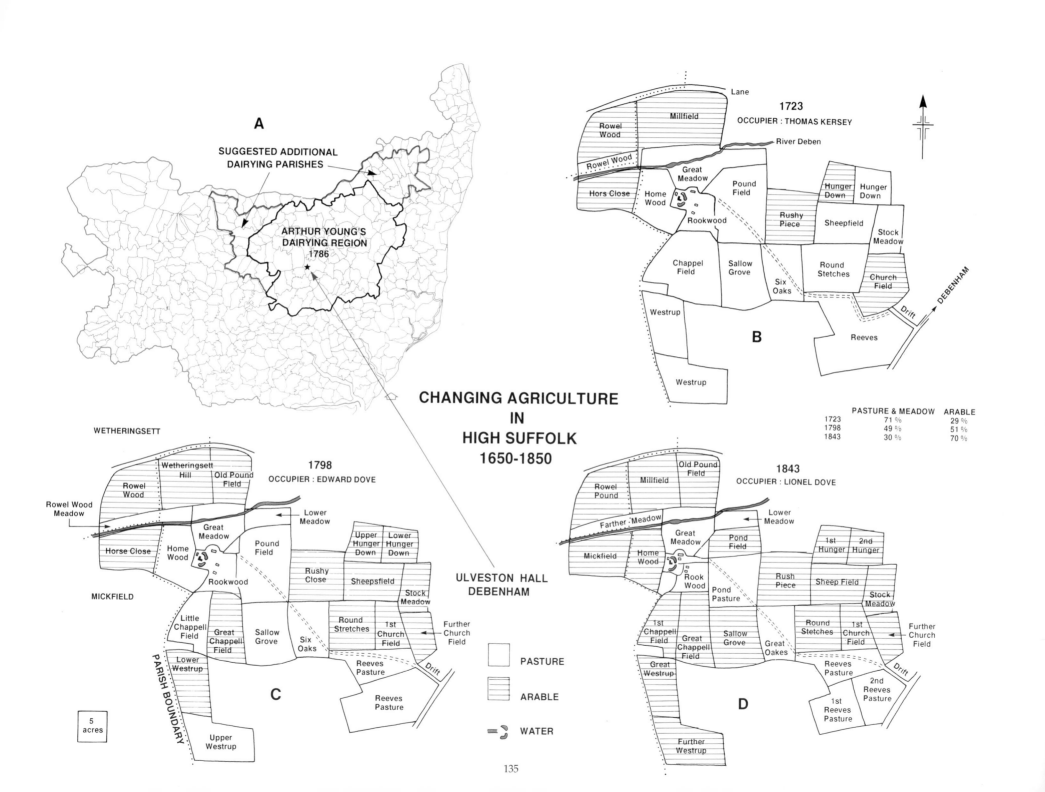

A

SUGGESTED ADDITIONAL
DAIRYING PARISHES

ARTHUR YOUNG'S
DAIRYING REGION
1786

1723
OCCUPIER : THOMAS KERSEY

Lane

Rowel
Wood

Millfield

River Deben

Rowel Wood

Great
Meadow

Hors Close

Home
Wood

Pound
Field

Hunger
Down

Hunger
Down

Rookwood

Rushy
Piece

Sheepfield

Stock
Meadow

Chappel
Field

Sallow
Grove

Round
Stetches

Church
Field

Six
Oaks

DEBENHAM

Westrup

Reeves

Drift

Westrup

B

CHANGING AGRICULTURE
IN
HIGH SUFFOLK
1650-1850

	PASTURE & MEADOW	ARABLE
1723	71 %	29 %
1798	49 %	51 %
1843	30 %	70 %

WETHERINGSETT

1798
OCCUPIER : EDWARD DOVE

Wetheringsett
Hill

Old Pound
Field

Rowel
Wood

Rowel Wood
Meadow

Lower
Meadow

Great
Meadow

Home
Wood

Pound
Field

Upper
Hunger
Down

Lower
Hunger
Down

Horse Close

Rookwood

Rushy
Close

Sheepsfield

Stock
Meadow

MICKFIELD

Little
Chappell
Field

Great
Chappell
Field

Sallow
Grove

Six
Oaks

Round
Stretches

1st
Church
Field

Further
Church
Field

Lower
Westrup

Reeves
Pasture

Drift

PARISH BOUNDARY

C

Upper
Westrup

Reeves
Pasture

5
acres

ULVESTON HALL
DEBENHAM

1843
OCCUPIER : LIONEL DOVE

Old Pound
Field

Rowel
Pound

Millfield

Farther Meadow

Lower
Meadow

Mickfield

Great
Meadow

Pond
Field

1st
Hunger

2nd
Hunger

Rook
Wood

Pond
Pasture

Rush
Piece

Sheep Field

Stock
Meadow

1st
Chappell
Field

Great
Chappell
Field

Sallow
Grove

Great
Oakes

Round
Stetches

1st
Church
Field

Further
Church
Field

Reeves
Pasture

Drift

Great
Westrup

2nd
Reeves
Pasture

1st
Reeves
Pasture

Further
Westrup

D

PASTURE

ARABLE

WATER

135

61. AGRICULTURE IN 1854

David Dymond*

Though at times afflicted by depression, farming has always been the basis of Suffolk's economy. Furthermore, local landowners and farmers have for centuries been notably willing to experiment with new crops, breeds and techniques. For example, turnips were being grown as a tithable field-crop in the Framlingham area by the early 1620s[1], and writers admired the highly productive dairy cows of High Suffolk from the 16th century onwards.[2] However, the study of local farming remains partial and impressionistic until the later 18th century when Arthur Young, himself a Suffolk squire and farmer, wrote a series of important articles and books; indeed it is not until the 19th century that the first broadly reliable statistics of farming become available.

The maps opposite are based on the first full-scale statistics of land-use, crops and animals, which were collected voluntarily in 1854.[3] In that year the Crimean War began, and agriculture was entering a 'Golden Age' which lasted for about 20 years. All those who occupied more than two acres were asked to make a return to a special Statistical Committee appointed in each Poor Law Union. Unfortunately the individual and parochial returns do not survive, but summaries for eighteen unions, wholly or partly in Suffolk, were published in 1855. Phillip Dodd wrote a useful article based on these returns in 1979, but the maps opposite are an attempt to present some of the statistics in a more detailed form.[4] (See Maps 5 and 54 for the names and boundaries of soil-regions and Unions, and Map 46 for enclosures.)

It has to be conceded that the returns are not wholly consistent. Sir John Walsham who supervised the survey issued 11,520 forms: 8,087 were filled in, and another 1,714 were completed by local enumerators, but 1,719 were returned blank. Nearly 1,600 of the refusals came from four unions—Mildenhall, Thingoe, Cosford

and Samford—which form a continuous strip across the county from north-west to south. Sir John was 'baffled by the hostility which he encountered' here, from landowners as well as farmers, especially as the east had responded so well.[5] To some extent the deficiencies were made up from other sources, but the livestock returns of Samford are certainly an underestimate, and all the figures for Thingoe must be treated with suspicion. In general, however, Dodd declared the returns of 1854 to be 'surprisingly good'.

The map showing the percentage of arable land is the most significant. The main concentration of arable farming (over 50% ploughed) was right across the centre of the county from south-west to east; the two unions of Cosford and Hoxne were over 70% arable. In about 70 years since Arthur Young's day, the farming economy of central or High Suffolk had been transformed (see Map 60). Then, it was noted for an intricate form of mixed farming, 'plough and pail', in which the most important single element was dairying,[6] but the high prices of grain during the Napoleonic Wares induced many farmers to plough up their pastures and to concentrate particularly on wheat and barley. Hundreds of tithe maps and apportionments show that this process of 'arabilisation' was well advanced by 1840. The heavy land was being made productive by widespread draining (pipe-drains were replacing the old bush-drains), by careful rotation, generous manuring and the use of large numbers of drills, hoes and other machines drawn by that powerful work-horse, the Suffolk Punch.[7] The figures for Thingoe in 1854 are certainly too low, and possibly for Mildenhall also; Thetford union is probably more typical of the Breckland as a whole (30-40%). On average 65% of the county was being ploughed in 1854.

The second map shows that most of the surviving 'permanent pasture' was in the centre-north and east of

Suffolk. The largest percentage was in Wangford: even here, permanent grass was below 25% of the total (about 26% if we include irrigated meadows not shown on this map). The Breckland and Sandlings are not prominent, partly because of under-recording; both areas also had considerable acreages of 'sheep walk' not illustrated here (10,500 acres in Mildenhall union, and 7,500 in Woodbridge union).

The third and fourth maps show the distribution of animals. The main concentration of cattle was from Sudbury and the Stour valley across to the north-eastern coast, with the highest counts in Hartismere, Hoxne and Mutford-cum-Lothingland; again the figures for Samford and Thingoe are suspect. Out of a total of 46,000 beasts, only 17,000 were dairy cows surviving from the old system: the rest were fat or 'store' cattle which farmers could keep because of the increased cultivation of green and root crops such as beans, clover and mangolds. As might be expected, the main concentrations of the county's 406,000 sheep were on the lighter soils of the north-west and south-east. The returns for Mildenhall, Thingoe and Samford unions are surely too low; Cosford may be in this category too. Again it should be noted that on the heavier land plenty of sheep were supported by fodder crops, in spite of the ploughing of so many old pastures.

Further details on p.211

Further details on p.211

* The statistics were mapped by Hilary Todd.

AGRICULTURE 1854

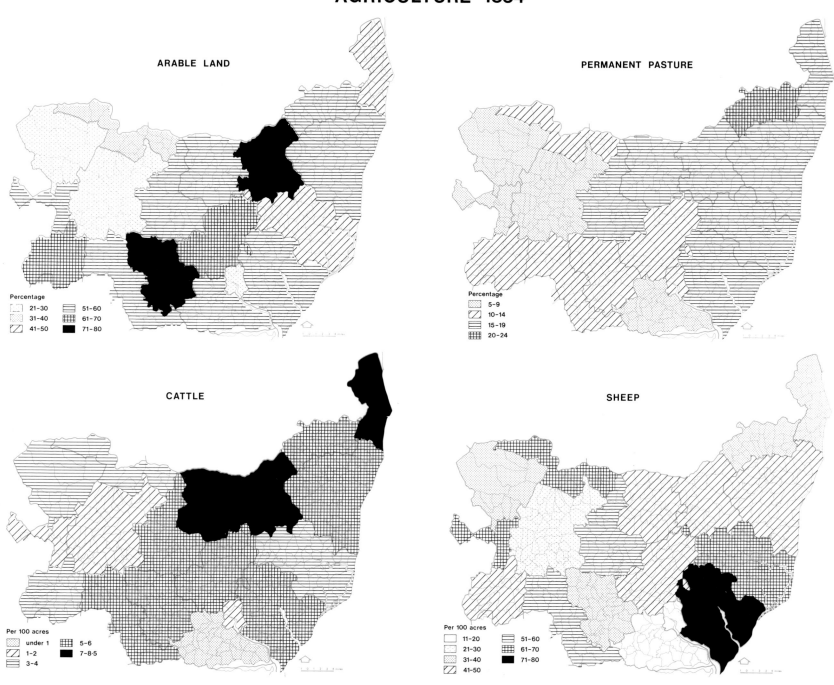

ARABLE LAND

Percentage
- 21-30
- 31-40
- 41-50
- 51-60
- 61-70
- 71-80

PERMANENT PASTURE

Percentage
- 5-9
- 10-14
- 15-19
- 20-24

CATTLE

Per 100 acres
- under 1
- 1-2
- 3-4
- 5-6
- 7-8·5

SHEEP

Per 100 acres
- 11-20
- 21-30
- 31-40
- 41-50
- 51-60
- 61-70
- 71-80

137

62. THE HERRING FISHERY

Robert Malster

Suffolk fishermen set off from the beach in search of herring in the Middle Ages, as is shown by the contents of wills such as that made by Robert Gylbanke the elder of Lowestoft in 1545. Besides leaving to his son Thomas 'my fish house and salt house beneath the cliff, with the billet and salt that is there' he bequeathed to him 'my boat called the Anthonie with all her tackle that belongeth to her, as anchors, cables, warples, nets both herring and mackerel, with waroppes and boye barrells and all manner of things'. The claim of the corporation of Great Yarmouth to control landings of herring at Lowestoft led to a long-lasting dispute between the men of Lowestoft and their neighbours to the north.[1]

In the mid-18th century Southwold became the base of the Society of the Free British Fishery, a short-lived attempt to challenge Dutch supremacy in the deep-sea herring fishery. For the most part Suffolk fishermen continued to go to sea in quite small boats launched off the beach. It was not until the 19th century that larger vessels were built and the herring trade grew strongly. The main stimuli were the spread of railways and an increasing demand for cheap food in the booming industrial towns of the midlands.[2]

As the fishing industry expanded, men were attracted not only from coastal villages but also from farming communities within reach of the main port, Lowestoft. After getting in the harvest, farmworkers sought work aboard the sailing drifters; their job was to turn the capstan which hauled the warp to which the fleet of nets was attached. 'The Home Fishing', the great East Anglian fishery that took place between September and December, coincided with a slack period on the farms. With the coming first of steam capstans in the 'luggers' and then of steam drifters many countrymen continued to serve in the boats as regular members of the crews.[3]

In the later part of the 19th century and the first half of the 20th, drifters from Lowestoft fished for herring and mackerel all around the British Isles. After the end of the home season, they fished from Newlyn (Cornwall) for mackerel and from Plymouth for herring; later in the year some boats went into the Irish Sea, fishing from Milford Haven, Dunmore East in Waterford Harbour, or Buncrana or Rathmullen in Lough Swilly. Those that did not take part in the spring fishing from their home port might fish from Stornoway on the Isle of Lewis, and then go on to Lerwick in the Shetlands for the summer season there. From Lerwick they went on to Aberdeen, Wick and Peterhead, then to North Shields, on to Scarborough or Grimsby, returning home in time to refit before the beginning of the Home Fishing in the autumn.[4]

For the Home Fishing from local ports the fishermen of East Anglia were joined by Scottish boats. Scotsmen began coming south towards the end of the 19th century in their sailing fifies and zulus, and the annual migration seems to have received a boost when the Scottish fleets switched from sail-power to steam and later to petrol and oil engines. With the Scottish fishermen there also came shore workers. These included the 'girls' who gutted the herring, a few of whom married Suffolk men and settled in the county.[5]

The peak of the East Anglian herring industry came in 1913, when 320 local drifters and 420 Scottish boats worked from Lowestoft and brought in nearly 535,000 crans of herring, but fishing virtually ceased during the First World War. When the work was resumed in the 1920s catches were lower, and they continued to decline until the industry came to an end in the 1960s.

Further details on p.212

Herring luggers leaving Lowestoft harbour in the late 19th century.

THE HERRING FISHERY

PORTS USED BY SUFFOLK HERRING FISHERMEN

Lerwick

Wick

Stornoway

Fraserburgh
Peterhead
Aberdeen

Caledonian Canal

North Shields

Scarborough

Grimsby

Great Yarmouth
Lowestoft

Buncrana

Dunmore East

Milford Haven

Padstow

Plymouth

Newlyn

100 miles

150 km

63. THE WOOLLEN CLOTH INDUSTRY

David Dymond*

To call Suffolk a merely agricultural county is to mis-read its history profoundly. Long before the Industrial Revolution of the 18th century, this county had developed a whole range of industries and crafts concerned mainly with the working of wood, metal, leather and textiles. The earliest established and longest lasting of these industries was the manufacture of woollen cloth. The hundreds of Babergh and Cosford were specialising in this trade by the end of the 13th century, while in the 1470s Suffolk produced more cloth than any other English county. The peak of production for these 'Old Draperies', which included broadcloth and kerseys,[1] came probably in the early 16th century. In the reign of Elizabeth, a far wider range of new, lighter and cheaper fabrics, the so-called 'New Draperies', was introduced by immigrants from the Low Countries and in turn reached a peak in the 17th century. These 'stuffs' as opposed to true 'cloths' were being woven, though on a diminishing scale, until the early 19th century.

The map opposite shows the number of 'clothiers' who, between about 1400 and 1700 left wills to be proved in the courts of the two Suffolk archdeacons.[2] Clothiers (or 'clothmakers', as they were also called) were the organisers and capitalists of the industry. They 'put out' work to a whole range of specialist workers who included wool-sorters, carders, spinners, weavers, dyers, fullers and cloth finishers. These employees lived in the same districts as the clothiers themselves, but could be as many as thirty miles away. The numbers of clothiers indicated on the map are, of course, no more than a sample because other clothiers, in general the more wealthy ones, left wills to be proved in the Consistory Court of the Bishop of Norwich and in the Prerogative Court of the Archbishop of Canterbury. The plotting of those missing persons is not likely to alter the general distribution, except for Monks Eleigh and Hadleigh. These two places were without doubt

involved with cloth-making, especially the major town of Hadleigh, but being ecclesiastical 'peculiars' most of their wills were proved in the court of the Dean of Bocking and unfortunately only a few have survived.[3]

The map shows a clear concentration of clothiers in the villages and small market towns of south-western Suffolk, from Clare in the west to East Bergholt in the east, and particularly in the rural hundreds of Babergh and Cosford.[4] Although Lavenham had an outstanding proportion of clothiers in 1522, when at the height of its prosperity,[5] the longer time-scale covered by probate indexes reveals that it was overshadowed by its near neighbour Glemsford and by East Bergholt. Another important point is that the distribution of clothiers was by no means exclusively rural: large numbers of them worked in the major towns of Ipswich and Bury St Edmunds. Indeed, it should never be forgotten that Bury was an industrial town of the first rank until the end of the 17th century. Finally, we see from the map that the industry spread geographically, particularly in its later phases, over the west, centre and north of the county. In the latter district it overlapped with another important textile industry which grew fast in the 17th century: the making of linen from the vegetable fibre of hemp (see Map 64). Equally striking is the almost entire absence of woollen clothiers from the eastern part of the county. Here too, textiles were certainly made but they were of the hempen variety—linen, sailcloth and sack-cloth.[6]

The probate indexes, which are the basis of this map, list a high proportion of clothiers at work in the 17th century. This reminds us that the Old Draperies, though under severe competition from the new fabrics, and suffering from recurrent slumps as in the 1620s, nevertheless took a long time to disappear. As late as 1676 Richard Blome talked of the 'decaying' (but not yet

dead) manufacture of broadcloth.[7] Indeed, while in decline, this industry seems to have spread itself thinner over a wider geographical area.

Another category of people is distinguished on the map by red symbols. These are 'baymakers' and 'saymakers' who were essentially similar in their organising role to the clothiers. In Suffolk bays and says[8] were undoubtedly the most important of the New Draperies, but their manufacture was geographically much more restricted than that of the older textiles. Most of the makers lived in the hundred of Babergh, with their largest concentration in the town of Sudbury. The earliest will in this category belongs to a baymaker of Stanstead who died in 1602.

Further details on p.212

Further details on p.212

* The figures on which the map is based were kindly supplied by Mrs Nesta Evans.

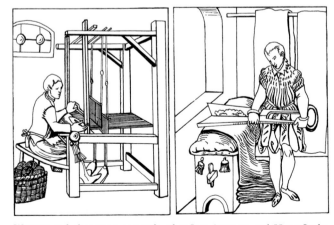

Weaver and shearman at work, after Jost Amman and Hans Sachs, *Book of Trades*, 1568. Note the padded bench on which the shearman delicately wields his heavy iron shears.

MAKERS OF WOOLLEN CLOTH
c. 1400 – 1700

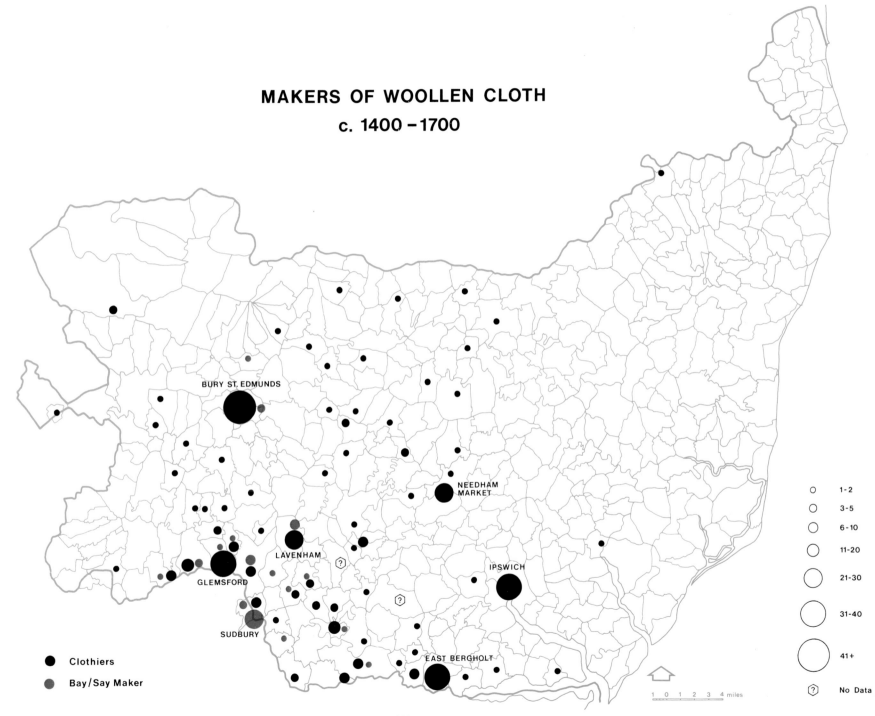

BURY ST. EDMUNDS

NEEDHAM MARKET

LAVENHAM

GLEMSFORD

IPSWICH

SUDBURY

EAST BERGHOLT

● Clothiers

● Bay/Say Maker

○ 1-2

○ 3-5

○ 6-10

○ 11-20

○ 21-30

○ 31-40

○ 41+

⬡ No Data

1 0 1 2 3 4 miles

64. THE LINEN INDUSTRY

Nesta Evans

The principal industrial areas of Suffolk were the south-west where woollen cloth was made, and the valleys of the Waveney and Little Ouse where linen was the chief product. The latter region extended some way on both sides of the two rivers, and was as important in south Norfolk as in north Suffolk. This can be clearly seen in a distribution map of Norfolk's linen weavers based on the same sources as for Suffolk.[1]

The linen weavers of Suffolk were concentrated in the area where more hemp was grown than anywhere else in the county. Arthur Young defined this district as lying between Eye in the west and Beccles in the east, and as being some ten miles in breadth.[2] In fact the cultivation of hemp spread further west into the valley of the Little Ouse and over most of eastern Suffolk. Proximity to its raw material probably encouraged the linen industry to grow during the 17th and 18th centuries, but cannot be the only reason. In all probability, weavers needed and used more hemp than could be grown locally, and therefore had to rely on imports from outside the region. In any case, the easy availability of raw materials is seldom the most important reason behind the development of any rural industry. The crucial factor here is probably demographic: that part of Suffolk where most linen weavers were to be found also had a large and growing population. The presence of many small farms in a weakly manorialized area not only supported an already dense population, but encouraged immigration as well. For an industry to grow, a workforce must be available, and the existence of work attracts yet more migrants. Linen weaving was labour intensive because it supplied much work for ancillary trades such as heckling, spinning and bleaching.[3] All these employ-ments combined well with part-time farming, while the cultivation of hemp fitted better with dairy farming which was already dominant in this district, than with arable.

Much evidence in wills, in tithe and estate maps and in manorial records supports the view that hemp was usually cultivated in small fields or enclosures. Arthur Young reached the same conclusion, saying 'it is very rare to see more than five or six acres [of hemp] in the occupation of any one man'.[4] Thus the growing and processing of hemp was often in the hands of small-holders and cottagers who were numerous in the linen-weaving region of Suffolk. Hemp grows well in river valleys, but it does not require the damp climate neces-sary for the successful cultivation of flax. Water was also needed for the retting or soaking of hemp so that the fibres could be peeled off the unwanted inner core of the stem. The use of running water for this purpose was usually prohibited because of the risk of pollution, but local people had no difficulty in digging suitable retting pits in the heavy clay soils of wood-pasture Suffolk, or in adapting earlier ponds and moats.

The map also indicates that linen weavers, although concentrated in north Suffolk, were also to be found scattered all over the county. As with many other rural manufacturers, their products were required every-where. The making of sailcloth can also be regarded as a branch of the linen industry. It flourished in and around Ipswich and Woodbridge from c.1575 until the middle of the 17th century when local ship-building went into decline. Bungay too was known for the pro-duction of sailcloth.

For most of its existence the Suffolk linen industry was predominantly rural, but in the 18th century it became more urban-based. The number of known weavers in towns increased, particularly in Beccles and Bungay, and in Diss just over the Norfolk border. This last town was an important linen market, and many of those who traded there must have been inhabitants of Suffolk; for this reason it appears on the map, as does East Harling,

the other principal market for linens in Norfolk.

The sources used to compile this map are listed in the notes. Over two-thirds of the known linen weavers were found in probate records.[5] In the 18th century the usefulness of wills and inventories declines, and few of the latter date from after 1750. Fortunately a new source becomes available from 1710 in the shape of the National Apprenticeship Registers.[6] They provided the names of a substantial number of linen weavers who were masters to young apprentices.

All sources have their defects and in this case the principal one is a bias towards the better-off; few jour-neymen or really poor weavers made wills, and it was those rich enough to employ others who registered apprentices. Only some 5% of the weavers were named in poor-law records, and almost all of those were mentioned after 1750. This is probably related to the decline of the linen industry in the later 18th century.

Further details on p.212

Stages in the production of hemp: breaking with a hinged bar and heckling with a rough iron comb, after C. Tomlinson, *The Useful Arts and Manufactures ... Textile Fabrics, c.*1850.

LINEN WEAVERS

E. Harling

Diss

Halesworth

Bury St. Edmunds

Woodbridge

- Below 5 weavers
- 6 – 10 "
- 11 – 20 "
- 21 – 30 "
- Linen market

1 0 1 2 3 4 miles

65. THE LEATHER INDUSTRY

Nesta Evans

Economic and local historians have written a considerable amount about the making of woollen textiles in East Anglia, but until recently have tended to overlook other important sources of employment and wealth. In Suffolk one of those 'forgotten' industries is the processing of hides and skins, and their conversion into leather goods of many kinds. The map opposite is an attempt to show the widespread extent of leather-working, and is based on probate records of local archdeaconries and to a lesser extent on marriage licence bonds.[1] No doubt the study of individual towns and villages will increase the number of known leather workers. For example, the parish registers of Halesworth from 1653 until the 1780s give occupations, including large numbers of men engaged in the leather industry.[2] However, most of them were not wealthy enough to leave wills, nor did they enter into marriage bonds.

Leather workers can be divided into two groups: those who prepared the raw materials such as tanners and curriers, and a larger group such as glovers, harness-makers (collar-makers) and shoemakers who manufactured goods from treated leather.[3] Not surprisingly, the two groups show a very similar distribution as they were closely reliant on each other. For the period from 1500 to about 1750, the numbers of each type of craftsman found in the two sources are as follows (again it should be stressed that the true numbers must be considerably higher):

Crafts preparing leather		Crafts using prepared leather	
Tanners	216	Cordwainers	318
Fellmongers	32	Glovers	173
Knackers	30	Shoemakers	144
Curriers	23	Collarmakers	59
Skinners	15	Saddlers	50
Leather dressers	6		

The map opposite shows the distribution of the *first* group only, that is those who prepared the leather.

The working of hides and skins was, on the whole, more urban-based than some other Suffolk industries. The principal reason for this may be that the skins of cattle, horses and other animals were most easily obtained in those places where large numbers of butchers and knackers congregated on market days. The dominance of butchers as holders of market stalls is noticeable in a number of towns such as Beccles and Halesworth.[4] Three towns stand out as particularly major centres of the industry: in descending order of importance, they

are Bury St Edmunds, Ipswich and Beccles. Tanners required water for their operations so it is not surprising that most of them lived in valleys. On the other hand, in spite of their concentration in towns, the preparation and working of leather were to be found in rural communities as well: they were widespread throughout the county, particularly in the clay lands of High Suffolk, where cattle rearing and dairying were a major feature of local farming. Not surprisingly they were less in evidence in the sheep-rearing districts of the Breckland and Sandlings.

Further details on p.212

The tannery of W. & A.J. Turner at Bures St Mary, *c.*1900.

CRAFTSMEN PREPARING LEATHER
c. 1500-1750

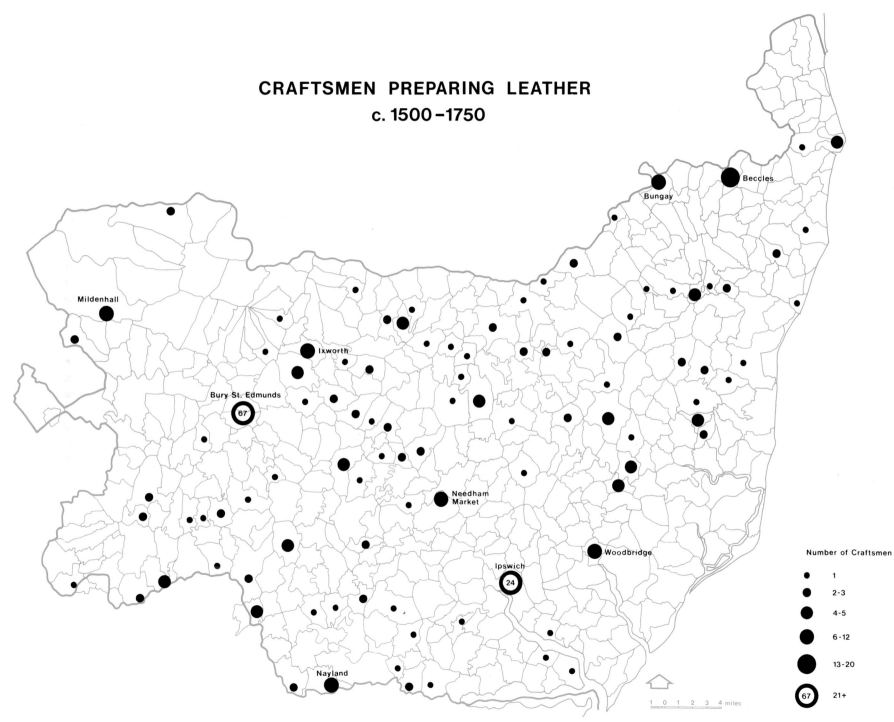

Mildenhall

Ixworth

Bury St. Edmunds 67

Beccles

Bungay

Needham Market

Woodbridge

Ipswich 24

Nayland

Number of Craftsmen

• 1

• 2-3

● 4-5

● 6-12

● 13-20

67 21+

1 0 1 2 3 4 miles

Charles Pankhurst

Kiln-fired bricks were made in England during the Roman occupation, and have been found on sites all over the country. In the 5th century AD when the Roman empire broke up, this widespread manufacture continued in parts of the continent but was abandoned in England. Therefore, any bricks used in Anglo-Saxon or Norman buildings were either reused from Roman sites or imported from the Low Countries.

The making of fired bricks began again in England in the 12th century, and first appeared in East Anglia which has little local stone suitable for building. The earliest surviving building using English bricks is probably the late-Norman aisled church of Polstead in Suffolk.[1]

The first medieval bricks were made in clamps close to the place where they were needed, probably by groups of itinerant brickmakers. Brickearth, which is a mixture of clay and sand, was dug from shallow pits, made malleable by treading and moulded into shape by hand. The 'green' bricks were partly dried in the air, and then stacked in heaps interspersed with fuel. After the heaps were covered in mud, the fuel was ignited and allowed to burn slowly for a week or more. The quality of the bricks produced by this method was variable, as the ones at the centre were fully burnt but the outer ones were still quite soft. Between the 16th and 18th centuries, large numbers of small brickworks were undoubtedly created all over the county to cater for local needs, because bricks were becoming cheaper and more fashionable, and were widely used in chimneys, in new facades and in the complete structure of an increasing number of domestic and agricultural buildings. The archaeological traces of medieval and early modern brickworks have sometimes been noted as clusters of pits or as mounds of fire-reddened clay and waste lumps of brick.[2]

By the 19th century, Suffolk bricks were mostly made in simple updraught kilns with open tops, which gave a good, uniformly fired product. At the bottom of the kiln was a fire-grate for burning the fuel, either coal or wood, and the air-dried bricks were stacked in the shaft above the fire-grate. If the brickearth contained iron oxide, the bricks emerrged with a red colour, but if it contained chalk they were a light buff colour, the so-called 'Suffolk whites'.[3] The only machinery used in most of the brickyards was a pugmill, driven by steam or turned by a horse, which mixed or churned clay, sand and water to the required consistency. The brickmaker threw the resultant mix or 'pug' into individual wooden moulds at a rate of about a thousand a day.

Brickyards were widely scattered, as can be seen in the map opposite which shows the situation in 1885. The small brickyards had a total output of about 100,000 bricks a year, and supplied purely local markets. The large brickyards had an output of several million bricks a year, and were close to a large town or had easy transport by road, rail or sea. Of about 250 sites identified in commercial directories between 1844 and 1937, more than seventy were working for more than twenty years, and twenty were working for over fifty years.

In the late 19th century, a tough shale clay which contained ten per cent of coal was found at Fletton near Peterborough. This material was easy to use in machinery, and the coal content burned in the kiln to give good uniform heating to all the bricks. Production of Fletton bricks began in 1881 using large Hoffman kilns which were economical on fuel. As a result the price of bricks fell from £1.10 per thousand in 1896 to 42p. per thousand in 1908. The wages of workers in the older brickyards were cut in an attempt to match the price of Flettons. However, after reaching a peak of 115 in 1885, the number of brickyards in Suffolk fell rapidly. Kilns were shut down during the First and Second World Wars because, in the final stages of firing, bricks became red-hot and the bright glow from the open tops of kilns was easily visible to enemy Zeppelins and aircraft. By 1994 Suffolk had only two brickyards still operating, at Aldeburgh and South Cove.

Further details on p.213

Bricks being made at Tuddenham St Martin, 1900

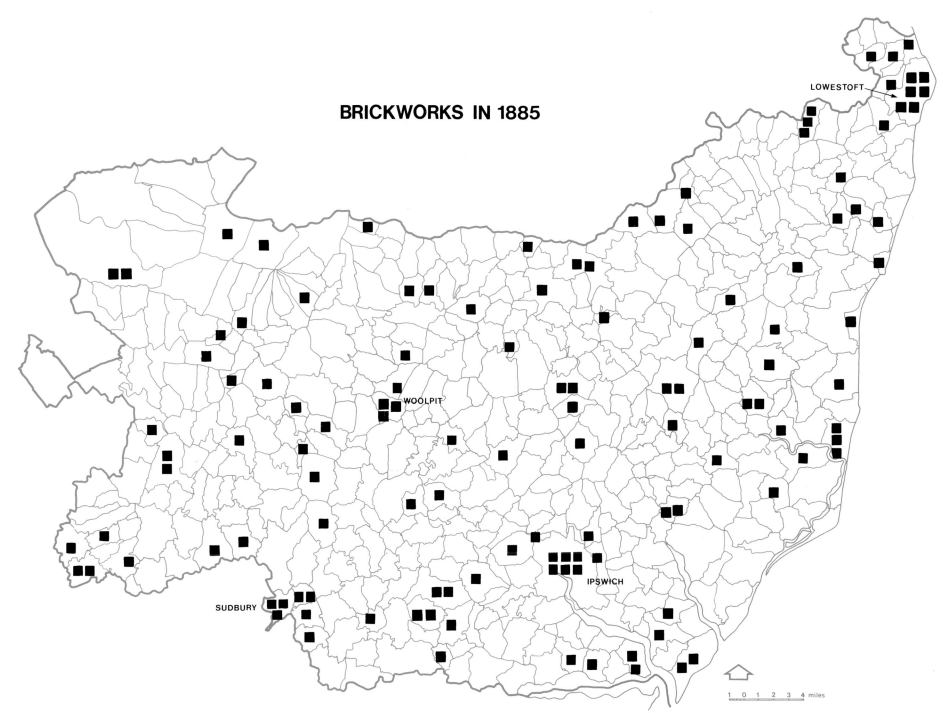

BRICKWORKS IN 1885

LOWESTOFT

WOOLPIT

IPSWICH

SUDBURY

1 0 1 2 3 4 miles

67. WINDMILLS AND WATERMILLS

Peter Dolman

In the early 19th century almost 500 windmills were at work in Suffolk, mostly grinding corn.[1] From then on their numbers declined, slowly at first but rapidly after 1900, in the face of competition from large steam-powered flour mills and smaller mills on farms driven by steam or internal combustion engines. Today just 20 windmills (remain four now in Norfolk due to boundary changes) and another 70 or so partially survive.

The earliest recorded windmill in Suffolk is generally held to be the one at Bury St Edmunds which so angered Abbot Samson in c.1191.[2] This was probably a *post* mill, the earliest type in Europe. By the late 13th century numerous documentary references suggest that such mills were commonplace.

The two other types of windmill found in Suffolk are the *tower* mill with its masonry tower, and the *smock* mill with its timber-framed tower.[3] The origin of the tower mill is not known but examples were recorded elsewhere as early as the 13th century.[4] In Suffolk they were really a product of the 19th century,[5] as only five or six stood in 1783.[6] Smock mills are thought to have been invented by the Dutch in the late 16th century; references to a 'Dutch windmill' at Lowestoft in the 1670s must indicate one of these.[7] However, the Dutch type differed in construction from the English, which seems to have become fashionable in the mid-18th century. In 1783 there were about 17, mostly used for drainage in the fens and broads, driving scoop-wheels rather than millstones.[8] The post mill was, and remained, the most common type, with about 200 standing in 1783.[9]

The 50 years after about 1780 saw a boom in the construction of windmills, some new, some rebuilt. The peak occurred in about 1840, by which time steam mills were already appearing.[10] New windmills were built after this date but the trend was ever downward.[11]

Watermills were much scarcer in Suffolk than windmills because of the lack of suitable rivers, with only about 100 standing in the 19th century. However, because they were larger structures than windmills, a higher proportion has survived. Today over 50 watermmills remain, of which about a third are complete with their machinery.

The Romans used water power[12] and it is possible that watermills were again being constructed from the 7th century at least. In 1086 Domesday Book recorded 178 mills in Suffolk-all watermills. This number may be misleadingly high, because a building with two or more sets of stones could have been counted as two or more mills. At this date all mills would have been for milling corn. With the rise of the cloth industry, water-powered fulling mills were built, sometimes on the sites of corn mills and sometimes next to them. By the 16th century the number of watermills had probably reached its peak, at about 200. Many sites were on little more than ditches, with water having to be impounded for a considerable period before accumulating sufficiently to work a wheel. The more marginal sites were abandoned until the early 19th century when numbers stabilized. When the cloth industry declined fulling mills disappeared, but in the early 19th century Suffolk could boast water-powered 'mills' for throwsting silk, paper-making, oil manufacture, spinning and possibly scutching flax, pumping water, grinding cement, and one for 'oil leather dressing, glue boiling and fellmongering' as well as for milling corn.[14]

Because of the relatively low fall on Suffolk's rivers, most mills had undershot or low-breastshot water-wheels. Some overshot and high-breastshot wheels were to be found, usually on smaller tributaries, but even at these a head of ten feet was the usual limit. In the late 19th century some larger mills replaced their wheels with more efficient water turbines. Suffolk has no record of 'horizontal' wheels such as those found elsewhere in the British Isles, but it is quite possible that the earliest mills used this kind of wheel, which required no gearing and so was easier to make.

Tide mills were found on the larger estuaries. One at Ipswich[15] and the well-known example at Woodbridge were true tide mills, relying totally on impounded salt water. Others at Ipswich, Stutton and Brantham were also supplied by freshwater streams or rivers.

Further details on p.213

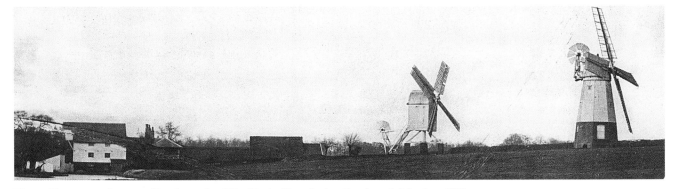

Watermill, open-trestle post mill and smock mill beside the River Lark at Fornham St Martin, c.1870.

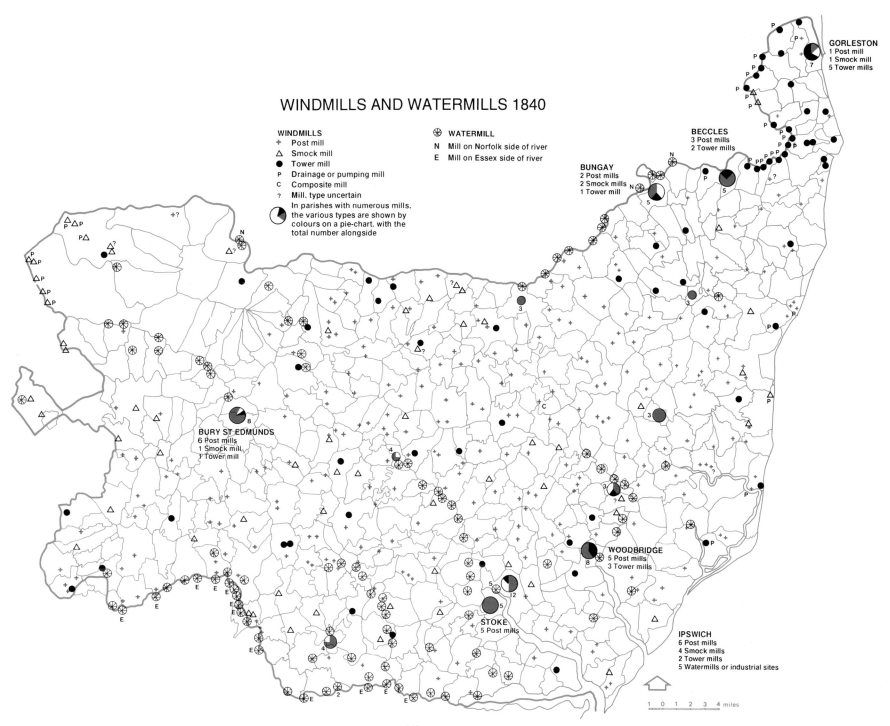

WINDMILLS AND WATERMILLS 1840

WINDMILLS
+   Post mill
△   Smock mill
●   Tower mill
P   Drainage or pumping mill
C   Composite mill
?   Mill, type uncertain

In parishes with numerous mills,
the various types are shown by
colours on a pie-chart, with the
total number alongside

⊛ **WATERMILL**
N   Mill on Norfolk side of river
E   Mill on Essex side of river

GORLESTON
1 Post mill
1 Smock mill
5 Tower mills

BECCLES
3 Post mills
2 Tower mills

BUNGAY
2 Post mills
2 Smock mills
1 Tower mill

BURY ST EDMUNDS
6 Post mills
1 Smock mill
1 Tower mill

WOODBRIDGE
5 Post mills
3 Tower mills

STOKE
5 Post mills

IPSWICH
6 Post mills
4 Smock mills
2 Tower mills
5 Watermills or industrial sites

1 0 1 2 3 4 miles

68. IRON FOUNDRIES, 1789-1900

Michael Lane

During the 18th and 19th centuries a total of 46 commercial iron foundries (the majority now extinct) are known to have been established in Suffolk. Most of them were inextricably connected with the needs of those making agricultural machinery.[1] Before the introduction of iron castings, the machine maker had relied almost entirely upon wood and wrought iron as his basic raw materials. Most metal-working was performed at the forge, but with the introduction of improved chill-cast ploughshares in the 1790s and the threshing machine and seed-drill in the early 1800s, the need for iron casting became imperative. But growth in demand was slow.

Between the end of the Napoleonic Wars and 1835, agriculture was not sufficiently stable to encourage large-scale investment in new or improved machinery. At the same time agricultural workers faced with major unemployment were often inclined to destroy any labour-saving devices (Map 55). The census of 1831 listed 676 men in Suffolk engaged in manufactures compared with 33,040 in agriculture. As late as 1844, White's *Directory* commented that 'the manufacturers of Suffolk are trivial compared with its agricultural importance'.

The two most important iron foundries in Suffolk are among the three oldest. Robert Ransome, a leading Quaker, established his foundry at Ipswich in 1789. Four years earlier he had been granted a patent for hardening the surface of ploughshares by wetting the sand-mould with salt water. In 1803 he obtained a further patent for inserting iron parts in the mould itself, at points where a particularly hard casting was sought. This invention proved to be of great importance. By mid-century J. R. & A. Ransome were said to be the largest manufacturer of metal goods in the country. Their products included a large range of agricultural machinery, the Budding patent lawnmower, cast-iron goods for railways and structural purposes, and agricultural steam-engines. In the 1850s they were closely associated with the building of an iron steamship on the River Orwell. They co-operated closely with John Fowler in developing a steam-plough which in 1858 won a coveted prize of the Royal Agricultural Society, and thereafter revolutionized methods of land cultivation. From this point the use of horses in ploughing began to decline.

In 1868 it was decided to separate railway work from agricultural machinery, and Ransomes & Rapier Ltd was formed at Waterside Works in Ipswich. Between 1847 and 1867 Ransomes had supplied more than 12,000 miles of railway materials for use worldwide. Ransome & Rapier, incorporated in 1896, continued this activity and also became famous for their large excavating and lifting machinery.

In 1884 Ransomes traded as Ransomes, Sims & Jefferies Ltd, and in 1911 became a publicly quoted company with a capital of £1 million. Their Orwell Works covered 25 acres and employed 2500 men. Throughout the second half of the 19th century, the company's striking success was based on worldwide exports.

The second most important iron foundry in Suffolk was that of Richard Garrett & Sons Ltd of Leiston. Founded in 1778 as bladesmiths and makers of sickles and edge-tools, the business prospered when in 1804 they started to manufacture John Ball's threshing machine. They started building portable steam-engines in 1840 and eventually became the third largest manufacturer of agricultural steam-engines in the UK. At their peak they employed nearly 1000 men, but in 1920 sadly fell victim to an ill-fated conglomerate called Agricultural & General Engineers Ltd which was liquidated in 1932.

Founded in 1780, Whitmore & Binyon Ltd of Wickham Market were the second oldest Suffolk firm and manufactured hand-tools and agricultural machinery. By 1839 they styled themselves engineers and millwrights, and it was at this time that their foundry was established. Thereafter they concentrated on making steam-engines including portables, beam engines, horizontal stationary engines and special flour-milling machines.

Undoubtedly the advent of the agricultural steam-engine in 1840 greatly stimulated the development of iron foundries in the region. Noteworthy firms include E. R. Turner Ltd of St Peter's Iron Works, Ipswich. Originally they traded as Bond, Turner & Hurwood, builders of portables and traction engines. Cocksedge & Co Ltd of Greyfriars Road, Ipswich, manufactured steam-engines and self-slewing derricks. James Smyth & Sons of Peasenhall, founded in 1800, were early patentees of seed drills and other special-purpose agricultural machinery, becoming important exporters to eastern Europe and winning many prizes at continental shows. Others worthy of mention are Woods & Co of Stowmarket, established in 1812, builders of stationary steam-engines and portables; Barton & Unwin's Stour Valley Iron Works in Sudbury, which has been replaced latterly by Brunton's Propeller Works; and George Cornish and R. & G. Boby in Bury St Edmunds.[2]

Ten iron foundries were established in the north-eastern corner of Suffolk, but these were mainly concerned with the boat-building and fishing industries.[3] Elliot & Garrood Ltd of Ingate Iron Works at Beccles, established in 1872, manufactured fine compound and triple-expansion marine engines developing up to 300 IHP, as well as steam-driven ships' capstans. Richards Iron Works at Lowestoft, established in 1872, were originally builders of boats and continued to manufacture steam marine engines until 1930.

Further details on p.213

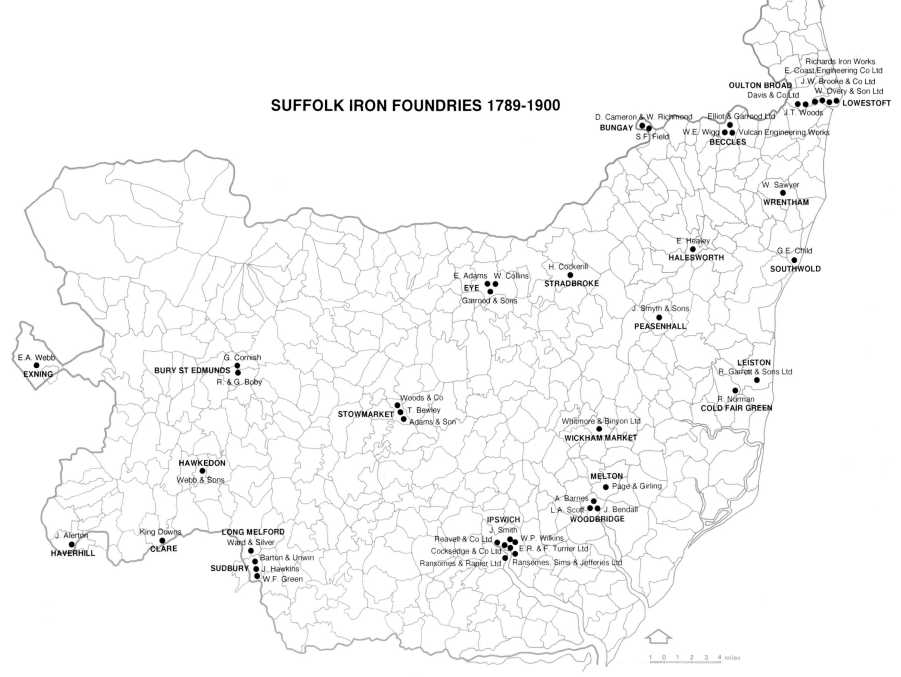

SUFFOLK IRON FOUNDRIES 1789-1900

Richards Iron Works
E. Coast Engineering Co Ltd
J. W. Brooke & Co Ltd
OULTON BROAD
W. Overy & Son Ltd
Davis & Co Ltd
LOWESTOFT
J.T. Woods

D. Cameron & W. Richmond   Elliot & Garrood Ltd
BUNGAY
S.F. Field   W.E. Wigg   Vulcan Engineering Works
BECCLES

W. Sawyer
WRENTHAM

E. Healey
HALESWORTH
G.E. Child
SOUTHWOLD

H. Cockerill
E. Adams W. Collins
EYE   **STRADBROKE**
Garrood & Sons

J. Smyth & Sons
PEASENHALL

E.A. Webb
EXNING

G. Cornish
BURY ST EDMUNDS
R. & G. Boby

LEISTON
R. Garrett & Sons Ltd

R. Norman
COLD FAIR GREEN

Woods & Co
STOWMARKET T. Bewley
Adams & Son

Whitmore & Binyon Ltd
WICKHAM MARKET

HAWKEDON
Webb & Sons

MELTON
Page & Girling

A. Barnes
L.A. Scott   J. Bendall
WOODBRIDGE

J. Alerton   King Downs   **LONG MELFORD**
HAVERHILL   **CLARE**   Ward & Silver

IPSWICH
J. Smith
W.P. Wilkins
Reavell & Co Ltd
Barton & Unwin   Cocksedge & Co Ltd   E.R. & F. Turner Ltd
SUDBURY J. Hawkins
W.F. Green   Ransomes & Rapier Ltd   Ransomes, Sims & Jefferies Ltd

1 0 1 2 3 4 miles

151

69. MALTING AND BREWING

Robert Malster

Like almost all Suffolk industries of any age, malting is based firmly on local agriculture; for centuries farmers in this county had specialised in the growing of good-quality barley. The making of malt was widespread in Suffolk in the 15th century, and in 1508 it was said of Ipswich that 'the maintenance of this Towne is much in malt'.[1] At such an early period, maltings were inevitably small and were often converted from buildings erected for quite different purposes. In Ipswich, for example, a malting was even made out of a redundant church.[2]

Malt was taxed continuously from 1711 to 1880, and strict Excise regulations militated against change. Nevertheless, a period of expanding trade in the mid-19th century did encourage such pioneers as Patrick Stead of Halesworth. He was the first to mechanise the process, building a new type of 'tower' malting in which he introduced new methods of handling the grain.[3] Removal of the tax in 1880 stimulated much faster expansion, and large new maltings were built at ports and alongside railway lines which provided a ready means of transporting malt to the big breweries of London and Burton-on-Trent. With the resulting change of scale came amalgamations and take-overs of malting firms, producing a revolution which is difficult to show on a map.

Much the same may be said of the brewing trade. Until the 19th century most breweries were small, and in many cases they consisted of no more than brewhouse attached to an inn or tavern. By 1900 few such brewhouses were operating, and a series of take-overs had already reduced the number of small breweries. This competitive process continued so that by the 1970s only three major firms survived: Adnams of Southwold, Greene King of Bury St Edmunds and Tollemache & Cobbold at Ipswich. Each of them was old-established

and had grown hugely since the 19th century. Since then a few new small breweries have sprung up to compete with the giants.

The distribution of maltings and breweries is mapped for 1855. The source of information is primarily William White's *Directory* of that year. This does not give an entirely accurate count of maltings, but does broadly clarify the distribution of the industry. In 1855 the majority of malting buildings were what is known in the trade as 'one-man maltings', operated by a single maltster with casual assistance from one or two others, whereas by 1904 many new multi-floor maltings were employing gangs of men on a shift-system. The first pneumatic maltings in the county was erected at Wainford in 1892. As in the case of breweries, the number of individual firms was declining, and the survivors were mainly those operating on a considerable scale.

Further details on p.214

A Newark-type malting in Princes Street, Ipswich, built 1866. This type of structure had three storeys: malting floors top and bottom with a barley store in between.

BREWERIES AND MALTINGS 1855

Brewery ●   Malting ○

○ 1

○ 2 - 5

◯ 6 - 10

◯ 11 - 15

1 0 1 2 3 4 miles

70. CAMPING CLOSES

David Dymond

From at least the 14th century until the mid 19th, the game of 'camping' or 'camp-ball' was popular in the eastern counties of Norfolk, Suffolk, Essex and Cambridgeshire.[1] This sport is normally described as a cross between football and handball because the ball could be kicked, thrown or carried as in modern rugby.[2] It was certainly energetic and dangerous, for local documents record frequent injuries and even deaths.[3] Just as the modern word 'football' covers several related but different games,[4] 'camping' referred to a whole cluster of games, variously called 'rough', 'savage', 'boxing', 'smooth' and 'civil'. Other important differences included the nature of the field, the size of teams, the kind of ball used, the length of games, and the type of goal. One variant was played cross-country using church-porches as goals, and another was more like modern hockey, because the players used sticks called 'camping crooks'.[5] Camping was indisputably an East Anglian phenomenon with clear western and southern limits, beyond which 'football' was the dominant term, but several variations need fuller clarification *within* the region.[6]

Virtually all popular sports were fiercely condemned by bishops' ordinances and by parliamentary statute. Nevertheless, so enthusiastic were East Anglians, as sportsmen and spectators, that many towns and rural parishes designated a special site for communal recreation. Normally called the Camping Close,[7] this was a grass field, less than four acres in size and sometimes as small as half an acre, enclosed by hedges and ditches. It could be in private or public ownership, and was often sited where lanes and footpaths converged. Here it was accepted that local people could enjoy themselves in their spare time, in practice often on Sunday. Similar sites can also be found under a range of other names. Good examples are the Game Place (Beccles), Playing Place (Hintlesham), Playstow (Gt Barton), Fairfield (Framsden), Buttland (Mettingham), Shooting Field (Layham), Brawling Piece (Stoke-by-Nayland), Wrestling Close (Claydon) and Maypole Pightle (Akenham).[8] Names could indeed be interchangeable, as at Gt Ashfield where a Camping Close was also known as the Playing Place.[9] This variable nomenclature strongly suggests that all these sites were used for multiple activities: games (including the much favoured camping), athletic contests, military exercises and social gatherings such as church-ales, fairs, pageants and plays.[10] Collectively these are surely the popular 'theatres' which literary historians have long sought in East Anglia.[11]

Evidence for Camping Closes is very patchy and unpredictable, and most known examples have been identified only in tithe apportionments of the 19th century. However, a significant minority have surfaced in much earlier documents (wills, glebe terriers, manorial surveys and early maps) which prove that this social institution originated in the second half of the 15th century—well before the Reformation. A late medieval origin is confirmed by the fact that Camping Closes, Game Places and other similarly named fields were not infrequently adjacent, or very close, to the parish church.[12] The likelihood is that whereas boisterous recreations had originally taken place in consecrated churches and churchyards, a change of sensibility by the mid-1400s demanded that they be moved *outwards*, in the interests of seemliness and respect.[13] This move, implicitly sanctioning activities which were technically illegal, must have been tolerated by all levels of local society: laity and clergy, peasantry and gentry.

On present evidence, one supposes that Camping Closes and the like remained in use after the Reformation and well into the 17th century, in the face of growing puritan and official opposition. Thereafter, the game of camping still throve in spite of continuing disapproval,[14] but was increasingly played elsewhere. By the early 18th century it was normally organised by innkeepers who advertised in local newspapers and provided prizes. Although the average Camping Close is unlikely to have been used for recreation after 1650,[15] the name often survived in popular memory to be recorded on tithe apportionments of the 1830s and '40s.

The map opposite shows about 70 Camping Closes so far discovered in Suffolk. Those known to have been adjacent to parish churches are distinguished, but it must be remembered that others, as at Drinkstone and Stoke-by-Nayland, were within a few hundred yards.[16] The general distribution raises many problems of interpretation. For example, the lighter lands of the Breckland and Sandlings seem to have fewer examples. Is this because a high acreage of common land made special provision unnecessary, or because large-scale enclosure in the 19th century obliterated earlier field-names? Even on the clayland where sites cluster more thickly, we do not know how many have disappeared without trace. Why are some examples identifiable in 19th-century sources but not in earlier ones, and *vice versa*? Why are three camping places identifiable in Bramfield,[17] and none in many other parishes? A large element of chance must be involved. At Hintlesham, one parson in 1613 recorded a field immediately west of the churchyard as 'the playinge place', but a few years later his successor simply referred to 'one peece of grownde heading upon the Church yarde east'.[18] Official disapproval of vulgar rowdyism must sometimes have encouraged the dropping of popular names. Furthermore some recreational sites may always have been hiding under general names like 'Church Croft' or 'Town Land'.[19] Certain strong concentrations, as in five adjoining parishes south of Bury St Edmunds, suggest that as yet we are seeing only the tip of an iceberg.[20]

Further details on p.214

CAMPING CLOSES

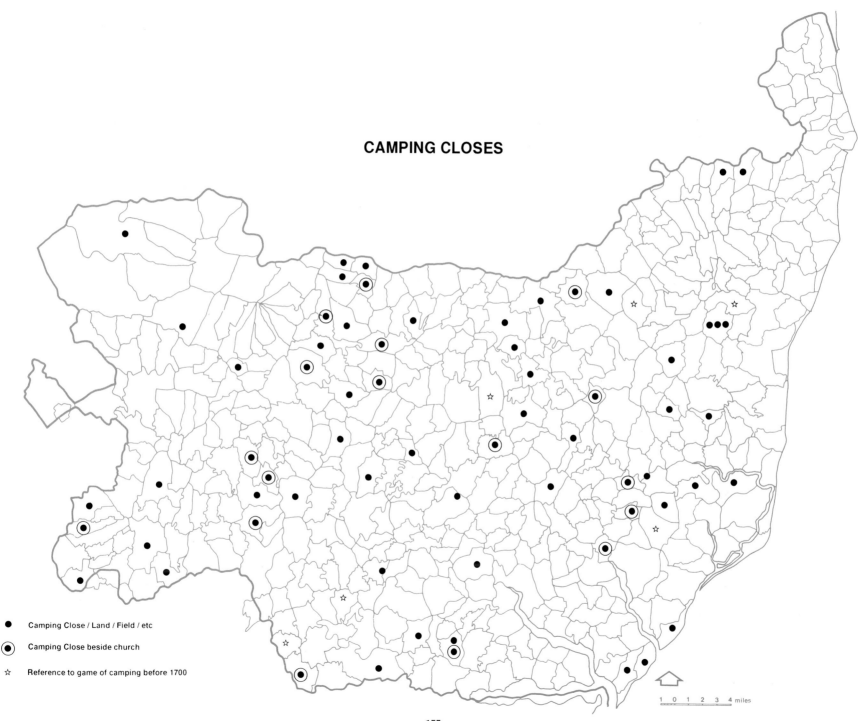

●   Camping Close / Land / Field / etc

◉   Camping Close beside church

☆   Reference to game of camping before 1700

1 0 1 2 3 4 miles

71. THEATRES AND CINEMAS

Alistair Robertson

By the 18th century, groups of strolling players began to form themselves into regional circuits, and to establish proper playhouses instead of using any convenient space such as an inn-yard or moot-hall. In East Anglia the leading group were the Norwich Comedians or the Duke of Grafton's Servants, who dated back to the period when, to avoid charges of vagrancy, actors attached themselves to the households of noblemen. This company, later based at the Theatre Royal in Norwich, was one of the leading provincial companies and continued to tour until 1852. Other companies were also touring East Anglia including that of Mr Scraggs which later, under the famous Fisher family, became the Norfolk and Suffolk Company of Comedians and continued until 1844.[1]

In 1786 the Norwich Company ceased to tour smaller towns, and concentrated its attention on Norwich, King's Lynn, Yarmouth, Barnwell (Cambridge), Bury St Edmunds, Colchester and Norwich. In the early 19th century, when this circuit was owned by the Wilkins family, several new theatres were built to the designs of the well-known architect, William Wilkins II (Ipswich in 1803; Bury St Edmunds in 1819). Finally, when the circuit closed, its theatres were sold off and run independently.

The Scraggs/Fisher Company took over the smaller towns and, in Suffolk, regularly visited Beccles, Bungay, Eye, Halesworth, Lowestoft, Newmarket, Sudbury and Woodbridge. Between 1812 and 1828 most of the theatres in those towns were built or rebuilt by David Fisher. When this circuit had to close in 1844, as a result of economic depression, the theatres were sold and converted to other uses (though the theatre at Eye was reportedly still running c.1850 and c.1870). In the late 19th century national touring groups did occasionally visit such towns but were forced to use alternative venues.

While the circuits were still working, theatres were used for only a few weeks in the year, usually coinciding with a fair (for example at Bury) or with races (for example at Beccles). At the same time assemblies and balls were often held, in order to make a social 'season'. Outside the main towns, smaller groups of players ocassionally erected temporary stages in such buildings as barns. On a still lower scale were the travelling booths.

When Felixstowe and Lowestoft developed strongly as holiday resorts in the late 19th century, theatres and multi-purpose halls were built to provide seasonal entertainment for visitors. Good examples are the Spa Pavilion at Felixstowe and the Marina at Lowestoft.

At the end of the 19th century, booths showing moving pictures began to appear at fairs and similar gatherings but, as equipment and techniques improved, buildings were adapted or built as the first proper cinemas. In 1909 Poole's Picture Palace opened in Ipswich, and by 1916 all the larger towns of Suffolk had at least one cinema (in Bungay the old theatre was used). Some cinemas, such as the Playhouse in Bury, were also equipped for stage shows and held mixed 'cine-variety' shows. Then in the 1920s the 'talkies' appeared, and many of the older cinemas were found to be too small or inadequate. They were replaced by larger and more luxurious establishments under such names as Odeon and Gaumont. The popularity of the cinema led to the closure of many theatres; some were converted into cinemas (for example the Marina at Lowestoft) and others were demolished (for example the Lyceum at Ipswich). When television became widely available in the 1950s and '60s, popular interest in films declined sharply and many cinemas followed their theatrical forbears into oblivion.

In spite of the enormous hold of modern television,

Suffolk has recently witnessed a rebirth of interest in theatre-going and live performances. The Theatre Royal in Bury has been restored and reopened; the Wolsey Theatre in Ipswich has been built to replace the old Arts Theatre; and a riverside warehouse at Sudbury has been converted into the Quay Theatre. Also in Ipswich the Corn Exchange has been converted into a large multi-purpose hall with stage facilities and a film theatre. In Lowestoft the Marina was reopened as a theatre in 1988, and recently the Gaumont cinema in Ipswich has become the Regent Theatre. Professional theatre has returned to Eye where the Assembly Room at the former White Lion is now the Eye Theatre. 'Strolling players' returned to Suffolk in 1982 with the formation of the Eastern Angles Theatre Company based in Ipswich.[1] Two of its regular venues, the Public Hall in Beccles and the Rifle Hall in Halesworth were originally built as theatres in the late 18th century! A new era of cinema building has begun with the introduction of multi-screen venues: two have opened in Ipswich and one is planned for Bury St Edmunds.

Further details on p.214

Theatre Royal, Bury St Edmunds: built 1819 to the designs of William Wilkins, the architect of the National Gallery and son of the lessee of the theatre. Closed in 1926, but re-opened again in 1965.

THEATRES AND CINEMAS

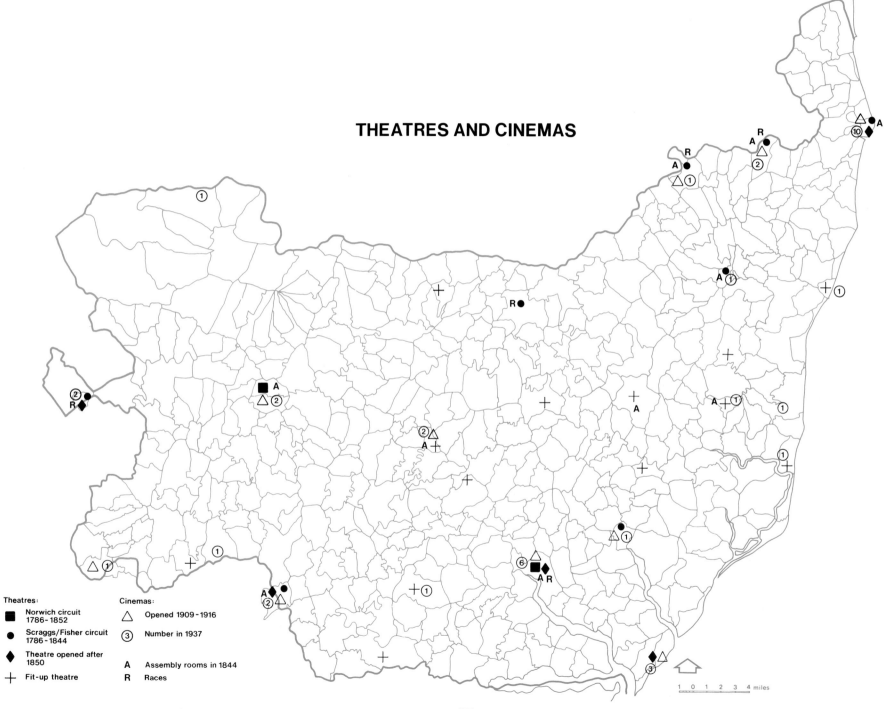

Theatres:

■ Norwich circuit 1786-1852

● Scraggs/Fisher circuit 1786-1844

◆ Theatre opened after 1850

+ Fit-up theatre

Cinemas:

△ Opened 1909-1916

③ Number in 1937

A Assembly rooms in 1844

R Races

72. ANGLO-SAXON AND MEDIEVAL IPSWICH

Keith Wade

Ipswich was founded in the late 6th or early 7th century on what had been open heathland on the north bank of the River Orwell, some twelve miles from the open sea. During the 7th century settlement was restricted to a few hectares immediately adjacent to the river, but in the early 8th century occupation spread over most of the present town-centre and south of the river, into Stoke. The economy was based on manufacturing and international trade. The most important industry was the production of pottery: kilns producing 'Ipswich Ware' supplied the whole East Anglian kingdom and other areas as far away as Kent and Yorkshire. Along the south side of Carr Street, dumps of wasters and traces of kilns have been found extending over 200 metres. Imports from abroad at this time included wine, pottery and millstones of lava, and came mainly from the Rhineland.

It can be plausibly suggested that the street system of the Anglo-Saxon town has largely survived to the present day. Once obvious modern insertions and distortions caused by the town's defences have been removed, the streets which remain seem likely to be of Anglo-Saxon origin. Little is known of the early churches but it can be argued, largely from their dedications, that St Mildred's and St Augustine's belong to the Middle Saxon period. St Peter's is also a likely candidate, and its large landholding at the time of Domesday Book strongly suggests that it was a minster from which a community of priests served a large area.[1] St Mary's at Stoke is another potentially early church, as Stoke was given to Ely Abbey in 970.

Ipswich was occupied by the Danes from about 879, and distinctively 'Viking' objects have been excavated within the town. Excavation has also shown that the town's first defences, consisting of an earthen rampart and ditch, were probably constructed by the Danes in the early 10th century, presumably in response to the West Saxon advance, but they were probably never used as the East Anglian Danes surrendered in 918 when King Edward occupied nearby Colchester.

The late Saxon economy continued to be based on industry and trade. From the middle of the 9th century, the pottery manufacturers in Carr Street turned to the production of Thetford Ware (named after the place where it was first recognised), and they continued in business until the middle of the 12th century. International trade appears to have ceased in the 10th century but revived in the 11th. However, during the 10th century, regional trade clearly became more important, especially with the area around St Neots and Bedford.

Domesday Book, compiled in 1086, recorded a further eleven churches in Ipswich. Three of them have long since been demolished (St Michael's, St Julian's and a second St Peter's). The churches of St George and Holy Trinity lay outside the town's defences, and probably indicate that suburbs already existed around them. The siting of the Norman castle in Ipswich still remains an enigma, largely because it was demolished as early as 1176.[2] Several sites have been suggested by previous writers, but all lie improbably outside the town's rampart and ditch. On the map opposite, a more plausible location is suggested within the town, where Elm Street appears to have been re-routed to avoid a large obstruction.

In the 13th century, the growth of three new suburbs led to the foundation of the churches of St Matthew, St Helen and St Clement. A fourth, around St John's at Cauldwell, lay one mile east of the town. St Margaret's church had replaced Holy Trinity in its suburb, and meanwhile two new churches had been built in the town-centre, St Nicholas and St Mary Quay.

Five monastic orders settled in the town during the medieval period. Austin canons were established at SS Peter and Paul in c.1130, and at Holy Trinity by 1162; the Blackfriars built their house in 1263, the Whitefriars in c.1278 and the Greyfriars before 1298. In the suburbs of Ipswich, four hospitals were built of which one, St Mary Magdalen, is not precisely located, as well as three chapels.

The town's defences were reconstructed in 1203, probably by the deepening of the existing ditch and raising of the rampart. Three gates are recorded, of which the west and north gates are easily located on later maps. The east gate is more problematical: it could have been where Carr Street or, more likely, Orwell Place crosses the medieval defences.

Further details on p.215

The first Common Seal of Ipswich, early 13th-century. This is one of the earliest depictions of a ship with a stern-post rudder.

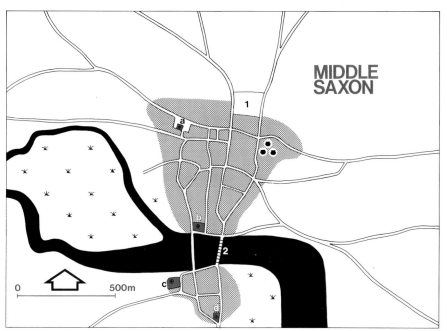

MIDDLE SAXON

1

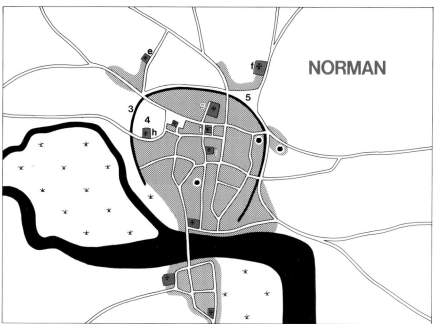

NORMAN

3
4
5

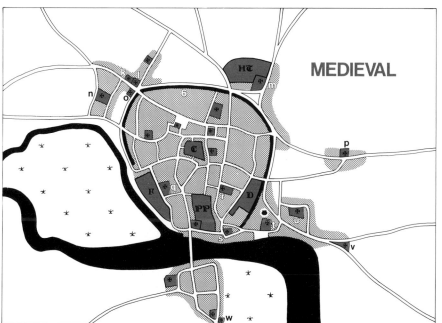

MEDIEVAL

THE EARLY DEVELOPMENT OF IPSWICH

1 Meeting Place?
2 Ford
3 First Town Defences
4 Castle (site of ?)
5 Thingstead
6 Later Town Defences

Pottery Kilns ◉

Marsh ⁙

Religious Houses

H𝕿 *Holy Trinity Priory*
𝕮 *Carmelite Friary*
𝕱 *Franciscan Friary*
P𝕻 *Priory of St Peter and St Paul*
𝕯 *Dominican Friary*

Churches, Chapels and Hospitals

✠a *St. Mildred's Church*
b *St. Peter's Church*
c *St. Mary's Church (Stoke)*
d *St. Augustine's Church*
e *St. George's Church*
f *Holy Trinity Church*
g *St. Mary Tower Church*
h *St. Mary Elms Church*
i *St. Lawrence's Church*
j *St. Stephen's Church*
k *St. John's Hospital (site of ?)*
l *All Saint's Chapel (site of ?)*
m *St. Margaret's Church*
n *St. Matthew's Church*
o *Chapel of Our Lady*
p *St. Helen's Church*
q *St. Nicholas's Church*
r *St. Edmund de Pountenay's Chapel*
s *St. Mary Quay Church*
t *Ostibolt Church (site of ?)*
u *St. Clement's Church*
v *St. James's Hospital*
w *St. Leonard's Hospital*

The growth of Ipswich can be usefully divided into phases by using maps which were printed in 1778, 1849, 1884, 1902-3, 1928 and 1938. Pennington's map of 1778 is a good starting point because it shows that the town had roughly the same size and shape as it had when depicted by John Speed in 1610. Continuity of townscape, not change, characterised Ipswich until the early 19th century.

c.1835-c.1850

Significant change begins with the building of the Wet Dock in the 1830s, the coming of the railways in 1846, the rapid expansion of Ransome's ironworks, and a population increase of over 30% in the 1840s. Expansion occurred on both sides of the dock. To the east and south-east, two areas of working-class housing were built around the Rope Walk and in the hamlet of Wykes Bishop, and housing for railway workers developed around the first railway station of 1846. The first suburbs of élite middle-class terraces and villas appear on the Woodbridge Road and especially to the north and west of the town. In the latter area a kind of 'West End' developed consisting of High Street, Berners Street, Fonnereau Road, Anglesea Road and Norwich Road, with poorer terraced housing on lower ground around Charles Street and between the Norwich and Handford Roads.

c.1850-c.1880

The industrial and commercial areas around the Dock and railway expand rapidly in this period, especially across the old Corporation Marshes north of the second railway station of 1860. Middle-class housing developed in the area around Burlington and London Roads, and in Christchurch Street and Tuddenham Road to the north-east. The most remarkable change, though, was extensive building by the Freehold Land Society to the east, in 'California' between Woodbridge Road and Foxhall Road and in the Rosehill area off the Felixstowe Road, with their grid-iron pattern of streets associated with smallholdings for artisans and others of the upper-working and lower-middle class.

c.1880-c.1914

In the late Victorian and Edwardian periods, suburban growth was of two kinds. An élite middle-class area grew up around Christchurch Park (Tuddenham, Westerfield, Park and Henley Roads), and above Anglesea Road to Constitution Hill. Meanwhile, a mass of modest terraced housing appeared between the Norwich and Bramford Roads to the north-west, and between the Foxhall and Nacton Roads to the south-east.

THE INTER-WAR YEARS

During the 1920s the pattern established previously did not change greatly, but by the late 1920s two developments began which are significant for the future. One of these was the building of the first large council estate on the former Racecourse between the Felixstowe and Nacton Roads. Policies of slum-clearance and re-housing in the 1930s led to the building of the Gainsborough, Priory Heath and Landseer Road estates to the south-east and the Whitton estate to the north-west. The second development was the growth of a large industrial estate between the Hadleigh Road and the river. After 1930, a major influence was the building of the Ipswich by-pass, and the consequent ribbon development of detached and semi-detached houses and bungalows around the northern and eastern perimeter of the town along the Valley, Colchester, Heath and Bixley Roads.

SINCE 1945

The main changes of the last 40 years focus on the south-western and north-western perimeter. They typify urban sprawl of the later 20th century, and have culminated in the mecca of out-of-town superstores. Massive post-war estates of council housing sprang up at Castle Hill, Whitton White House, Chantry and Maidenhall, interspersed with private housing on the Crofts estate and off the Belstead Road and in Stoke Park. In addition, the whole area between Whitton and the Hadleigh Road, and extending out to the new A14 by-pass, has become an industrial estate. To the east, towards Rushmere and out along the Foxhall Road, expansion of the residential area has been rapid since the 1960s and will soon fuse Ipswich with Kesgrave and Martlesham. The most recent development is to the south-east with the growth of an industrial and business park between Warren Heath and the Nacton Road.

The economic development of the port, the concentration of industrial and commercial activity and the long-term growth of population have thus transformed the physical shape and size of Ipswich in the last 150 years. This is particularly obvious after 1930 when first housing, both by private developers and the council, began to reach out to the borough boundary and, more recently, when industrial estates emerged on both the western and south-eastern periphery. From a population of some 11,000 in 1801, the population trebled by 1850 to 32,000 and thereafter has grown to today's total of about 116,000. The resulting pressure on land for housing has meant expansion from its Anglo-Saxon core to the limits of Ipswich's ancient Liberty, approximately the present boundary of the administrative borough.

Further details on p.215

THE GROWTH OF MODERN IPSWICH

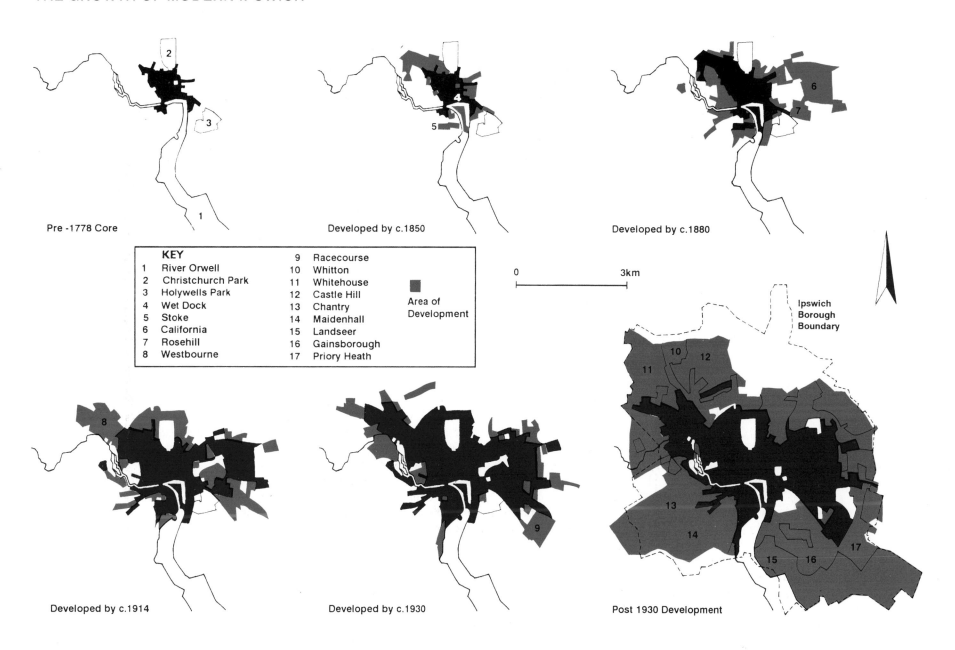

Pre -1778 Core

Developed by c.1850

Developed by c.1880

KEY

1	River Orwell	9	Racecourse
2	Christchurch Park	10	Whitton
3	Holywells Park	11	Whitehouse
4	Wet Dock	12	Castle Hill
5	Stoke	13	Chantry
6	California	14	Maidenhall
7	Rosehill	15	Landseer
8	Westbourne	16	Gainsborough
		17	Priory Heath

Area of Development

0   3km

Ipswich Borough Boundary

Developed by c.1914

Developed by c.1930

Post 1930 Development

74. SMALLER MEDIEVAL TOWNS

Keith Wade & David Dymond

With the collapse of the Roman Empire in the early 5th century, town life disappeared from England and the whole of north-western Europe, and did not reappear until the early 7th century. In eastern England, only one town, Ipswich, appears to represent this rebirth of urban life, and from the 7th to 9th centuries it may have been the only town in the whole region. During the later Anglo-Saxon period, however, other towns were founded, and by the early 11th century the basic modern pattern of major towns was established.

In Domesday Book (1086), six places were described as having burgesses and were undoubtedly towns. In order of their populations, they were Ipswich, Dunwich, Eye, Sudbury, Beccles and Clare. To them we can add Bury St Edmunds which, although described as a *villa*, had a population of about 3000 and was clearly urban. Five other places were mentioned as having markets but no burgesses—Blythburgh, Haverhill, Hoxne, Kelsale and Thorney (now Stowmarket). Lastly we can add Bungay which also appears to have been a defended settlement of some size.

How many of the Domesday places, other than Ipswich, evolved as towns *before* the Norman Conquest is a matter of debate. Bury, Sudbury and Dunwich were minting coins in the 10th century and it must be assumed, therefore, that they were small, defended towns. At Sudbury the line of the 10th-century defences is clearly fossilised in the street-plan, beyond which the town expanded in the 12th century by adding a new market and two new churches. In Bungay, the castle built by the Bigod family between 1103 and 1140 was clearly imposed on an earlier planned grid of streets, with defences to north and south.[1] Scarfe has suggested that this may have been a *burh* created in the early 11th century by Ulfcytel, earl of East Anglia.[2] Commanding an important crossing of the River Waveney, Beccles too

appears to have an Anglo-Saxon planned nucleus around an early market-place; later developments on its uphill side coincided with the immigration of burgesses from Norwich. Clare contained a late Anglo-Saxon college of priests and a market was recorded in 1066, but its urban status was undoubtedly enhanced by the construction of a castle by 1090.

Other small towns emerged after the Norman Conquest, and into the 12th century, and were associated with the construction of castles. At Eye, the castle, market-place and church were all laid out together on a low promontory within a bend of the River Dove. At Framlingham the powerful Bigod family established their main stronghold by 1157 and a thriving town beside it. Orford is a planned town laid out by Henry II in 1165; it comprises a grid of streets surrounded by a castle, church, market-place and quay.

By the year 1547 when Aldeburgh's market was licensed, Suffolk had no fewer than 98 places which had received royal charters licensing weekly markets, and very often annual fairs as well (see Maps 33 and 34). Most of the charters were granted in the 13th century, which was obviously a period of great commercial and industrial development. The large number of such charters does not, however, give a totally accurate picture of the wealth and prosperity of Suffolk during the Middle Ages. Some places had functioning markets without any official, chartered basis, as at Walsham le Willows and Lidgate. The latter is an extreme example, for it not only had a physical market-place but some of its inhabitants bore the rank of burgess—all without a charter. On the other hand many markets quickly failed, or had a relatively short commercial life so that they had petered out by the end of the Middle Ages. About a third of the places given market charters developed into permanent small towns: good examples are Wood-

bridge, Halesworth, Mildenhall and Nayland. The cloth-making towns of Lavenham and Hadleigh are particularly noteworthy. In both cases, the industrial expansion appears to have been catered for by planned extensions tacked on to the original nucleus surrounding the parish church. In Hadleigh's case, the plan was over-ambitious and was not fully built-up until modern times.

At the lower end of the scale, it is important to recognise the surviving urban qualities of places like Mendlesham, Bildeston and Ixworth. Today such places are often regarded as 'villages', yet they display a tightness of plan characteristic of towns and have identifiable market-places no longer in use. Another group of towns well worth special attention are those which developed organically along major roads. Thus Botesdale grew up beside the main road between Bury and Scole, with its own market, fairstead and chapel-of-ease, while Newmarket is a true 'frontier town' set astride the Icknield Way which is the boundary between Suffolk and Cambridgeshire. Soon after 1200, Needham Market was begun speculatively by the Bishop of Ely in one corner of his large manor of Barking, taking advantage of the highroad between Bury and Ipswich. By the middle of the century its chapel-of-ease had been built within a rectangular market-place; it remained subordinate to Barking church until granted parochial status in 1907.

Further details on p.215

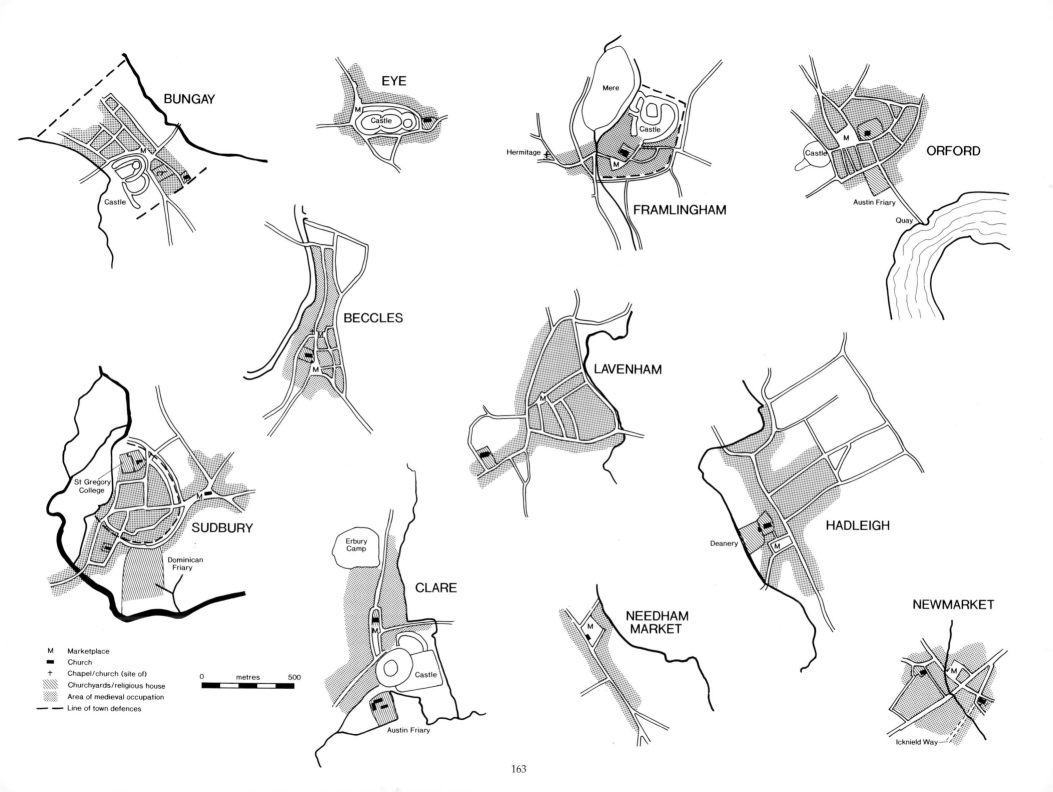

BUNGAY

EYE

Castle

FRAMLINGHAM

Mere

Castle

Hermitage

ORFORD

Castle

M

Austin Friary

Quay

BECCLES

M

M

L

LAVENHAM

M

HADLEIGH

Deanery

M

SUDBURY

M

St Gregory
College

M

Dominican
Friary

CLARE

Erbury
Camp

M

Castle

Austin Friary

NEEDHAM
MARKET

M

NEWMARKET

M

Icknield Way

M   Marketplace
■   Church
+   Chapel/church (site of)
▨   Churchyards/religious house
▨   Area of medieval occupation
--- Line of town defences

0   metres   500

163

75. LISTED BUILDINGS

Sylvia Colman

Suffolk has a great many buildings considered to be of historic and architectural interest; their variable distribution and density are illustrated in the map opposite. The original Statutory Lists were made in the early 1950s, often very superficially, but from the later '60s revision was carried on intermittently, beginning with the larger towns and following in the early '70s with the three southern Rural Districts of Clare, Melford and Cosford. By the early 1980s the coverage of England as a whole was so uneven that a national programme for re-listing all the remaining rural areas and small towns was set in train. This is now complete, and has resulted in a large increase in the number of listed items in virtually all the Suffolk parishes under review. The new lists, issued for small groups of rural parishes or for single towns, have far more detailed descriptions than formerly, and cover interiors as well as exteriors. Information for the map has necessarily been drawn from lists of several different dates.

Buildings are listed for a great variety of reasons including age, architectural merit, traditional interest, unusual features, rarity, or association with a well-known person or historical event. The scope and date-range are constantly being widened; buildings can be selected up to the middle of the present century, so that a spread of over 1000 years may be covered by the items in one list.

Items fall into Grade I if they are considered of national importance: this includes the majority of the county's medieval churches and a selection of outstanding secular buildings such as the mansion at Hengrave built for Sir Thomas Kitson in the early 16th century, or Brockley Hall which is an aisled manor house of about 1300. Only about 1 per cent of all listed buildings are in Grade I. Grade II has a much broader coverage, ranging from items not quite good enough for Grade I to those which are only just listable, or listable simply as part of

a group. In Suffolk many timber-framed buildings are included, especially in rural areas. If a Grade II building has outstanding features such as fine carvings, plasterwork or good architectural details, this may be recognised by a star (Grade II*). Altogether 9 per cent of Grade II buildings are starred.

In addition to houses and churches, many other kinds of building can be listed. These include monastic remains, nonconformist chapels, barns and other farm buildings (ranging from traditional forms to model farmsteads of the 19th century), follies, summer-houses (like the charming 18th-century Tea House at Great Saxham Hall), windmills and watermills, industrial buildings, granaries, maltings and warehouses, harbour installations, bridges (at Homersfield is the oldest pre-cast concrete bridge in England, built about 1870), railway stations, schools and police stations. The list of potential candidates is enormous and varies from one part of England to another. Suffolk, obviously, is relatively thin on industrial items. Even if it has historical associations, no building can normally be listed unless it has some intrinsic structural quality. This often excludes minor industrial items, lesser farmstead buildings or village smithies.

Listing also recognises the value of other lesser features which are associated with buildings, or which contribute to a landscape, village centre or street scene. For example, garden walls, gate piers and wrought-iron gates can enhance the setting of a major house. If the house is very grand the grounds may also have classical statuary, urns, sundials and balustraded terraces. These can all be listed in their own right, as have many items in the grounds of Somerleyton Hall. Boundary walls are important in many contexts, sometimes to exclude no less than to enhance. Churchyard monuments by virtue of age, design or historic associations can add to the

interest of the church itself. Milestones, signposts (an attractive example stands beside the churchyard at Yoxford), drinking troughs, old lamp-posts, even some telephone kiosks, may all be visually significant and potentially listable. The new list for Framlingham includes two fine Victorian pillarboxes and some cast-iron bollards near the church.

The aim of listing is to draw attention to the very wide range of important buildings and other features and, through the associated planning procedures, to control what happens to them. Rules and regulations can be helpful, but the best protection that any listed building can have is a sympathetic, caring owner.

Further details on p.215

Laxfield Guildhall, built *c*.1520. For the original function of gildhalls see Map 32; this one is now a local museum.

LISTED BUILDINGS

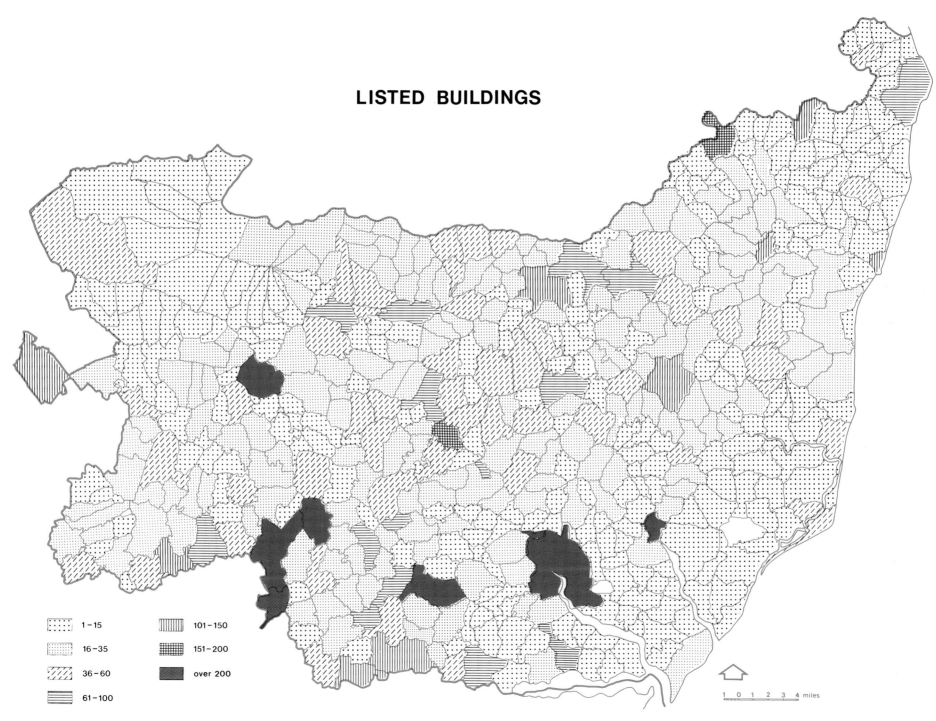

1 – 15
16 – 35
36 – 60
61 – 100
101 – 150
151 – 200
over 200

1 0 1 2 3 4 miles

76. THE ROMANESQUE CHURCH OF BURY ST EDMUND'S ABBEY   Eric Fernie

The ruins of the abbey church belong almost entirely to the building begun by Abbot Baldwin in the 1080s, after King William pronounced in his favour and rejected the claims of Herfast, bishop of East Anglia, who had attempted to gain control of the monastery. The east arm is likely to have been ready for the translation of the body of St Edmund in 1095, and the whole church was largely complete by 1140, except for the towers on the west front which were finished by Abbot Samson in the late 12th century. It consisted of an east arm with a crypt below and presbytery above (both levels with an ambulatory and three radiating chapels), aisled transept arms of five bays each, a twelve-bay nave and a western massif almost as wide as the nave is long. This building belongs to the tradition of great Norman pilgrimage churches of the decades following the Conquest, but even among these examples it is one of the largest. As such, along with only a handful of contemporary churches in western Europe, it rivals the scale of the Constantinian basilicas of Early Christian Rome.

Despite their largely robbed state the remains provide a large enough number of accurate measurements to indicate that the building was laid out, apparently like most of the largest Norman churches in England, using the ratio between the side of a square and its diagonal, or one to the square root of two. The best preserved structure is St James's tower (or Norman Tower) which stands on the boundary wall on the axis of the church. All the elements on its entrance face are determined by this proportion, while its external width of 10.74m (35ft 3 in) is the same as the width of the nave and half of the width of the main vessel and aisles in the crypt. The main dimensions of the church appear to be based on a small number of lengths such as this, namely 7.62m, 10.74m, 18.34m, 25.95m and 36.6m (25ft, 35ft 3in, 60ft 2in, 85ft 1in and 120ft), all of which are related to the proportion in question. There is also evidence that the root-two system was used in the setting out of the town, something which might be expected from the fact that Churchgate St both continues the axis of the church and forms the axis of the town.

One of the most striking features of the plan is the displacement to the north-west of the north side of the crossing and the north walls of the nave. The angle begins in the misalignment between the west pier of the presbytery and the adjacent north-east crossing pier, and is underlined by the fact that the crossing pier is much thicker than the presbytery pier. These distortions could be the result of a blunder on the part of a builder uncertain how to set out a design in which the western arm was intended to be nearly 4.5m (almost 15ft) wider than the eastern, but this is unlikely, especially when the angled wall is taken in conjunction with another oddity which provides the basis for a more far-reaching possibility.

The westernmost pier of the presbytery is much larger than any likely reconstruction of the lost piers to the east, and is in fact almost identical to the equivalent parts of the crossing piers of the cathedral at Norwich. This suggests that the westernmost presbytery pier at Bury was the original crossing pier and that the building has been lengthened by a whole bay. This enlarging of the church in both width and length would have been carried out shortly after the translation of the saint's body in 1095, in order to make Bury substantially larger than the rival church at Norwich, which had been begun in 1096 on lines very similar to those already established in the original eastern arm of Bury.

Further details on p.215

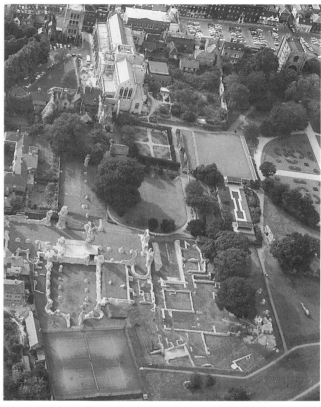

The ruins of the abbey church, from the east, 1969. This huge church was one of the largest of its time in western Europe. It dwarfs the present cathedral (at the top of the picture) which was formerly the parish church of St. James. Also at the top are the two principal gates into the abbey princinct: the Norman Tower or St. James's Gate (left) and the Abbey or Great Gate (right). To the right of the abbey church are the remains of the claustral buildings.

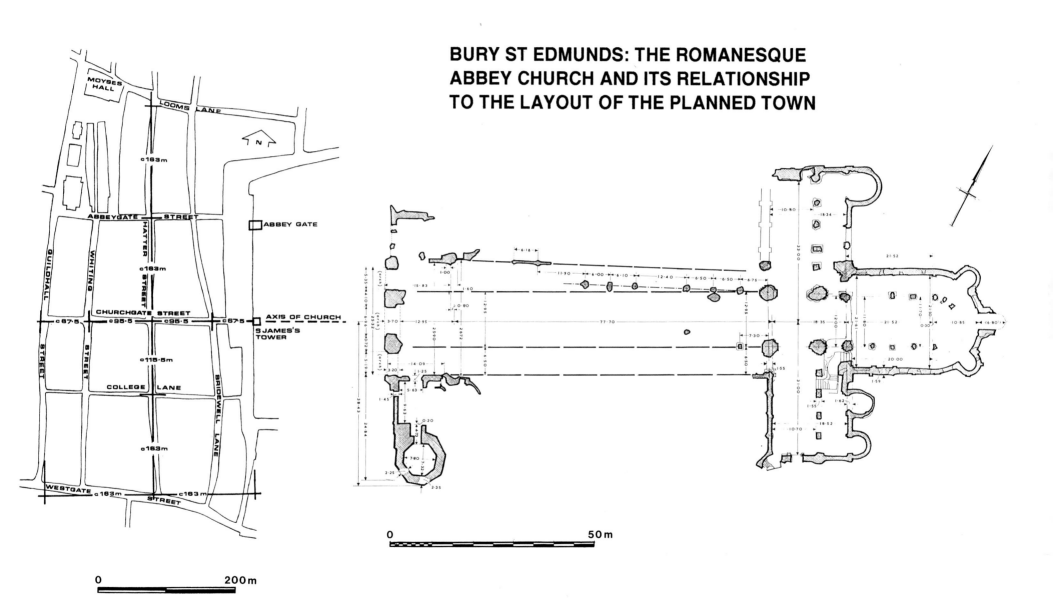

BURY ST EDMUNDS: THE ROMANESQUE ABBEY CHURCH AND ITS RELATIONSHIP TO THE LAYOUT OF THE PLANNED TOWN

77. MEDIEVAL MASONS

Birkin Haward

Over 400 medieval churches remain in Suffolk, and approximately another 100 are known to have existed. All these, along with a few large castles and some public works, represent most of the permanent stone buildings erected in the county before 1550. The majority of other structures, various types of houses and agricultural buildings, were made largely of timber. The churches therefore are the most advanced examples of the art of building in the medieval period: they are mainly the work of masons and to a lesser extent of carpenters.

The leading architect-masons were held in highest esteem. They were very skilled in geometry and in manipulating a straight edge, square and compasses; and in establishing three-dimensional forms and setting out accurate plans and proportions. They had learned the secrets of laying good foundations, of calculating loads on walls and piers, of buttressing the thrust of arches and vaults, and of resisting the pressures of wind and storm. It appears that few such leading designers were to be found among the masters of practical mason-craft, and they were in great demand for their conspicuous talents. The master mason was clearly responsible for establishing much decorative detail as well as the main lines of·each design. On any large project, medieval building accounts record the early establishment of a 'tracing house', and the procuring of parchment for drawings and of special board panels for templates.[1] It is therefore of great interest, wherever possible, to identify the men who designed and supervised these buildings in East Anglia and who, until recently, have remained largely unknown.

There were various grades of mason. At the top were the on-site warden and supervising mason; below them came the ordinary master mason, and then the more numerous carvers, setters, layers, journeymen and labourers, for whom the scales of pay are well recorded.[2] A few leading architect-masons, while maintaining their appointment as king's mason or master mason to an abbey or cathedral, also acted as consultants for more distant projects.[3] Examples recorded for Suffolk include Simon Clerk and John Wastell, both of Bury St Edmunds and successively masters to Bury Abbey between 1440 and 1515. Clerk also carried out important work at Eton in Berkshire, at King's College chapel and Great St Mary's church in Cambridge, and at Saffron Walden in Essex. Wastell followed at the same churches in Cambridge and Essex, and with prestigious works at the cathedrals of Canterbury and Peterborough. On stylistic evidence, it can be argued that both men were almost certainly involved with the parish churches indicated on the map opposite, as well as with major works at Bury Abbey, now unfortunately lost.

At the level of ordinary parishes, documents recording building work rarely survive. In Suffolk building contracts remain only for the towers of Walberswick, Thornham Parva and Helmingham, and an estimate for work only for the chancel at Wingfield. Fortunately, from the late 14th century onwards, wills have been preserved in large numbers in the records of ecclesiastical courts, and they frequently contain bequests towards work in local churches. Many such wills have now been transcribed, and the results so far provide a valuable though incomplete resource for dating the fabric of churches, especially in rural areas.[4] As a substantial number of Suffolk churches were built or rebuilt after 1350, wholly or partly, individual projects identified from wills provide valuable fixed points for the purpose of dating. Leading Suffolk masons identified by these various means include William Layer (fl.1420-44), Simon Clerk (fl.1440-89) and John Wastell (fl.1480-1515), all three of Bury, Reginald Ely of Cambridge (fl.1438-71), John Melford of Sudbury (fl.1490-1509), Hawes of Occold (fl.1410-40), Richard Russell and Adam Powle of Dunwich and Blythburgh (fl.1420-?70), Thomas Aldrych of North Lopham in Norfolk (fl.1487-1508), and John Barbour of Ipswich (fl.c.1520-51).[5]

The principal resource is of course the buildings themselves, and what can be learnt from them by close examination of details, by making comparative measured drawings and by cross-reference to documents which may indicate precise or approximate dates. Stylistic dating was widely practised by architectural historians in the past, though they mostly failed to provide verifiable evidence or to quote sources. While surviving contracts indicate that clergy and parishioners often prescribed the main design of a proposed new building, by referring to buildings elsewhere as models, the master mason was generally free to follow his own preferences when it came to deciding proportions, patterns and mouldings. Consequently it is these elements that are most likely to indicate a particular mason's hand, and to justify an attribution. A recently published survey, which covers all Suffolk arcades with moulded piers, has been found to support most of the attributions shown on the map.[6] It has also been used to identify several groups of churches near Ipswich, Bury St Edmunds and Sudbury respectively, which have marked similarities of design. Further research may make it possible, one day, to name the masons responsible.

Further details on p.215

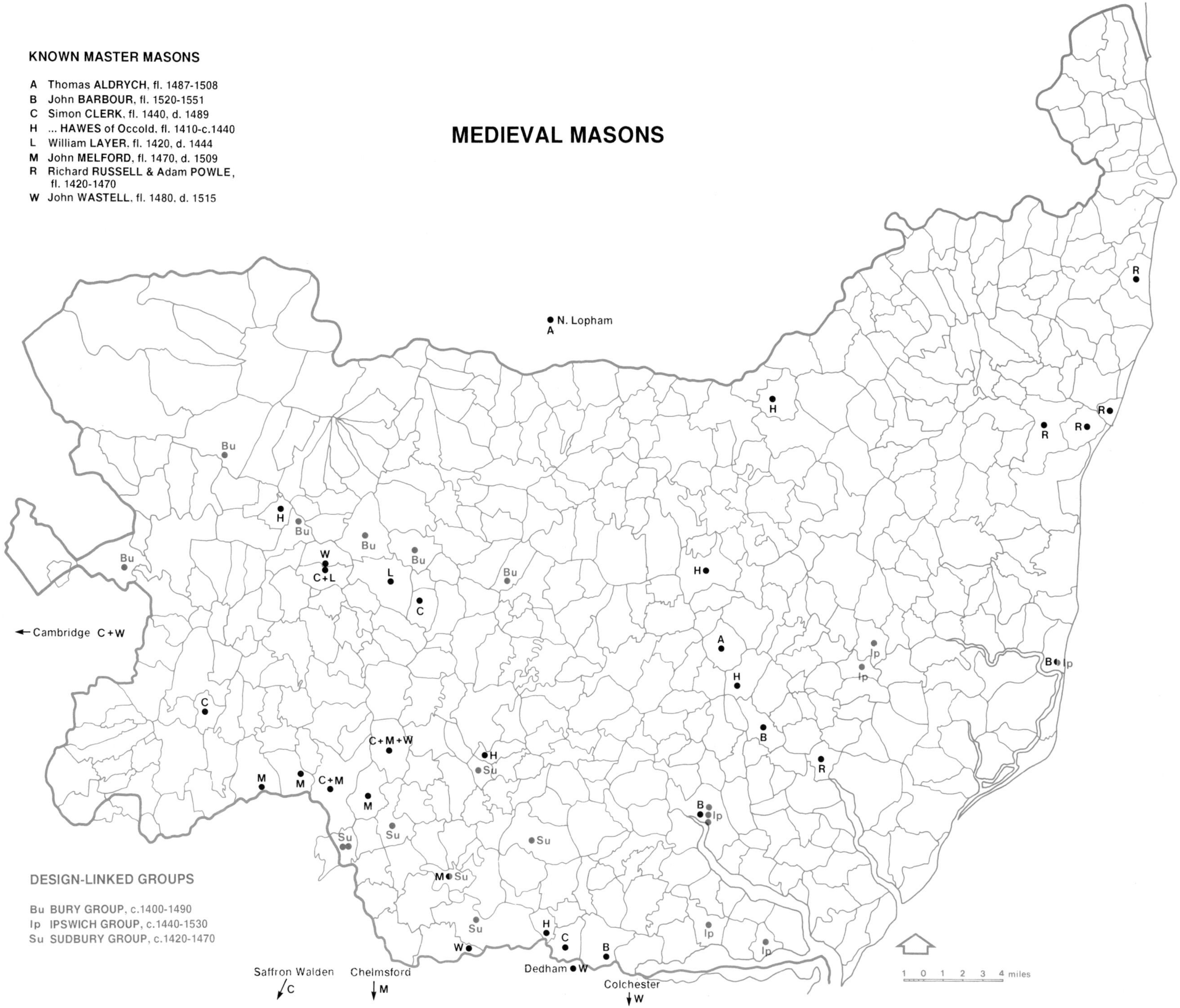

MEDIEVAL MASONS

KNOWN MASTER MASONS

A Thomas ALDRYCH, fl. 1487-1508
B John BARBOUR, fl. 1520-1551
C Simon CLERK, fl. 1440, d. 1489
H ... HAWES of Occold, fl. 1410-c.1440
L William LAYER, fl. 1420, d. 1444
M John MELFORD, fl. 1470, d. 1509
R Richard RUSSELL & Adam POWLE, fl. 1420-1470
W John WASTELL, fl. 1480, d. 1515

N. Lopham
A

DESIGN-LINKED GROUPS

Bu BURY GROUP, c.1400-1490
Ip IPSWICH GROUP, c.1440-1530
Su SUDBURY GROUP, c.1420-1470

← Cambridge C + W

Saffron Walden
C

Chelmsford
M

Dedham W

Colchester
W

1 0 1 2 3 4 miles

78. MEDIEVAL CHURCH ROOFS

Birkin Haward & Philip Aitkens

The eminent Victorian architect George Street wrote that 'churches erected by the English medieval builders are more remarkable for the beauty and variety of their wooden roofs than those of any other race of builders in the world',[1] while Pevsner said that 'for open timber roofs Suffolk stands supreme'.[2] A new index of medieval hammerbeam roofs in England, compiled from Nikolaus Pevsner's 'The Buildings of England', shows that Street's bold judgement applies especially to East Anglia. Out of 188 single-hammerbeam roofs in England, 124 (or 66 per cent) occur in the four eastern counties. Even more remarkably, all 32 double-hammerbeam roofs surviving nationally occur *only* in the same area (21 in Suffolk; 4 in Norfolk; 4 in Essex and 3 in Cambridgeshire). These figures surely imply that the double-hammerbeam construction was developed by Suffolk carpenters in the 15th century, and was then exported to neighbouring counties.[3] The church roofs of medieval Suffolk are justly renowned,[4] yet surprisingly they have attracted little detailed attention from architectural historians. In fact, nine main types of medieval church roof can be distinguished (A-H); the maps and diagrams on the following pages show their profiles, numbers and distribution. Out of 495 medieval churches in the county, some 200 (nearly 40 per cent) retain enough of their original roof timbers to make their design-type recognizable.

MEDIEVAL HAMMERBEAM ROOFS IN ENGLAND

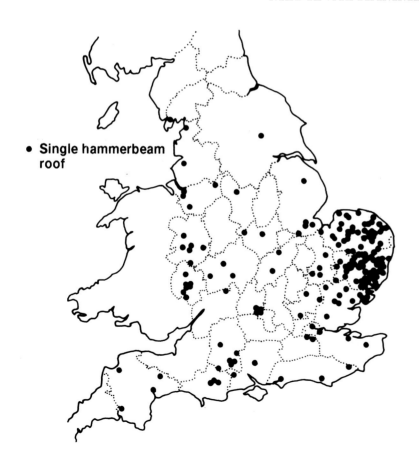

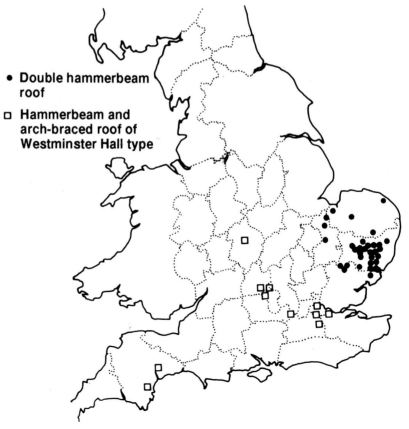

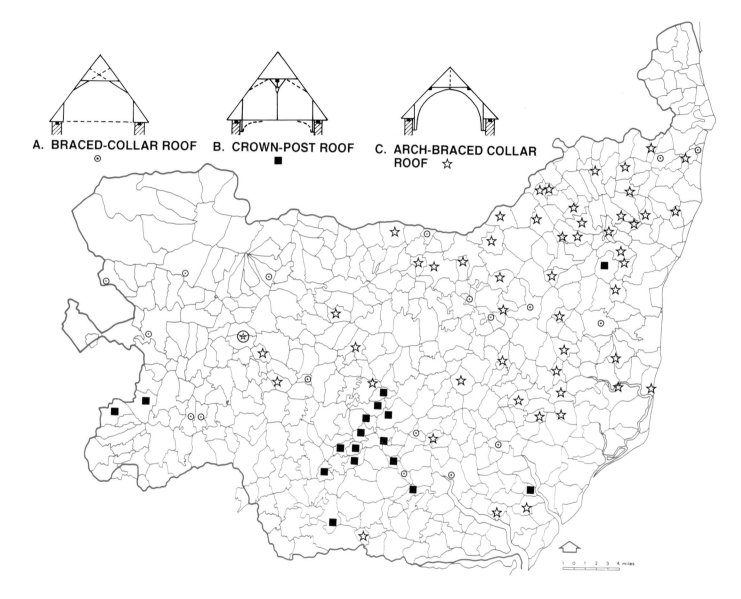

A. BRACED-COLLAR ROOF

B. CROWN-POST ROOF

C. ARCH-BRACED COLLAR ROOF

A. BRACED-COLLAR ROOF (17 examples): the earliest in date, 13th-15th century, and originally the most numerous type; spread fairly evenly in the county. With fairly steep pitch, and no doubt originally thatched.

B. CROWN-POST ROOF (17 examples): from early 14th to early 16th century, always a minority type; occurs mostly in a small area of south-mid Suffolk where the same roof-form appears in domestic buildings; is not found in north or east (see Map 81).

C. ARCH-BRACED COLLAR ROOF (51 examples): one of the most numerous groups, probably dating mainly from late 14th and 15th centuries; occurs most strongly in the eastern half of Suffolk, particularly in the north-east. Contains many variations of structure and detail: a few lack collars, and some have trusses alternating with tiebeams.

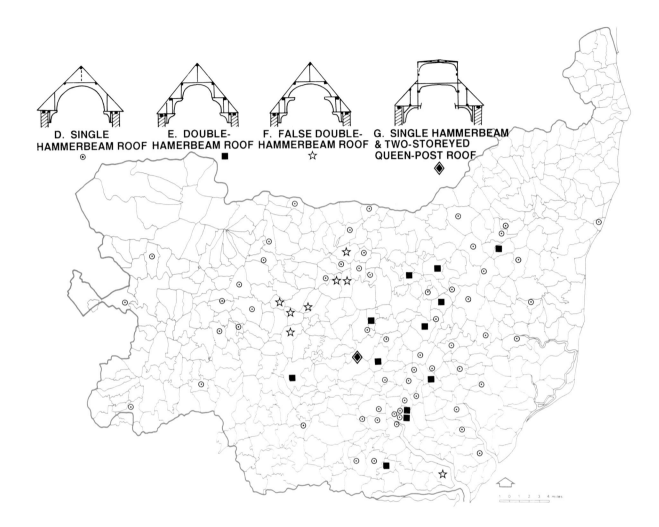

D. SINGLE-HAMMERBEAM ROOF (53 examples): the largest group, popular from the late 14th to 16th century. Concentrated in the middle and south-east of Suffolk; may be related to secular buildings in the northern part of the same area which have raised-aisles and queenposts. Considerable variety in richness of detail; some like Earl Stonham and Badingham compare favourably with elaborate double-hammerbeams. The hammers offer seatings for winged angels; spandrels, braces and cornices are often carved. Sometimes the trusses alternate with arch-braces or tiebeams.

E. TRUE DOUBLE-HAMMERBEAM ROOF (12 examples): 15th and 16th century in date; occurs largely in the south-east, often contemporary with the peak development of Types C and D. Represents the highest point of timber, open-roof design in medieval England; implies a concentration of leading native craftsmen. Ipswich is the only large town in England with these magnificent church roofs.

F. FALSE DOUBLE-HAMMERBEAM ROOF (8 examples): forms a close group around Bacton; described as 'false' because the upper hammers carry no vertical posts. May have been produced by local craftsmen, including the Rollesby family who are recorded as working in Norfolk and Suffolk in the early 15th century.[5]

G. SINGLE-HAMMERBEAM & TWO-STOREYED QUEEN-POST ROOF (1 example): the unique roof of Needham Market dating from c.1470 has no obvious prototype, although in detail it has similarities with local double-hammerbeam roofs such as Wetherden and Tostock.

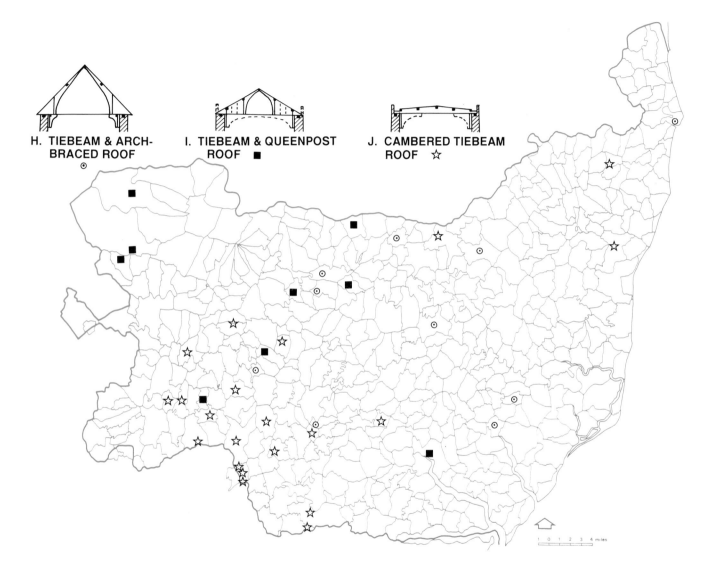

H. TIEBEAM & ARCH-BRACED ROOF (10 examples): separately defined because it was favoured by master mason Hawes of Occold in the 1420s as at Debenham and Bildeston.[6] Tiebeams alternate with arch-braced or hammerbeam principals, generally without collars.

I. TIEBEAM & QUEEN-POST ROOF (9 examples): popular in north-west Norfolk in the early 15th century; in Suffolk a few dispersed examples such as Lakenheath and the famous roof of Mildenhall which is strongly linked to St Nicholas, King's Lynn.[7] Generally, a strong and reliable construction with low pitch.

J. CAMBERED TIEBEAM ROOF (21 examples): the only type concentrated in west Suffolk; relates specifically to the wealth generated by the late-medieval cloth trade. An important component in comprehensive designs for naves in the final phase of Perpendicular architecture; occurs in all churches attributed to master masons John Wastell, Simon Clerk and John Melford.

Further details on p.216

79. AISLED HALLS

Philip Aitkens

In the high Middle Ages, the aristocratic household was large and lived in a cluster of buildings resembling a tightly packed village. At the centre was a Great Hall where meals were eaten, servants slept and courts were held. Local lords of manors copied features of this design in their smaller halls, of which hundreds must have been built in Suffolk during the 13th century. The hall was frequently aisled—pairs of vertical posts supported horizontal beams halfway up the sloping roof, and allowed for a much wider building. About six of these aisled halls remain reasonably intact, about 10m long and 8m wide, each of two bays with a pair of central arcade posts, and with ancillary rooms at one or both ends.

For centuries this very important class of early buildings was forgotten, until in 1958 John Smith of the Royal Commission on Historical Monuments walked into Edgar's Farm at Combs. During the next decade, a few similar buildings were identified, mostly in East Anglia, but by 1988 the total in lowland England was approaching 200.

Away from East Anglia other forms of construction were employed by vernacular builders in the 13th and 14th centuries, but here in Suffolk lesser men also desired the status of an aisled house—even though they were not always in need of the space provided. At Cookley (c.1200) and later at Levington, parish priests built smaller houses of aisled form. In towns, where building sites were tighter, only one aisle might be built at the rear while the wall along the street was higher and well-windowed, as at 88 High Street in Lavenham. As late as c.1500, a peasant living beside the village green at Depden built his little house with aisles.

In the earlier halls, long overlapping braces rose from the side walls, parallel to the roof-slope, interlocking with posts and beams to form a series of strong triangles at the open truss across the centre of the hall, and similarly in the wall behind the dais. The decorative value of these passing-braces was used to the full: visitors to high-quality halls like the Woodlands at Brundish and the Priory Hall at Great Bricett would have been greatly impressed by soaring geometrical patterns of chevrons and saltires.

By about 1300, the diagonal passing-braces were giving way to fan-shaped patterns of shorter curved braces, in end and side walls alike. Fashion now dictated the use of a crownpost over the centre of all open halls, while at the same time omitting the additional tiebeams seen in many earlier examples. This is is well displayed at Edgar's Farm, the frame of which is now preserved at the Museum of East Anglian Life at Stowmarket.

The lighting of the larger halls was probably provided by an oriel—a tall dormer window—breaking the line of the aisle near the dais, but all have now gone and mostly without trace. When from the late 14th century fashion favoured taller, narrower and more dignified open halls, the aisles of earlier houses were likely to be reduced or altogether removed because of their lowness—especially at the front. Of the manor houses, only Brockley Hall retains the profile of an unaltered aisle which, significantly, is at the rear.

With most aisled halls, in fact, one is able to observe only fragments. For instance, nine of the examples mapped opposite have lost their original roofs, and nine their aisles, while in six others the main body of the hall was almost or entirely destroyed at an early date. Some, as at Worlingworth Hall and Wingfield College, were converted into 'raised aisles' by the introduction of a massive beam across the centre of the hall. Many later houses and barns contain re-used timbers which clearly show that an aisled hall once existed nearby and has been demolished.

Aisled halls survive in the areas which were wealthier and more populous in the Middle Ages; this excludes the Breckland and Sandlings where poorer soils always supported fewer and poorer inhabitants. Most of the finest aisled halls are in the mixed farming belt of mid-Suffolk, but even here the scattered distribution shows the factor of chance. Many must have been swept away by wealthy owners in Tudor times. Very early houses only survive when their successive owners had money enough for essential maintenance, but not enough to afford a complete rebuilding. Much of southern Suffolk remains to be searched for survivals, and the number may yet be doubled. The 25 examples so far found since John Smith's foray in 1958 are shown on the accompanying map. They form the second highest total in England, second only to neighbouring Essex.

Further details on p.216

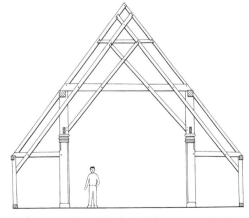

Reconstructed cross-section of the late-13th-century aisled hall at Purton Green, Stansfield.

MEDIEVAL AISLED HALLS

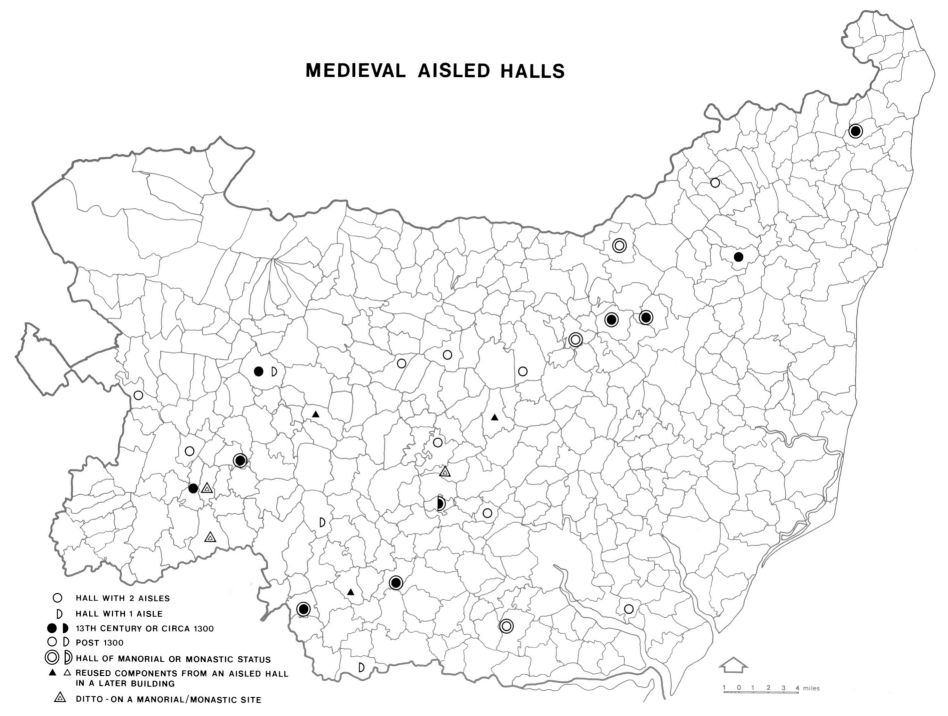

○   HALL WITH 2 AISLES

◗   HALL WITH 1 AISLE

● ◖   13TH CENTURY OR CIRCA 1300

○ ◖   POST 1300

◎ ◖   HALL OF MANORIAL OR MONASTIC STATUS

▲ △   REUSED COMPONENTS FROM AN AISLED HALL
IN A LATER BUILDING

△   DITTO - ON A MANORIAL/MONASTIC SITE

1 0 1 2 3 4 miles

80. AISLED BARNS

Philip Aitkens

The English climate forces every farmer to put his annual crop of corn under cover with haste, so he needs a strong, capacious and accessible building. For 700 years at least, this need was met in Suffolk by the largest and most valuable of all farm buildings—a timber-framed barn. By extending the roof slopes down to about 2 or 2.5 metres from the ground, extra space could be made behind the main posts along each side. At first these aisled barns only appeared on manorial and monastic sites, where resources enabled them to be built on a massive scale.

About fifteen medieval aisled barns remain in Suffolk, but only three have original roofs, and most have undergone major alterations. The few complete survivors are therefore immensely precious. Other barns were completely rebuilt at a later date, but from the same components. For example, a vanished medieval barn shown on a map of 1594 at Lower Farm, Risby, was rebuilt in the 17th century 30 metres from its original site: it incorporates parts of the old barn and of the old farmhouse. A 17th-century barn at Whepstead Hall (now converted into houses) has twelve main posts, five tiebeams and many other timbers taken from a manorial barn of *c.* 1300 which must have stood on the same site.

The accompanying map also shows about 70 post-medieval aisled barns, nearly all within the boundaries of West Suffolk. This must reflect the greater emphasis in the west on the growing of grain, and the pattern continues into adjacent grain-producing areas in Essex and Cambridgeshire. An interesting group of about 30 aisled barns lies west of Bury St Edmunds, many on poor soils, and must have been built to serve large estates. In the east of Suffolk, farms were generally smaller and their farming was more mixed; they normally relied on a three-bay unaisled barn, which often incorporated stabling at one end.

Gaps in the map need some explanation. The area north and east of Ipswich may have had aisled barns on many medieval manors, but if so the tradition died out early. The Breckland had huge acreages of arable land but few of its barns are earlier than 1800; perhaps the region was not prosperous enough to build large barns before then. The south-west of the county has not yet been properly surveyed: this is an area with medieval houses, and some fine early barns are likely to be found.

All Suffolk barns have certain features in common. Smaller barns were entered at the centre of one side by a pair of divided doors, high enough to take wagons loaded with sheaves. The sheaves were thrown to one side, and later brought back onto the paved floor inside the doors for threshing. Larger barns of six or more bays had two doorways, and smaller doors were normally provided opposite in the rear wall. Half of the later barns have only one aisle, at the rear: the extra space won by this aisle was at the expense of a row of obtrusive posts and braces, but was considered worthwhile—even after 1800 in a few cases.

All those aisled barns so far surveyed were timber-framed, the earlier ones with an infill of wattle and daub, but nearly all have been re-clad with hardwood weather-boarding and later with softwood. By the 17th century, boarding was becoming the more normal material because of its durability in a working building. Apart from the south of the county where plaintiles were more readily available, and apart from the very finest barns, roofs were usually thatched.

In the mid-20th century, many of Suffolk's best barns have been destroyed. It is vital that new uses be found for those which remain.

Further details on p.217

Interior of a 14th-century aisled barn at Rectory Farm, Gazeley. Demolished *c.* 1965.

AISLED BARNS

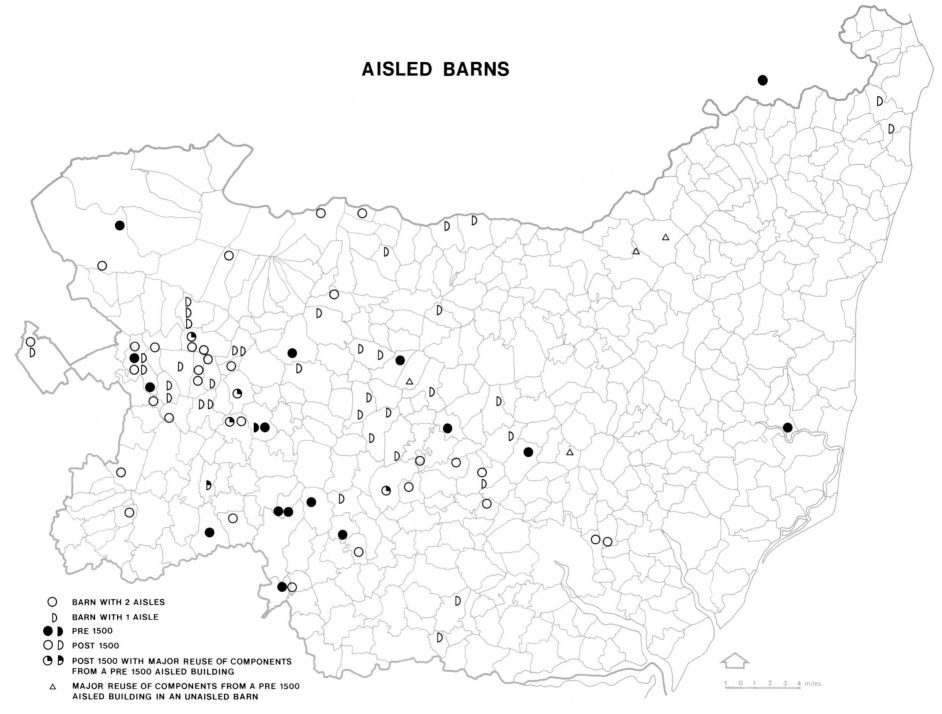

BARN WITH 2 AISLES

BARN WITH 1 AISLE

PRE 1500

POST 1500

POST 1500 WITH MAJOR REUSE OF COMPONENTS
FROM A PRE 1500 AISLED BUILDING

MAJOR REUSE OF COMPONENTS FROM A PRE 1500
AISLED BUILDING IN AN UNAISLED BARN

1 0 1 2 3 4 miles

81. CROWN-POST ROOFS

Sylvia Colman

The crown-post is the best known and most widely distributed component of Suffolk roofs, and is found in timber-framed buildings from the beginning of the 14th century until the end of the 16th. It is normally seen as the main, often the only, decorative focus of a medieval hall, but although it was frequently carved and moulded in an eye-catching manner, its underlying purpose was strictly practical. The carpenter's intention was to tie the roof together lengthwise (see diagram): he placed a long horizontal timber (collar-purlin) linking individual pairs of rafters below their collars, which was in turn supported by a post which stood on the tie-beam spanning the hall: this was the crown-post. Above the cap of the post, upwardly inclined braces to the collar and collar-purlin added further stability, as did substantial arched braces below the tie-beam. The term 'crown-post' was coined by the late Professor R.A. Cordingley in 1961.

The map shows the known distribution of crown-post roofs throughout Suffolk. The vast majority were domestic, with the crown-post set high above an open hall of the 14th or 15th century, or over the upper room of an associated wing. A separate symbol has been given for those completely storeyed houses which still have a crown-post roof, often, though not invariably, plain. These are usually considered to belong to the 16th century, but in urban settings can date from the later 15th. A few barns are also included, and a group of churches which have crown-posts in nave or porch: a small enclave of these is centred on Barking near Needham Market.

Much new information about these roofs has emerged from the Listed Building Re-Survey of the 1980s (see Map 75), which covered rural areas and small towns in all but the extreme south of the county, where the former Rural Districts of Clare, Cosford and Melford have

had only sporadic investigation. Work on the larger towns has continued into the 1990s, but amendments to the map have only been possible in those cases where new lists have already been issued.

In no part of the county was the crown-post the only form of medieval roof, but in the rich commercial and agricultural region of south and south-central Suffolk it was clearly a dominant status symbol, particularly in towns. However, in the south-west and to the north of the Gipping an even longer-lasting type was strongly entrenched, reducing the overall incidence of crown-posts there: this was the simple coupled-rafter roof which persisted from the 13th century through to the 17th. To the north and west of Bury St Edmunds, and in the south-eastern quarter of the county, a paucity of medieval survivals is partly responsible for a sparse distribution of crown-posts, while in the north-east of Suffolk raised-aisled halls (whose two-tiered structure could incorporate a crown-post) dominated in the 14th century, and queen-posts in the 15th century and later (Map 82).

In conjunction with other structural elements, crown-posts are important in the dating of timber-framed buildings. Mouldings on the cap and base can be related to those used by contemporary stone-masons. Upward braces from the head of the post, sometimes two-way but more often four-way, change gradually in form from wide and solid in the 14th century to thin and plank-like by the 16th, although the overall quality of the framing should always be taken into account. Downward-sloping braces from the post to the tie-beam can occur throughout the period in south-west Suffolk. Shafts can be square, chamfered and stopped in the angles, octagonal, fluted, cruciform or cross-quadrate in section. The earliest, from the early 14th century may be short and slender, with a disproportionately heavy cap

and bracing, but by the late 14th and 15th centuries shafts tended to be longer and more substantial. There is scope for a detailed study of the distribution and dating of different styles of crown-post within the whole of East Anglia.

Set on a tie-beam with a marked central camber, the medieval crown-post soared into a roof in which the collars were set high for visual effect, though not necessarily for maximum stability. Even in the upper room of a fully storeyed house it could look impressive in an open timber roof. However, as the roof-space of houses, both in towns and the countryside, came increasingly into use, the inconvenience of a central post within the attic led carpenters to abandon the crown-post in favour of roofs with side-purlins.

Further details on p.217

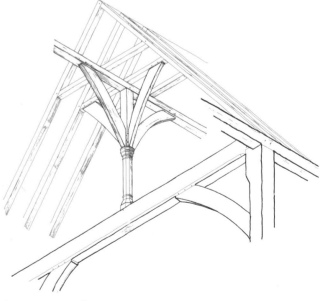

A crown-post roof.

CROWN POST ROOFS

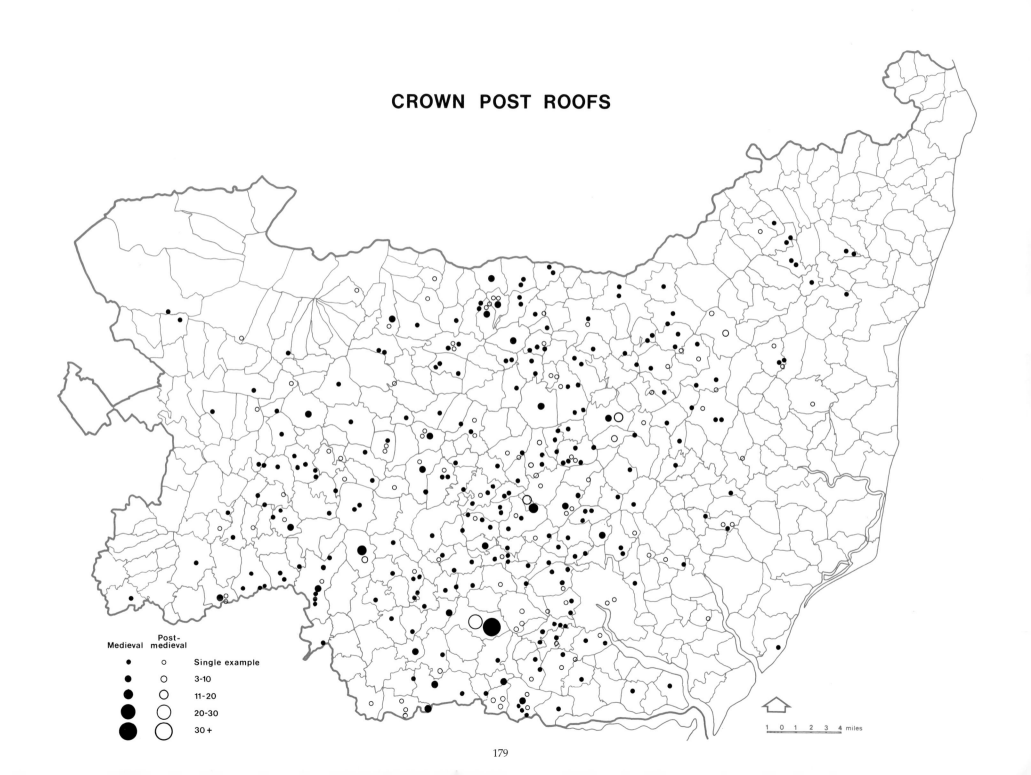

Medieval | Post-medieval
● | ○ Single example
● | ○ 3-10
● | ○ 11-20
● | ○ 20-30
● | ○ 30 +

1 0 1 2 3 4 miles

82. RAISED-AISLED HALLS AND QUEEN-POST ROOFS   Sylvia Colman & Mark Barnard

Many timber-framed houses of the 14th century, representing a wide cross-section of society, survive in Suffolk. Their halls are higher and narrower, admit more light and, in prosperous contexts, are a good deal more ornate than their 13th-century predecessors which were built in the aisled tradition. One particular group with a distinctive distribution is of especial interest: the so-called 'raised-aisled' halls.

In them, a truss of two tiers spans the hall, resembling an aisled truss lifted upon a tie-beam (see drawing). The tie-beam, supported by large solid braces, is set low, just above head height. It is morticed into the sides of the main posts, rather than linking their tops in the usual way: the truss thus creates a particularly marked division between the two bays of the hall. Most of these houses are of high social status, and by implication this deliberate division, as well as being structural, has social significance also.

The upper truss usually incorporates a crown-post, as in the drawing, but a raised-aisled hall of the early 15th century at Worlingworth had a king-post rising to a ridge-piece. A fascinating fragment of an important building at Church Farm, Fressingfield, has the most ostentatious of these roofs: its lower tier forms an arcade along the tie-beam and the upper tier has a crown-post and triple tie-beams.

A few raised-aisled halls are known in other parts of England, notably in the neighbouring county of Essex, while in Norfolk further research seems likely to add to the present small total of prestigious examples there. Currently, however, the greatest concentration is in north-central Suffolk. One notable tendency is for them to be sited in isolated positions and near parish boundaries; this, and their specific grouping, poses many unanswered social and economic questions. In

particular, the possibility of continental influences over their unusual structural form is so far completely unexplored, although Dutch influence on our brickwork has been long acknowledged. The widespread conversion of earlier aisled houses into raised-aisled halls, by narrowing or removing the aisles and inserting a low tie-beam into the open truss of the hall accompanied, or perhaps preceded, the adoption of developed raised-aisled forms.

A number of two-tier roofs are carried on tie-beams set at normal height. These tend to be later than raised-aisled forms and may be seen as an intermediate stage between raised-aisled and single-tier queen-post construction. Some are over open halls, while others are over first-floor accommodation; in each case upper trusses with crown-posts and king-posts are recorded. A few high quality barns of the 15th and early 16th centuries have two tiers of queen-posts. Perhaps the most impressive of these barns is at Park Farm, Somerleyton, where both tiers of queen-posts are arch-braced to the purlins.

Within the same tradition, but arguably at a lower social level, are the simpler single-tier queen-post roofs (see drawing). Their distinctive assembly of paired posts, collar and square-set purlins clearly indicates a derivation from aisled buildings, and distinguishes them from the queen-posts of other regions, where the posts act simply as additional supports below the collars; 'queen-strut' roofs like these, which occur in Suffolk, have not been plotted on the map.

Queen-post roofs occur most frequently in the same areas of central and northern Suffolk as raised-aisled halls, but their overall distribution is wider and they are more numerous (upwards of 250 still survive). One westerly instance is at Great Barton, a 16th-century

replacement over a 13th-century monastic aisled barn. Another, at Mildenhall, belongs to a small grouping across the border in Cambridgeshire. Some farm buildings can also have queen-post roofs, but the bulk are domestic. Medieval examples, in which the posts can be decorated similar to crown-posts, are rare in Suffolk, although commoner in Norfolk; most Suffolk examples are plain, and set above two-storeyed houses of the 16th century.

Parishes like Mendham and Laxfield, where queen-posts are most thickly scattered, are within the dairying area which boomed in the 16th and early 17th centuries and saw the widespread building and rebuilding of houses. Many seem initially to have had open timber roofs to their upper storey. But in later examples the upper rooms were ceiled over from the outset, giving a usable attic space above. As this happened, side-purlin roofs, which did not impede the roof area, replaced the more intrusive queen-posts.

Further details on p.217

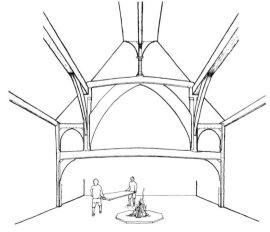

Interior of a raised-aisle hall.

180

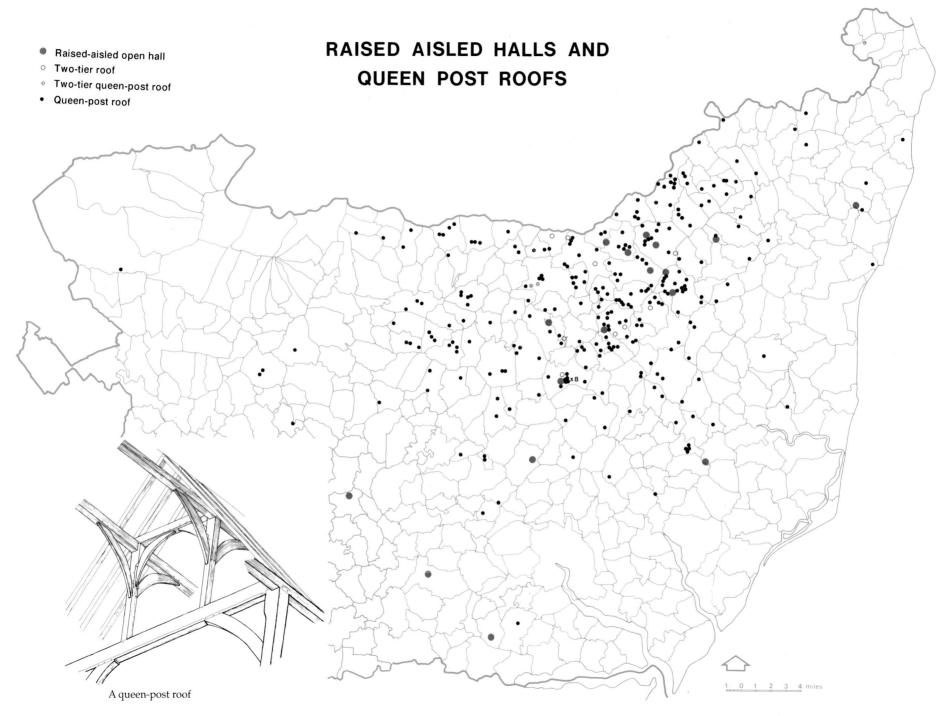

RAISED AISLED HALLS AND
QUEEN POST ROOFS

- ● Raised-aisled open hall
- ○ Two-tier roof
- ◉ Two-tier queen-post roof
- • Queen-post roof

x8

1 0 1 2 3 4 miles

A queen-post roof

83. WEALDEN HOUSES

Leigh Alston

Wealden houses are distinctive in appearance, and are perhaps the most famous and well-researched type of medieval house. They are commonly found, as the name suggests, in the Weald of Kent and Sussex. By 1970 some 350 had been identified in Kent alone, and others have been found since.[1] Forty examples are known in Suffolk, representing by far the largest concentration in any county north of the Thames, and others doubtless await discovery.

Although variants exist, the standard Wealden house conforms to the ubiquitous late-medieval plan of an open hall flanked by floored and jettied parlour and service rooms. The jettied ends of more typical Suffolk houses are built as cross-wings at right angles to the hall, while a Wealden house uses a single large roof to span the entire structure. Since the front wall of the open hall cannot be jettied in the absence of ceiling joists, it is characteristically recessed behind its roof. This creates a unitary facade which must have seemed fashionably novel and imposing when it first appeared, and even today is very satisfying.

The term 'Wealden house' is a modern one, and we have no knowledge of any earlier name. The Wealdens of Suffolk were built by local carpenters for local purposes, and there is no evidence to suggest that the style was developed in the south-east and exported elsewhere. No more than 25 examples have so far been found in Essex, and a relatively small number in other counties as far afield as Yorkshire and Herefordshire. Norfolk boasts only four. The earliest firmly dated Wealden is in Winchester, well outside the main area of concentration, and was built during the 1340s.[2] The oldest example in Kent, at Chart Sutton, has been dated by tree-ring analysis to 1379-80.[3] Although no Suffolk Wealdens have yet been accurately dated in this way, a number pre-date the earliest Kentish examples on stylistic

grounds. The oldest surviving Wealden in the county is probably Hill House in Woolpit, which was apparently built in 1350-75. Suffolk carpenters have at least as great a claim to have invented the Wealden style as those of Kent.[4]

The construction of a Wealden house presents a number of technical difficulties. The roof-plate over the hall requires additional support to withstand the burden placed upon it, and the hall's crown-post cannot be central to both hall and roof. The ingenious and sometimes unique solutions of local carpenters make Wealdens as fascinating to the student of historic carpentry as to the social historian. Reversed assembly is common in Suffolk, where the tiebeam lies beneath rather than above the roof-plate and therefore supports it, and in certain technically dubious cases the two timbers are simply tenoned together. The most dramatically indigenous Wealden is at Debenham where a native raised-aisled hall is built in Wealden form.

The origins of the Wealden lie in the development of domestic architecture during the High Middle Ages. Until the end of the 13th century most vernacular houses were completely unfloored, with relatively large halls and small, aisled end bays. As more functions such as storage and sleeping were removed from the hall during the later 13th and 14th centuries, the end bays became larger and were more likely to be floored over. The Wealden was a logical extension of this development, particularly in urban locations where jetties were both fashionable and pragmatic. As the map demonstrates, the majority of Suffolk's Wealdens are in towns. Although some are large and of high status, many occupy restricted sites where the Wealden form was a sensible alternative to houses with cramped cross-wings or without fashionable jetties. The single roof of a Wealden is more economical to build than the multiple

roofs required by other forms, and is therefore ideal for urban 'terracing'. At least one pair of semi-detached open halls in Suffolk is built in Wealden form, and this phenomenon is common in other counties.

Of the few rural Wealdens in Suffolk, most seem to be in the vicinity of wealthy towns and may well represent the country retreats of urban merchants. In contrast to Kent and Sussex where Wealdens proliferated in the late medieval countryside, they never became fashionable among the yeoman farmers of Suffolk. After 1440, when Wealdens became the norm in the south-east,[5] choosing to build a Wealden in Suffolk remained a bold statement of confidence and innovation, even where a restricted plot all but dictated the decision.

The county's Wealdens are remarkably diverse, ranging from substantial and imposing merchant's houses to small tenanted halls. Stowmarket boasts probably the largest example in East Anglia, at a length of 56 feet, while the hall of the Cock Inn in Clare is just 11 feet long. Perhaps the grandest Wealden of all, at Barton Mills, dates from c.1520; built with a chimney-stack to heat its open hall it was something of an anachronism from the beginning. It should not surprise us that no manor houses, where a natural conservatism might be expected, are known to have been Wealdens. The Wealden form belongs primarily to the county's urban élite, and to those among them who wanted their houses to be a little different from those of their neighbours.

Further details on p. 217

WEALDEN HOUSES

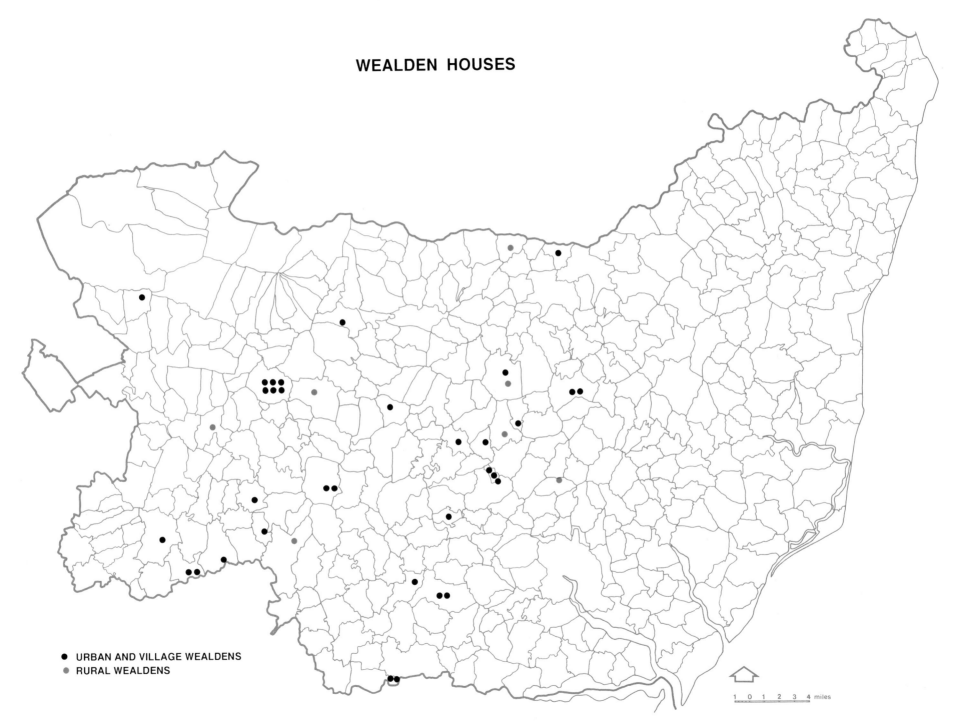

● URBAN AND VILLAGE WEALDENS
● RURAL WEALDENS

1 0 1 2 3 4 miles

84. COASTAL FORTIFICATIONS, 1500-1900

Peter Kent

Since 1500 the fortifications of Suffolk have been almost exclusively coastal, for the qualities which make the Suffolk shore so alluring to weekenders—a succession of beaches and low cliffs, close to London—were exactly those which attracted potential invaders. Apart from Harwich Haven, three anchorages might enable a fleet to lie offshore and disembark an invading army: Hollesley Bay, Sole Bay and Lowestoft Roads. It is in those areas that defences have been concentrated.

The first recorded fortification was a small battery built at Dunwich in 1479,[1] but the first real attempts at coordinated coastal defence began in the reign of Henry VIII. In 1539, in response to a serious threat from France and the Holy Roman Empire, the king ordered a survey of the whole English coast from the Humber to Cornwall. The plans for Suffolk included forts at Lowestoft, Southwold, Minsmere, Aldeburgh and Landguard Point.[2] Much of this scheme remained on parchment, but three small batteries were built at Lowestoft, some entrenchments dug at Minsmere and two 'bulwarkes of earth and wood' constructed on Landguard Point. The latter, despite their importance, were dismantled in 1552.[3]

Over the next fifty years various schemes were proposed and a few guns were emplaced, but the coast was practically defenceless when the Spanish Armada threatened in 1588. A survey listed twenty-nine vulnerable points but only a few new works were built.[4] The surviving earthworks at Landguard were restored and new batteries built at Lowestoft, Southwold and Aldeburgh.

The defences subsequently fell slowly into ruin, until the 17th century when privateers from Dunkirk attacked towns and coastal shipping. This prompted urgent petitions for new artillery. A new eight-gun battery was raised at Southwold and ten new guns sent to Aldeburgh.[5] On Landguard Point the first real fort was built in 1625. Designed by a Dutch engineer, this was a conventional four-bastioned fort with turf ramparts and brick barracks. It was this fort, with some repairs and additions, which was attacked by the Dutch in 1667, the last time that an enemy force landed in Suffolk. Afterwards it became so derelict that it was demolished and completely rebuilt in 1717, to a surprisingly innovative design.[6]

In 1744 during the War of the Austrian Succession an invasion scare resulted in a new fort at Lowestoft, a battery at Pakefield, six 18-pounders which still survive on Gun Hill at Southwold, and two new batteries at Aldeburgh. But the most important work was the rebuilding, yet again, of Landguard Fort with five bastions.[7]

The War of American Independence, in which both Holland and France joined to discomfort Britain, produced a new threat. Several batteries were erected at Aldeburgh, three new forts at Lowestoft and a complex system of earthworks around Landguard Fort.[8]

Most of these works were maintained during the Napoleonic Wars, although the outer earthworks at Landguard were condemned and demolished. The danger of invasion was never greater than in 1803. Floating batteries armed with four guns, hastily improvised from barges, were moored in the mouths of the Deben and Alde, while a 64-gun warship was anchored at Hollesley Bay.[9] This, however, was only a temporary solution, and work began on building Martello towers in 1809. Twenty were proposed with two large eight-gun towers at Orford and Aldeburgh, but only seventeen were built with ten associated batteries. Each tower had three guns, and the batteries either three, five or

seven. The last and most northerly of the towers stood at Slaughden south of Aldeburgh, and was of unique quatrefoil design with four guns.

With the defeat of Napoleon, most of the earthwork batteries were allowed to decay, though the Martello towers were still maintained and armed. In 1860 a Royal Commission investigating Britain's defence did not make any recommendations concerning Landguard Fort, but in 1862 a small seven-sided fort with fourteen guns, costing £10,000, was built on Shotley Point to cover the harbour.[10]

In 1870 growing fears of German naval power prompted a reassessment of the defences of Harwich harbour. Landguard Fort was extensively rebuilt as a fine casemated battery, mounting ten heavy muzzle-loaded guns firing through armoured shields. All other batteries along the coast had been dismantled and the only other guns in Suffolk were the six ancient cannon at Southwold. Landguard Fort was soon obsolescent and every successive decade saw additions to its armament. A battery with two 6-inch guns and one 10-inch gun on disappearing carriages was built outside the fort in 1888, followed by another similar battery in 1898. Finally in 1900 a small battery mounting two 4.7-inch guns was built in front of the fort and named after Captain Darell who had defended the fort in 1667.[11] The harbour was also defended by an elaborate system of submarine mines that were stored in a special building beside the fort. At the turn of the century Landguard Fort was at its zenith, 'the bulwark of the most important harbour between the Thames and the Humber, as hard a nut to crack as was discovered by our Dutch foemen'.[12] As for the rest of the Suffolk coastline, the War Office felt that its defence could be safely left to mobile columns of cavalry and artillery.

Further details on p.217

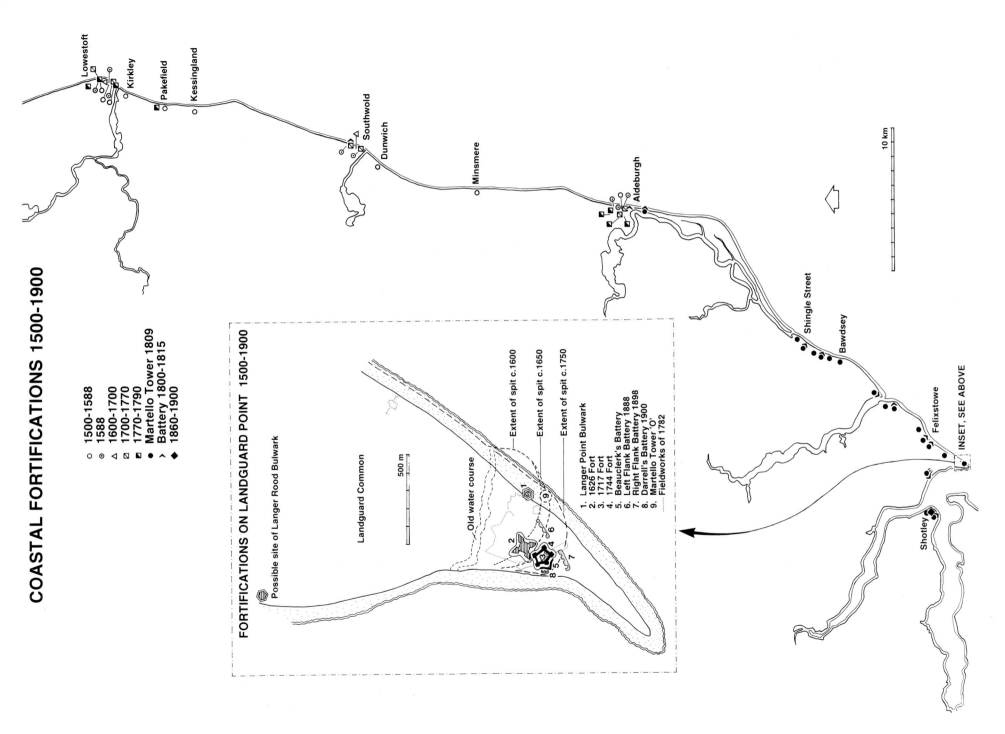

COASTAL FORTIFICATIONS 1500-1900

Legend:
- ○ 1500-1588
- ◎ 1588
- △ 1600-1700
- ◩ 1700-1770
- ▨ 1770-1790
- ● Martello Tower 1809
- ➤ Battery 1800-1815
- ◆ 1860-1900

Lowestoft
Kirkley
Pakefield
Kessingland
Southwold
Dunwich
Minsmere
Aldeburgh
Shingle Street
Bawdsey
Felixstowe
INSET, SEE ABOVE
Shotley

10 km

FORTIFICATIONS ON LANDGUARD POINT 1500-1900

- Possible site of Langer Rood Bulwark
- Landguard Common
- Old water course
- Extent of spit c.1600
- Extent of spit c.1650
- Extent of spit c.1750

500 m

1. Langer Point Bulwark
2. 1626 Fort
3. 1717 Fort
4. 1744 Fort
5. Beauclerk's Battery
6. Left Flank Battery 1888
7. Right Flank Battery 1898
8. Darrell's Battery 1900
9. Martello Tower 'O'
.... Fieldworks of 1782

In the early 1900s, most of the elaborate and expensive artillery assembled at Landguard Fort was scrapped, and by 1910 the fort's armament had been reduced to two 6-inch and two 4.7-inch guns. It was soon realised, however, that the reduction was too great for safety and a new work, Brackenbury Battery, armed with two modern 9.2-inch guns, was begun in 1914 at North Felixstowe.[1]

When war came in August 1914 an invasion was officially discounted, although it was thought that the Germans might launch a disruptive raid. Troops were sent to guard likely landing-places, but trenches were not immediately dug as the war was expected to be short. In 1916 fears of invasion were renewed when Lowestoft was bombarded by German battle-cruisers. In response a battery of six 60-pounders and two monitors were sent to the town.[2] More trenches were dug along the coast, a few guns emplaced and the first concrete pillboxes were built. More of the latter were constructed south of Lowestoft in April-May 1918, when the General Staff thought that the Germans might attempt to resolve the military stalemate by invading eastern England.[3] After the Armistice, when the field works and temporary batteries were dismantled, only the pillboxes remained.

At the beginning of the Second World War in 1939, no-one feared a German landing. Holidaymakers still frolicked on the beaches, and the only use envisaged for the pillboxes of 1916-18 was as air-raid shelters. The fall of France and occupation of the Netherlands changed the situation abruptly. Although the Germans were expected to land on the south coast, it was thought that a diversionary assault might be attempted on East Anglia. This prompted the most ambitious programme of fortification ever undertaken in Suffolk. The coast and small ports were again fortified and extensive defences constructed inland.

The defensive strategy called for a strong coastal crust to hold invaders on the beaches. If this was pierced, several 'stop-lines' would be defended before the GHQ line, guarding London and the industrial Midlands, was reached. All road-junctions were to be heavily defended and small towns made into 'tank proof islands' to prevent 'the enemy rushing about and tearing the guts out of the country'.[4] Most towns were defended to some extent, and Ipswich and Lowestoft became fortresses ringed by anti-tank obstacles and pillboxes. In Suffolk five stop-lines were planned. The first was based on the River Waveney, the second on the Hundred River from Beccles to Kessingland, the third on the River Blyth from Southwold to Halesworth, the fourth from Euston to Stowmarket, while the fifth and most important ran from Mildenhall through Bury St Edmunds to Lavenham and Sudbury.

The main features on the coast were emergency batteries rapidly installed in June-July 1940, armed with elderly guns from scrapped warships. Thirteen batteries were built along the coast from Felixstowe to Lowestoft, although not all were operational at the same time. Early 1943 saw Suffolk's coastal defences at their strongest with two 9.2-inch and twenty-two 6-inch guns, two 12-pounders, two 4-inch guns and two twin 6-pounders. After this the artillery was gradually reduced as the threat of attack dwindled.

The emergency batteries were all similar in design and construction, although with local variations in materials and detail. Two guns were emplaced in separate gunhouses to give protection from splinters, aerial straffing and small-arms fire. Between the gunhouses was a semi-underground corridor lined with magazines and shelters. On either side of the guns were two searchlights in shelters with armoured shutters. Both guns and lights were controlled from a battery observation post. The batteries were camouflaged with foliage, nets, hayricks, and false roofs which unfortunately tended to blow off when the guns fired.

Other shoreline defences included miles of scaffolding on the water's edge, thousands of concrete blocks along the beaches and obstructing every exit, tens of thousands of anti-tank mines buried in the sand, while clifftops and dunes were heavily entrenched and festooned with barbed wire. The most permanent components were pillboxes: nearly one hundred were built along the coast, and even larger numbers inland. The basic designs were issued by the War Office, but numerous local adaptions resulted in a bewildering variety of shapes, sizes and materials. The standard was a small hexagon built of reinforced concrete with walls eighteen inches thick, although many were also rectangular. The largest of these, sited mainly along the stop-lines, was designed to take an anti-tank gun.

From 1943 the coastal defences were gradually reduced and many batteries closed. Work began on clearing the beaches before the German surrender. As soon as the war in Europe was over, the whole system was quickly dismantled. In the winter of 1945-6 all guns were removed from the batteries and scrapped, but the emplacements were only demolished if they interfered with civilian activities. Only the guns at Landguard and Brackenbury Battery were retained, but not for long because fixed defences were increasingly redundant. In 1956 the concept of coastal artillery was officially abandoned, and the 6-pounders and two remaining 6-inch guns were removed from Landguard. Coastal defence, in a form comprehensible to Henry VIII's 'sad and expert men' who first surveyed the coast of East Anglia in 1539, had ended for ever.

Further details on p.218

FIRST AND SECOND WORLD WAR DEFENCES

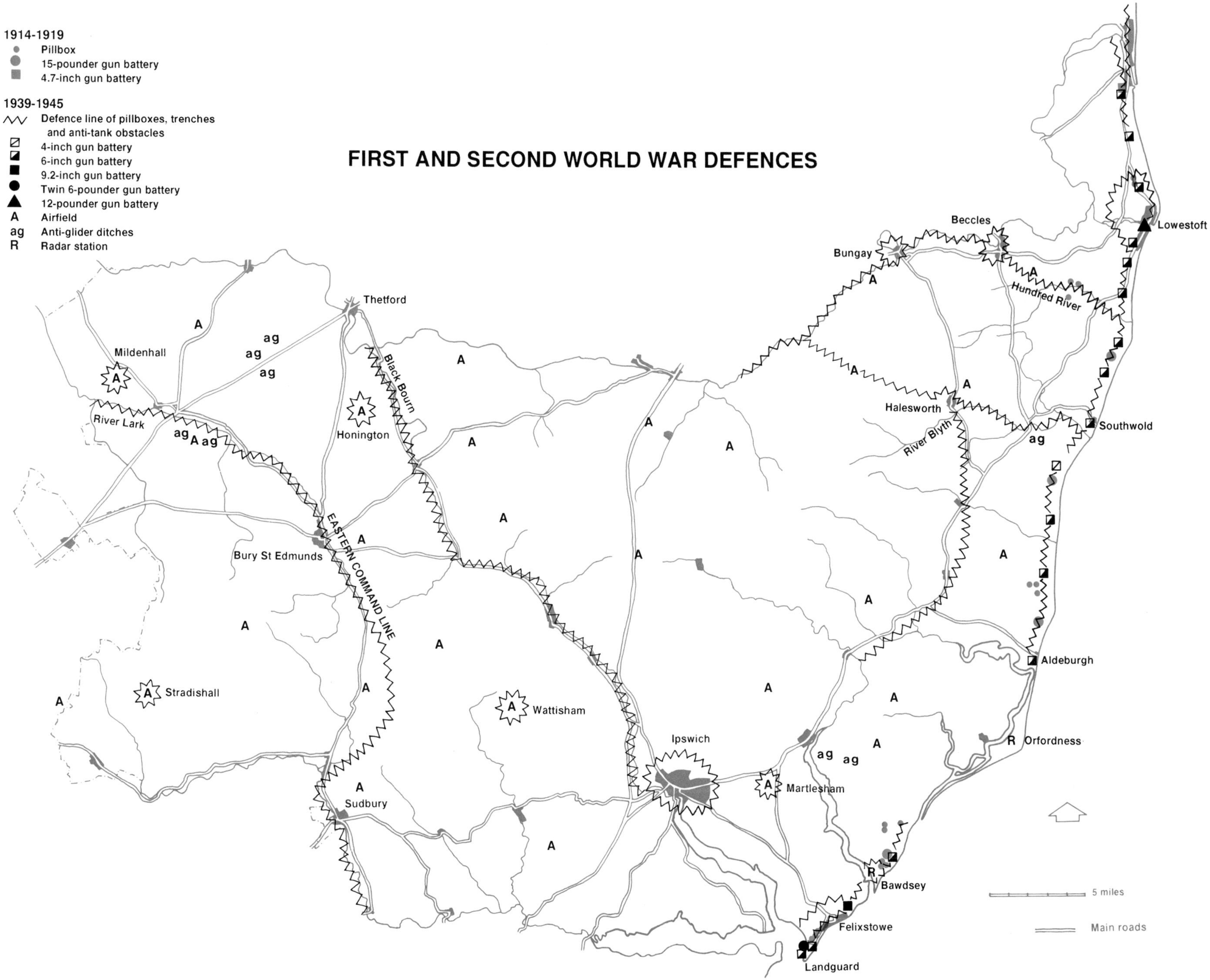
1914-1919
Pillbox
15-pounder gun battery
4.7-inch gun battery
1939-1945
Defence line of pillboxes, trenches and anti-tank obstacles
4-inch gun battery
6-inch gun battery
9.2-inch gun battery
Twin 6-pounder gun battery
12-pounder gun battery
A Airfield
ag Anti-glider ditches
R Radar station
Thetford
Mildenhall
River Lark
Honington
Black Bourn
Bury St Edmunds
EASTERN COMMAND LINE
Stradishall
Wattisham
Sudbury
Ipswich
Martlesham
Bungay
Beccles
Lowestoft
Hundred River
Halesworth
River Blyth
Southwold
Aldeburgh
Orfordness
Bawdsey
Felixstowe
Landguard
5 miles
Main roads

When the First World War broke out, the value of having aircraft to aid military and naval forces was quickly realized. This led to the creation of a Royal Flying Corps (RFC) and a Royal Naval Air Service (RNAS). From 1914 to 1918 take-offs and landings still relied on any large pasture or open space devoid of trees or buildings. As Suffolk was well removed from France, the RFC had little interest in establishing installations here during the first year of hostilities. However, the Royal Navy had set up a seaplane base on the Orwell estuary at Felixstowe in 1913; this was a major marine centre for operations across the North Sea, also for the design and construction of large flying boats and, after the war, home to the Marine Aircraft and Experimental Establishment. The RNAS also operated land-based aircraft, and from 1916 nearby Trimley served as its airfield.

Suffolk's coast first attracted the RFC in 1915, which moved its Armament Experimental Flight to Orford Ness. In the same year the policy was begun of selecting sites for night landings. Zeppelins raided at night, and the limited range of intercepting aircraft demanded airfields close to the enemy's likely objectives, the main east-coast ports. The first in Suffolk is believed to be Covehithe, used by the RNAS from March 1915 to defend Yarmouth. Another opened at Aldeburgh in August that year. Other night landing grounds were established at Lakenheath, Newmarket, Elmswell, Hadleigh and Martlesham Heath. These were merely landing areas at least 400 yards square. Most were used only rarely, but a few were given extra facilities.

Faced with increased Zeppelin activity the RFC placed No 75 Squadron with one flight of biplanes at Elmswell in September 1917, another flight at Hadleigh and a third in Norfolk. Meanwhile Martlesham Heath had developed into a true aerodrome, on which the RFC's Experimental Aircraft Flight took up residence in January 1917. Soon after, the RNAS abandoned Trimley in favour of Martlesham, and a landing ground at Butley became another experimental station. Newmarket racecourse also received a fully fledged aerodrome where two squadrons trained for night-flying.

With the exception of Martlesham, Felixstowe and Orford Ness, all other military landing grounds in Suffolk were abandoned after 1918.[2] It was not until the 1930s, when war threatened again, that military aviation was revived. Funding for a new bomber airfield resulted in the selection of Mildenhall. Opened in October 1934, it was the first of four bomber airfields built in Suffolk. The others were Honington (opened May 1937), Stradishall (February 1938) and Wattisham (March 1939). All had grass surfaces, four hangars and permanent buildings.

When the Second World War broke out, two civilian airfields at Ipswich and Westley were taken over by the RAF. Both were too restricted for regular operations, although Ipswich served as a satellite and became a base for target-towing. Westley hosted army co-operation units but appears to have been little used after 1943. The RAF again took over Newmarket racecourse, moving in Wellington bombers a few days before war was declared. Of the five regular RAF aerodromes in Suffolk in 1939, only Martlesham Heath served Fighter Command; its squadrons were active in the Battle of Britain. Because Felixstowe was in the front line, its experimental units were moved north. Later, however, the station was used for modifying flying boats. Orford Ness retained a landing strip but this was for special use.

During the first two years of the war no new airfields were built in Suffolk. However, in the next two years, no fewer than twenty-four were completed or under construction. The Air Ministry had identified many possible sites and in 1941 construction began at Chedburgh, Horham and Lakenheath, the latter already a satellite of Mildenhall. These were to be bomber bases with concrete runways. The specification for new bomber airfields was amended several times, but by the summer of 1942 a Class A airfield required three intersecting runways, the main one 6000 ft long and the others 4200 ft. With accommodation for 3000 personnel, each airfield cost £1 million to construct.

When the USA joined the war and decided to base an enormous offensive airforce in England, the Air Ministry had to find 75 sites in East Anglia for bomber airfields, of which 21 were in Suffolk. In fact 19 were on virgin sites, while Honington and Wattisham were upgraded. RAF Bomber Command retained its existing airfields in the west of the county, with new bases at Tuddenham and West Wickham (later re-named Wratting Common). Additionally a fighter airfield was to be built at Leiston and an emergency runway of 9000 ft at Woodbridge. By December 1942, it became obvious that contractors did not have enough labour, equipment or materials to complete the programme in the specified time. So one airfield, at Crowfield, was postponed indefinitely and work stopped at Hepworth and Butley. Later, the last two were re-started and re-named Shepherd's Grove and Bentwaters.

Many airfields extended into two or three parishes, and often the official name was not chosen with conspicuous accuracy. Prominent examples are 'Framlingham' which was three miles away from the town in Parham and Great Glemham, 'Bury St Edmunds' which was in Rougham, and 'Lavenham' which was largely in Alpheton.

Further details on p.218

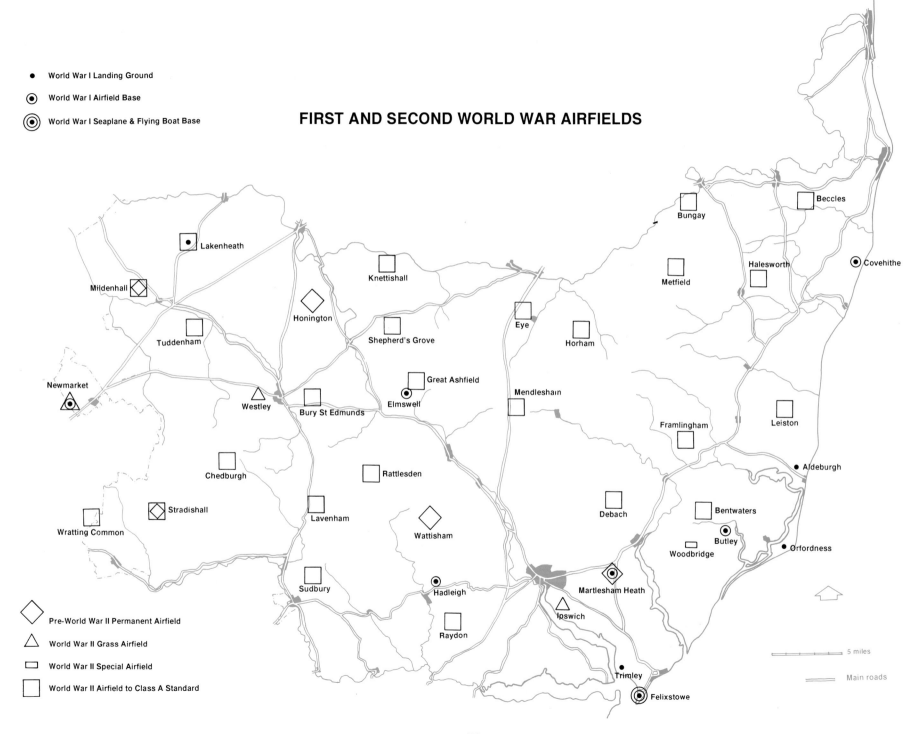

FIRST AND SECOND WORLD WAR AIRFIELDS

● World War I Landing Ground

◉ World War I Airfield Base

◎ World War I Seaplane & Flying Boat Base

◇ Pre-World War II Permanent Airfield

△ World War II Grass Airfield

▭ World War II Special Airfield

☐ World War II Airfield to Class A Standard

Beccles
Bungay
Lakenheath
Mildenhall
Knettishall
Halesworth
Covehithe
Metfield
Honington
Tuddenham
Shepherd's Grove
Eye
Horham
Newmarket
Great Ashfield
Mendlesham
Westley
Elmswell
Bury St Edmunds
Framlingham
Leiston
Chedburgh
Rattlesden
Aldeburgh
Stradishall
Lavenham
Debach
Bentwaters
Wratting Common
Wattisham
Butley
Woodbridge
Orfordness
Sudbury
Hadleigh
Martlesham Heath
Ipswich
Raydon
Trimley
Felixstowe

5 miles

Main roads

189

FURTHER INFORMATION

Abbreviations:

AJ	*Archaeological Journal*
BPP	*British Parliamentary Papers*
BAR	British Archaeological Reports
BRS	British Record Society
CBA	Council for British Archaeology
CUL	Cambridge University Library
EAA	*East Anglian Archaeology*
JBAA	*Journal of the British Archaeological Association*
NA	*Norfolk Archaeology*
NRS	Norfolk Records Society
PPS	*Proceedings of the Prehistoric Society*
PRO	Public Record Office, London
PSIAH	*Proceedings of the Suffolk Institute of Archaeology & History*
RCHME	Royal Commission on the Historical Monuments of England
SR	*Suffolk Review*
SRO(B)	Suffolk Record Office (Bury St Edmunds)
SRO(I)	Suffolk Record Office (Ipswich)
SRS	Suffolk Records Society
SMR	Sites and Monuments Record, maintained by the Archaeology Service of Suffolk County Council
UEA	University of East Anglia
VCH	*Victoria County History*

1. EARLY PRINTED MAPS OF SUFFOLK

REFERENCES

1. Parks are shown at or near Westwood, Henham, Yoxford (to the south-west), Heveningham, Huntingfield, Letheringham, Framlingham, Wingfield, Monk Soham, Debenham (?Crows Hall), Thwaite, Denham (?Brome misplaced), Burgate, Redgrave, Westhorpe, Nettlestead, Hintlesham, Tendring, Smallbridge, three near Lavenham, Ickworth, Cavendish, Chilton and three between Stradishall and Hundon. The parishes of Easton 'Gosbek' and Gipping 'Newtowne' have since lost their first and second names respectively.

2. Easton Ness was shown uneroded on maps long after the church was lost in the mid-17th century. John Kirby, a local man, knew better in 1736. Aldringham stayed on the coast on Thomas Kitchin's map of 1747, but was moved inland by Emanuel Bowen in 1750. Kirby included parks, churches (including those in ruin), windmills, watermills and woods. Other cartographers such as Bowen developed this approach and added other features and marginal notes.

3. All scales are expressed in miles *to the inch.*

4. His two corrections: Shelley from Samford to Babergh and, in an afterthought, Butley from Plomesgate to Loes. Then, in a foolish late move, he brought Chilton by Sudbury into Risbridge by means of a long corridor. See *PSIAH*, xxxiii, 318-22.

5. John Ogilby's *Britannia*, vol.1, has seven maps which pass through Suffolk (Plates 46, 52, 54, 73-5 and 92). It was Ogilby who on his road from Colchester to Yarmouth (Pl.54) first marked the park of Seckford Hall, the mansion in Bealings where Saxton's patron was brought up. As Cosmographer Royal, Ogilby set out to cover the whole country in road maps (which he did), county maps (few exist) and town plans. Of the latter, only London, Lynn, Canterbury and Edinburgh were published; Ipswich and Maldon were surveyed by Gregory King and Robert Felgate in 1674, but of their Maldon work all trace is lost. As late as 1698 the plan of Ipswich was engraved on nine sheets and published by the herald painter, Thomas Steward of Brook Street, Ipswich. This detailed plan at 100 feet to the inch is an under-exploited resource for the 17th-century county town.

6. He added nine more parks, the first six culled from Ogilby's roads: Euston, Haughley, Little Glemham, Darsham, Weston, Erwarton, also Hurt's Hall, Assington and another near Stoke-by-Nayland. As measurements varied according to local custom, great, middle and small miles are shown. A smaller map (7.5 miles) was engraved for Cox's *Magna Britannia* of 1720. Again, copying was rife. Henry Overton, putting roads on a copy of Speed in 1713, failed to show the direct route from Ipswich to Woodbridge and left the traveller to meander through Westerfield, Tuddenham, Culpho and Grundisburgh. He did, however, add distances along post roads as figures in circles.

7. The *Traveller* of 1764 also has four strip-maps of roads all prepared for the engraver by Andrew Baldrey, Joshua Kirby's partner as house and herald painters. A plan of Ipswich, reduced from Ogilby, and maps of separate hundreds which Baldrey had drawn exist only as originals. The title page still proclaims John Kirby as author of the much improved book.

8. Most extant prints from the plates of 1766 were made in 1825 when Stephen Piper of Ipswich, claiming to have revised them, merely added his name as publisher. The half-scale map reappeared, unrevised and still dated 1737, but bearing the imprint of John Shave, an Ipswich printer and bookseller of the 1760s.

9. Printed on twelve sheets, ed. D. Dymond (SRS, xv, 1972)

10. The author is grateful to Raymond Frostick for valuable advice in the preparation of this survey.

2. THE SHAPING OF SUFFOLK

SOURCES

The succession of climatic changes is recorded in deep-sea cores extracted from the ocean floors in different parts of the globe. Analysis of the oxygen isotope in these sediments demonstrates a consistent pattern of oscillating cooler and warmer periods of sea temperature. These are considered to reflect the complex sequence of glacial advances and recessions, especially evident in the northern hemisphere during the last 700,000 years. Past environments can be partly reconstructed by the study of fossil pollen in the sediments of marshes and lakes.

REFERENCES

1. Named after a site at Castle Bytham, Lincs., where the extinct river was first identified (also sometimes

called the Ingham River).

2. This date is based on the so-called 'long chronology' which identifies the Anglian Glaciation with a particular dated stage of the oxygen isotope's temperature scale, mainly based on numbers of buried soils found in the loess of central Europe. Clear, unequivocal correlation of marine episodes with terrestrial events has still to be demonstrated.

3. The number of times that Suffolk has suffered glacial or periglacial conditions is not known in detail, but the fourfold scheme of glaciation based on early studies of the Alpine sequence is no longer tenable.

4. As the Quaternary geology of Britain is more fully represented here than elsewhere, its various stages have been named mainly from East Anglian sites. The stages which cover the periods of known human occupation are, from oldest to youngest:

Cromerian	mainly warm
Anglian	mainly cool
Hoxnian	mainly warm
Wolstonian	mainly cool
Ipswichian	mainly warm
Devensian	mainly cool
Flandrian	mainly warm (the stage in which we live now)

BIBLIOGRAPHY

Ashton, N., Healy, F. & Pettitt, P. (eds.), *Stone Age Archaeology. Essays in Honour of John Wymer* (1998)

Bridgland, D.R., *Quaternary of the Thames* (1994)

Evans, J.G., *The Environment of Early Man in the British Isles* (1975)

Murphy, P., 'Prehistoric Environments and Economies' in Barringer, C. (ed.), *Aspects of East Anglian Pre-history* (1984)

Rose, J., 'Major River Systems of Central and Southern Britain during the Early and Middle Pleistocene', *Terra Nova*, 6, 435-43

Stuart, A.J., *Pleistocene Vertebrates* (1982)

Sutcliffe, A.J., *On the Track of Ice Age Mammals* (1985)

3. SOLID GEOLOGY

SOURCE

British Geological Survey, map of solid geology at scale 1:625,000 (South sheet, 3rd edition, 1979). More detailed geological maps at a scale of 1:63,000 or 1:50,000 are only available for parts of the county (Woodbridge & Felixstowe, Ipswich, Sudbury, Bury St Edmunds, Newmarket, Diss and Lowestoft).

BIBLIOGRAPHY

British Geological Survey Memoirs:

Bristow, C.R., *Geology of the Country around Bury St Edmunds* (1990) [for sheet 189]

Gallois, R.W., *Geology of the Country around Ely* (1988) [for sheet 173]

Mathers, S.J., Horton, A. & Bristow, C.R., *Geology of the Country around Diss* (1993) [for sheet 175]

Pattison, J., Berridge, N.G., Allsop, J.M. & Wilkinson, I.P., *Geology of the Country around Sudbury* [Suffolk] (1993) [for sheet 206]

4. SURFACE GEOLOGY

SOURCE

British Geological Survey, map of surface geology at scale of 1: 625,000 (South Sheet, 1st edition, Quaternary, 1977). More detailed geological maps at a scale of 1:63,000 or 1:50,000 are only available for parts of the county (Woodbridge & Felixstowe, Ipswich, Sudbury, Bury St Edmunds, Diss, Newmarket and Lowestoft).

REFERENCE

1. Until recently, much of the glacial till of Suffolk was thought to be more recent than the Lowestoft Till and was described as the Gipping Till, but the latter is now considered to be only a weathered part of the former.

BIBLIOGRAPHY

Chatwin, C.P., *British Regional Geology, East Anglia and Adjoining Areas* (4th edition, 1961): a good outline, although the chapters on the Quaternary are now outdated.

Spencer, H.E.P., 'A Contribution to the Geological History of Suffolk', *Trans. Suffolk Naturalists' Soc.*, vol. 13 (1967), 197-209, 290-313, 366-89; vol. 15 (1970), 148-96.

Wymer, J.J., 'East Anglian Palaeolithic Sites and their Settings' in Barringer, C. (ed.), *Aspects of East Anglian Pre-history* (1984)

5. SOIL REGIONS

SOURCES

The map is based on the *Soil Map of England and Wales 1:250,000*, Sheet 4 (eastern England) by the Soil Survey of England and Wales, 1983. For more detailed studies see W.M. Corbett, *Breckland Forest Soils* (Soil Survey, 1973), and R.S. Searle & C.A.H. Hodge, *Soils of the Cambridge and Ely District* (Soil Survey, 1976)

REFERENCES

1. R. Hoppitt, 'A Relative Relief Map of Suffolk', *Trans. Suffolk Naturalists' Soc.*, 25 (1989), 80-5.

2. D.N.J. MacCulloch (ed.), *The Chorography of Suffolk*, SRS, xix (1976), 19. In 1669 Sir Philip Skippon noted that the country around Eye was called 'high Suffolk': C.M. Hood, 'An East Anglian Contemporary of Pepys', *NA*, xii (1926), 168.

3. J. Kirby, *The Suffolk Traveller* (1735), 1-2

4. A. Young, *General View of the Agriculture of the County of Suffolk* (1797), 3-5. Young refers to sand blows in both the east and west sand areas. A notorious 'sand-flood' which overwhelmed Santon Downham is recounted by the local squire, Thomas Wright, in *Philosophical Transactions*, 3 (1668), 722-5.

5. W. & H. Raynbird, *On the Agriculture of Suffolk* (1849), 2-5

6. Anonymous contribution in H. Stevenson, *The Birds of Norfolk* (1866), i, xlviii-liv.

7. There are 14th-century references to lands called *le Brech*, *le Breach* and even *Brechelond*, but they become more common from the 16th century onwards as *brake*, *break* or *breck*. The origin is Old English *brec*, 'breaking, breach, land broken up for cultivation'.

8. W.G. Clarke, 'A Breckland Ramble', *The Naturalists' Jour.*, 3 (1894), 90-107.

9. The Broads (designated 1986), Breckland (1988) and Suffolk River Valleys (1988).

10. Breckland, Broads, East Anglian Chalk, Fens, South Norfolk and High Suffolk Claylands, South Suffolk

and North Essex Claylands, Suffolk Coast and Heaths. The descriptions of the 'Character Areas' have not yet been published.

11. The published profiles are: Breckland (1998), Broads (1996), East Anglian Chalk (1997), East Anglian Plain (1997), Fens (1997) and Suffolk Coast and Heaths (1997), Suffolk Coast Maritime (1997).

BIBLIOGRAPHY

Beardall, C. & Casey D., *Suffolk's Changing Countryside* (1995)

Clarke, W.G., *In Breckland Wilds* (1925), revised by his son, R. R. Clarke (1937)

Trist, P.J.O., *A Survey of the Agriculture of Suffolk* (1971)

6. SUFFOLK AND THE EAST ANGLIAN KINGDOM

REFERENCES

1. D. Whitelock, *Anglo-Saxon Wills* (1930), xxxi; C. Hart, *The Early Charters of Eastern England* (1966), p. 69. The names are recorded as *Suffolke* and *Norfolke*. Thurstan was the great-grandson of Ealdorman Brihtnoth of Essex.

2. B. Colgrave & R.A.B. Mynors (eds), *Bede's Ecclesiastical History of the English People* (1969), 4.

3. S.E. West, 'A Gold Bracteate from Undley', *PSIAH*, xxxvi, pt 1 (1985), 37; J. Hines, *The Scandinavian Character of Anglian England in the Pre-Viking Period*, BAR 124 (1984), 204-9; R. Derolez, 'Runic Literacy among the Anglo-Saxons' in A. Bammesberger & A. Wollmann (eds), *Britain 400-600: Language and History* (1990), 416.

4. The last earl, the Breton Ralph Guader, fled into exile after rebelling in 1075. When the earldom was re-established 1140-41 for Hugh Bigod, it was normally referred to as 'Norfolk' but occasionally as 'East Anglia' or 'Norfolk and Suffolk'.

5. D. Whitelock, 'The Pre-Viking Age Church in East Anglia' in P. Clemoes (ed.), *Anglo-Saxon England*, i (1972), 1-22; J. Campbell, 'The East Anglian Sees before the Conquest' in I. Atherton *et al.* (eds), *Norwich Cathedral, Church, City and Diocese, 1096-1996* (1996), 1-21.

6. The province of the South Gyrwe was rated at 600 hides in the Tribal Hideage, which compares with Bede's description of Ely as a district (*regio*) of 600 families. This invites speculation that the territory of the South Gyrwe can be equated with the later two hundreds of the Isle of Ely. By the early 8th century the Gyrwe came within the Middle Anglian diocese with its see at Dorchester-on-Thames, but the abbey at Ely claimed to be free of diocesan control, and after about 1000 it professed obedience to the East Anglian see.

7. E.O. Blake (ed.), *Liber Eliensis*, Camden Soc., 3rd ser., xcii (1962), 3-4; E. Miller, *The Abbey and Bishopric of Ely* (1951), 8-15.

8. M. Parker Pearson, R. Van de Noort & A. Woolf, 'Three Men and a Boat: Sutton Hoo and the East Anglian Kingdom' in *Anglo-Saxon England*, 22 (1993), 27-50.

9. The East Saxon royal line is unparalleled in Anglo-Saxon dynastic history for its sibilant names, particularly compounds with *Seax-*, *Sae-* and *Sige-*. The Wuffingas' line contains individuals called Seaxburg, Seaxwulf, Saethryth and Sigeberht. The place-names Saxmundham (Seaxmund's *ham*) and Saxtead (Seaxa's *stede*) in south-east Suffolk could also be relevant.

10. S. Newton, 'Beowulf and the East Anglian Royal Pedigree' and L. Hines 'The Scandinavian Character of Anglian England: An Update' in M. Carver (ed.), *The Age of Sutton Hoo* (1992), 65-74, 315-29. For a suggestion that the Icelingas, the Mercian royal dynasty, were the original rulers of East Anglia, see E. Martin, 'The Icelingas', *EAA*, 3 (1976), 132-4.

7. ECCLESIASTICAL JURISDICTIONS

REFERENCES

1. A 'peculiar' is a parish or church exempt from the jurisdiction of the local bishop, and therefore subject to a bishop elsewhere or to the Crown. The origins of 'peculiars' go back to at least the early Norman period: in 1086 Freckenham was held by the bishop of Rochester, while Moulton, Hadleigh and Monks Eleigh were in the hands of Archbishop Lanfranc. Peculiars were abolished in 1847.

2. The situation in Suffolk, and in much of eastern and north-eastern England, was different from that in the south and west where ecclesiastical and secular divisions diverged to a much greater extent. The formation of rural deaneries seems to have been part of an attempt to separate ecclesiastical and civil courts in the years after the Conquest.

3. For example, the Archdeacons' Transcripts of parish registers in Norfolk and Suffolk were arranged by deanery.

4. The close correlation between some parish boundaries and Bronze Age burial mounds, especially in the Felixstowe peninsula, is particularly striking. See E.A. Martin, 'The Barrows of Suffolk' in *EAA*, 12 (1981), pp.84-7.

5. The extra-parochial places of Suffolk included Alnesbourn Priory, Halfway House and Purdis Farm (near Nacton), Nowhere House (Thorington), Chimney Mills (West Stow), Southwood Park (sometimes called Southwell Park, Hargrave), Dallinghoo Wield, Gedgrave, Hardwick, Havergate Island, Monks Risbridge, Rymer Point, Stratton Hall (Trimley St Martin), and small areas in or adjoining Ashbocking, Botesdale, Bungay, Ipswich and Sudbury. Several of these extra-parochial places were made into civil parishes in 1858. I am indebted to Peter Northeast for this list.

6. In the 19th and 20th centuries many changes were made to parish boundaries. Most of these were relatively minor but major changes did affect Halesworth, Leiston, Westley and the environs of Ipswich. Some new parishes were also created—Higham (1861 out of Gazeley), Leavenheath (1863 out of Stoke-by-Nayland, Assington, Polstead and Wissington) and Needham Market (1901 out of Barking and Creeting St Mary). Meanwhile a few parishes were abolished—Hazlewood (1934 to Aldeburgh and Friston), Hadleigh Hamlet (1935 to Boxford and Kersey), whilst others were subsumed into neighbouring parishes—the Suffolk part of Rushford was incorporated into Euston in 1894, Walton was taken into Felixstowe in 1914, and

Southwood Park became part of Hargrave in 1927. Nedging and Naughton were amalgamated in 1936. In the 19th century the recognition of civil as opposed to ecclesiastical parishes complicated the picture, as on occasions the two are not identical. For instance, the civil parish of Lowestoft contains the ecclesiastical parishes of Lowestoft, Gunton, Kirkley and Pakefield.

BIBLIOGRAPHY

Campbell, J., 'The East Anglian Sees before the Conquest' in Atherton, I. *et al.* (eds), *Norwich Cathedral, Church, City and Diocese, 1096-1996* (1996), 3-21

Lunt, W.E., *Valuation of Norwich* (1926)

Rumble, A. (ed.), *Domesday Book, Suffolk* (1986)

Thompson, A.H., 'Diocesan organisation in the Middle Ages', *Proc. British Academy*, xxix (1943), 153-94

Wade-Martins, P. & Rigold, S., 'North Elmham', *EAA*, i (1980), 3-11

White, William, *Directory of Suffolk* (1855)

Whitelock, D., 'The pre-Viking age church in East Anglia' in P. Clemoes (ed.) *Anglo-Saxon England*, i (1972), 1-22

8. HUNDREDS AND LIBERTIES

REFERENCES

1. Old English *(ge)mot* and Old Norse *thing*, both terms meaning an assembly or meeting.

2. Meeting places at fords are implied by Lackford, Wilford and Mutford ('moot-ford'); at lakes or meres by Bosmere, Bradmere and Hartismere; the head of a stream—Blackbourn; a bridge—Risbridge; mounds—Thingoe ('thing-mound') and Babergh; a hill—Claydon; a promontory—Colneis; and a tree —Thedwastre. The *stow* or meeting-place of Stow Hundred was probably at a crossing of the river Gipping at present-day Stowmarket. Hundreds named after settlements were limited to Ipswich, Parham and Hoxne. The last was annexed to an episcopal manor at Hoxne—hence its Domesday name of 'Bishop's Hundred'. Older 'folk' names seem to lie behind Blything ('the people of the Blythe'), Lothing (the Domesday name of Mutford

Hundred, possibly meaning 'Hluda's people') and Lothingland ('the land or island of Hluda's people'). Thredling was formerly a third (Old English *thridling*) of Claydon Hundred. Rather curiously, Loes means a 'pig-sty' and Plomesgate 'gate at/near plum trees'.

3. Comprising the parishes of Akenham, Barham, Claydon, Helmingham, Henley, Swilland, Thurleston, Westerfield and Whitton.

4. Comprising Blaxhall, Dunningworth, Parham, Tunstall and Wantisden.

5. The two original hundreds were divided by Oulton Broad and Lake Lothing.

6. In fact, several hundreds, particularly in the east, had detached portions. Kelsale was an isolated part of Hoxne while Butley, Kenton and Woodbridge were detached parts of Loes. At the time of Domesday, Aldringham was part of Hoxne, Gedgrave part of Loes, Alnesbourne part of Carlford and Diss in Norfolk was part of Hartismere.

7. Beccles served the hundreds of Blything, Wangford, Mutford and Lothingland, while Ipswich served the remaining hundreds of the Geldable.

8. It passed into royal hands in 1460 and was annexed to the Duchy of Lancaster by Queen Mary, together with the manor of Mildenhall and the borough of Sudbury.

BIBLIOGRAPHY

Anderson, O.F., *The English Hundred Names*, Lunds Universitets Arsskrift (1934)

Jewell, H.M., *English Local Administration in the Middle Ages* (1972)

VCH, Suffolk, 1 (1911)

Whitfield, J.H., The Evolution of Local Government Authorities and Areas in Suffolk. 1555-1894, MA thesis, Univ. of Kent (1970)

9. LOCAL GOVERNMENT SINCE 1872

REFERENCES

1. ALTERATIONS TO COUNTY BOUNDARIES, 1889-96:

    1889 Gorleston to Gt Yarmouth CB; Newmarket All

    Saints to West Suffolk

    1894 Thetford St Mary to Norfolk

    1895 Brandon and Kedington: whole parishes to West Suffolk

    1896 Haverhill and Ballingdon: whole parishes to West Suffolk

2. URBAN SANITARY DISTRICTS, 1872-94

    1872 *Boroughs*: Bury St Edmunds, Beccles, Eye, Ipswich, Southwold, Sudbury
          Local Boards: Newmarket (1851), Stowmarket (1866), Hadleigh (1869)
          Improvement Commission: Lowestoft (borough in 1885)
    1878 Haverhill (Local Board)
    1885 Aldeburgh (borough)
    1887 Felixstowe and Walton (Local Board)
    1894 Woodbridge (Local Board)

3. URBAN DISTRICTS, 1894-1934

    1894 Felixstowe and Walton (Felixstowe from 1914), Hadleigh, Haverhill, Newmarket, Stowmarket, Woodbridge
    1895 Leiston-cum-Sizewell
    1896 Glemsford
    1900 Halesworth, Saxmundham
    1904 Oulton Broad (absorbed by Lowestoft MB in 1919)
    1910 Bungay

BIBLIOGRAPHY

First General Review of County Districts by the East Suffolk County Council (1932)

First General Review of County Districts and Parishes by the West Suffolk County Council (1934)

Local Government Boundaries Commission: Report of the Boundary Commissioners of England and Wales, 1888—County of East and West Suffolk

Local Government Boundary Commission for England, Report No. 1 (1972) (Cmnd 5148)

Local Government Commission for England, Report No. 9—Lincolnshire and East Anglia General Review Area (1965)

Report of the Royal Commission on Local Government in England, 1966-9 (Cmnd 4040)

Whitfield, J.H., 'The Evolution of Local Government Authorities and Areas in Suffolk, 1555-1894', MA thesis, Univ. of Kent (1970)

Youngs, F.A., Jr, *Guide to the Local Administrative Units of England, Vol. i: Southern England* (Roy. Historical Soc., 1979)

10. PARLIAMENTARY CONSTITUENCIES

REFERENCES

1. Parts of Suffolk were at times in non-Suffolk constituencies: *Newmarket All Saints* was in Cambridgeshire until 1885, then in Cambridgeshire Eastern Division until 1918 when it joined the Bury Division; *Gorleston* was part of the Gt Yarmouth borough seat; *Thetford St Cuthbert and Saint Mary* were in the Thetford borough seat until 1885, and then in the Stowmarket Division until 1918.

2. The size of the electorate in the whole of Suffolk: *c.*1830—*c.*6200; 1832—10,394; 1884—26,662; 1906—72,272; 1924—201,499; 1929—255,142.

BIBLIOGRAPHY

Craig, F.W.S., *British Parliamentary Election Results, 1918-49* (1983)

Craig, F.W.S., *British Parliamentary Election Results, 1950-70* (1971)

Electoral Registers, Suffolk constituencies, SRO (B) & (I)

Hanham, H.J., *The Reformed Electoral System in Gt Britain, 1832-1914* (1968)

Murrell, P.E., 'Suffolk: the Political Behaviour of the County and its Parliamentary Boroughs from the Exclusion Crisis to the Accession of the House of Hanover', unpublished PhD thesis, Univ. of Newcastle upon Tyne, 1982.

Page, W. (ed.), *VCH*, ii (1907)

Vincent, J. & Stenton, M. (eds), *McCalmont's Parliamentary Poll Book—British Election Results, 1832-1918* (1971)

Youngs, F.A., Jr, *Guide to the Local Administrative Units of England, I, Southern England* (1979)

11. THE PALAEOLITHIC

SOURCE

The distribution of sites is based on J.J. Wymer, *The Palaeolithic Sites of East Anglia* (1985).

BIBLIOGRAPHY

Ashton, N.M., Cook, J., Lewis, S.G. & Rose, J., *High Lodge: Excavations by G. de G. Sieveking, 1962-8 and J. Cook, 1988* (1992)

Ashton, N.M. *et al.*, 'Excavations at the Lower Palaeolithic Site at East Farm, Barnham, Suffolk, 1989-92', *Jour. Geological Soc. London*, 151 (1994), 599-605

Ashton, N., Healy, F. & Pettitt, P. (eds.), *Stone Age Archaeology. Essays in Honour of John Wymer* (1998)

Singer, R., Gladfetter, B.G. & Wymer, J.J., *The Lower Palaeolithic Site at Hoxne, England* (1993)

Wymer, J., *The English Rivers Palaeolithic Project, Regions 8 (E. Anglian Rivers)* and *11 (Trent Drainage)*, (Wessex Archaeology, 1997) and *Regions 9 (Great Ouse Drainage)* and *12 (Yorks. and Lincs. Wolds)*, (Wessex Archaeol., 1996)

12. LATE GLACIAL AND MESOLITHIC HUNTERS

SOURCES

The distribution of sites is based on J.J. Wymer (ed.) *Gazetteer of Mesolithic Sites in England and Wales* with C.J. Bonsall (ed.), *Gazetteer of Upper Palaeolithic Sites in England and Wales*, CBA Research Report no. 20 (1977).

REFERENCE

1. Recent radiocarbon accelerator dates for the two Sproughton barbed points are 10,700 years before present plus or minus 160 years, and 10,910 plus or minus 150 years.

BIBLIOGRAPHY

Jacobi, R.M., 'The Mesolithic of Northern East Anglia and Contemporary Territories' in Barringer, C. (ed.), *Aspects of East Anglian Pre-history* (1984)

13. THE NEOLITHIC

SOURCES

The map was compiled from information in the SMR.

REFERENCES

1. The causewayed enclosures at Fornham All Saints and Freston consist of double circuits of discontinuous ditches (giving an hyphenated appearance), each approximately 300m in diameter. The one at Fornham also has a subsidiary enclosure, of about the same size, attached to its southern side. The enclosure at Kedington is smaller, just over 100m across, and consists of a single length of ditch across a riverside spur.

2. The cursus at Fornham consists of the cropmarks of two parallel ditches 40m apart x 1.9 km long. The one at Stratford was 60m wide x 290m long, but was largely destroyed when a bypass was built in the 1970s. At Bures the cursus is 30m wide x 250m long.

3. E. Martin, 'When is a Henge not a Henge?', *PSIAH*, xxxv (1982), 141-43.

4. See *PSIAH*, xxxix (1997), 96

BIBLIOGRAPHY

Barringer, C. (ed.), *Aspects of East Anglian Pre-history* (1984)

Clark, J.G.D., Higgs, E.S. & Longworth, I.H., 'Excavations at the Neolithic site at Hurst Fen, Mildenhall', *PPS*, 26 (1960)

Cummins, W.A., 'Stone axes as a guide to Neolithic communications and boundaries in England and Wales', *PPS*, 46, (1980)

Martin, E., 'Grasping at straws? The interpretation of ritual and religion in prehistoric East Anglia', *Bull. CBA, E. Anglia* 36 (1994)

Mercer, R.J., *Grimes Graves, Norfolk, Excavations 1971-2*, Dept. of the Environment Archaeol. Rep. no. 11 (1981)

Mercer, R.J., *Causewayed Enclosures* (1990)

Whittle, A., *Neolithic Europe: A Survey* (1985)

14. THE BRONZE AGE

SOURCES

The map was compiled from information in the SMR. Additional information on metalwork from Forest Heath District was provided by Dr Colin Pendleton.

BIBLIOGRAPHY

Barringer, C. (ed.) , *Aspects of East Anglian Pre-history* (1984)

Lawson, A.J., Martin, E.A. & Priddy, D., 'The Barrows of East Anglia', *EAA*, 12 (1981)

Martin, E. & Murphy, P., 'West Row Fen, Suffolk: A Bronze Age Fen-edge settlement site', *Antiquity*, 62, no. 235 (1988), 353-8

Pearson, M. Parker, *Bronze Age Britain* (1993)

Pendleton, C.F., *Bronze Age metalwork in Northern East Anglia*, BAR 279 (1999)

15. THE IRON AGE
SOURCES
The map was compiled from information in the SMR.
BIBLIOGRAPHY

Brailsford, J, *Early Celtic Masterpieces from Britain in the British Museum* (1975), contains an excellent chapter on the Ipswich gold torcs.

Clarke, R.R., 'The Iron Age in Norfolk and Suffolk', *AJ*, 95 (1939)

Cunliffe, B., *Iron Age Communities in Britain* (3rd edition 1991)

Dunnett, R., *The Trinovantes* (1978).

Martin, E., 'Burgh: the Iron Age and Roman Earthwork', *EAA*, 40 (1988)

Martin, E., 'Settlements on hill-tops: seven prehistoric sites in Suffolk', *EAA*, 65 (1993)

Martin, E., 'Suffolk in the Iron Age' in J. Davies & T. Williamson (eds.), *Land of the Iceni: The Iron Age in Northern East Anglia* (forthcoming).

16. THE ROMAN PERIOD
SOURCES
This map was compiled from information in the SMR.
BIBLIOGRAPHY

Bland, R. & Johns, C., *The Hoxne Treasure: An Illustrated Introduction* (1993)

Brown, A.E. (ed.), *Roman Small Towns in Eastern England and Beyond* (1995)

Johnson, S., *Later Roman Britain* (1980)

Millett, M., *Roman Britain* (1995)

Moore, I., 'Roman Suffolk', *PSIAH*, xxiv (1948), 163-81

Moore, I.E., Plouviez, J. & West, S., *The Archaeology of Roman Suffolk* (1988)

Potter, T.W. & Johns, C., *Roman Britain* (1992)

Swan, V.G., *The Pottery Kilns of Roman Britain*, RCHME, sup. series 5 (1984)

17. THE EARLY ANGLO-SAXON PERIOD
SOURCES
The map was compiled from information in the SMR.
BIBLIOGRAPHY

Carver, M. (ed.), *The Age of Sutton Hoo* (1992)

Carver, M., 'The Anglo-Saxon Cemetery at Sutton Hoo: An Interim Report' in Carver, M. (ed.), *The Age of Sutton Hoo* (1992)

Carver, M., *Sutton Hoo: Burial Ground of Kings?* (1998)

Filmer-Sankey, W., 'Snape Anglo-Saxon Cemetery: The Current State of Knowledge' in Carver, M. (ed.), *The Age of Sutton Hoo* (1992)

Scull, C.J., 'Before Sutton Hoo: Structures of Power and Society in Early East Anglia' in Carver, M. (ed.), *The Age of Sutton Hoo* (1992)

West, S.E., 'West Stow Anglo-Saxon Village', *EAA*, 24 (2 vols, 1985)

West, S.E., 'A Corpus of Anglo-Saxon Metalwork from Suffolk', *EAA*, 84 (1998)

18. THE LATER ANGLO-SAXON PERIOD
SOURCES
This map was compiled from information in the SMR. The note on round towers was contributed by R.D. Carr.
REERENCES

1. J. Newman, 'East Anglia Kingdom Survey: Interim Report on the South-East Suffolk Pilot Field Survey', *Bull. Sutton Hoo Research Committee*, 5 (1988).
2. R.D. Carr & A. Tester, 'The Middle Saxon Settlement at Staunch Meadow, Brandon', *Antiquity*, 62, no.235 (1988), 371-77.
3. V. Fenwick, 'Insula de Burgh: Excavations at Burrow Hill, Butley, Suffolk, 1978-81' in S. C. Hawkes, J. Campbell & D. Brown (eds), *Anglo-Saxon Studies in Archaeology and History* (1984), 35-54.
4. N. Scarfe, *The Suffolk Landscape* (1972), 106.
5. Christians lived at Icklingham, Suffolk in Roman times: see S.E. West & J. Plouviez, 'The Romano-British Site at Icklingham', *EAA*, 3 (1976), 63-125.
6. R. Cramp, 'Anglo-Saxon Monasteries of the North', *Scottish Archaeol. Forum*, 5 (1973), 104-24.
7. S.E. West, N. Scarfe & R. Cramp, 'Iken, St Botolph and the Coming of East Anglian Christianity', *PSIAH*, xxxv (1984), 279-301.
8. Round towers are essentially an East Anglian phenomenon. The great majority—over 120—are in Norfolk, and the 41 in Suffolk are clearly on the margins of this homeland. The date of these structures is the subject of speculation. The earliest examples are 11th century and some may be pre-Conquest, as at Little Bradley and Thorington; the majority are probably Norman, but it is clear that round towers continued to be built in the 13th century and even into the early 14th. The recently demolished and partly rebuilt tower at Onehouse has yielded archaeological evidence of a 14th-century origin, while others such as Syleham can be dated from their architectural details. The long history of construction was identified by John Gage as early as 1829 ('Observations on the Ecclesiastical Round Towers of Norfolk and Suffolk', *Archaeologia*, 23, 10-17). There is no positive evidence that any of them was intended as defensive. Two extensive published surveys of round towers are C.J.W. Messent, *The Round Towers to English Parish Churches* (1958) and W.J. Goode, *East Anglian Round Towers and their Churches* (1982).

BIBLIOGRAPHY

Johnson, S., 'Burgh Castle, Excavations by Charles Green, 1958-61', *EAA*, 20 (1983)

Taylor, H.M. & J., *Anglo-Saxon Architecture*, i-iii (1965 and 1978)

Warner, P., *The Origins of Suffolk* (1996)

Whitelock, D., 'The Pre-Viking Age Church in East Anglia' in P. Clemoes (ed.), *Anglo-Saxon England*, i, 1-22

Whitelock, D., Douglas, D.C. & Tucker, S.I. (eds), *The Anglo-Saxon Chronicle* (1961)

Wilson, D.M. (ed.), *The Archaeology of Anglo-Saxon England* (1976)

19. ANCIENT LANDSCAPES
REFERENCES

1. O. Rackham, *Trees and Woodland in the British Landscape* (1976), pp. 16-17.
2. A. Fleming, 'The Prehistoric Landscape of Dartmoor: Wider Implications', *Landscape History*, 6 (1984), 5-19.
3. T.M. Williamson, 'Sites in the Landscape: Approaches to the Post-Roman Settlement of South-Eastern

England', *Archaeol. Review from Cambridge*, 4:1, 51-64.

4. N. Scarfe, *Suffolk in the Middle Ages* (1986), 6.

5. W.G. Hoskins, *Fieldwork in Local History* (1967), 143; T. Williamson, 'Early Co-axial Field Systems on the East Anglian Boulder Clays', *PPS*, 53 (1987), 4 1 9 - 31.

6. T.M. Williamson, 'Parish Boundaries and Early Fields: Continuity and Discontinuity', *Jour. of Historical Geography*, 12, 3 (1986), 241-8.

20. PLACE-NAME PATTERNS

SOURCES

E. Ekwall, *The Oxford Dictionary of English Place-Names* (4th ed., 1960).

E. Martin, 'Suffolk Minor Place-Names: An Annotated List' (typescript 1985; copy in SRO).

REFERENCES

1. A.H. Smith, *English Place-Name Elements*, English Place-Name Soc., vol. xxvi (1956).

2. K. Cameron (ed.), *Place-Name Evidence for the Anglo-Saxon Invasion and Scandinavian Settlements* (1975).

3. In both the Suffolk and Norfolk parts of Breckland, names in -*ham*, -*ing* and -*ton* are largely confined to the eastern and southern edges of the region. In the dry central area, several names end in -*ford* and -*well* (OE *wella*, a spring or stream), perhaps revealing an understandable preoccupation with water.

4. Market Weston and Coney Weston have different meanings: Coney Weston is really *Cunegeston*, king's *tun*.

5. About half a dozen -*ham* names and a similar number of -*ing* names are non-parochial (eg. Whittingham in Fressingfield, Benningham in Occold and Chickering in Wingfield), but over forty -*ton*s are non-parochial.

6. The seven Boytons in the county may also be significant, for five occur on or near a parish boundary and contain, as their first element, the word *boia*, a boy or servant.

7. Wilby has been excluded because early forms of the name point to Old English *beg* meaning 'ring' as the second element, rather than Old Norse *by* meaning

'village'

8. T. Williamson, 'Place-name patterns' in P. Wade-Martins (ed.), *An Historical Atlas of Norfolk* (1993), 44-5.

9. Eg. Bradfield *St Clare* (family from Saint Claire-sur-Elle, Manche), Carlton *Colville* (family from Colleville, Seine Inferieure), Easton *Bavents* (family from Bavent, Calvados) and Thorpe *Morieux* (family from Morieux in Cotes-du-Nord). Anglo-Norman lords are commemorated in Ash *Bocking* (family from Bocking, Essex) and Stonham *Aspal* (family from nearby Aspal). In Suffolk it was more common to use the church dedication as a suffix to distinguish similarly named places, as Creeting *St Peter*, *St Mary*, etc. See J.H. Round, 'The Origin of Essex Parishes' in *Family Origins and Other Studies* (1930), 266-74.

BIBLIOGRAPHY

Copley, G., *Early Place-Names of the Anglian Regions of England*, BAR, British Series, 185 (1988)

Gelling, M., *Signposts to the Past: Place-Names and the History of England* (1978)

Gelling, M., *Place-Names in the Landscape* (1984)

Gelling, M., 'A Chronology for Suffolk Place-Names' in M. Carver (ed.), *The Age of Sutton Hoo* (1992), 53-64

21. DOMESDAY CHURCHES

SOURCES

Page, W. (ed.), *VCH Suffolk*, vol. 1 (1911); *Domesday Book: Facsimile of the Part relating to Suffolk* (Ordnance Survey, 1861-3); Rumble, A. (ed.), *Domesday Book: Suffolk* (2 vols, 1986).

REFERENCES

1. I intend to publish, in the *PSIAH,* a full catalogue of the Suffolk churches in Domesday Book, with the acreages of their glebes and folio references.

2. The vill of Claydon has only a brief mention in Domesday, and it must be presumed that most of it was included in Akenham.

3. The foundations of this small unaisled church, with an apsidal east end and western round tower, were excavated by R.D. Carr in 1980 (SMR no. NHC004). The site is now in North Cove parish.

4. Churches at Brantham and Exning were granted to Battle Abbey by William II in 1094 (W. Dugdale, *Monasticon Anglicanum*, III, 1986, 246). The church at Ixworth Thorpe is recorded in the near contemporary *Feudal Book of Abbot Baldwin* (D.C. Douglas (ed.), *Feudal Documents from the Abbey of Bury St Edmunds* (1932), 22).

5. D. Dymond, *The Norfolk Landscape* (1990 edn.), 81.

6. N. Scarfe, *The Suffolk Landscape* (1987 edn.), 122-8.

7. Old English *mynster* derived from the Latin *monasterium*, meant both a monastery and a major church served by a group of clergy.

8. J. Blair, *Minsters and Parish Churches: The Local Church in Transition, 950-1200*, Oxford Univ. Comm. for Archaeol. Monograph, 17 (1988); E. Martin, 'St Botolph and Hadstock: A Reply', *Antiq. Jour.*, lviii, pt 1 (1978), 153-9; N. Scarfe, *Suffolk in the Middle Ages* (1986), ch. 3.

9. The wills of Bishop Theodred, 942-51, of Ealdorman Ælfgar, 946-51, and of his daughters Æthelflæd, 975-991, and Ælfflæd, 1000-2.

10. The collegiate church of St John at Clare was founded by 'earl' Ælfric son of Wihtgar, c.1045; the monastery at Rumburgh was founded by Bishop Æthelmar of Elmham and Abbot Thurstan of St Benet at Holme, 1047-64.

11. Oulton is not named in Domesday, but the entry for a church of St Michael at Flixton probably refers to St Michael's at Oulton. See N. Scarfe, *The Suffolk Landscape*, (1972), 124-27.

12. The second church was at Sproughton (see *PSIAH*, xxxvii, pt 2 (1990), 173 for the 13th-century separation of Sproughton from Bramford). In 1094 Burstall was also a 'berewick' or outlying part of Bramford, as was the chapel of St Æthelbert at *Albrihtestou* (a lost place, originally in Bramford, now in Ipswich as a result of boundary changes).

13. Domesday records Bergholt as an important royal manor with berewicks at Shelley, Bentley and Shotley. Confusingly, the grant of Brantham church (not recorded in Domesday) to Battle Abbey by William II in 1094 lists Bergholt, Shotley, Shelley and Bentley as berewicks of Brantham (*Mon. Anglic.*, III, 246; C.

Harper-Bill, 'Battle Abbey and its East Anglian Churches' in Harper-Bill (ed.), *Studies in Medieval History presented to R. A. Brown* (1989), 159-72).

14. An apparent Viking burial *c.*953 in the churchyard strengthens the possibility of Hundon being a minster (B. & M. Biddle, 'Coins of the Anglo-Saxon Period from Repton, Derbyshire, II', *Brit. Numismatic Jour.,* 56 (1986), 27).

15. Both valued at £63 in 1291 (*Ecclesiastical Taxation, 1291*) when most other churches were valued at £10 to £20.

16. Fieldwalking by M. Hardy located a Middle Saxon settlement, contemporary with the earliest bishops of Elmham, near South Elmham Hall (*PSIAH,* xxxvi, pt 3 (1987), 232-4), but the ruin known as South Elmham Minster is probably an early Norman monastic foundation associated with Bishop Herbert Losinga, 1091-1119 (S. Heywood, 'The Ruined Church at North Elmham', *JBAA,* 135 (1982), 1-10; J. Ridgard, 'References to South Elmham Minster in the Medieval Account Rolls of South Elmham Manor', *PSIAH,* xxxvi, pt 3 (1987), 196-201; N. Scarfe, *The Suffolk Landscape* (1987), 118-21.

BIBLIOGRAPHY

Blair, J., *Minsters and Parish Churches: The Local Church in Transition, 950-1200,* Oxford Univ. Comm. for Archaeology Monograph 17 (1988)

Morris, R., *Churches in the Landscape* (1989)

22. CHURCHES AND CHURCHYARDS
SOURCES

The plans of churches are taken from Ordnance Survey 25-inch maps of 1884 and 1904, supplemented by larger-scale plans of churches (early 19th century) from David Elisha Davy's 'Collections for the History of Suffolk' (British Lib: Add. 19,109; microfilm in SRO(B): J534/3). Small details like buttresses have been omitted, but the main components of churches should be visible as distinct 'boxes'. The plans of churchyards are taken from OS 25-inch maps, checked against tithe maps of *c.*1840 and the occasional enclosure map.

REFERENCES

1. H.M. Cautley, *Suffolk Churches and Their Treasures* (5th edn, 1982); D.P. Mortlock, *The Popular Guide to Suffolk Churches, No.1: West Suffolk* (1988); N. Pevsner, *The Buildings of England: Suffolk* (1974); N. Scarfe, *The Suffolk Guide* (1988).

2. B. Carr, 'A Survey of the Church of St Peter, Ubbeston', *EAA,* 3 (1976), 155-69; B. Haward, *Suffolk Medieval Church Arcades* (1993); various summaries of recent work in 'Archaeology in Suffolk', *PSIAH,* and in *Medieval Archaeology.*

3. E. Duffy, *The Stripping of the Altars: Traditional Religion, 1400-1580* (1992); B. Kumin, *The Shaping of a Community: The Rise and Reformation of the English Parish, c.1400-1560* (1996); K. French, G. Gibbs & B. Kumin, *The Parish in English Life, 1400-1600* (1997).

4. A. Rumble (ed.), *Domesday Book: Suffolk* (2 vols, Phillimore, 1986). One church is mentioned in Bradfield, which later became three parishes. The other two churches not mentioned in Domesday were at Rushbrooke and Beyton. Interestingly, Beyton church has the earliest surviving tower in the district, of circular 'Saxo-Norman' type; it must presumably postdate 1086.

5. Bradfield St Clare takes its name from its manorial lords, the St Clare family, and not from the dedication of its church which is All Saints.

6. For groups of other small-scale plans of churches see RCHME, *North Northants,* 6, pp.lxxvi-vii. A map of 1769 shows the church of Fornham St Genevieve in a rectangular churchyard; another map of 1788 shows that the yard had been made oval in a newly

---

22. THEDWASTRE DEANERY, A PAROCHIAL ANALYSIS: KEY TO COLUMNS BELOW

1. Name of parish, in order of acreage (asterisk means church mentioned in Domesday Book)
2. Status of benefice (R=rectory; V=vicarage)
3. Acreage of parish as recorded in White's *Directory of Suffolk* (1855)
4. Size of church (0=no aisle; 2=two aisles; N=north aisle; S=south aisle)
5. Acreage of churchyard, 1894-1904
6. Orientation of church: degrees north (N) or south (S) of east
7. Total value of benefice in 1291 (to nearest £): from *Taxatio Ecclesiastica* (1802)
8. Number of people recorded in 1086: from Domesday Book
9. Number of taxpayers in Lay Subsidy of 1524 (Suffolk Green Books, x)

1	2	3	4	5	6	7	8	9
GT BARTON*	V	4030	2	2.1	5N	30	103	34
ROUGHAM*	R	3840	2	1.9	17N	40	127	52
PAKENHAM*	V	3696	0	1.5	4N	32	119	49
RATTLESDEN*	R	3254	2	1.3	2S	20	71	—
THURSTON*	V	2200	2	2.0	3N	20	75	28
DRINKSTONE*	R	2172	2	0.9	5S	17	38	42
BRADFIELD ST GEORGE	R	1980	N	0.6	7N	11	+	37
WOOLPIT*	R	1877	2	1.4	8N	13	60	59
FELSHAM*	R	1630	0	1.2	6N	9	39	32
HESSETT*	R	1568	2	1.1	4S	13	76	31
GT LIVERMERE*	R	1549	0	0.9	4N	15	52	16
GT WHELNETHAM*	R	1493	0	1.2	15N	19	†	9
STANNINGFIELD*	R	1455	0	1.0	5N	8	25	15
BRADFIELD ST CLARE*	R	1428	0	0.6	1N	7	+	13
TIMWORTH*	R	1358	0	0.9	13S	10	38	16
FORNHAM ST MARTIN*	R	1230	0	0.7	21N	8	27	16
RUSHBROOKE	R	1060	S	0.3	5N	8	?32	23
TOSTOCK*	R	945	0	0.7	4N	6	57.5	20
BRADFIELD COMBUST	S	818	S	0.5	2S	11	+	12
FORNHAM ST GENEVIEVE*	R	790	0	—	—	8	30	17
AMPTON*	R	736	0	0.3	4S	—	22	7
BEYTON	R	625	0	0.3	4N	4	1	14
LT WHELNETHAM*	R	592	0	0.7	6S	5	†	16
GEDDING*	R	521	0	0.8	19N	5	18	4

+ Only one Bradfield is listed in Domesday, with a single church and a recorded population of 76; in later sources it is mentioned as three separate parishes.

† Whelnetham appears in Domesday as one vill with a recorded population of 54, but already it had two churches.

landscaped park (SRO(B): 373/23 and 24). The church itself was burnt and finally demolished in 1813; only the tower remains.

7. These measurements include western towers, but exclude buttresses.

8. The architectural histories of nave and chancel were often different, because the first was maintained by parishioners and the second by a rector (clerical, monastic or lay). Good examples of these structural differences can be seen at Great Barton and Little Whelnetham.

9. The two exceptions are Pakenham with a central Norman tower (and 13th-century transept), and Timworth which has a tower-cum-porch to the south.

10. Orientation was measured from 25-inch maps. Because walls were not necessarily parallel, I chose a line which seemed the 'best fit' in each church. Fortunately, none of the 23 churches was seriously skewed. Even so, one cannot claim a high degree of precision for this method. A better, more time-consuming approach would be to measure the orientation of each wall separately, at the same time assessing its probable (or minimum) date by architectural or archaeological criteria.

11. For earlier work, see C.J.P. Cave, 'The Orientation of Churches', *Antiq. Jour.*, 30 (1950), 47-51; B. Somerville, 'Orientation', *Antiquity*, 1 (1927), 31-41; and F.C. Eeles, *Proc. Soc. of Antiqs. of Scotland*, 48 (1913-14), 169-83. A modern study by P.G. Hoare & C.S. Sweet, 'The Orientation of Early Medieval Churches in England', is forthcoming.

12. At Great Barton the eastern edge of the churchyard was probably re-aligned when, as part of enclosure after 1805, a new road was created adjacent to it: SRO(B), Q/RI/5.

13. Human bones were found under the SW corner of this building in 1995 (SMR: GDD 011).

14. Map, le Heup estate, 1723: SRO(B), E3/22/2.18.

23. MEDIEVAL CHAPELS
SOURCES
Wills, *Valor Ecclesiasticus,1535* (Record Commissioners, 1817), volumes of the SRS (Charter Series), cartularies, the chantry certificates of 1548, and official calendars (especially *Calendar of Patent Rolls* and *Letters & Papers of the Reign of Henry VIII*).

REFERENCES
1. S. Neave & S. Ellis, *An Historical Atlas of East Yorkshire* (1996), 102-3.

2. A fine example survives in Hengrave Hall.

3. Parish churches once having the status of chapel include the following (the relevant mother church is shown in brackets):
   Boxted (Hartest); Brundish (Tannington); Burstall (Bramford); Crowfield (Coddenham); Darmsden (Barking); East Bergholt (Brantham); Gedgrave (Orford); Haverhill (Haverhill Upper Church, destroyed in 16th cent.); Hazlewood (Aldeburgh); Higham Green (Gazeley); Kentford (Gazeley); Metfield (Mendham); Nayland (Stoke-by-Nayland); Needham Market (Barking); Newbourn (Martlesham); Newmarket St Mary (Exning); Orford (Sudbourne); Peasenhall (Sibton); Rushmere St Michael (Reydon); Saxtead (Framlingham); Shelland (Haughley), Shotley (Brantham); Southolt (Worlingworth); Southwold (Reydon); Sudbury St Peter (Sudbury St Gregory); Walberswick (Blythburgh).

4. D. Dymond, 'Chapels-of-Ease and the Case of Botesdale' in A. Longcroft & R. Joby (eds), *East Anglian Studies: Essays presented to J. C. Barringer on his Retirement* (1995), 58-65. Botesdale did, however, become a separate *civil* parish in 1866.

5. C. Paine, 'The Chapel and Well of Our Lady of Woolpit', *PSIAH*, xxxviii (1993), 8-12.

6. V.B. Redstone, 'The Ancient Chapel of Bures', *PSIAH*, xv (1914), 218-24.

7. M.C. Evans, 'The Contribution of Hoxne to the Cult of St Edmund, King and Martyr in the Middle Ages and Later', *PSIAH*, xxxvi (1987), 182-95.

8. M. Clegg, 'The Chapel of St Edmund de Pountenay in Ipswich', *PSIAH*, xxxiv (1979), 171-9.

9. S. Smith, *The Madonna of Ipswich* (1980).

BIBLIOGRAPHY
Hair, P., 'The Chapel in the English Landscape', *The Local Historian*, 21 (1991), 4-10

Morley, C., 'A Check-list of the Sacred Buildings of Suffolk', *PSIAH*, xix (1926), 168-211

Orme, N., 'Church and Chapel in Medieval England', *Trans. Royal Hist. Soc.*, 6th ser., vi (1996), 75-102

Redstone, V.B., 'Chapels, Chantries and Gilds in Sufolk', *PSIAH*, xii (1904), 1-87; continued in *PSIAH*, xxiii (1937), 50-78

24. MEDIEVAL CASTLES
REFERENCES
1. This may have been a free-standing stone house surrounded by an ringwork, similar to the first phase at Castle Acre, Norfolk.

2. Butler, H.E. (ed.), *Chronicle of Jocelin of Brakelond* (1949), 138.

3. Ashfield castle belonged to the Blund family, who held part of their lands as tenants-in-chief and part as tenants of Bury Abbey. Denham Castle served the important de Clare manor of Desning and in the time of King Stephen there were knights under the constable of the Honour of Clare there. Freckenham Castle belonged to the bishops of Rochester. Ilketshall St John belonged to the knightly de Ilketshall family, who may have been inspired to build a castle because of the destabilising threat of the Bigod castle at Bungay. Lidgate was probably erected by Maurice de Windsor, who was steward to Bury Abbey during the reign of Stephen, though the surrounding bailey may have been added in the 13th century by the Hastings family. Otley seems to have been erected by the de Otteley family, as knights of the Honour of Lancaster.

4. By the early 13th century Burgate was held by the de Burgate family, possibly descendants of Adelhelm, who held it in 1086 as tenant of Aubrey de Vere. Peter de Valognes, sheriff of Essex in 1086 and constable of Hertford Castle, had his most important Suffolk estate at Fakenham Magna (in addition

to the main ringwork at Burnthall Plantation, there is a second ring, smaller and unbanked, a short distance to the north in Castle Fen). Nayland was the head of the Suffolk estate of Peter's predecessor as sheriff, Swein of Essex. The estate that became Colt's Hall in Cavendish was held in 1086 by Roger de St Germain, one of the 'barons' of Richard Fitz-Gilbert of Clare. Great Cornard was a royal possession in 1086, but was later granted to Robert Fitz-Hamo, a major landowner in Kent and Glamorgan, who gave it to Malling Abbey, Kent, c.1100; a small embanked ring on the edge of Abbas Hall Wood may have been an attempt to fortify the manor in the time of Stephen. The earthworks in Grange Wood, Wissington may relate to the estate given by Hugh de Hosdene to Thetford Priory in the late 11th century. Bramfield belonged in the 12th century to the de Branfeld family, as knights of the Honour of Richmond. In 1086 Creeting St Peter was held by William de Boeville, a tenant of the Essex magnate Geoffrey de Mandeville.

5.   The traditional ascription of the building to Sir John de Vaux is untenable—he was feudal overlord but not resident lord (see Bibliography).

6.   In 1371 a licence was granted to Helming Legat, constable of Windsor Castle, to 'embattle' his mansion at Pond Hall, Hadleigh, and 1387 the warlike bishop of Norwich, Henry Despencer, was permitted to fortify South Elmham Hall, but in both cases it is not clear what works were actually undertaken on these moated sites.

BIBLIOGRAPHY

Braun, H., 'Some notes on Bungay Castle' and 'Report on the excavations', *PSIAH*, xxii (1936), 109-19, 201-23, 334-8

Brown, R. Allen, *English Castles* (3rd ed, revised, 1976)

Coad, J.G., 'Recent excavations within Framlingham Castle', *PSIAH*, xxxii, pt 2 (1971), 152-63

Heslop, T.A., 'Orford Castle: nostalgia and sophisticated living', *Archit. Hist.*, 34 (1991), 36-58

King, D.J.C., *Castellarium Anglicanum* (1983)

Martin, E., 'Little Wenham Hall: a reinterpretation', *PSIAH*, xxxix (1998), 151-64

Pounds, N.J.G., *The Medieval Castle in England and Wales* (1990)

Raby, F.J.E. & Reynolds, P.K.B., *Framlingham Castle* (Guide) 1959

Renn, D.F., *Norman Castles in Britain* (1968)

Renn, D., 'Defending Framlingham Castle', *PSIAH*, xxxiii, pt 1 (1973), 58-67

25. MEDIEVAL MOATS

SOURCES

The map was compiled from information contained in the SMR, and from the author's own notes. Information on some of the buildings has been supplied by Philip Aitkens.

REFERENCES

1.   A similar high platform, surrounded by a dry ditch, occurs at Lidgate Castle and is probably contemporary.

2.   It was probably built by the knightly de Bramfeld family, manorial lords in the later 12th century. A now-levelled site at Creeting St Peter appears to have been similar in shape and size.

3.   The 'bailey' has now been flattened. The moats, together with a priory church, lay on the northern edge of a large rectangular area (c.7 acres) that may have functioned as a market place. The Fitz-Brian family were the resident manorial lords from the time of Domesday down to 1233.

4.   The de Wachesham family were manorial lords from the mid-12th to mid-14th century. Circular moats are are recorded at Acton Hall, Aspal Hall and Earl Soham Lodge.

5.   Both are likely to have been built by Sir Alexander de Walsham, who acquired the manor in 1302/3.

6.   All probably built for Robert Hotot, a justice 1381-c.1402.

7.   Built for Sir William Burgate (d. 1409). The original hall no longer exists, but the gatehouse now functions as the farmhouse.

8.   Difficult to date, possibly built either for Sir Robert Chamberlain (executed 1491) or his grandson, Sir Ralph, in the 1530s. A three-storey gatehouse lavishly decorated with moulded terracotta ornaments was built at Westhorpe Hall in the 1520s by Charles Brandon, Duke of Suffolk, but demolished c.1750. Brick gatehouses are also recorded at Crow's Hall at Debenham, Denston Hall, Helmingham Hall, Hengrave Hall, Hoxne Hall, South Elmham Hall and West Stow Hall.

9.   'Chambers in the newe works' were referred to by Sir Thomas Jermyn in his will of 1552. The porch bore the arms of Sir Ambrose Jermyn (d. 1577) and his wife Ann Heveningham (d. 1567). Demolished 1961.

BIBLIOGRAPHY

Aberg, F.A. (ed.), *Medieval Moated Sites*, CBA Research Rep. 17 (1978)

Gunn, S.J. & Lindley, P.G., 'Charles Brandon's Westhorpe: an Early Tudor Courtyard House in Suffolk', *AJ*, 145 (1988), 272-89

Martin, E., 'Two exceptional Tudor Houses in Hitcham: Brick House Farm and Wetherden Hall', *PSIAH*, xxxvii, pt 2 (1991), 186-207

Paine, C.R., *Moated Sites in West Suffolk* (MS in SRO(B)), 1969)

West, S.E., 'Brome, Suffolk. The Excavation of a Moated Site, 1967', *JBAA*, 3rd ser. 33 (1970)

Wilson, D., *Moated Sites* (1985)

'Excursion Notes', *PSIAH* (especially those for 1990-9), contain details of a number of moated sites

26. GREENS, COMMONS AND TYES

SOURCES

Maps of the Ordnance Survey, 1:10560 scale, published c.1957-8. All examples of the words 'green', 'common' and 'tye' were noted.

REFERENCES

1.   Since the Commons Registration Act of 1965, commons have been defined as areas of land subject to common rights, principally the pasturing of animals; village and town greens are used for exercise, recreation or sport.

2.   As in the case of the former Allwood Green in the parishes of Rickinghall Superior and Inferior, Wal-

sham-le-Willows, Gislingham and Finningham (enclosed in 1819).

3. Mellis Green at 218 acres and Wortham Long Green at 102 acres are the two largest surviving examples.
4. As at High Street Green, Great Finborough, now partly enclosed.
5. Mellis and St Michael South Elmham are notable exceptions.
6. As at Buttonhaugh Green, where four parishes (Elmswell, Great Ashfield, Hunston and Norton) shared common rights.

BIBLIOGRAPHY
Clayden, P., *Our Common Land, the law and history of commons and village greens* (1985)

Dymond, D.P., 'The Suffolk Landscape' in L. M. Munby (ed.) *East Anglian Studies* (1968)

Hodskinson, J., *The County of Suffolk* (map of 1783; reprinted as SRS, xv, ed. D. Dymond, 1972)

Hoskins, W.G. & Stamp, L.D., *The Common Lands of England and Wales* (1963)

Martin, E., 'Greens, Commons and Tyes in Suffolk' in A. Longcroft & R. Joby (eds.) *East Anglian Studies* (1995), 167-78

Smith, A.H., *English Place-Name Elements* (English Place-Name Soc., vols. xxv-xxvi, 1956)

Tate, W.E., 'Handlist of Suffolk Enclosure Acts and Awards', *PSIAH*, xxv, pt. 3 (1951)

Warner, P., *Greens, Commons and Clayland Colonization: The Origins and Development of Green-side Settlement in East Suffolk* (1987)

27. MEDIEVAL WOODS

BIBLIOGRAPHY
Rackham, O., *Trees and Woodland in the British Landscape* (1976)

Rackham, O., *Ancient Woodland: its History, Vegetation and Uses in England* (1980)

28. DEER-PARKS, 1086-*c*.1600

REFERENCES
1. Possible dates for the introduction of fallow deer are discussed by N. & D. Chapman in *Fallow Deer*, British Deer Soc. Pub. No. 1 (1970), 5, and in *Fallow Deer* (1975), ch. 3.
2. Three maps of Hundon, dating from the end of the 16th century, show lodges centrally within the Great Park, Easty Park and Broxted Park (PRO, MPC 1, 2 & 3). Earlier documents of 1370-1 record the 'lord's lodge', a lodge 'for the gatekeeper at Stradeslegate' in the Great Park, and a lodge at the gate to Broxted Park (PRO, SC 6/999/25).
3. Fishponds were located in a number of parks. Remains can be seen at, for example, Hawstead, Hundon, Kelsale and Wetheringsett. A licence of 1479 allowed the construction of a fishpond of half an acre at Rishangles Park in Thorndon (SRO(I) XI/5/5.1 & 5.2). In 1408-10 Easty park in Hundon was recorded as having a warren within it (PRO, SC6/1112/18).
4. At Bradfield St Clare, in the former Monks Park of the abbot of Bury, 240 acres described as the 'Old Wood' were exempt fom tithe (SRO(B) T105/1,2). In the 17th century the woods of the parish were the subject of a tithe dispute (PRO, E134, Deposition 21 Chas II, no. 7). In the parishes of Wickhambrook and Lidgate, the park of Badmondisfield was the subject of another dispute over tithes (enclosure award of 1817, SRO(B) 1201/5; PRO, DL/43/14/3, fols 12, 22 & 24; SRO(B) T128/1,2).
5. This terminal date is chosen to include the parks listed in the *Chorography of Suffolk, 1602*, ed. D.J.N. MacCulloch (SRS xix, 1976).
6. H.E. Butler (ed.), *Chronicle of Jocelin of Brakelond* (1949), 28.
7. In Domesday Book (ed. A. Rumble, Pt 1, 1986), Robert Malet's holdings are listed on fols 304a to 330a. He held parks in his manors of Eye, Dennington and Leiston. Roger Bigod's parks were listed in his inquisition post mortem (IPM) of 35 Edward I (*Cal. IPM, IV, Edward I*, no. 434, 292-3).
8. IPM, 13 Edward II; *Cal. Close Rolls, Edward II, 1323-27*, 107.

BIBLIOGRAPHY
Cantor, L., *The Medieval Parks of England: A Gazetteer* (1983)

Farrer, E., *Suffolk Deer Parks* (1923), SRO(I) S712.644

Hoppitt, R., 'The Development of Parks in Suffolk from the Eleventh to the Seventeenth Centuries', PhD thesis, UEA (1992)

Rackham, O., *The History of the Countryside* (1986), 62-152

Shirley, E.P., *Some Account of English Deer Parks* (1867)

29. RABBIT WARRENS

REFERENCES
1. Grants of free warren appear in the Charter Rolls. In some cases they were for individual manors, but in others for whole estates. For example, in 1252-3 Roger de Huntingfield was granted free warren over all his lands.
2. In medieval documents the Latin for rabbit is *cuniculus*, from which the Old English 'coney' is derived. 'Rabbit' or 'rabbet' refers to the young. The place for keeping rabbits is *cunicularium*. An alternative is the French *garenne*, from which the English 'warren' is derived. For background detail on rabbits and warrens, see J. Sheail, *Rabbits and their History* (1971) and O. Rackham, *The History of the Countryside* (1986), 47-9, 292-3; for their local significance, see M. Bailey, 'The Rabbit and the Medieval East Anglian Economy', *Agric. Hist. Rev.*, 36, 1 (1988), 1-20.
3. At Elmswell in 1378, 16% of the sown demesne was destroyed by rabbits (SRO-B, 613/686/1, quoted in M. Bailey, *op. cit.*). 'The whole country is mere rabbit warren... a man could fall up to his waist in the holes made by collapsed tunnels and it was dangerous to ride a horse over the ground': G.T. Keppel, *Fifty Years of My Life* (1876), describing the Breckland.
4. The myxoma virus was introduced from South America in 1952 to an estate near Paris, whence it spread across the rest of Europe. The first British record was in Kent in Aug. 1953; within five years

around 96% of rabbits had died. M. Leach, *The Rabbit* (1989), 4-5.

5. M. Bailey, *op. cit.* (1988).
6. J. Sheail, 'Rabbits and Agriculture in Post-medieval England', *Jour. of Hist. Geography*, 4 (1978), 350-1.
7. At Lakenheath the warren covered 930ha and extended some 7.5kms across the higher eastern part of the parish where soil conditions are driest and most sandy. The warrens at Mildenhall and Santon Downham cover 505ha and 283ha respectively.
8. At Covehithe aerial photography has revealed 47 rectangular marks (possibly pillow mounds) on the warren. The mounds at Sutton Common and the mound at Knettishall are accessible from public footpaths. At Knettishall the warren contains a circular mound with an encircling bank.
9. M. Bailey, *op. cit.*, (1988), 16-19.
10. Thetford Warren Lodge (the lodge of Westwick warren belonging to Thetford Priory) lies south of the B1107 road, from which it is signposted. The building is of flint with ashlar dressings and slit windows, and dates from the early 15th century (National Monuments Record). The lodge is briefly described in F.J.E. Raby & P.K.B. Reynolds, *Thetford Priory* (1979), 22-3. An illustration of the lodge in the middle of its warren is included in H. Stevenson, *The Birds of Norfolk* (1866). It gives a clear picture of the nature of the Breckland before afforestation, and in particular the commanding position of the lodge. A similar lodge was constructed at Brandon in the 1380s and is documented in manorial accounts: it consisted of a two-storey flint tower costing over £20. Remains of other Breckland lodges, some of which have been incorporated into, or been replaced by, later farmhouses, are recorded in K. Sussams, *The Breckland Archaeological Survey* (1996), 96-7, 118-9.
11. Compiled from gazetteers produced by Suffolk Biological Records and E. Martin, based on large-scale OS maps and various documentary references such as field-names from Tithe Apportionments.
12. M. Bailey, 'Sand into Gold: The Evolution of the Foldcourse System in West Suffolk, 1200-1600', *Agric. Hist. Rev.*, 38, 1 (1990), 40-57.
13. M. Bailey, *op. cit.* (1988), 6.
14. P. Armstrong, *The Changing Landscape* (1975), 80.
15. M. Bailey, *A Marginal Economy? East Anglian Breckland in the Later Middle Ages* (1989); Sussams, *op. cit.*

30. RELIGIOUS HOUSES
SOURCES
Chapter on 'Religious Houses' by J.C. Cox in *VCH*, 2 (1907); D. Knowles & R. Neville Hadcock, *Medieval Religious Houses: England and Wales* (1971); W.A. Copinger, *Manors of Suffolk* (1907-11).

REFERENCES
1. The Crutched (Crossed) Friars at Whelnetham were an exception, with only a small handful of inmates.
2. This excludes the friars who were 'mendicants' and therefore not allowed possessions.
3. For example, Nicholas Bacon whose father was a yeoman from the Drinkstone area and who became solicitor to the Court of Augmentations, was able to set up each of his five sons with a comfortable estate. But recent work has shown that we should place less emphasis on the advancement of such 'new men', for in the majority of cases the land went to those already established in social and governmental circles. By far the greatest beneficiary in Suffolk, for instance, was the Duke of Norfolk.
4. Some of the wealthier chantries (for example, at Wingfield and Eyke) had been endowed with land or manors, to support chantry priests who were to say masses for the soul of the donor.

BIBLIOGRAPHY
Kitching, C., 'The Disposal of Monastic and Chantry Lands' in F. Heal and R. O'Day, *Church and Society Henry VIII to James* (1977)
Youings, Joyce, *The Dissolution of the Monasteries* (1971)

31. VICARAGES AND APPROPRIATE CHURCH LIVINGS
SOURCES
The map shows the situation in 1535, with a few more examples mentioned in the 13th century. See *Valor Ecclesiasticus* [1535], iii (Record Commissioners, 1817); W. E. Lunt, *Valuation of Norwich* [1254] (1926); *Ecclesiastical Taxation of Pope Nicholas* [1291] (Record Commissioners, 1802). John Kirby, *Suffolk Traveller* (1st edition, 1735) has a list of rectories, vicarages and impropriations, but it is incomplete and contains inaccuracies.

REFERENCES
1. This process should not be confused with patronage, or the right of advowson, which is the power to appoint an incumbent. This right, too, was frequently acquired by religious houses and often led to impropriation.
2. For example, in 1187-93 the parish of Clare was impropriated by the Benedictine monks of Stoke-by- Clare. By a Deed of Appropriation, the Bishop of Norwich ordained that a vicar was to receive the lesser tithes and offerings; the monks retained every other endowment, and even received an annual pension of £1 from the vicar: C. Harper-Bill & R. Mortimer, *Stoke by Clare Cartulary*, Part 1 (1982), 82 (see pp.64-66 for other impropriations at Cavenham and Bures). Vicars were responsible for the spiritual care of their parishes ('cure of souls') but impropriating rectors were liable for the upkeep of chancels.
3. Thus, Ixworth Priory acquired the rectory of Badwell Ash and appointed a priest; after the Reformation this living remained, for centuries, a poorly-paid curacy.
4. T. Cox, *Britannia* (c.1730), 310-24
5. In 1380, when Theberton was impropriated, Leiston Abbey was said to be 'destroyed by inundation of the sea and its goods largely wasted... burdened with debt and no longer able to offer hospitality...': R. Mortimer, *Leiston Cartulary* (1979), 127. Religious houses sometimes preferred to keep a valuable living intact to promote favoured clergy. For example, Bury Abbey never impropriated Long Melford or Beccles, though it was patron in both places.
6. Of the impropriated livings listed in 1535, roughly three quarters were vicarages and the rest had

salaried priests. In 1835 Suffolk contained 334 rectories, 98 vicarages, 69 perpetual curacies, 11 other curacies and 4 donatives. The 182 non-rectories then formed 35 per cent of the total (*BPP*, 1835, xxii).

7. Some vicarages later acquired 'augmentations' both in the Middle Ages and after the Reformation, to boost their depleted endowments. At Moulton, which was a 'peculiar' under the jurisdiction of the Archbishop of Canterbury, the Valor lists two beneficed clergy, a rector and a vicar. This kind of anomaly occurred when an absentee or incapacitated rector endowed an official substitute in the form of a vicar.

8. For example, the rector of Woolpit had an annual income of £20 15s. 0d., but he had to pay £13 6s. 8d. in pensions to officers of Bury Abbey. See *Ecclesiastical Taxation* [1291], 119.

9. Long before the Reformation, Cambridge colleges had received benefices in Suffolk, which they then impropriated. For example, in the mid-14th century 'Gonville Hall' acquired Mutford, and Trinity Hall took control of Cowlinge.

10. For example, Bardwell, Preston and Ubbeston. See White Kennett, *Impropriations and Vicarages* (1704). This had also happened much earlier: a few parishes mentioned as impropriated in the 13th century were rated as rectories by 1535—for example, Yaxley, Culpho and Glemsford.

11. Compare 'Report on Ecclesiastical Revenues' in *BPP*, 1835, xxii, with Kelly's *Directory of Suffolk* (1888).

12. For example at Higham in 1894 and St John's, Lowestoft, in 1854.

13. Laxfield was the most valuable living in Hoxne Deanery and was impropriated by Eye Priory; Debenham was the most valuable in Claydon and Thredling and was impropriated by Butley Priory. In Dunwich Deanery, eight parishes were worth more than £20 a year: of these five became impropriated, including the three wealthiest. Similar opportunism can be seen in areas where impropriations were not so common. In Thedwastre deanery which had 22 parishes, only three were impropri-ated but they were among the five wealthiest. In Clare Deanery, of the four wealthiest parishes, three became impropriated.

14. More work is needed on the value of individual livings. These details are recorded for each parish in *BPP*, 1887, lxiv. In this source, the effects of medieval impropriation are still clearly visible.

32. PARISH GILDS
SOURCES
Wills of local people, tax-lists (especially lay subsidies of 1524 and 1543), gild certificates of 1389, chantry certificates of 1548 (see Bibliography below, *sub* Redstone)

REFERENCES
1. The spelling GILD has been preferred because it was used by earlier writers, and because it helps to distinguish social and religious gilds from those which were occupational and urban.

2. Other groups, sometimes known as 'fellowships', also existed, often making themselves responsible for maintaining certain lights in the church, e.g. 'bachelors', 'maidens', 'ploughmen', etc.

3. In wills, especially where the testator has property in more than one parish, an added complication is the mention of 'a gild' in an unspecified parish.

4. Listed in abstract in H.F. Westlake, *The Parish Gilds of Mediaeval England* (1919), 225-31.

5. Accounts of a gild in the Creetings also survive in the PRO, and await publication. A microfilm copy is available in SRO (I), J436.

BIBLIOGRAPHY
Betterton, A., & Dymond, D., *Lavenham: Industrial Town* (1989), 20-3, 110-12

Morley, C., 'A Check-list of the Sacred Buildings of Suffolk, to which are added Gilds', *PSIAH*, xix (1926), 168-211

Northeast, P., 'Suffolk' in K. Farnhill (ed.), *English Gilds: Regional Studies of the Fraternities in Later Medieval England* (forthcoming)

Redstone, V.B., 'Chapels, Chantries and Gilds in Suffolk', *PSIAH*, xii (1904), 1-87; xxiii (1937), 50-78

Warren, F.E., 'Gild of St Peter in Bardwell', *PSIAH*, xi (1902), 81-110, 134-47

Westlake, H.F., 'The Origin, Purposes and Development of Parish Gilds in England', *PSIAH*, xvii (1921), 163-74

33. MEDIEVAL AND LATER MARKETS
REFERENCES
1. N. Scarfe, *SR,* 3, no. 1 (1965), 4-11.
2. N. Scarfe, *The Suffolk Landscape* (1972), Fig. 133.
3. 'Grants of Markets and Fairs from 1 John to 22 Edward IV', *BPP* 1888, liii, 108-3. This calendar proved to be very unreliable. Twenty of the grants listed under Suffolk were found to refer to other counties. In addition, some place-names were transcribed in a puzzlingly misleading form: for instance, *Tuwand*, granted a market in 1221, was found to be *Suwaud* or Southwold.
4. I have still not found time to check the list exhaustively against all the very extensive printed sources used by R.H. Britnell for Essex in 1981. His is the model for anyone beginning such a search. See R.H. Britnell, 'Essex Markets before 1350', *Essex Archaeol. & Hist.*, 13, 15-21. See also his 'The Proliferation of Markets in England 1200-1349', *Econ. Hist. Rev.*, 2nd series, xxxiv (1981), 209-221. Wendy Walker's *Essex Markets and Fairs* (1981) is a well illustrated, thoroughly researched and stimulating booklet of 44 pages, no. 83 of the Essex Record Office's Publications. I hope to produce a more definitive version for Suffolk in the *PSIAH*. A model discussion of such material in one county is D. Dymond, *The Norfolk Landscape* (1985), 152-64.
5. *Calendar of Patent Rolls*, 51 Edward III, m.18.
6. Domesday Book, f.379.

34. MEDIEVAL AND LATER FAIRS
REFERENCES
1. MS of Robert Reyce, SRO(I): 474/4237.
2. William Owen, *Book of Fairs* (1759 and 1805). In 1764, a further count of 96 fairs in 66 different places was given in the 2nd edition of John Kirby's *Suffolk Traveller* (1764), Appendix, 70-72.
3. It should be noted that new fairs continued to appear regularly in the post-medieval period:

Hartest for example started its first fair on 23 April 1789, the day when the nation gave thanks for George III's recovery from madness, and Bardwell's fair, which is still held each spring, appears to have been entirely a 20th-century creation!

4. D. Dymond (ed.), *Register of Thetford Priory*, ii (1996), 388; William Harrison, *Description of England* [1577] (edn of 1968), 308.
5. Enclosure Map of Newmarket, SRO(B): FL 610/1/6a,6b; information on Halesworth from Dr J. Middleton-Stewart.

35. POPULATION DENSITIES, 1327 AND 1524

SOURCES
The published Lay Subsidies of 1327 and 1524.

NOTES
SUFFOLK HUNDREDS: RELATIVE RANKINGS

A. By density of population per acre	1327	1524
Babergh	8	2
Blackbourn	11	20
Blything	14	9
Bosmere & Claydon	6	14
Carlford	15	6
Colneis	12	13
Cosford	9	4
Hartismere	3	9
Hoxne	5	15
Lackford	21	21
Loes	10	7
Mutford & Lothingland	4	5
Plomesgate	20	18
Risbridge	19	8
Samford	18	17
Stow	7	11
Thedwastre	13	16
Thingoe	2	1
Thingoe (without B. St E.)	4	15
Thredling	17	12
Wangford	1	3
Wilford	16	19

B. By tax paid per acre	1327	1524
Babergh	6	1
Blackbourn	11	20
Blything	15	10
Bosmere & Claydon	7	9

	1327	1524
Carlford	15	13
Colneis	13	16
Cosford	12	4
Hartismere	4	15
Hoxne	9	12
Lackford	18	21
Loes	17	5
Mutford & Lothingland	5	11
Plomesgate	19	17
Risbridge	10	18
Samford	14	7
Stow	3	6
Thedwastre	8	14
Thingoe	1	2
Thingoe (without B. St E.)	4	10
Thredling	20	8
Wangford	2	3
Wilford	21	19

REFERENCES
1. S.H.A. Hervey, (ed.) *Suffolk in 1327* (1906); S.H.A. Hervey, (ed.) *Suffolk in 1524* (1910).
2. D.P. Dymond & R. Virgoe, 'The Reduced Population and Wealth of Early 15th Century Suffolk', *PSIAH*, xxxvi, pt 2 (1986), 73-99.
3. Dymond & Virgoe, *op. cit.*, (1986), 77, Fig.13.
4. To make them more manageable, the figures actually represent *acreage per taxpayer*. The acreage of parishes has been taken from Kelly's *Directory* of 1912 or, in cases where boundaries have been revised, from White's *Directory* of 1844.
5. See also J. Pound (ed.), *The Military Survey of 1522 for Babergh Hundred* (1986).
6. N. Evans, 'Farming and Landholding in Wood-Pasture East Anglia, 1550-1650', *PSIAH*, xxxv, pt 4 (1984), 303-15.
7. See W.G. Hoskins, *Local History in England* (2nd ed. 1972), 239. Between 1327 and 1524, Babergh, at the heart of the textile-manufacturing area, rose from sixth to first place among the hundreds of Suffolk in terms of tax paid, even though, as John Pound shows, two-thirds of its parishes were still predominantly agricultural.

36. MOBILITY AND SURNAMES

SOURCE
Published Lay Subsidy of 1327.

NOTES
LOCATIVE SURNAMES OF 1327 NOT CERTAINLY IDENTIFIED

BURY ST EDMUNDS	IPSWICH
Borugh (?Barrow)	*Bour* (also occurs at Groton)
Haverlond (also in Cockfield, Sudbury, Yaxley, etc.)	*Collesdon* (?Coulsdon, Surrey)
Meryhel (?Merryhill Green,Berks; surname also at Barrow, Polstead, etc.)	*Hondelane* (prob. local)
	Newtone (common place-name/ surname)
Neulyn (?Newlyn Cornwall)	*Plomcherd*
Northenton (?Northington, Hants)	*Rodlond* (also at Eyke, Felsham, etc.)
Thornton (?Lincolnshire)	*Roughbrok/Roubrok*

REFERENCES
1. R. McKinley, *Norfolk and Suffolk Surnames in the Middle Ages* (1975); also *Norfolk Surnames in the 16th Century*, Dept. of English Local History, Leicester Univ., Occ. Papers, 2nd ser., no. 2 (1969); see also P.H. Reaney, *A Dictionary of British Surnames* (1958) and P. McClure, 'Surnames from English Place names as Evidence for Mobility in the Middle Ages', *The Local Historian*, 13, no. 2 (1978), 80-86.
2. *Suffolk in 1327*, Suffolk Green Books, ix, vol.11 (p.91 for Mutford).
3. *Ibid*, 215-20.
4. Other local names from places in, or close to, the two towns are *Hennecote* (Hencote, an area to the south of Bury), *Caldewalle* (probably Coldwell Brook which ran on the line of St Helen's Street in Ipswich), *Godelesford* (Gusford lies in Stoke, on the opposite side of the river from Ipswich). *Hondelane* is another probable example from Ipswich.
5. Reaney, *op. cit.*, (1958), 285-86.
6. McKinley, *op. cit.*, (1975), 78.

37. THE STRUCTURE OF A MEDIEVAL MANOR
SOURCES
Map of *c*.1606 and various manorial records of Worlingworth. The remarkable accuracy of the map is only slightly compromised by some shrinkage of the vellum, and perhaps by some inventive surveying by the anonymous cartographer in the area north of the Great

Green and Fingle Street. Most of the manorial records, which include a good series of medieval court rolls, accounts and surveys, are to be found in the Henniker collection (SRO(I), S1/2). Additional information is available in the registers, customaries and cartularies of the abbey of Bury St Edmunds, to which Worlingworth belonged from 1020 to 1539.

REFERENCES

1. The easternmost strip of *Carrfeld* appears to have survived to the present day as a thicket.
2. Field-names incorporating the British element *Wal-* fuel such speculation, especially *Walhill* on which *le letecote* was situated, and the demesne close called *Walworttes*.
3. The isolation of *le letecote* could again be an important piece of evidence in this respect.
4. Now Cross Cottage.

38. DESERTED, DISPERSED AND SMALL SETTLEMENTS

SOURCES

The map was compiled from information in the SMR, together with the author's own notes. The data on households in 1428 is taken from D. Dymond & R. Virgoe, 'The Reduced Population and Wealth of Early 15th Century Suffolk', *PSIAH*, xxxvi, pt 2 (1986), 73-100. Information on ruined churches can be found in J. Blatchly & P. Northeast, 'The Lost and Ruined Churches of Suffolk' in H.M. Cautley, *Suffolk Churches* (5th ed., 1982).

REFERENCES

1. S. Podd, *Earthwork Reconaissance in Suffolk: Rapid Identification Survey*, Suffolk County Council (1995).
2. M.R. Postgate, 'Field Systems of East Anglia' in A.R.H. Baker & R.A. Butlin (eds), *Studies of Field Systems in the British Isles* (1973), 281-324; M. Bailey, *A Marginal Economy? East Anglian Breckland in the Later Middle Ages* (1989), 40-5.
3. Some has been claimed at West Stow (S.E. West, 'West Stow, The Anglo-Saxon Village', *EAA*, 24 (1985), 102) and some very slight traces could survive in Little Saxham, in an area that was emparked by 1638 and is now part of Ickworth Park. It is also rare in Norfolk: see R.J. Silvester, 'Ridge and Furrow

in Norfolk', *NA* (1989), 286-96.
4. In 1573 Thomas Tusser referred to Suffolk and Essex as places 'where enclosure is most' in his *Five Hundred Points of Good Husbandry* (OUP, 1984).
5. B.K. Roberts & S. Wrathmell, *Terrain and Rural Settlement Mapping*, English Heritage rep. (1995).
6. For example, the work of Mike Hardy in the South Elmhams and of Edward Savery in Bardwell, Stanton and Ixworth Thorpe. Summaries are published in 'Archaeology in Suffolk' in *PSIAH* for 1985-90 and 1993; see also M. Hardy, 'The Waveney Valley Survey', *Current Archaeol.*, 115 (1989), 266-9.
7. P. Wade-Martins, 'The Archaeology of Medieval Rural Settlement in East Anglia' in M. Aston, D. Austin & C. Dyer (eds), *The Rural Settlements of England* (1989), 149-65.
8. K. Sussams, *The Breckland Archaeological Survey* (1996), 86-8.
9. Information from Clive Paine.
10. M. Bailey, '*Per Impetuum Maris*: Natural Disaster and Economic Decline in Eastern England, 1275-1350' in B.M.S. Campbell (ed.), *Before the Black Death: Studies in the Crisis of the Early Fourteenth Century* (1991).

39. THE UPRISING OF 1381

SOURCES

Rolls of Parliament, Pardon Rolls and Commissions (e.g. of the Peace); printed extracts from registers of the abbey of St Edmunds. *Not* included are the parishes of over 1,500 rebels mentioned in the proceedings of King's Bench and of Common Pleas: information on these men and women, together with those recorded in manorial records (for example, for Felixstowe-cum-Trimley and Tangham), will be collated in the author's forthcoming volume *The Roots of Freedom*.

REFERENCES

1. Thomas Sampson of Harkstead and Kersey had shipping interests, and had previously been a tax-collector himself.
2. Thomas de Bedingfield is another good example.
3. Military action taken by Henry Despenser, soldier-bishop of Norwich, resulted in the alleged defeat of

the Norfolk rebels at North Walsham.
4. This document gave the findings of a commission led by Thomas de Morieux.
5. Men from Norfolk, Cambridgeshire and Lincolnshire were present in Suffolk.
6. One of the Suffolk riding-men (élite horsemen who co-ordinated the revolt) was Robert Cavell or Tavell of Lavenham, later killed in Huntingdonshire.
7. John Wrawe had declined the crown, saying that as a priest he already had a hat. The ritual was no doubt conducted in the spirit of Corpus Christi.
8. Cambridge had been executed at Mildenhall; he had been caught trying to escape, carrying papers which incriminated him, probably, in the trial of the popular but illegal candidate for the vacant post of abbot, Edmund Brounfield.
9. The duration and suppression of the rebellion in Suffolk will inevitably be a prominent focus for future investigation, as will its survival in 'folklore'.
10. Like Thomas de Walsingham.
11. At Hollesley, for example, John Reynold was killed.
12. In 1385 de la Pole obtained licence to fortify his castle at Wingfield.
13. This time at Parham and Framlingham.
14. One of the leaders was John Bette, very active in 1381 in Suffolk, and possibly in Norfolk.
15. For example, on Friday after Corpus Christi, 1393.
16. Against the mayor and burgesses of Thetford, for example.
17. Westbrom was a mercer by occupation, and very probably came from a villein family of Drinkstone.

40. GREAT HOUSES OF THE 16th AND 17th CENTURIES

SOURCES

S.H.A. Hervey, (ed.), *Suffolk in 1674, being the Hearth Tax Returns*, Suffolk Green Books, no. xi, vol. 13 (1905); Richard Blome, *Britannia* (1673), 427-31. Descriptions of many of the houses mentioned can be found in the excursion reports published in the *PSIAH*.

REFERENCES

1. Nine peers (the Duke of York, renting Lord Cornwallis's house at Culford; the Earl of Arlington at

Euston; the Earl of Norwich at Whittingham Hall; the Earl of St Albans at Rushbrook; Viscount Hereford at Christchurch Mansion and Sudbourne Hall; Lord Cornwallis at Brome; Lord Crofts at Little Saxham; and Lord North at Tostock Place), 57 baronets, knights and ladies, 62 esquires, 218 gentlemen, misters, madams and mistresses, six doctors, one major, seven captains and one alderman.

2. R. Blome, *Britannia* (1673), 427-31.
3. Though none is in the direct male line. The Henham estate still belongs to a direct male descendant of its owner in 1674, Sir John Rous, but the house has been demolished.
4. A sketch of this now-demolished house on a map of 1702 suggests that it was one of the fashionable 'tower' houses so characteristic of the Commonwealth period.
5. Curiously, although the house at Fakenham was Sir Lionel Tollemache's principal residence in this period (Helmingham being occupied by his brother Robert), he did not own an extensive estate there and was not the manorial lord. It is possible that the house was only rented, for in 1674 it was in the possession of Thomas Rushbrook, who was lord of the manor 1613-85. Rushbrook belonged to the lowest rank of the gentry and occupied a much smaller house of 11 hearths in Fakenham. Another house with 11 hearths in Fakenham, possibly also a lodge, was sold in 1651 by Sir Lionel to his brother-in-law, Sir Henry Felton of Playford. Felton resold it in 1673 to Thomas Jermyn of Rushbrook. Presumably the attraction was the hunting available on the open heaths stretching from Fakenham to Thetford. In 1636 Tollemache was entrusted with the preservation of the king's game within 12 miles of Thetford.
6. Colvin, H. & Newman, J. (eds), *Of Building: Roger North's Writings on Architecture* (1981), 142-3.

BIBLIOGRAPHY
Airs, M., 'The Designing of Five East Anglian Country Houses, 1505-1637', *Architectural Hist.*, 21 (1978), 58-67
Airs, M., *The Tudor and Jacobean Country House: a Building History* (1995)
Colman, S., 'The Hearth Tax Returns for the Hundred of Blackbourne, 1662', *PSIAH*, pt 2 (1971), 168-92
Gunn, S.J. & Lindley, P.G., 'Charles Brandon's Westhorpe: an Early Tudor Courtyard House in Suffolk', *AJ*, 145 (1988), 272-89
Howard, M., *The Early Tudor Country House; Architecture and Politics, 1490-1550* (1987)
Kenworthy-Browne, J., Reid, P., Sayer, M. & Watkin, D., *Burke's and Savills Guide to Country Houses, Vol. III, East Anglia* (1981)
Mowl, T. & Earnshaw, B., *Architecture without Kings; the Rise of Puritan Classicism under Cromwell* (1995)
Pevsner, N. & Radcliffe, E., *Buildings of England—Suffolk* (1974)
Sandeen, E.R., 'The Building of Redgrave Hall, 1545-54', *PSIAH*, xxix, pt 1 (1961), 1-33
Sandon, E., *Suffolk Houses; A Study of Domestic Architecture* (1977)

41. THE GENTRY OF SUFFOLK DURING THE CIVIL WAR
SOURCES
For lists of Suffolk gentry in the reign of Charles I, see PRO, E178 (Knighthood Composition Lists, 1631-2); E179 (Lay Subsidy Rolls, 1628 and 1641); E377/49 (Recusant Roll, 1641). For gentry allegiances in the Civil War, see PRO, E113 (Bills and Answers against Defaulting Accountants); SP19 (Committee for Advance of Money); SP23 (Committee for Compounding); SP28 (Commonwealth Exchequer Papers); SP29/68, fols 48-87 (List of Officers claiming £60,000, 1633); BL, Additional MS 15520 (Candler's Notes on the History of Suffolk, written mainly 1655-7). A full list can be found in articles by G. Blackwood in *SR*, 1992 and 1994.

REFERENCES
1. Ipswich and Bury St Edmunds are excluded from the agricultural districts, and are considered separately.
2. The Fielding also included the parishes of Moulton, Kentford, Gazeley and Dalham in Risbridge hundred.
3. Excluding the parishes named in Note 2.

BIBLIOGRAPHY
Banks, C.E. (ed.), *Able Men of Suffolk, 1638* (1931)
Everitt, A.M. (ed.), *Suffolk and the Great Rebellion, 1640-60* (SRS iii, 1960)
Holmes, C. (ed.), *The Suffolk Committee for Scandalous Ministers, 1644-6* (SRS xiii, 1970)
Metcalfe, W.C. (ed.), *The Visitations of Suffolk, 1561, 1577, 1612* (1882)
Redstone, V.B. (ed.), *Suffolk Ship Money Returns, 1639-40* (1904)
Rylands, W.H. (ed.), *The Visitations of Suffolk, 1664-8* (Harleian Soc., 1910)
The County of Suffolk divided into... Classical Presbyteries (1647)

42. PEOPLE AND POOR IN 1674
REFERENCES
1. S.H.A. Hervey, *Suffolk in 1674*, Suffolk Green Books, No 11 (1905).
2. It is occasionally possible to compare hearth-tax returns with other listings of the same period, such as probate records or lists of ratepayers. This can show, rather disconcertingly, that persons known to have been living in a particular place in 1674, are not mentioned in the returns. So the returns cannot be relied upon as an absolutely full census of heads of households, and omissions certainly occur. See for example a list of charitable payments made in the village of Fornham St Martin.
3. K. Schurer & T. Arkell, *Surveying the People* (1992).
4. These brackets do not appear in the original manuscript. They are the editor's convention for showing names grouped on the same line of the original, in each case with a total number of hearths for the group rather than for each individual household.
5. The subdivision of houses into tenements was becoming a major problem in 17th-century Suffolk. For example, special by-laws were passed to restrict the practice in Hadleigh in 1618 and at Mendlesham in 1635 (Hadleigh Borough Archives, 3/2; SRO(I) FB 159/L2/1). At Bramford the vestry petitioned Quarter Sessions in 1677, saying that the pressure of population had required the conversion of 'antient

houses of habitacion into cottages for the necessary reception of theire poore' (S. Colman, *Vernacular Architecture*, 12 (1981), 54).

43. COUNTRY-HOUSE BUILDING IN SUFFOLK, 1700-1900
REFERENCES
1. J. Bateman, *The Great Landowners of Gt Britain and Ireland* (1883) based on *BPP*, 1874, lxxii, Pt 2. By selecting houses according to the size of estates, one excludes examples which might by other criteria be considered significant. Some estate-owners lived in modest houses, for example in Exning and Pakenham where houses are not shown on the map. Bateman split a few holdings between different family members, and this accounts for three estates and seats in Icklingham. Some of the selected houses at the time of building would have been associated with smaller estates, no more significant than others which did not grow to over 1000 acres. Strictly speaking, the survey of 1873 is concerned with land-ownership and not with the history of houses. If it is used to throw light on the size of earlier estates and on earlier building activity, uncertainty increases with distance in time. However, it is generally true that large estates tended to get larger, and the rankings are relatively stable.
2. N. Scarfe (ed.), *A Frenchman's Year in Suffolk, 1784*, SRS xxx, 1988).
3. R. Hoppitt, 'A Relative Relief Map of Suffolk, *Suffolk Natural History*, 25 (1989), 80-5.
4. Mackley, A.L., 'The Construction of Henham Hall', *The Georgian Group Jour.*, vi (1996), 85-96.

BIBLIOGRAPHY
Mackley, A.L., 'An Economic History of Country-House Building, with particular reference to East Anglia and the East and West Ridings of Yorkshire, c.1660-1870', unpublished PhD thesis, UEA, 1993

Pevsner, N., *The Buildings of England: Suffolk* (2nd ed., 1974)

Reid, P., 'Suffolk' in *Burke's and Savills Guide to Country Houses, III, East Anglia* (1981), 211-70

Returns of Owners of Land, 1872-3 (England & Wales), *BPP*, 1874, lxxii, Pt 2
Sandon, E., *Suffolk Houses* (1977)

44. PARKS OF THE 18th CENTURY
BIBLIOGRAPHY
Jaques, D., *Georgian Gardens: The Reign of Nature* (1983)
Stroud, D., *Capability Brown* (1965)
Williamson, T., *Polite Landscapes: Gardens and Society in Eighteenth-Century England* (1995)

45. THE COUNTY VOTERS OF 1705
SOURCE
A copy of the Poll for Knights of the Shire for the County of Suffolk, taken at Ipswich, May 9, 1705. Photocopies are available in the SRO(B), open shelves 0.55.7, and in the Institute of Historical Research, London. An original is to be found at the Society of Genealogists, London.
REFERENCES
1. For a fuller discussion of Suffolk's electoral scene in the late 17th and early 18th centuries, see P.E. Murrell, 'Suffolk: the Political Behaviour of the County and its Parliamentary Boroughs from the Exclusion Crisis to the Accession of the House of Hanover', unpublished PhD thesis, Univ. of Newcastle upon Tyne, 1982. Copy in SRO(B).
2. G. Holmes & W.A. Speck (eds), *The Divided Society: Party Conflict in England, 1694-1716* (1967); W.A. Speck, *Tory and Whig: The Struggle in the Constituencies, 1701-15* (1970).
3. The battle for this shire, a microcosm of the feelings which gripped the country at large, has earned a place in various historical surveys: E. Cunnington, 'The General Election of 1705', unpublished MA thesis, Univ. of London, 1939; D.M. Reed, 'The Tackers in the Election of 1705', in J. Murray (ed.), *Essays in Modern European History* (Indiana, 1946), 22-23; J.O. Richards, *Party Propaganda under Queen Anne: The General Elections of 1702-13* (Georgia, 1972), 70-71; W.A. Speck, *Tory and Whig* ...(1970), 104-05.
4. G. Holmes, *British Politics in the Age of Anne* (revised, 1987), 102-03, 336.

5. SRO(B), E2/18, Cullum Correspondence: A. Pitches to Sir D. Cullum, 11 May 1705.
6. SRO(B), D4/1/3a, f.217; W. Sussex Record Office, Shillinglee MSS, Ac. 454, no. 876: Sir E. Bacon to Sir E. Turnour, 20 March 1705; SRO(I) HA 247/5/4, Commonplace Book of the Tory JP, Devereux Edgar.
7. Bodleian Library, Rawlinson D., 863, no. 89, *A Collection of several Paragraphs out of Mr Dyer's Letters* (1705), *sub* 12 May 1705.
8. Several poll figures exist for this election. All vary slightly in the number of votes cast for each candidate, though the victory is always for the Tories and their majority in the region of 500 votes apiece. For example Dyer (*op. cit.*) reported Dysart with 2,883 votes, Davers 2,877, Cullum 2,318 and Barnardiston 2,286; *The Daily Courant*, 15 May 1705 (in British Library) gave the final poll as Dysart 2,877, Davers 2,883, Cullum 2,386 and Barnardiston 2,310. Each voter could cast two votes. Coming so early in the national campaign, Suffolk's results, and particularly that for the county itself, did two things. First, they gave a great boost to High Church morale. Secondly, they proved to be a very emotive 'red herring'. The divisions in Suffolk reflected those in the country generally, but the results were atypical of what was to happen in most other places. Consequently, when Suffolk's early returns were seized upon and dangled in front of the national electorate by the propaganda presses of both parties, they gave a misleading picture both of how the two parties were faring, and of the true support given to the Tackers and their adherents in the more popular constituencies.
9. The exact count of parishes is obscured by vagaries within the Poll Book. For example, the poll clerks grouped the voters of Fornham All Saints, Fornham St Martin and Fornham St Genevieve under the single heading 'Fornhams'. For statistical purposes, therefore, the Fornhams are counted as one parish.
10. For the extent of Puritanism in Suffolk, see J. Browne, *History of Congregationalism in Norfolk and Suffolk* (1877); *Cal. State Papers Domestic, 1683*, 83 for conventicles in Bury St Edmunds and Ipswich;

SRO(B), D8/1/1, presentments; D. MacCulloch, 'Power, Privilege and the County Community: County Politics in Elizabethan Suffolk', unpublished PhD thesis, Univ. of Cambridge, 1977; D. MacCulloch, *Suffolk and the Tudors: Politics and Religion in an English County, 1500-1600* (1986); P. Collinson, *The Elizabethan Puritan Movement* (1967).

11. While newspapers developed by leaps and bounds during 'The First Age of Party', the press and Grub-Street journalism still could not equal the pulpit for the dissemination of propaganda on a large scale. The vocal support of the clergy was something to be coveted, and here the Tories possessed an inbuilt advantage. Becoming 'the Church party', they found themselves with a potential propaganda outlet in virtually every parish in the country. Few places were without an Anglican church though scores were without dissenting meeting houses, which were to become the breeding ground of many Whig supporters. For an analysis of how Suffolk's clergy voted in 1705, see Murrell, *op. cit.*, Table 33, Scatter Map 11 and notes on pp. 423-28.

12. W.A. Speck, *Tory and Whig* ...(1970), 36.

46. ENCLOSURE AND RECLAMATION
REFERENCES

1. 'Enclosures' can also turn out to be a replacement for *earlier* enclosures.

2. W.E. Tate & M.E. Turner, *Domesday of Enclosures* (1978), 242-46.

3. On the Elveden and Euston estates, large-scale reclamation has been carried out since 1940. See P.J.O. Trist, *A Survey of the Agriculture of Suffolk* (1971), 143-44, 146-47 and G. Martelli, *The Elveden Enterprise* (1952).

4. F. Hervey (ed.), *Suffolk in the 17th Century* (1902), 14: in about 1603 Robert Reyce referred to 'our deep myrie soyle, our narrow and fowle landes, our manifold inclosures, severed with so many deep ditches, hedges, and store of wood, bushes and trees...' For a local study, see D.P. Dymond, 'The Parish of Walsham-le-Willows: Two Elizabethan Surveys and

their Medieval Background', *PSIAH*, xxxiii, 195-211.

5. For example, a detailed study of the surviving probate inventories for Long Melford reveals that the main wealth of local yeomen, husbandmen and farmers, from Elizabethan times until the mid-18th century, lay in their dairy cattle.

6. Trist, *op. cit.*, 120-22, 129-32.

47. POPULATION TRENDS, 1811-1981
REFERENCES

1. For example, the populations of Ipswich and Lowestoft both rose by 100%. Similar though smaller increases can be seen in and around Bury St Edmunds, Sudbury, Mildenhall, Haverhill and Leiston with Aldeburgh.

2. The growth of seaside resorts can also be seen at places like Aldeburgh, Kessingland and Southwold. Other towns expanded because they had important industries such as the making of agricultural machinery at Leiston and of textiles at Haverhill. Another group grew because they were successful marketing and service centres like Stowmarket and Beccles or, to a lesser extent, Brandon and Sudbury.

3. We can, of course, find exceptions to these general trends, particularly towards the end of this long period. A relatively early example is Brantham which grew after a xylonite works was established there in 1887. During the First World War the naval training establishment at Shotley and, from the 1930s, the 'Aeroplane Experimental Establishment' at Martlesham explain the increase of local populations. Similarly, the presence of airbases during the Second World War, and their maintenance afterwards, account for the growth of Honington, Stradishall and Ringshall (next to Wattisham), as well as Bawdsey.

48. RURAL SETTLEMENT IN THE MID-19th CENTURY
REFERENCES

1. B.K. Roberts & S. Wrathmell, 'The Monuments Pro-

tection Programme: Medieval Settlements Project', *Medieval Settlements Research Group, Annual Report*, 9 (1994-5); B.K. Roberts, D. Stocker & S. Wrathmell, 'Rural Settlement in England: and the English Heritage Mapping Project', *Pamatky Supplementum*, 5, Prague (1966); B.K. Roberts & S. Wrathmell, 'Dispersed Settlement in England' in P. Everson & T Williamson, *The Archaeology of Landscape: Studies Presented to Christopher Taylor* (1998).

2. H. Margery (publisher), *The Old Series Ordnance Survey Maps of England and Wales*, 8 vols (1975-81): J.B. Harley, *The Historian's Guide to Ordnance Survey Maps* (1964).

3. B.K. Roberts, *The Making of the English Village* (1987).

4. D. Stamp (ed.) *The Land of Britain*, Parts 72-73 (1941), 309-371; H.C. Darby, *The Domesday Geography of Eastern England*, (1952), 153-208: J. Thirsk, *England's Agricultural Regions and Agrarian History, 1500-1750* (1987).

49. ROMAN CATHOLIC RECUSANCY
REFERENCES

1. Darkyn of Chippenham near Newmarket was 'taken to be a carrier fo[r] letters from one papist to another', 1598.

2. Dallison, a priest, was schoolmaster at Wetherden Hall, 1578.

3. Nicholas Gellibrand, ordained in 1546, was still working in 1588.

4. John Fenn, High Master of Bury St Edmunds' grammar school in Mary's reign, was ordained in 1574 after a period of writing and publishing for the English recusant presses.

BIBLIOGRAPHY

Anstruther, G., *The Seminary Priests, 1558-1800*, 4 Vols (1966)

Bellenger, D. A., *English and Welsh Priests, 1558-1800* (1984)

Bellenger, D. A., *The French Exiled Clergy* (1986)

Blackwood, B.G., 'Cavalier and Roundhead Gentry of Suffolk', *SR*, new ser. 5 (1985)

Bowler, H., 'Some Notes on the Recusant Rolls of the

'Exchequer', *Recusant History*, 4 (1958)

Catholic Records Soc., vols. 1-71 (1905-86)

Dymond, D.P., 'Suffolk and the Compton Census of 1676', *SR*, 3, no. 4 (1966)

Estcourt, E.E. & Payne, J.O., *The English Catholic Non-Jurors of 1715* (1885)

Foley, H., *Records of the English Province of the Society of Jesus*, 7 vols (1877)

MacCulloch, D., *Suffolk and the Tudors* (1986)

McGrath, P.V., *Papists and Puritans under Elizabeth I* (1967)

McGrath, P.V. & Rowe, J., 'The Recusancy of Sir Thomas Cornwallis', *PSIAH*, xxviii, pt 3 (1961)

McGrath, P.V. & Rowe, J., 'The Marian Priests under Elizabeth I', *Recusant History*, 17, no. 2 (1984)

Norman, E., *Roman Catholicism in England* (1985)

Rowe, J., *Catholic Bury St Edmunds, Coldham and the Surrounding District* (1980)

Williams, J.A., 'Recusant Rolls: Short Guides to Records, No. 11', *History*, 50 (1965)

50. PROTESTANT NONCONFORMITY

SOURCES

The licences of 1672; Quaker records, 1669-74; Census of Religious Worship, 1851. See References below.

NOTES

NONCONFORMITY IN SUFFOLK, 1851

Key to columns below:
1. No. of places of worship, from *Report and Tables of the 1851 Census* (1853)
2. No. of places of worship, including omissions noted by Timmins (1997)
3. Estimated total membership in 1851
4. Actual membership of each sect

	1.	2.	3.	4.
CONGREGATIONAL (or INDEPENDENT)	90	100	20,300-29,600	5018 (in 1863)
PRESBYTERIAN		1		
WESLEYAN METHODIST	84	94	8200-10,500	c.2500
WESLEYAN REFORM	5	9		
WESLEYAN ASSOCN	2	3		
PRIMITIVE METHODIST	72	87	6600-8800	c.1800
BAPTIST UNION		15		
STRICT & PARTICULAR BAPTIST	78	54	19,600-30,000	c.6400
BAPTIST, Unspecified	13	25		
QUAKER	8	8		
UNITARIAN	3	3		
MORMON	3	5		
PLYMOUTH BRETHREN	3	7		
SWEDENBORGIAN		1		
Non-Denominational	10	3		

Note: The map and table above include all places of worship listed in 1851, and those omitted but identified by Timmins. The three-fold division of the Baptists is also based on Timmins. The Strict and Particular Baptists include 39 congregations belonging to the Calvinistic Norfolk and Suffolk Association. The number given for the Plymouth Brethren is larger than Timmins', and is based on personal knowledge.

REFERENCES

1. Independent congregations were first established in Suffolk at Bury in 1646-8 and Walpole in 1647 (J. Brown, *History of Congregationalism in Norfolk and Suffolk* (1877), 395, 437). The first Quaker meeting was at Botesdale in 1655, when George Whitehead was on his way to Robert Duncan's house at Mendlesham (G. Whitehead, *Christian Progress* (1722). Quakers were to establish meetings at Bury, Woodbridge and other places in the same year. Baptists were first recorded in 1644-5 at Beccles, when two believers were charged with being Anabaptists and 'dipping' other adults (A.J. Klaiber, *The Story of the Suffolk Baptists* (1931), 18).

2. G. Lyon Turner, *Original Records of Early Nonconformity under Persecution and Indulgence* (3 vols, 1911-14), vol.1, 613-5 and vol.2, 903-22.

3. The Compton Census of 1676, however, which survives for the archdeaconry of Sudbury alone, gives the number of nonconformists in each parish. Though it probably underestimates the true figures, the Census shows that hard-line nonconformists existed in many towns and villages, and no doubt 'gathered' for worship in convenient centres. For example, 37 dissenters in Hepworth probably worshipped with 49 other Independent brethren in adjoining Wattisfield. However as the map is concerned with known *places* of worship, the people listed in 1676 have not been shown. See D. Dymond, 'Suffolk and the Compton Census of 1676', *SR*, vol.3, no.4 (1966), 103-18; 'Mapping Nonconformity in Suffolk' in E.S. Leedham-Green, *Religious Dissent in East Anglia* (Cambridge Antiq. Soc., 1991), 113-24; Anne Whiteman, *The Compton Census of 1676*, Records of Social & Economic History, new ser. x (1986).

4. In the early 18th century Baptist congregations were established at Bildeston and Ipswich by members from Colchester.

5. Including the minutes of Monthly Meetings, and records of 'Sufferings' in the period 1669-73. See J. Besse, *The Sufferings of the People called Quakers* (1753); G. Lyon Turner, *Original Records*; PRO: RG 6/1213 and RG 6/1492; SRO(I): FK 6/3/68.

6. No records survive for the north-west of Suffolk, which is represented by only two meetings.

7. Of those, 16 had more than one denomination: Aldeburgh, Beccles, Bungay, Bury, Haverhill, Hepworth, Ipswich, Kelsale, Nayland, Needham, Rattlesden, Spexhall, Sudbury, Walpole, Wattisfield and Woodbridge.

8. This growth included the older, 17th-century sects. For example, in the period 1715-29, the Presbyterians at Hadleigh claimed 250 members, and the Independents at Beccles 350 (Dr Williams Library: John Evans' List of Dissenting Congregations and Ministers, 1719-29, MS 34.4).

9. For example, out of 405 licences granted in Suffolk between 1791 and 1810, only 48 were for formal chapels: Returns relating to Dissenters' Places of Worship (including Roman Catholic), *BPP*, 1870, liv. See also *Religious Dissent in East Anglia*, 124.

10. Of the chapels, 40 were Wesleyan Methodist, 35 were Particular Baptist and 33 were Independent or Congregational. Sadly the original returns of this important survey do not survive for Suffolk, but the figures were summarised in W. White, *Directory of Suffolk* (1844), 29 and *BPP*, 1836, xl.

11. The returns have been published in T.C.R. Timmins (ed.), *Suffolk Returns from the Census of Religious Worship, 1851* (SRS, vol.39, 1997). Microfilms of originals: SRO(B) J 501/3/1 & 2; SRO(I) J 430/102/1 & 2. Contemporary summaries can be found in *Report and Tables of the 1851 Census* (1853) and J. Glyde, *Suf-*

folk in the 19th Century (1856), 275-6.

12. From information supplied by Heather Spencer of Tostock.

13. The rise of nonconformity in the late 18th and early 19th centuries must be seen against the background of a sharply rising population nationally. Even at its peak, around 1840, it has been estimated that Methodism was embraced by only 2.78% of the nation (R. Currie, A. Gilbert & L. Horsley, *Churches and Churchgoers*, 1977, 65). Our admiration for the dogged persistence of nonconformists should not blind us to the danger of exaggerating their actual and relative numbers, at all periods. If, alternatively, the strength of nonconformity is measured by the number of purpose-built chapels, the apogee probably comes in the period 1900-14. For an estimate of the strength of nonconformity in the 1980s, see *Religious Dissent in East Anglia*, 117.

51. EDUCATION BEFORE 1750

SOURCES

Reports of Charity Commissioners, 1819-1840, known as the 'Brougham Report' (Suffolk is covered in the reports of 1828-30); records of the Society for Promoting Christian Knowledge, and the annual 'Accounts of Charity Schools', 1707-33; the Venns' *Alumni Cantabrigienses*, Part 1 (1922-27).

REFERENCES

1. Generally speaking, it was not considered necessary for girls to receive formal education before the 18th century. Although many endowments referred to 'children', it is clear that only boys were really meant. None of the grammar schools admitted girls; of the endowed schools, only at Long Melford did part of the endowment include girls, and that dated only to 1713. Some charity schools provided for girls, but only a small proportion of the total did so in the early years of their establishment.

2. P. Northeast, 'The Provision of Elementary Education in 19th Century Rural Suffolk', *SR*, 5, no. 2 (1981), 90-96.

BIBLIOGRAPHY

Jones, M.G., *The Charity School Movement* (1938)

Leach, A.F. & Steele Hutton, E.P., chapter on 'Schools' in *VCH, Suffolk*, 2 (1907)

52. ELEMENTARY EDUCATION IN THE 19th CENTURY

SOURCES

Government reports and returns (see refs. below); commercial directories; reports of the National Society.

REFERENCES

1. Estimated from *Abstracts of Returns of Charitable Donations, made in 1787-8* (BPP, 1816, xvi.B) and *Reports of Charity Commissioners set up by Act 58 Geo. III, c.91* (1819-40).

2. See various reports in the *Bury Free Press*, June-November 1903.

3. *BPP*, 1819, ix.B, 877-928.

4. *BPP*, 1835, xlii, 424-62.

5. *BPP*, 1852-3, xc, 106-10.

6. *BPP*, 1871, lv, 694-713.

7. *BPP*, 1904, lxxv, 102-3.

BIBLIOGRAPHY

Goldstrom, J.M. (ed.), *Education: Elementary Education 1780-1900* (1972)

Northeast, P., 'The Provision of Elementary Education in 19th Century Rural Suffolk', *SR*, 5 (1981), 90-96

Serjeant, R., 'Joshua George Newman and the Ipswich Ragged School', *SR*, 5 (1981), 79-89

Sutherland, G., 'Education' in Thompson, F.ML. (ed.), *The Cambridge Social History of Britain, Vol. 3, 1750-1950* (1900), 119-69

Sutherland, G., *Elementary Education in the 19th Century* (Hist. Assoc., 1971)

53. PARISH AND HUNDRED WORKHOUSES, BEFORE 1834

SOURCE

Abstracts of the Returns made by the Overseers of the Poor, *Sessional Papers*, 31 (1777).

REFERENCES

1. In 1579 East Bergholt created a 'store house' for food, which it bought to re-sell cheaply to the poor. By 1610 Mendlesham had a similar 'stockehouse', probably to store the food and cloth which it was buying in quantity. Such buildings could also have stored materials for the poor to work on.

2. Indenture of 26 Nov. 1747 conveying Weathercock Farm in Gt Wratting to trustees for benefit of Gt Thurlow, Gt Wratting and Barnardiston (SRO(B): Fl 638/11/1).

3. A 'town-house' is a property owned by the parish, in which poor families were merely housed. Suffolk had a large number of town-houses, usually bequeathed by charitable individuals. Genuine workhouses can only be identified where the language of documents is unequivocal, as at Mendlesham in 1714: a workhouse accommodating adults and children had to provide a stock of wool to supply 'full work for the said workhouse' (SRO(I): FB 159/A1/2).

Houses of Correction were frequently called Bridewells after a famous example in London, once a royal palace. These were virtually prisons, set up by an Act of 1576, to house and reform the so-called 'sturdy beggars', the able-bodied and undeserving poor. Bridewells are known to have existed at Bury St Edmunds, Mildenhall, Honington, Clare, Sudbury, Lavenham, Ipswich, Witnesham, Needham, Woodbridge, Melton, Beccles, Blythburgh and Botesdale, but much more work remains to be done on the dates of their foundation and closure.

4. Abstracts of the Returns made by Overseers of the Poor, *Sessional Papers*, 31 (1777).

5. *BPP*, 1803-4, xiii.

6. *BPP*, 1818, xix.

7. A. Young, *General View of the Agriculture...of the County of Suffolk* (1813), 234-86.

8. See Map 54. Parishes occasionally opted out of Incorporated Hundreds, as did Playford in 1813.

9. *BPP*, 1834, xxviii.

54. POOR LAW UNIONS, 1834-1930
SOURCES
W. White, *History, Gazetteer and Directory of Suffolk* (1874), 167, 209, 231, 270-1, 299, 300, 308-9, 324, 349, 369, 398, 425, 484, 505, 524, 539, 608, 625 and 650; *Report of the Committee appointed to enquire into the present state of the poor and the workhouses in the town of Ipswich* (1822), SRO(I): S.Ips 362.5; *Remarks on the expediency of applying to Parliament for a bill to incorporate the several parishes of the Borough of Ipswich* (1815), SRO(I): S.Ips. 362.5; S.G. & E.O.A. Checkland, *The Poor Law Report of 1834* (1974).

55. RURAL PROTEST, 1815-51
REFERENCES
1. PRO, HO 40/27/3 (13 Dec., 1830).
2. *Times*, 21 June 1844.

56. TURNPIKES AND STAGECOACHES
SOURCES
The map is based in C. & J. Greenwood's map of Suffolk (London, 1825). Patrick Taylor supplied additional information on toll-houses.
REFERENCES
1. TURNPIKE ACTS

Date	Routes covered
1711-12	Ipswich-Scole; Claydon-Haughley; Yaxley-Eye
1724	Chesterford-Newmarket
1745	Cambridge-Newmarket
1762	Sudbury-Bury St Edmunds
1763	Fulbourn-Newmarket
1766	Shelford-Haverhill
1768	Newmarket-Thetford
1769	Bury St Edmunds-Scole
1770	Newmarket-Bury St Edmunds
1770	Barton Mills-Brandon
1775	Yarmouth Bridge-South Town
1785	Ipswich-Lowestoft-South Town; Darsham-Halesworth-Bungay
1792	Yoxford-Aldeburgh; Farnham-Aldeburgh
1792	Bury St Edmunds-Thetford-Brandon
1796	Blythburgh-Beccles-South Town; Brampton-Halesworth
1802	Woodbridge-Debenham-Eye
1812	Ipswich-Helmingham; Ipswich-Debenham; Otley-Hemingstone
1812	Ipswich-Stratford St Mary
1828	Mildenhall-Littleport; Mildenhall-Hockwold

2. W. White, *Directory of Suffolk* (1885), 2.
3. *A Century of Service: The County Councils of Suffolk, 1889-1989* (1989), 23.

BIBLIOGRAPHY
Albert, W., *The Turnpike Road System in England, 1663-1840* (1972)

Bates, A., *Directory of Stage Coach Services, 1836* (1969)

Cossons, A., 'The Turnpike Roads of Norfolk', *NA*, 30 (1952), 189-212 (includes roads into Suffolk)

Kennett, D. H., 'Coaching Routes of the Cambridge Region, 1820-50', *Proc. Cambridge Antiq. Soc.*, 68 (1978), 89-104

Kennett, D.H., 'The Pattern of Coaching in Early 19th Century Norfolk', *NA*, 36 (1977), 355-72

Serjeant, W.R. & Penrose, D.G. (eds), *Suffolk Turnpikes* (1973)

Taylor, Patrick, 'Toll-houses: A Last Fling in Local Distinctiveness', MA thesis, Univ. of York, 1995

57. RAILWAYS
NOTES
BRANCH RAILWAYS IN SUFFOLK:

Branch	Opening	Closure (P=Passenger; G=Goods)
Bentley-Hadleigh	1847	P 1932; G 1965
Marks Tey-Sudbury	1849	G 1966
Tivetshall-Beccles	1855-63	P 1953; G 1960-6
Wickham Mkt-Framlingham	1859	P 1952; G 1965
Snape Junction-Snape Bridge	1859	P — ; G 1960
Saxmundham-Aldeburgh	1859-60	P 1966; G *
Oulton Broad South-Kirkley	1859	P — ; G 1966-7
Chappel-Haverhill (Colne Valley Railway)	1860-3	P 1962; G 1962-5 (Haverhill North, P 1924)
Sudbury-Cambridge (Shelford Junction)	1865	P 1967; G 1966
Long Melford-Bury St Edmunds	1865	P 1961; G 1961-5
Mellis-Eye	1867	P 1931; G 1964
Bury St Edmunds-Thetford	1876	P 1953; G 1960
Westerfield-Felixstowe	1877	
Halesworth-Southwold (Southwold Railway)	1879	P & G 1929
Cambridge (Barnwell Junction)-Mildenhall	1884-5	P 1962; G 1964-5
Yarmouth-Lowestoft	1903	P 1970; G 1967
Haughley Junction-Laxfield (Mid-Suffolk Light Railway)	G 1904 P 1908	P & G 1952

* Sizewell Siding to Aldeburgh closed G 1959

The original records of the Great Eastern Railway Company and its constituents are in the PRO at Kew. Lists of these have been published by the Gt Eastern Railway Society in its *Information Sheet*, M102 (1978).
REFERENCES
1. Former railway lines have left many archaeological traces in the modern landscape, especially where they ran in cuttings or on embankments. They are often visible as linear woods, footpaths, nature reserves and soil marks in arable fields. One of the most obvious, because of its chalky embankments across arable fields, is the line which ran from Chesterford to Newmarket.
2. But the Ipswich-Peterborough service continues.
BIBLIOGRAPHY
Allen, C.J., *The Great Eastern Railway* (5th edn, 1968)

Clinker, C.R., *Register of Closed Passenger Stations and Goods Depots, 1830-1977* (new edn, 1978, plus supplements)

Gordon, D.I., *Regional History of the Railways of Great Britain, Vol.5: The Eastern Counties* (2nd edn, 1977)

Joby, R.S., *Eastern Counties Railway and its Associates* (1996)

Joby, R.S., *Forgotten Railways: East Anglia* (1977, reprint 1986), with useful bibliography of branch lines

Moffat, H., *East Anglia's First Railways* (1987)

58. RIVERS AND NAVIGATIONS
REFERENCE
1. NAVIGATIONS IN SUFFOLK

	Act	Opened	Disused by	Abandoned by
Little Ouse, Brandon-Thetford	1670	c.1677	1914	
Waveney, Beccles-Bungay	1670	?	1934	Open to Shipmeadow or Geldeston Lock
Breydon-Beccles	1722	?		
Lark, Mildenhall-Bury	1700	c.1720	1920s	
Stour, Manningtree-Sudbury	1705	c.1709	1928	1937

	Act	Opened	Disused by	Abandoned by
Blyth,				
Southwold-Halesworth	1757	1761	1911	1934
Gipping,				
Ipswich-Stowmarket	1790	1793	1922	1932
Norwich & Lowestoft Navn,				
Lowestoft-Reedham	1827	1833		
Beccles Navn	1831	?1833		
Lakenheath Lode			1910s	

BIBLIOGRAPHY

Arnott, W.G., *Suffolk Estuary* [Deben] (1950)

Arnott, W.G., *Alde Estuary* (1952)

Arnott, W.G., *Orwell Estuary* (1954)

Boyes, J. & Russell, R., *The Canals of Eastern England* (1977)

Clark, R., *Black Sailed Traders* (reprint 1972)

Lawrence, R., *Southwold River* (1990)

Malster, R., *Wherries and Waterways* (1971)

Pluck, D.F., *The River Waveney, its Watermills and Navigation* (1994)

Waller, A.J.R., *The Suffolk Stour* (1957)

Weston, D.E., 'West Suffolk's Forgotten Waterway: The Story of the River Lark Navigation' (typescript in SRO(B), 1975)

Wrenn. W.J., *Ports of the Eastern Counties* (1976)

59. NAVIGATION, PORTS AND TRADE

REFERENCES

1. J.W. Norie, *New and Extensive Sailing Directions for the Navigation of the North Sea* (1826) gives a 'Full and Accurate Description of the Various Channels from London to the South Foreland and Orfordness'.

2. *The North Sea Pilot*, Pt iii (The Hydrographic Office of Admiralty, 7th edn, 1905), chs vii & viii for Suffolk coast.

3. N. Long, *Lights of East Anglia* (1983).

4. D. Defoe, *Tour through the Whole Island of Great Britain* (1724), 107-8.

5. N. Williams, *The Maritime Trade of the East Anglian Ports, 1550-1590* (1988), Chs 3 & 4.

6. D. Defoe, *Tour* (1724), 57.

7. R. Malster, 'The 19th-Century Maritime Trade of

Cromer and other minor East Anglian Ports' in A. Longcroft & R. Joby (eds), *East Anglian Studies* (1995).

8. R. Jones & R. Malster, *A Victorian Vision* (1992).

9. R. Malster, *Lowestoft, East Coast Port* (1982), 19-37.

10. *The East Anglian*, Jan. 1814, 23-5.

11. R. Malster, *Felixstowe: A Hundred Years a Working Port* (1986).

60. CHANGING AGRICULTURE IN HIGH SUFFOLK, 1650-1850

REFERENCES

1. A. Young, *Annals of Agric.* (1786), 193-224

2. A. Young, *Annals of Agric.* (1786), 196; PRO, C112/181.

3. Herts. Record Office, xi.13; Northants. Record Office, ASL 1143; SRO (I), C14/1/7.

4. Stocking figures taken from ongoing research by J. Theobald. The colour of these cattle was either red, brindle (brown with other streaks), or cream.

5. A. Young, *Annals of Agric.* (1786), 195

6. SRO(I), FC102/C1/3, FB19/C4/1,2, FC90/C1/15-27, HA87/C8/1/1.

7. CUL, Vanneck Collection, box of maps; SRO(I), HA24/50/19.4.5 (16 & 17), C13/12(4).

8. SRO(I), FB19/C4/1, 2 & 3.

9. SRO(I), HA24/50/19/4.5 (16 & 17); A. Young, *General View* (1813), 56.

10. SRO(I), *Ipswich Jour.*, 5 Nov. 1814, p. 3, col. 2; 22 Sept. 1817, p. 1, col. 3; 5 Dec. 1818, p. 3, col. 4; 18 Sept. 1819, p. 1, col. 3; 9 Oct. 1819, p. 3, col. 2.

11. W. & H. Raynbird, *On the Agriculture of Suffolk* (1849), 94.

12. SRO(I), map P461/82; apportionment FDA82/A1/1a.

BIBLIOGRAPHY

Overton, M., *Agricultural Revolution in England* (Cambridge, 1996)

Raynbird, W. & H., *On the Agriculture of Suffolk* (1849)

Theobald, J., PhD thesis, UEA (forthcoming)

Young, A., 'Minutes relating to the Dairy Farms, etc., of High Suffolk, taken at Aspal, in January 1786', *Annals of Agriculture* (London, 1786), 193-224

Young, A., *Tours in England and Wales* (London, 1932), 102-21

Young, A., *A General View of the Agriculture of the County of Suffolk* (London, 1813)

61. AGRICULTURE IN 1854

SOURCE

Agricultural Statistics of 1854, in *BPP*, 1854-55, liii.

REFERENCES

1. Diary of Rev. Richard Golty of Framlingham and Saxstead, 1628-77: SRO(I), JC1/29/1, f.166.

2. D.N.J. MacCulloch (ed.), *The Chorography of Suffolk* (1976), pp. 19-20; F. Hervey, *Suffolk in the 17th Century: The Breviary of Robert Reyce* (1902),. 37-42; R. Blome, *Britannia* (1673), 207; N. Scarfe, *A Frenchman's Year in Suffolk, 1784* (SRS xxx, 1988).

3. Limited returns of crops were made as early as 1802 (PRO, HO 67; see List & Index Soc., 195, 13-14). In 1853, a pilot scheme was organised for Norfolk and Hampshire alone. From 1866 onwards, agricultural returns were made annually and survive in parish summaries; they were organised by the Board of Inland Revenue.

4. J.P. Dodd, 'The Suffolk Crop Returns of 1854', *PSIAH*, xxxiv, pt 3 (1979), 191-204. Dodd's article contains one map in which the Poor Law Unions are grouped into five large areas cutting across natural boundaries. Individual unions often include more than one kind of countryside and soil.

5. Out of 1,287 occupiers in the large union of Blything, only 34 refused to make a return.

6. The best account of Suffolk dairying was written by Arthur Young in 1786 (*Annals of Agriculture, 27*). The heartland of dairying, as he saw it, was from Wyverstone in the west to Bramfield in the east; from the Waveney valley in the north to Otley in the south.

7. W. & H. Raynbird, *On the Agriculture of Suffolk* (1849), esp. 7-24.

BIBLIOGRAPHY

Caird, J. *English Agriculture in 1850-51* (1852), 151-61

Dodd, J.P., 'The Suffolk Crop Returns of 1854', *PSIAH*, xxxiv, pt 3 (1979), 191-204

Evans, N., 'Farming and Land-holding in Wood-pasture East Anglia, 1550-1650', *PSIAH*, xxxv, pt 4 (1984), 303-15

Holt, H.M.E. & Kain, R.J.P., 'Land Use and Farming in Suffolk about 1840', *PSIAH*, xxxv, pt 2 (1982), 123-39

Raynbird. W. & H., *On the Agriculture of Suffolk* (1849)

Thirsk, J. & Imray, J., *Suffolk Farming in the 19th Century* (SRS, i, 1958)

Young, A., *General View of the Agriculture of Suffolk* (1813)

62. THE HERRING FISHERY

REFERENCES

1. R. Malster, *Lowestoft, East Coast Port* (1982), 9.
2. Samuel Morton Peto, the railway contractor and entrepreneur who settled at Somerleyton Hall in 1843, is said to have promised at a public meeting in Lowestoft that the building of a railway line from the town to Reedham, thereby linking into the railway system, would enable fish to be delivered to the industrial areas on the same day it was landed.
3. G. Youell, *Lower Class* (1938), 113-36.
4. D. Butcher, *The Driftermen* (1979), 121-31; Bill Soloman, 'Steam Drifters' in *The Norfolk Sailor*, 12 (1966).
5. D. Butcher, *Following the Fishing* (1987).

63. THE WOOLLEN CLOTH INDUSTRY

REFERENCES

1. It is now virtually certain that the Suffolk village of Kersey did *not* give its name to a kind of cloth. The word *kersey* as applied to a narrow ribbed cloth possibly derives from an Arabic word which can be traced back to at least the 12th century. This referred to a kind of head-dress, or long strip of cloth wound like a turban. (*Ex inf.* Peter Northeast who intends to publish an article on this subject).
2. M.E. Grimwade (ed. W.R. & R.K. Serjeant) *Index of the Probate Records of the Court of the Archdeacon of Suffolk, 1444-1700*, 2 vols. (BRS 1979); *Index of the Probate Records of the Court of the Archdeacon of Sudbury 1354-1700*, 2 vols. (BRS 1984). Both these publications have a valuable index of 'Trades and Conditions' from which the figures for this map have been taken. Unfortunately the eight volumes listing wills

proved at the Bishop's Consistory Court at Norwich (NRS) have no such index of occupations—except for the period 1819-57.

3. An outstandingly large number of wills was proved for Hadleigh in the Archbishop's Prerogative Court of Canterbury (PCC) and must include a considerable proportion of clothiers. See T.W. Oswald-Hicks (ed.), *A Calendar of Wills relating to ...Suffolk, proved in PCC, 1383-1604* (1913).
4. The same concentration of clothiers no doubt continued over the River Stour into northern Essex. This is a classic example of the disadvantage of plotting historical features within counties only, and not in wider regions.
5. B. McClenaghan, *The Springs of Lavenham* (1924), 59; J. Pound, *The Military Survey of 1522 for Babergh Hundred* (SRS xxviii, 1986), 75-82; D. Dymond & A. Betterton, *Lavenham, 700 years of Textile Making* (1982), 25.
6. R. Blome, *Britannia* (1673), 207-8: 'In the Woodlands also, and North-east part of the County, a considerable trade is driven in linnen made into Huswivescloth, or sale-cloth. In the Track [tract] between Woodbridge and Saxmundham, with their neighbouring Towns, is a good trade in Pouldavys for sail-cloth, and in sack-cloth'. For a summary map, see D. Dymond & P. Northeast, *A History of Suffolk* (1985), 66-7.
7. R. Blome, *op. cit.*, 208: 'In the Southern Track [tract, of Suffolk], the great but decaying trade is in broadcloth for beyond Sea ... '.
8. A 'bay' was lighter and finer than modern baize, and made of a worsted warp (combed fibres) and a woollen weft (carded). In the 17th century, Colchester and Sudbury had special Bay Halls for the inspection and sale of this material. A 'say' was a fine durable cloth, entirely of carded wool, with a texture resembling serge.

64. THE LINEN INDUSTRY

SOURCES

Probate records of the Norwich consistory court and of the Suffolk and Sudbury archdeaconry courts; marriage

licence bonds; Quarter Sessions records; newspapers, principally the *Ipswich Journal* and *Bury and Norwich Post*; National Apprenticeship Registers; census returns, poor-law records; parish registers.

REFERENCES

1. N. Evans, *The East Anglian Linen Industry: Rural Industry and the Local Economy, 1500-1850* (1985), Map 3; 'Worsted and Linen Weavers' in *An Historical Atlas of Norfolk* (ed. P. Wade-Martins, 1993),150-1.
2. A. Young, *General View of the Agriculture of the County of Suffolk* (1813), 141.
3. Heckling is a process similar to the combing of wool, carried out with long-toothed combs called heckles.
4. A. Young, *op. cit*, 141.
5. Index of probate records for:
   The Court of the Archdeacon of Sudbury, 1354-1700 (BRS, 2 vols, 1984); *The Court of the Archdeacon of Suffolk, 1444-1700* (BRS, 2 vols 1979); *Index of Wills Proved at Norwich, 1550-1603* (NRS xxi); *Index of Wills Proved at Norwich, 1604-1686* (NRS xxviii); *Index of Wills Proved at Norwich, 1687-1750* (NRS xxxiv); *Index of Wills Proved at Norwich, 1751-1818* (NRS xxxviii); *Index of Wills Proved at Norwich, 1819-1857* (NRS xliv).
6. PRO, IR 1.

65. THE LEATHER INDUSTRY

REFERENCES

1. Grimwade, M.E. (ed. W.R. & R.K. Serjeant) *Index of the Probate Records of the Court of the Archdeacon of Suffolk, 1444-1700*, 2 vols (BRS 1979); *Index of the Probate Records of the Court of the Archdeacon of Sudbury, 1354-1700*, 2 vols (BRS 1984); marriage licence bonds, originals in SRO(B & I).
2. SRO (Lowestoft), 124/D2/1.
3. A tanner converts skins or hides into leather by steeping them in an astringent liquid made from crushed oak-bark; a currier dresses and colours tanned leather; a fellmonger is a dealer in skins and hides. See Norman Smedley, *East Anglian Crafts* (1977), 50-66.
4. N. Evans (ed.), *Beccles Rediscovered* (1984), 21.

66. THE BRICKMAKING INDUSTRY

SOURCES
Commercial directories of Suffolk by White, Kelly, Harrod and Morris, from 1844 to 1937

REFERENCES
1. At Polstead thin red bricks (10-11 x 5-7 x 1.75 inches) were used in the chancel arch and nave arcades. Not far away is Little Wenham Hall, built *c.*1270-80, the earliest house in England to be constructed largely of brick.
2. For example, at Wyken in the parish of Bardwell, close to the significantly named Kiln Wood, a large red mound containing countless fragments of brick is annually visible after ploughing at TL 961721. Documentary evidence confirms that bricks were being made at Wyken in the 16th and 17th centuries.
3. Many of these white bricks were made at Woolpit, where brickmaking is recorded as early as 1573-7. In the early years of the 20th century, the Woolpit brickworks were linked to the main rail network by their own branch-line to Elmswell station. Traces of the embankment for this line can still be seen to the north of the A14.

BIBLIOGRAPHY
Hammond, M., *Bricks and Brickmaking* (1981)

Malster, R.W., 'Some Suffolk Industries', *SR,* vol. 5, no. 4 (Summer, 1983)

Woodforde, J., *Bricks to Build a House* (1976)

67. WINDMILLS AND WATERMILLS

SOURCES
The prime source is the 1st edition of the Ordnance Survey's one-inch map (1837), backed up by Tithe Apportionments held in the SRO. At the time of writing, not all tithe maps have been examined, but it is unlikely that any sites have been missed. Information as to type of mill has been derived from sale advertisements in local newspapers, particularly the *Suffolk Chronicle, Norwich & Norwich Post* and *Ipswich Journal*, together with photographic records and fieldwork from many sources, particularly the Lummis Collection and Suffolk Photographic Survey in the SRO. In a few cases no evidence exists for the type of windmill: in these cases an 'educated guess' has been made.

REFERENCES
1. Apart from drainage, windmills were also used for cement manufacture, dressing seed and sawing timber. One at Brandon may have been used for making whiting, but this is speculative. In Ipswich one ground drugs but had gone by 1840.
2. *Jocelin of Brakelond's Chronicle* (1989), 53. Dean Herbert's new windmill was ordered to be destroyed because it infringed the abbey's manorial rights.
3. In 1840 another type existed called the *composite* or 'bastard' mill. Later in the 19th century several post mills were converted to composite mills by having their posts removed and their bodies set on brick towers. The mill at Monk Soham, however, was built as a composite. As it resembled a normal post mill it is so recorded on the map. Some of the smallest drainage or pumping mills were of a type known as *hollow post mill*, in which the drive is taken in a bore through the post; an example was the brine pump at Southwold's saltworks.
4. In 1294-5 a *stone windmill* was mentioned at Dover. In the church of Stoke-by-Clare a tower mill is depicted in stained glass dated to the 1470s, although this is now thought to be of continental origin.
5. A mill shown on a map of Kedington in 1724 stood on *Stone Mill Common*, but otherwise the earliest recorded tower mill is at Theberton, standing by 1756.
6. Hodskinson's map of Suffolk, 1783.
7. I am indebted to David Butcher for this reference.
8. Hodskinson's map of Suffolk, 1783.
9. Hodskinson's map of Suffolk, 1783.
10. A steam mill existed at Ipswich by 1822, and another at Barningham by 1826. The watermill at Nayland gained a steam mill in 1821.
11. The last to be built were a post-mill at Wetheringsett (1882-3), a smock-mill at Lattice Barn, Ipswich (1879-80) and a tower-mill at Cockfield (1891). The small wind-pump at St Olaves was erected in 1910. With the exception of that at Ipswich, all these replaced earlier mills.
12. Tantalising evidence of millstones and watercourses was discovered on a Roman site at Stuston in 1993: *PSIAH*, xxxviii, pt 2 (1994), 220-2.
13. At least two wheels on farms drove threshing machines and other machinery, but they are not shown on the map because of their late date.
14. The main tide mill at Ipswich stood next to Stoke Bridge and was also fed by the River Gipping. The second and true tide mill was at Tovell's Roman Cement works, with a mill-pond to the west of what became the wet dock.

BIBLIOGRAPHY
Bennett, R. & Elton, J., *History of Corn Milling* (4 vols, 1898-1904)

Dolman, P.C.J., *Windmills in Suffolk, A Contemporary Survey* (1978)

Flint, B., *Suffolk Windmills* (1979)

Hodskinson, J., Map of Suffolk, 1783 (SRS xv, 1972)

Holt, R., *The Mills of Medieval England* (1988)

Kealey, E.J., *Harvesting the Air; Windmill Pioneers in 12th-Century England* (1987)

Pluck, D., *The River Waveney, its Navigation and Watermills* (1994)

Wailes, R., *The English Windmill* (1954)

Wailes, R., 'Suffolk Windmills' and 'Suffolk Watermills', *Trans. Newcomen Soc.,* xxii (1942), xxiii (1943) & xxxvii (1965).

Watts, M., *Corn Milling* (Shire, 1983)

Woolford, A., 'Windmills, with special reference to those in Suffolk', *PSIAH*, xx, pt 2 (1930)

68. IRON FOUNDRIES, 1789-1900

REFERENCES
1. Blacksmiths, millwrights and small machine-makers continued to meet local needs and to grow in numbers throughout the 19th century, but they are not included in this survey. They were concerned with the production of basic and unsophisticated agricultural machinery, with wind- and water-mills, irrigation and drainage projects, the making of carts and wagons, and serving firms engaged in textiles, silk, horsehair and bell-hanging. Nor are white-

smiths or brassfounders included, although many of the iron foundries also worked in brass.

2. Other jobbing iron foundries were located in Ipswich (3), Woodbridge (3), Melton (1), Saxmundham (1), Southwold (1), Halesworth (1), Stowmarket (2), Sudbury (2), Long Melford (1), Clare (1), Haverhill (1), Hawkedon (1), Exning (1), Eye (2), Bungay (2) and Stradbroke (1).

3. At Beccles (3), Wrentham (1), Oulton Broad (2) and Lowestoft (4).

69. MALTING AND BREWING

SOURCE

William White, *Directory of Suffolk* (1855)

REFERENCES

1. N. Bacon, *Annalls of Ipswiche* (1884), 180.
2. When the Suffolk Archaeological Unit excavated the church of St Edmund de Pounteney in Rose Lane, numbers of early malt-kiln tiles were found on the site.
3. W. White, *Directory of Suffolk* (1845), 371-2.

BIBLIOGRAPHY

Bristow, C.R., *A Directory of 19th and 20th Century Suffolk Breweries* (1985)

Brown, J., *Steeped in Tradition* (1983)

Malster, R., *Drink and Be Merry: A History of the Drinks Industry in East Anglia* (Hadleigh, n.d.)

Malster, R., *Malting in Suffolk* (Suffolk Industrial Archaeol. Soc., 1984)

70. CAMPING CLOSES

REFERENCES

1. The word 'camping' is derived from the Middle English verb *campen* meaning 'to fight, contend, or strive'. For the game and its background, see D. Dymond, 'A Lost Social Institution: The Camping Close', *Rural History*, I (1990), 165-92; 'Place-Names as Evidence for Recreation', *Jour. English Place-name Soc.*, 25 (1992-3), 12-18; 'God's Disputed Acre', *Jour. Ecclesiastical Hist.* 50 (1999), 1-34.

2. The best parallel is probably with American football with its multiple scrimmages all over the field—on

and off the ball. In June 1668 John Long of Charlestown, Massachusetts, told the Middlesex County Court, 'I will camp the ball to the devil' (*ex inf.* Roger Thompson), so we may yet learn of a Camping Close in the New World.

3. On 10 Oct. 1612 a man was killed during a game of 'the campeing ball' in St Giles parish, Colchester: Essex Record Office, Colchester Borough Sessions, Roll 17.

4. Soccer is played primarily with the feet, but why are American football, rugby union and rugby league all classed as forms of 'football'?

5. *NA* xxiv, 317; J.L. Fisher & A. & R. Powell, *A Medieval Farming Glossary* (1997), 7.

6. At present the most westerly Camping Close known is at Orwell, 10 miles south-west of Cambridge. The most southerly is at Canewdon in Essex.

7. The second word could also be Field, Place, Meadow, Land, Ground, Pightle, etc.

8. For the dangers inherent in using these words, see Dymond, 'Place-names as Evidence for Recreation', 17.

9. F. Blomefield, Suffolk Collection: CUL, Add.MS 3390, f.215.

10. At both Walsham le Willows and Beccles, an open-air theatre called the Game Place lay in the corner of a Camping Close.

11. 'Most of the towns and villages of Norfolk and Suffolk seem to have had their games. . . In the sense that all games were presumably held somewhere, 'game-places' for them must have existed': David Galloway, *REED Newsletter*, 1979: 1, 25).

12. Dymond, 'Place-names as Evidence for Recreation', 14-17. The French game of 'soule', which also had at least three main variants, was often played 'près d'une église': J-P. Leguay, *La Rue au Moyen Ages* (1984), 211.

13. Dymond, 'God's Disputed Acre'.

14. In 1700, the Quarter Sessions of Woodbridge and Bury issued orders against disorderly sports associated with alehouses, including camping.

15. By 1621 the Camping Close at Debenham was divided and used as two orchards (SRO(I),

S1/2/31.6), while at Ufford a hempland was described as 'hertofore called Campeinge Close' (SRO(I), FAA 270/19/133). Yet at Pakenham, the Camping Close was still being used by footballers in the late 18th century (SRO(B), FL 614/3/35).

16. The comparable numbers are 36 so far identified in Norfolk, 29 in Cambridgeshire and 14 in Essex.

17. Presumably the three sites were used at three different periods.

18. Glebe terriers of Hintlesham, SRO(I), FAA 2701/19/2 & 89.

19. At Weybread in 1617, 2 shillings were paid 'for a merriment upon the towne close': *East Anglian*, i (1864), 409.

20. The author will always be pleased to hear of new examples, and of any evidence bearing on camping and other popular recreations.

71. THEATRES AND CINEMAS

REFERENCE

1. The Fisher Theatre Collection is now in the UEA library in Norwich.

BIBLIOGRAPHY

Ambrose, R., 'The Theatre Royal [Bury St Edmunds]' (typescript in SRO(B), nd)

Burley, T.L.G., *Playhouses and Players of East Anglia* [mostly Norfolk] (1928)

East Anglian Theatre: [Catalogue of] an Exhibition devoted to the History of the Players and Playhouses of Norfolk and Suffolk (1952)

Field, M., *The Lamplit Stage: the Fisher Circuit, 1792-1844* (1985)

Grice, E., *Rogues and Vagabonds; or the Actors' Road to Respectability* (1977, with good bibliography)

Lingwood, H.R., *Ipswich Playhouses: Chapters of Local Theatrical History* (1936)

Macintosh, I., *Pit, Boxes and Gallery: the Story of the Theatre Royal, Bury St Edmunds, 1819-1926* (1979)

Peart, S., *The Picture House in East Anglia* (1980)

72. ANGLO-SAXON AND MEDIEVAL IPSWICH

SOURCES

The map has been compiled from information in the Ipswich section of the SMR.

REFERENCES

1. N. Scarfe, *The Suffolk Landscape* (1972), 101, 122
2. L.J. Redstone, *Ipswich through the Ages* (1948), 109

BIBLIOGRAPHY

Wade, K., *Origins of Ipswich* (1981)

Wade, K., 'Ipswich' in Hodges, R. and Hobley, B. (eds), *The Rebirth of Towns in the West, AD 700-1050*, CBA Research Rep., 68 (1988), 93-100

Wade, K., 'The Urbanisation of East Anglia: The Ipswich Perspective' in Gardiner, J. (ed.), 'Flatlands and Wetlands: Current Themes in East Anglian Archaeology', *EAA*, 50 (1993), 144-51

73. THE GROWTH OF MODERN IPSWICH

SOURCES

Maps of Ipswich by Joseph Pennington (1778), Edward White (1849 and 1867), and the Ordnance Survey (six-inch series dated 1884, 1902-3, 1928 and 1938). Fuller description in Frank Grace, *Old Ordnance Survey Maps: Ipswich 1902* (OS sheets 75.11 and 75.12, published by Alan Godfrey, 1998).

74. SMALLER MEDIEVAL TOWNS

SOURCES

The maps are based on the earliest maps of each town, the distribution of timber-framed buildings and information in the SMR.

REFERENCES

1. K. Penn, 'Bungay and its Early History', *Quarterly Jour. Norfolk Archaeol. & Hist. Research Group*, 29 (1998), 3-7
2. N. Scarfe, *The Suffolk Landscape* (1972), 109

BIBLIOGRAPHY

Atkin, M., 'The Anglo-Saxon Urban Landscape in East Anglia', *Landscape History*, vii (1985), 27-40

Dymond, D. & Northeast, P., *A History of Suffolk* (1995)

Scarfe, N., *The Suffolk Landscape* (1972)

75. LISTED BUILDINGS

SOURCES

The map has been compiled from the totals in the new Statutory Lists, issued after the resurvey of 1982-87, whenever these were available. For the former Rural District of Samford, and for parts of the present Districts of Mid-Suffolk and Coastal, new lists have not yet been issued by the Dept. of the Environment, although resurveying has been completed. Here the original lists from the early 1950s have had to be used. To provide the best comparison, all the items on those lists, whether Grades I, II or III, have been included in the total. This is not as haphazard as it might seem, since in resurveyed parishes the total of Statutory items (Grades I, II* and II) has risen considerably, often by 75%, or even by more than 100%. Many buildings formerly of Grade III have been upgraded, and a number of previously unlisted buildings included. For the larger towns, and for the former Rural Districts of Clare, Melford and Cosford, the revised lists issued in the 1960s and 70s have been used. In spite of these discrepancies in the sources, the map does bring out clear differences in the incidence of listed buildings from one part of the county to another, and even in some cases between adjacent parishes. Thanks are due to Mark Barnard and Hilary Todd for extracting many of the totals on which the distribution map is based.

NOTE

Although the issuing of a new Statutory List can be delayed after the resurvey of an area, owners of listed buildings are notified in due course by English Heritage and by their District Council, and are given the essential information regarding their rights and obligations. No demolition of a listed building, or its alteration outside or within, should take place without Listed Building Consent from the District Council. Applications are advertised in the local press and by a notice on the building itself. Further information, either general or on a particular application, may be obtained from the Planning Department of the relevant District Council. General information about listing can also be had from English Heritage at 23 Savile Row, London W1X 2HE, or from the Environment & Transport Department of Suffolk County Council, St Edmund House, County Hall, Ipswich IP4 1LZ.

76. THE ROMANESQUE CHURCH OF BURY ST EDMUND'S ABBEY

SOURCES

All measurements up to 40m. (130ft) used in this paper were taken on site by the author. Only those above 40m. were derived from plans. The best measured drawings of the site were prepared by the Dept of the Environment in 1972, and of the town the 1:500 series prepared by the Borough Council.

BIBLIOGRAPHY

Arnold, T. (ed.), *Memorials of St Edmunds Abbey*, Rolls Series, xcvi (1890-6), i, 84

Crummy, P., 'The System of Measurement Used in Town Planning from the 9th to the 13th Centuries' in S. Chadwick Hawkes (ed.), *Studies in Archaeology and History*, BAR 72, i (1979), 160-1

Fernie, E.C., 'The Romanesque Church of Bury St Edmunds Abbey' in A. Gransden (ed.), *Bury St Edmunds: Medieval Art, Architecture, Archaeology and Economy* (British Archaeol. Assoc. Conference Trans., xx (1998), 1-15

Gilyard Beer, R., 'The Eastern Arm of the Abbey Church at Bury St Edmunds', *PSIAH*, xxxi (1969), 256-62

James, M.R., 'The Abbey of St Edmund at Bury', *Cambridge Antiquarian Soc.*, xxviii (1895)

Whittingham, A.B., 'Bury St Edmund's Abbey: The Plan, Design and Development of the Church and Monastic Buildings', *AJ*, cviii (1951), 168-87

77. MEDIEVAL MASONS

NOTES

CHURCHES ATTRIBUTED TO NAMED MASONS

Aldrych, Thomas	Helmingham; also North Lopham (Norfolk)
Barbour, John	Aldeburgh, Grundisburgh, East Bergholt, Ipswich St Stephen
Clerk, Simon	Bury St Mary, Denston, Hessett, Lavenham, Long Melford, Stratford St Mary; also King's College and Great St Mary in Cambridge, and Saffron Walden (Essex)
Hawes, [...]	Bildeston, Debenham, Hengrave, Higham, Otley, Wingfield
Layer, William	Bury St Mary, Rougham

Melford, John	Acton, Boxford, Cavendish, Glemsford, Lavenham, Long Melford; also Chelmsford (Essex)
Russell, Richard	Blythburgh, Kessingland, Southwold, Walberswick, Wangford, Woodbridge
Wastell, John	Bury St James, Lavenham, Nayland; also King's College and Great St Mary in Cambridge; Colchester St James the Great, Dedham and Saffron Walden (Essex)

GROUPS OF DESIGN-LINKED CHURCHES

Ipswich group	Ipswich St Mary le Tower, St Mary Quay and St Clements, Hasketon, Wickham Market
Bury St Edmunds group	Fornham All Saints, Great Barton, Icklingham St James, Moulton, Thurston, Wetherden
Sudbury group	Boxford, Bradfield St George, Chelsworth, Great Waldingfield, Hadleigh, Stoke-by-Nayland, Sudbury All Saints and St Peter.

REFERENCES

1. J.H. Harvey, *The Medieval Architect* (1972), ch.4; L.F. Salzman, *Building in England down to 1550* (1967), ch.1.
2. L.F. Salzman, *op. cit.*, ch.4.
3. J.H. Harvey, *English Medieval Architects: A Biographical Dictionary down to 1550* (1987), 55-61, 316-24.
4. Peter Northeast has transcribed many hundreds of late-medieval wills for Suffolk. His edition of the first surviving register of wills for the archdeaconry of Sudbury will be published by the SRS.
5. See J.H. Harvey, *Biographical Dictionary* (1987), and B. Haward, *Suffolk Medieval Church Arcades* (1993).
6. B. Haward, *Arcades* (1993).

BIBLIOGRAPHY

Cattermole, P. & Cotton, S., 'Medieval Parish Church Building in Norfolk', *NA*, xxxviii, pt iii (1983), 235-79

Coulton, G.C., *Art and the Reformation* (1928)

Davis, R.H.C., 'A Catalogue of Masons' Marks', *JBAA*, xvii (1954), 43

Gimpel, J., *The Cathedral Builders* (1988)

Harvey, J.H., *Medieval Architect* (1972)

Harvey, J.H., *The Perpendicular Style, 1330-1485* (1978)

Harvey, J.H., *English Medieval Architects: A Biographical Dictionary down to 1550* (revised 1987)

Haward, B., *Suffolk Medieval Church Arcades* (1993)

Salzman, L.F., *Building in England down to 1540* (1967)

78. MEDIEVAL CHURCH ROOFS

SOURCES

Descriptions given in H.M. Cautley (1982) and N. Pevsner & E. Radcliffe (1974), augmented by information from R. & J.A. Brandon (1860) and by personal study in local churches. Information on single and double hammerbeam roofs in other counties has been obtained from the CD-Rom index of Pevsner's county volumes of 'The Buildings of England' (English Heritage, 1995).

NB. The number of recorded examples of each roof-type inevitably depends on modern survivals, in some cases probably less than half the original numbers. Generally the later types of roof are more likely to have survived than the earlier.

REFERENCES

1. F. Bond, *English Church Architecture*, vol. 2 (1913), 789.
2. N. Pevsner & E. Radcliffe, *Buildings of England—Suffolk* (2nd edn, 1974), 37.
3. The hammerbeam and arch-braced roofs typified by Westminster Hall (1493-9) form a distinct group of large royal or aristocratic halls created by master masons and carpenters from London and Westminster.
4. N. Pevsner & E. Radcliffe, *Buildings of England—Suffolk* (1974), 37: 'For open timber roofs Suffolk stands supreme'.
5. J.H. Harvey, *English Medieval Architects: A Biographical Dictionary down to 1550* (1984), 258.
6. B. Haward, *Suffolk Medieval Church Arcades* (1993), 168-9, 210-11.
7. B. Haward, *ibid.*, 308-10.

BIBLIOGRAPHY

Bond, F., *English Church Architecture*, vol. 2 (1913)

Brandon, R. & J.A., *Open Timber Roofs of the Middle Ages* (1860)

Cautley, H.M., *Suffolk Churches and their Treasures* (1982)

Harvey, J.H., *English Medieval Architects: A Biographical Dictionary down to 1500* (1984)

Haward, B., *Suffolk Medieval Church Arcades* (1993)

Pevsner, N. & Radcliffe, E., *The Buildings of England—Suffolk* (1974)

Salzman, L. F., *Building in England down to 1540* (1967)

Smith, J.T., 'Medieval Roofs: A Classification', *AJ*, cxv (1958), 111-49

79. AISLED HALLS

SOURCES

Lists of Buildings of Architectural or Historic Interest are produced by English Heritage, and give brief descriptions of each individual building. Booklets known as 'Greenbacks' cover groups of parishes. Copies are available for examination at the Environment & Transport Department of Suffolk County Council in Ipswich, and at the planning offices of District Councils for their own areas. Copies are held for the area formerly within East Suffolk at the SRO(I), and for West Suffolk at the SRO(B).

BIBLIOGRAPHY

Aitkens, P., 'Mid-Suffolk Houses, 1250-1530', in D.F. Stenning & D.D. Andrews (eds.) *Regional Variation in Timber-Framed Building in England & Wales Down to 1550* (1998), 40-46.

Colman, G. & S., 'A Thirteenth Century Aisled House: Purton Green Farm, Stansfield', *PSIAH*, xxx, pt 2 (1965), 149-65

Colman, S, & West, S.E., 'Edgar's Farm, Stowmarket: A Re-appraisal', *EAA*, I (1975), 39-45

Hewett, C.A., 'Aisled Timber Halls and Related Buildings, chiefly in Essex', *Trans Ancient Monuments Soc.*, n.s. 16 (1968-9), 45-99

Hewett, C.A., *The Development of Carpentry, 1200-1700: An Essex Study* (1969)

Hewett, C.A., *English Historic Carpentry* (1968)

Sandall, K., 'Aisled Halls in England and Wales', *Vernacular Architecture*, 17 (1986), 21-35

Smith, J.T., 'A 14th Century Aisled House: Edgar's Farm, Stowmarket', *PSIAH*, xxviii, pt 1 (1959), 54-61

Walker, J.L., 'Purton Green, Stansfield: Some Later Observations on the Early Aisled Hall', *PSIAH*, xxxviii, pt. 2 (1994), 126-137

Wood, M., *The English Medieval House* (1965)

80. AISLED BARNS
SOURCES
See those for 'Aisled Halls' (No.79, above)
BIBLIOGRAPHY
Hewett, C.A., *The Development of Carpentry, 1200-1700: An Essex Study* (1969)

Hewett, C.A., *English Historic Carpentry* (1980)

81. CROWN-POST ROOFS
SOURCES AND ACKNOWLEDGEMENTS
All the Historic Buildings Inspectors who worked in Suffolk on the re-survey of listed buildings have contributed information for the distribution map. In particular I should like to thank Philip Aitkens, Mark Barnard and Peter Guillery for much detailed material and fruitful discussion. In addition, John Bloomfield generously shared the results of his investigations in Hadleigh, and Timothy Easton kindly passed on information from the Debenham area. It is felt that coverage for the areas re-surveyed is reasonably complete.

REFERENCES
1. R.A. Cordingley, 'British Historical Roof-types and their Members: A Classification', *Trans. Ancient Monuments Soc.*, n.s. 9 (1961), 73-118. This gives illustrated definitions.
2. Plain, undecorated crown-posts of square section can occur at all periods, but most frequently in small urban houses of the late 15th and early 16th centuries, well built but restricted in plan. Two-way bracing to the collar-purlin only is common in this context, and becomes usual in 16th-century houses which still retain a poor form of crown-post roof.

BIBLIOGRAPHY
Harris, R., *Discovering Timber-Framed Buildings* (1979). A short but remarkably comprehensive introduction to timber-framing which cannot be bettered.

Fletcher, J.M. & Spokes, P.S., 'The Origin and Development of Crown-Post Roofs', *Medieval Archaeol.*, 8 (1964), 152-83

Smith, J.T., 'Medieval Roofs: A Classification', *AJ*, cxv (1958), 111-49. This is one of a series of fundamental studies of timber construction, with numerous illustrations, drawings, maps and references.

NB: No specific work deals with crown-post roofs in Suffolk, but the feature is of such wide national significance that it is certain to feature in any general work on timber-framed buildings.

82. RAISED-AISLED HALLS AND QUEEN-POST ROOFS
NOTES
We are indebted to colleagues on the Listed Buildings Survey, especially Philip Aitkens and Peter Guillery, for much of the information which has enabled us to produce the distribution map. Material for the Debenham area was kindly passed on by Timothy Easton.

It seems unlikely that further investigation will alter the distribution fundamentally, although more raised-aisled halls may exist in south Suffolk, as they do in northern Essex. No detailed work has been published on either of these distinctive types of roof. Further research, especially into their social and economic background, will be needed before they can be dealt with adequately. As far back as 1958, J.T. Smith, on the basis of only two known examples (Gate House Farmhouse, Felsted, Essex, and the fragment at Church Farm, Fressingfield, Suffolk), identified raised-aisles as a specific form for the first time. See 'Medieval Roofs: A Classification', *AJ*, cxv (1958), 114-49.

83. WEALDEN HOUSES
SOURCES
The distribution map is based upon the List of Buildings of Special Architectural or Historic Interest compiled by the Department of the Environment, upon information received from Philip Aitkens, Sylvia Colman and John Walker, and upon the author's own surveys. Of the 34 urban and rural examples, 27 occur in the larger towns such as Bury St Edmunds and Needham Market. Those in the solidly-built 'streets' of villages cannot meaningfully be separated from their truly urban counterparts.

REFERENCES
1. J.T. Smith 'The Evolution of the English Peasant House', *JBAA*, 3rd ser., 33 (1970), 123. Having recognised 350 Wealden houses in Kent, Smith estimated

that the true total, including disguised examples, was probably closer to 700.
2. Personal communication from David Martin of the Rape of Hastings Architectural Survey.
3. S. Pearson, *The Medieval Houses of Kent: An Historical Analysis* (1994), 70.
4. It is sometimes claimed that the Wealden form originated in medieval London. The surviving stock of Wealdens does not focus on London, but the possibility is difficult to debate given the absence of positive evidence.
5. S. Pearson (1994), 69. Of some 134 Wealdens analysed in the laudable survey of Kent by RCHME, all but 19 were estimated to have been built after 1440. Between 1440 and 1510 Wealdens represented approximately 37% of new houses being constructed, and between 1476 and 1510 almost twice as many were built as any other type of house. Unfortunately the survey was restricted to rural Kent, and avoided the larger towns.

84. COASTAL FORTIFICATIONS, 1500-1900
REFERENCES
1. T. Gardner, *An Historical Account of Dunwich* (1754), 179.
2. *Letters & Papers of the Reign of Henry VIII*, xiv (1), 398.
3. *Cal. State Papers (Dom.), 1547-65*, vi, 424; *Acts of Privy Council, 1552-4*, 286.
4. *Hist. Manuscripts Comm.*, 4, 5th Rpt, 67.
5. PRO, SP 16, 249, 49.
6. P. Kent, *The Fortifications of East Anglia* (1988), 101-09.
7. Kent, *op. cit.*, 109.
8. Kent, *op. cit.*, 111-12, 161.
9. PRO, WO/1548/2.
10. Kent, *op. cit.*, 91.
11. Kent, *op. cit.*, 121-4.
12. J.F. Leslie, *The History of Landguard Fort in Suffolk* (1898), 89.

BIBLIOGRAPHY
Hussey, F., *Suffolk Invasion* (1983)

Kent, P., *The Fortifications of East Anglia* (1988)

Leslie, J.F., *The History of Landguard Fort in Suffolk* (1898)

Trollope, C., 'The Defences of Harwich', *Fort*, 11 (1983), 5-30

Wood, D., *Landguard Fort, Felixstowe* (1983)

85. FORTIFICATIONS OF THE TWO WORLD WARS

REFERENCES

1. P. Kent, *The Fortifications of East Anglia* (1988), 93.
2. These were *HMS Glowworm*, armed with two 6-inch guns, and the larger *HMS Havelock* with two 14-inch and two 6-inch guns.
3. Kent, *op. cit.*, 10.
4. W.E. Ironside, D. Kelly & R. Macleod (eds), *The Ironside Diaries, 1937-40* (1962), 368-9.

BIBLIOGRAPHY

Dobinson, C.S., *Twentieth Century Fortifications in England* (CBA 1996, vols. i-iv)

Hussey, F., *Suffolk Invasion* (1983)

Kent, P., *The Fortifications of East Anglia* (1988)

Leslie, J. F., *The History of Landguard Fort in Suffolk* (1898)

Lowry, B. (ed.), *20th Century Defences in Britain: An Introductory Guide* (CBA, Practical Handbook 12, 1995)

Trollope, C., 'The Defences of Harwich', *Fort*, ii (1983)

Wood, D., *Landguard Fort, Felixstowe* (1983)

86. AIRFIELDS OF THE TWO WORLD WARS

REFERENCES

1. With grateful acknowledgement to E.F. Cheesman.
2. Although a few remained as civilian airfields.

BIBLIOGRAPHY

Bowyer, M.J.F., *Action Stations: Military Airfields of East Anglia, 1939-45* (1979)

Freeman, R.A., *Airfields of the Eighth: Then and Now* (1978)

INDEX